An expanded and up-dated revision of the
original 1887 edition to which has been added
new recipes and brief biographies
ladies up to Mrs. Johnson.

The White House Cookbook

THE

WHITE · hOUSE
COOK · BOOK

COOKING, TOILET AND HOUSEHOLD RECIPES,

MENUS, DINNER-GIVING, TABLE ETIQUETTE,

CARE OF THE SICK, HEALTH SUGGESTIONS,

FACTS WORTH KNOWING, Etc., Etc.

THE WHOLE COMPRISING

A COMPREHENSIVE CYCLOPEDIA OF INFORMATION FOR THE HOME

BY

MRS. F. L. GILLETTE

AND

hUGO ZIEMANN, Steward of the White house

CHICAGO:
R. S. PEALE COMPANY.

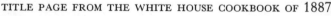

TITLE PAGE FROM THE WHITE HOUSE COOKBOOK OF 1887

The White House Cookbook

EDITED BY

Janet Halliday Ervin

Follett Publishing Company

Chicago 1964

Library of Congress Catalog Card Number: 64-23612

FIRST PRINTING

Manufactured in the United States of America
Designed by Gordon Martin

Follett Publishing Company
1000 West Washington Boulevard
Chicago, Illinois 60607

To Rosemary Doucette
who thought her old cookbook made interesting reading

To Mother
who loves to read

To Howard, Howard, Jr., Dennis, and David
who would rather eat than read cookbooks any day

And to my grandmother
who would say: "Writing a cookbook? With four hungry
men waiting to be fed? Land sakes!"

—J.H.E.

Author's Preface

THE FIRST WHITE HOUSE COOKBOOK

THE YEAR IS 1887 and you, Mrs. Newlywed, have just "gone to house-keeping." Your ivory satin wedding gown with bustle has been stored away in muslin and brown paper. The silk suit and velvet hat, crowned with ostrich plumes, which you wore to Niagara Falls, have been exchanged for a Mother Hubbard apron and dustcap.

As you happily unpack your hope chest, you come upon a prize wedding gift. It is a handsome book on whose enameled cover the White House and the Capitol are traced in silver. Proudly, you lay the book on the shawl-covered table in the parlor, beside the Bible, the family album, and the kerosene courting lamp. Its presence will prove to all callers that you are an up-to-date homemaker, one who has everything—a husband, a stove that draws, a shiny washtub and scrub-board, and a copy of *The White House Cookbook*, this year's runaway best-seller.

Not that you need a cookbook! You're handy in the kitchen. Even your mother admits that you have a light hand with pie crust. For years you've been learning to cook by *cooking*, under the watchful eyes of Mama, Grandma, Auntie, Older Sister, and Hired Girl. You're a "tasting cook"—the best kind. You're thrifty but not stingy. Low-calorie diet? You never heard of it. Butter, cream, eggs, flour, sugar—those are the keys to a man's heart. To your way of thinking, kitchen thrift lies in the quality of the product. No inedible failures. No unused leftovers. No weak or bitter coffee (can't afford to waste it at 12 cents a pound!). Remember what Mama always says: "A woman can throw out more with a teaspoon than a man can bring in with a shovel."

Still, it's fun to own the cookbook, even if you don't need it, and to know that your idol, Frances Cleveland, "The Bride of the White House," owns a copy, too. (A handsome portrait of her graces the book.) Everything is *Frances* this year. It was her wedding dress and traveling costume you copied for your trousseau. And aren't you wearing your hair in the style they call "à la Cleveland"—in a low knot at the nape of the neck? Most young women your age are.

But your older neighbors may think you are putting on airs. "Learn-ing to cook from a book?" they'll sniff. "Well, I never—!"

They—and you—would be shocked to know how much your great-granddaughter will depend on printed recipes. Far from home and family, leading a more mobile life than you ever dreamed of, she will stumble over the basics of cookery that you take for granted:

She will pour beaten eggs directly into hot sauce and wonder why they curdle.

She will fail to add that pinch of sugar that your Mama says always makes the tasty difference in any tomato dish.

One day three-quarters of a century from now—say, 1965—bored with TV dinners (no, you wouldn't understand), she may turn for inspiration to your *White House Cookbook*. As she pores over its fragile, yellowed pages, she will read in bewilderment: "Add butter the size of a walnut and enough flour to make a stiff dough."

"How much is that exactly?" she will ask helplessly. "And how long do I bake it? At what temperature?"

Then your spirit, dear wasp-waisted Good Cook of 1887, will put hands on hips and say in exasperation: "For goodness' sakes, I could *show* you but I can't *tell* you! Just add the ingredients until it seems about right, then cook it till it's done. And taste, Girl, taste!"

That is what my grandmother, a turn-of-the-century bride, told me, a World War II bride. Because that's the way they cooked in nineteenth-century America—even at the White House.

In 1887, when good store teeth sold for $4 and a pretty French corset for $1, when well-bred ladies did not twirl their watch chains in public and a gentleman did not take undue liberties with his fiancée—such as borrowing money from her family—two good cooks put their heads together and dreamed up *The White House Cookbook*, an encyclopedia of good eating, good health, and gracious living (typical cookbook authors of the time did not restrict themselves to kitchen lore but added their thoughts on etiquette, clothes, health, and happiness). The book was an immediate success and thereafter was republished, more or less unchanged, every two or three years into the twentieth century.

The authors were Mrs. Fanny Gillette, an authority in domestic science, and Hugo Ziemann, the steward of the White House. The publishers pointed out that Mr. Ziemann was particularly well qualified, having been at one time "caterer for that Prince Napoleon who was killed while fighting the Zulus in Africa." Later, at the Hotel Richelieu in Chicago, according to the 1891 edition, he "laid the famous spread to which chiefs of the warring factions of the Republican Convention sat down in June, 1888, and from which they arose with asperities softened, differences harmonized, and victory organized."

The book was "affectionately dedicated":

To the Wives of Our Presidents
Those Noble Women
Who Have Graced the White House
and Whose Names and Memories
Are Dear to All Americans

In this new edition, for the first time—thanks to the generous help of members, relatives, descendants, and friends of the First Families—favorite recipes of the First Ladies and other White House hostesses have been included. Where such information was not available, recipes typical of the period were used. Biographies of the Presidents' wives, from Martha Washington through Lady Bird Johnson, are featured. Wives and hostesses, family groups, and official and private occasions through the history of the White House are pictured, and the selection of official and private menus has been brought up to date.

Mrs. Gillette's original recipes from her editions of 1887 and the 1890s make up the general Recipes section of this book. They have been augmented by selections from other Victorian cookbooks. To anyone fortunate enough to have "eaten after" a nineteenth-century cook, these recipes bring back mouth-watering memories of vegetable soup served from a big black kettle, not a can, of homemade bread that *was* bread, of cake that was a bit heavier than our modern mix-cakes and ever so much richer. They recall leisurely summer afternoons enhanced by sugar and molasses cookies, fresh from the oven, not the box, and delectable, sweet-sour lemonade that came from a real lemon—you could tell by the seeds.

Some of Mrs. Gillette's recipes and the recipes of early Presidents' Wives and Hostesses may seem a bit vague to cooks of today. Little attempt has been made to modernize them. Cooking was an art before it was a science. When good cooks of fifty or a hundred years ago got together to swap "receipts," it wasn't necessary to tell all. Mrs. Theodore Roosevelt, for example, explains how to mix her Indian Pudding, but she does not mention that it must be baked. If we were to point out this oversight, I'm sure Mrs. TR would reply impatiently: "Well, anybody knows that!" And if we were to change "saleratus" to "baking soda," or if we were to brown a sugar-topped cake under the broiler instead of with a *salamander*, the recipes would be ours, not their originators'.

Those were the golden days of cooking when meals were not easy nor instant nor even "vitamin-rich"—an hour's boiling certainly took care of all the Vitamin C in a head of cabbage!—but just delicious and soul-satisfying to both producer and consumer. The recipes, like the old Etiquette and Household hints in this book are fun to read. Some are fun to try, and you have Mrs. Gillette's solemn promise that they were tested and proved—in 1887.

By way of contrast and in the interest of good eating, as well as good reading, modern recipes have been included in the new edition. Some are my own favorites, some were contributed by friends who are good cooks. Mrs. Gillette might not admit that the modern recipes are *better* than hers, but she could not fail to be amazed and impressed by the ease and speed with which good meals can be prepared in 1964.

The modern recipes and the old-timers that are still practical for today's cook have been starred. All recipes not starred are originals of the 1890s or earlier and may be tried at the reader's discretion! Some are curiosity pieces—kitchen heirlooms as quaintly appealing and impractical as a *turk's head*. Others are classics that "age cannot wither nor custom stale," as good today as they were many days before yesterday.

One thing might perplex Mrs. Gillette about modern cooking. With all the automatic kitchen equipment at its command, why does a mid-twentieth-century family persist in cooking its meat over an old-fashioned outdoor grill, pioneer-style? Because that's the "modern way," Mrs. Gillette. *The more things change, the more they remain the same.*

—J.H.E.

Contents

The Laws of Etiquette

THE RULES AND HABITS OF POLITE SOCIETY, CIRCA 1887

Recipes

Prescriptions, Recipes

AND SUCH FOR HEALTH, HOUSEHOLD, AND HAPPINESS, CIRCA 1887

The Presidents' Wives

AND OFFICIAL HOSTESSES OF THE WHITE HOUSE 1789–1964

The Laws of Etiquette

THE RULES AND HABITS

OF POLITE SOCIETY

CIRCA 1887

"God may forgive sins, but awkwardness has no forgiveness in Heaven or Earth."

—Hawthorne

A SIMPLE LIFE RECIPE

Thought for self, one part; thought for family, two parts; equal parts of common sense and broad intelligence, a large modicum of the sense of the fitness of things, a heaping measure of living above what the neighbors think of you, twice the quantity of keeping within your income, a sprinkling of what tends to refinement and aesthetic beauty, stirred thick with the true brand of Christian principle and set it to rise.

Good Manners

GOOD MANNERS are very closely allied to good morals. The Messiah himself, in His great moral teachings, frequently touches upon mere manners. He teaches that modesty is the true spirit of decent behavior and rebukes the forward manner of His followers in taking the upper seats at banquets.

Socrates and Aristotle have left behind them a series of ethics that might easily be turned into a "Guide to the Complete Gentleman."

Lord Bacon reminds us that a stone must be of very high value to do without a setting. Dr. Johnson doubtless considered himself one of these unset gems with his speech, "Sir, you are a fool!" Unfortunately, Johnson has too many imitators among those of inferior value.

Lord Chesterfield's manners, fine as they appear, have not the ring of true metal about them.

The motive of good manners is to make one better than he is, to render him agreeable to everyone with whom he has to do, and to improve the society in which he is placed.

A man is a better citizen for being a gentleman.

THE ART OF CONVERSATION

Avoid associating with those who express themselves incorrectly and vulgarly. Nothing is so infectious as bad speech.

Affectations of foreign accent and mannerisms are detestable.

Absolute suppression of emotion, *whether of anger, laughter, mortification, or disappointment*, is one of the most certain marks of good breeding.

The voice should never be loud, no gesticulation should accompany the speech, and the features should be under strict control. Nothing is more ill-bred than a half-opened mouth, a vacant stare, a wandering eye, or a smile ready to break into a laugh at any moment.

Be genial, animated, sympathetic, and cheerful, or do not go into society. Dull and stupid people are but so many clogs to the machinery of social life.

Flattery is suggestive of snobbery, particularly if it be paid to people of great wealth and high position.

The habit of "fishing" for compliments is notably vulgar, and it is one in which a certain class of vain young people are very apt to indulge, especially among themselves in private.

All "slang" is vulgar. The alarming prevalence of slangy phrases among the young people of this day is enough to cause our decorous fore-fathers and mothers to rise in their graves. It is a grand mistake to imagine slang to be a substitute for wit. This habit is more reprehensible in young ladies than in the opposite sex.

Scandal is a sin against morality as well as good taste.

Punning is a most objectionable habit. Unless a pun amounts to a positive witticism, it should never be propounded in company.

Religion and politics are two subjects to be avoided.

Be a good listener. Give your companion the impression that you are in perfect sympathy with and highly entertained by what he is saying.

Topics especially interesting to gentlemen, such as the farm and business matters, should be excluded in general society.

Be very careful of introducing long-winded anecdotes into the con-versation. Nothing is more awkward than to find an array of bored faces when one is not more than half through a long story.

Repartee should be indulged in only moderately. Otherwise it may degenerate into flippancy, a habit much to be condemned in certain young ladies who think themselves clever or, as our American word goes, "smart."

Names should be used as little as possible. Few solecisms give greater offense than a liberty taken with a name.

People take more interest in their affairs than in anything else. Having furnished the topic, you have but to listen to acquire a reputation for being intelligent and well-bred.

If you would not be unpopular, do not always be witty, no matter what your natural abilities may be in that line. People do not like to be always outshone.

Never correct a fault if you wish to retain a friend.

Avoid such colloquialisms as "says I."

In telling a joke, do not laugh yourself before the point is reached.

In *tête-à-tête* conversation, it is always ill-bred to drop the voice to a whisper.

In speaking of husband or wife, do not use last name alone.

It is exceedingly bad taste to parade the fact that you are an acquain-tance of distinguished or wealthy people or that you have been to college or that your family is noted for gentility and blue blood.

4

THE ETIQUETTE OF SALUTATION

Acquaintances of every degree of intimacy, from the closest to the slightest, are entitled to a bow.

Never fail to return a bow. It is extremely rude. An intimate friend may be more cordially greeted.

The custom of nodding to everyone you meet in thinly settled neighborhoods is a very pleasant one, as it evinces kindliness of feeling and should be generally followed out.

SALUTATION IN THE STREET

If a gentleman is smoking when he meets a lady, he should remove the cigar from his mouth in bowing. None but a boor will puff a cloud of tobacco smoke in the face of a lady who is honoring him with a salutation.

If passing on the street, the hand farthest from the lady should be used in removing the hat.

On meeting a number of persons, you should greet all alike. To gush exuberantly over one and bow stiffly to another would be making a distinction that could not fail to be remarked and might wound the feelings.

A gentleman should not bow from a window to a lady, but if a lady recognizes him from a window, he should return the salutation. It is best, however, for a lady to avoid such recognitions. It is not in the best

5

taste for her to sit sufficiently near her windows to recognize and be recognized by those passing on the street.

ETIQUETTE OF THE STREET

A lady will bow first. She will not stop on the street to converse with a gentleman. If he wishes to chat with her, he will turn and walk by her side until he has finished his conversation, then raise his hat and leave her.

It is not etiquette for a lady to take the arm of a gentleman on the street in the daytime, unless he be a lover or husband, and even then it is seldom done.

In walking with a lady, a gentleman should take charge of any small parcel, book, etc., with which she may be burdened.

Never recognize a gentleman unless you are perfectly sure of his identity. Nothing is more awkward than a mistake of this kind.

The body should not be bent at all in bowing.

Ladies should avoid walking rapidly on the street, as it is ungraceful.

Staring at people, expectorating, looking back on the street, calling in a loud voice, laughing, etc., are very bad manners.

A gentleman may assist a lady from an omnibus or over a bad crossing without the formality of an introduction. Having performed the service, he will bow and retire.

STREET PROMENADE SCENE

ETIQUETTE OF DRIVING

The art of driving is simple enough but requires practice. No one should pretend who does not understand every part of the harness and cannot harness and unharness a horse himself.

LADY ALIGHTING

A good driver will use his horse well, whether it be his own or another's. He will turn corners gently and know when to drive fast and when to ease him up.

In the carriage, a gentleman places himself with his back to the horses, leaving the best seat for the ladies. Only very elderly gentlemen are privileged to take the back seat. No gentleman driving alone with a lady should sit beside her, unless he is her husband, father, son, or brother. Even an affianced lover should remember this rule of etiquette.

To get in and out of a carriage gracefully is quite an accomplishment. A gentleman should be careful to avoid stepping on the lady's dress. He should always get out of a carriage first to assist her in alighting.

When a gentleman intends taking a lady driving in a one-seated vehicle, he should be sure his horse is a safe one, as he is obliged to get out to assist the lady in and out of the vehicle. He should always hold the reins so that he can check the animal in case it should start suddenly.

The dress should never be lifted in alighting from a carriage but left to trail upon the ground.

7

ETIQUETTE OF TRAVELING

It is only courteous for a gentleman to offer a lady the seat beside him, as she scarcely likes to seat herself beside him without such invitation.

A courteous gentleman will also relinquish his place to two ladies or a gentleman and lady together. Such a sacrifice always receives its reward in grateful admiration of his character.

Ladies traveling alone, when addressed in a courteous manner by gentlemen, should reply politely. In long journeys it is even allowable to enter into conversation without the formality of an introduction. But a true lady will always know how to keep the conversation from bordering on familiarity and by a quiet dignity and sudden *hauteur* will check any attempt at presumption on the part of her strange acquaintance.

LADIES TRAVELING WITHOUT ESCORT

Very young ladies are not allowed to travel without the attendance of some older person, either male or female.

A lady should enter a hotel by way of the ladies' entrance.

A lady will not, of course, enter into conversation with any but friends at a public table. A simple request to the waiter, particularly if it be backed by a slight remuneration, will ensure his meeting her at the dining-room entrance and preceding her to her seat, thus obviating the slight awkwardness of crossing a full dining room without an escort.

While waiting to be served, it is permissible to read a newspaper. All orders should be given in a low but clear and distinct tone of voice. Never ask anyone at the table to pass you anything nor point to any article wanted; a glance at the waiter is usually sufficient.

Loud and ostentatious dressing is out of place in a hotel dining room. A quiet, unassuming dress of cloth or plain black silk is the most ladylike.

When a lady is without escort, it would be best for her not to take her supper in the dining room late in the evening. She can have a meal sent to her room at a trifling extra cost.

A lady should never loiter in the halls nor stand alone at a hotel window.

She should never hum to herself while going through the halls nor play on the piano nor sing in a hotel parlor unless invited to do so.

If she be naturally of a lively and chatty disposition, she must beware how she indulge these innocent propensities, lest they be misunderstood.

Chester's Livery, Sale and Boarding Stable, Turnouts for Funerals a Specialty. Terms Cash. —(*old adv.*)

RAILWAY CAR SCENE, PROPER

RAILWAY CAR SCENE, IMPROPER

ETIQUETTE OF THE LADY'S TOILET

Cleanliness is the outward sign of inward purity. It is not to be supposed that a lady washes to become clean but simply to remain clean. Bathe the entire body once a day. It is not necessary to have a bathtub for this purpose, merely an ordinary basin of tepid water, with soap, sponge, and clean towels.

Teeth should be brushed night and morning and after each meal. The best tooth powder is a simple preparation of chalk.

A sweet breath is one of the essentials of happiness.

Much care is given the nails by those who are particular in matters of the toilet. Of late years the care of the nails has been elevated to a profession, and persons calling themselves "manicures" make it their business to dress the nails of ladies of fashion.

The hair should be brushed morning and evening and cleansed occasionally with a mixture of glycerine and lime juice. Your own hair, as nature colored it, is apt to be the only shade that will correspond with your eyes, eyebrows, and complexion. The use of hair dyes, false hair, etc., is almost as much to be condemned as painted cheeks and penciled brows.

A NEATLY DRESSED LADY   AN OVERDRESSED LADY

Milk baths, pearl powders, and complexion lotions would never be needed if ladies were always careful to take exercise in the open air, wear broad-brimmed hats in the sun and veils in the wind.

Perfumery should properly be used only in the evening, and then it should be of the most *recherché* kind.

How Lumped Sweetness May Gain in Grace

The stout woman is always asking what she shall wear. Now these, according to the New York *Sun*, are some of the things she should not wear:

She should not wear a tailor-made suit fitting her figure closely. It brings out every pound of flesh for the benefit of the looker-on.

She should not wear a rosette at her belt.

She should not wear a lace or ribbon ruche about her neck, though the soft feather one is permissible if it have long ends.

She should not wear a short skirt.

She should not wear her hair low on her neck.

She should not wear a string of beads about her neck, rings in her ears, or, if her fingers are short and fat, many rings on them.

She should avoid high sleeves and loose gloves.

She should shun champagne.

She should hate ice-cream.

> OBESITY *safely cured by a Fellow Sufferer. Stout Abdomens Reduced. Debility and Short Breath a Specialty. Dr. Burdon, Patterson, N.J. — (old adv.)*
>
> THINACURA *for Thin People. Flesh made with Thinacura Tablets is a Scientific Process. Produces 12 to 15 pounds per month, containing no arsenic. Pamphlet, "How to Get Fat," free. The Thinacura Co., New York City. — (old adv.)*

ETIQUETTE OF THE GENTLEMAN'S DRESSING ROOM

The first requisite of the male toilet is, of course, the bath. This should be as bracing as the constitution will allow. The cold-water bath is best, but there are very few physiques, especially among Americans, that will admit of it.

A sponge bath once a day, with a liberal use of the flesh brush and a coarse huckaback towel, will answer every purpose.

Long nails are vulgar.

11

The beard should be kept will trimmed and well combed, and plenty of warm water and soap should be used on it.

Do not indulge in long hair, thinking it gives you an artistic look. Except in painters and poets, flowing locks are a ridiculous affectation.

The mustache should be neat and not overlarge. A mustache à l'Empereur is absurd and smacks of the fop.

When fashion dictates tight pantaloons, do not have them so tight you cannot bend in them; nor, if broad ones be the mode, shall they resemble your wife's gown.

Loud patterns in cloth and glittering trinkets on the watch chain are indications rather of the gambler than the gentleman.

Bulwer says, "A gentleman's coat should not fit too well," and he is right, as no self-respecting man wants to be taken for a tailor's dummy.

Regulation dress for evening wear—but never before sundown—is black swallow-tail coat, black trousers, black vest, cut low to show the shirt front, thin patent-leather boots, a white cravat, and light kid gloves.

Sleeve buttons and collar studs should be of plain gold but genuine.

O'Connell's Barber Shop—Next Door to the Postoffice, Baths Day and Night. —(old adv.)

NEATLY DRESSED GENTLEMAN

THE DUDE

"WELL LATHERED IS HALF SHAVED."

Spanish Proverb.

That which distinguishes "SHAVING SOAP" from Toilet or Washing Soaps is the LATHER.
What is lather *for*? What does it *do*? What *should* it do?
The use of Soap in Shaving is to penetrate, moisten, and soften the beard that it may present the least possible resistance to the keen edge of the razor. Failing in this—it fails utterly!
But it has other uses!!
Shaving is naturally an irritating process to the skin. The soap applied should contain properties to soothe and allay irritation.
Many "*so-called*" Shaving Soaps have a very opposite effect. They *draw* and parch the skin, and after shaving impart to the face a feeling similar to that caused by the cutting of a sharp wind.
A TRUE Shaving Soap should contain *germicide* properties.
Gentlemen who are shaved by barbers are unconsciously exposed to the most distressing cutaneous diseases.
For HALF A HUNDRED YEARS WILLIAMS' SHAVING SOAPS have ranked as the PUREST, RICHEST, and BEST.
Compare the lather with that of *any* other.
Mild and Delicate, it penetrates and softens the beard, and renders shaving a positive luxury. Unlike other Shaving Soaps, the *lather will not dry on the face while shaving*.
WILLIAMS' SHAVING SOAPS have a *Soothing* effect upon the Skin. Like rich cream, the lather cools, softens, and heals.
GENTLEMEN WHO ARE SHAVED BY BARBERS should *insist upon it* that WILLIAMS' BARBERS' BAR SOAP is used. Rich and refreshing, it contains properties destructive to disease germs, and renders SAFE the luxury of *being* shaved.

"GENUINE YANKEE" SOAP, UNSURPASSED for Use of Gentlemen who shave THEMSELVES, STANDARD for QUALITY in U. S. NAVY. **15c.**

WILLIAMS' SHAVING STICK, EXCELLING all other Shaving Sticks in Richness of LATHER, DELICACY of PERFUME, and superior strength and Style of Package. **25c.**

WILLIAMS' BARBERS' BAR SOAP, USED in THOUSANDS of FAMILIES AS A TOILET SOAP. ABSOLUTELY PURE! SURE Preventive of "Chapped Hands." A Perfect NURSERY SOAP. 6 cakes for 40c. **40c.**

WILLIAMS' SHAVING SOAPS are SOLD by all DRUGGISTS.
FOR 75 CENTS we will mail, postpaid, a package of each of the 3 kinds.
Sample of any one kind mailed on receipt of price. Stamps or Currency.

Address communications to

The J. B. WILLIAMS CO., Glastonbury, Conn.

(Originally WILLIAMS & BROS., Manchester, 1840.)

(old advertisement)

13

ETIQUETTE OF ENGAGEMENTS

The Proposal

No wise man will intrude himself upon the presence of a lady; neither will a modest woman receive the attentions of a man too eagerly, however agreeably she may regard them. Unless a woman is a downright coquette, a man of sense ought to be able to judge whether his proposal will be favorably received or not. It is exceedingly dishonorable, not to say cruel, for either a man or a woman to trifle with the affections of the other.

The manner of making the proposal must always be regulated by circumstances. If the gentleman be ready of speech and attractive in person, it is best for him to plead his cause in *persona propria* and receive his acceptance with the added sweetness of smile and blush and love-lit glance, or his rejection with the tender, saving grace of sadly murmured regrets.

If the suitor, however, be of a nervous temperament or "fears his cause too much" to risk a personal interview, he should make his proposal in writing.

In making his offer of marriage, a man should always bear in mind that he is a petitioner, that he is begging of the woman to grant him her liberty, her obedience, her very life, and he should comport himself with suitable humility and accept her acquiescence with becoming gratitude.

Advice to Brides

The girls that are wanted are home girls,
Girls that are Mother's right hand,
That fathers and brothers can trust to
And the little ones understand.

The girls that are wanted are careful girls
Who count what a thing will cost,
Who use with a prudent, generous hand
But see that nothing is lost.

Deportment of the Engaged

The gentleman fortunate enough to be engaged should be careful always to observe the following directions regarding his conduct:

14

He should be tender and devoted to his bride-elect.

He should treat her family with the greatest respect.

He should always be on the alert to do any member of her family a service, play devoted friend to his betrothed and all her relatives, be kind to the children and courteous toward the servants.

He should particularly guard against taking liberties that he is not justified in taking, such as borrowing money from the family.

He should not compromise his fiancée's reputation by keeping her up until a late hour. His visits may be frequent but short. The custom of lovers staying until a late hour of the night is no longer permitted in genteel society.

He should be gallant toward other ladies but not sufficiently to excite the jealousy of his betrothed. He should not monopolize her company but should be watchful of all her wants.

He may keep her supplied with flowers, books and with sweetmeats if she has a taste for bonbons, or with more costly gifts if his means are not limited and her family does not object. A sensible man will not give more than he can afford nor run into debt.

If there is an engagement ring, it should be worn upon the first finger of the left hand.

The lady must be careful not to excite the jealousy of her lover by flirting with other men. She must avoid undue familiarity on his part and effectually check any attempt toward such.

A Lady's Chances of Marrying

Every woman has some chance of marrying. It may be one to fifty, or it may be ten to one that she will. Representing her entire chance at one hundred, at certain points of her progress in time it is found to be in the following ratio:

Between the ages of 15 and 20 years.	14½ per cent
Between the ages of 20 and 25 years.	52 per cent
Between the ages of 25 and 30 years.	18 per cent
Between the ages of 30 and 35 years.	15½ per cent
Between the ages of 35 and 40 years.	3¾ per cent
Between the ages of 40 and 45 years.	2½ per cent
Between the ages of 45 and 50 years.	⅜ of 1 per cent
Between the ages of 50 and 55 years.	¼ of 1 per cent

After sixty it is 1/10 of 1 per cent—or one chance in a thousand. A pretty slender figure. But figures are often slender at that age. [*Note:* And the figures in the right-hand column add up to more than one hundred per cent!]

15

ETIQUETTE OF THE HOUSE

Every mistress of a house is a sovereign queen whose court is the home circle. No lady, however gifted, can afford to neglect the management of her household. No tastes, no pleasures should be allowed to stand in the way of this important duty.

Children should speak respectfully to parents and obey the slightest command immediately. Parents should address a child in a mild, pleasant, but firm manner. Issue no orders but those of a just and reasonable nature, then see that they are obeyed, and home will be indeed a little heaven on earth.

Elegance adds greatly to the enjoyment of life if it is not purchased at the expense of peace of mind. To affect a better income than you have, to ape the manners of your richer neighbors, proclaims you are vulgar and ill-bred in the highest degree. Shams are contemptible. Every young housekeeper should build her house upon a superstructure of sincerity, and she will never have to blush at awkward discoveries.

One good engraving is better than half a dozen cheap chromos.

A house without books is a house without a soul.

Thorns and ferns are ornamental and may be obtained at a very slight expenditure.

Be careful not to overload your rooms with cheap knick-knacks and gaudy tidies.

In this day of artistic furniture, art magazines, and art crazes generally, there need be no excuse for bad taste in furnishing. The day of one stiff sofa, six stiff chairs, and one straight table, all placed rigidly against the wall, is over.

Offer good wages, take a well-recommended girl, and patiently teach her your way. The servant question is the most difficult one housekeepers have to contend with in America.

A housewife should use her head to save her heels.

ETIQUETTE OF THE BALL AND THE "GERMAN"

The invitations to a ball should be delivered by a footman at least two weeks before the appointed evening.

As you wish your ball to be the event of the season, you must have your rooms handsomely decorated. An abundance of cut flowers should be artistically scattered around, with here and there a tropical plant. The fireplaces should be screened by flowers in summer.

The most favorable room for dancing is one which is nearly square but rather longer than wide. Such a room will admit of two quadrille parties at once. The top of a ballroom is the part nearest the orchestra; the top couples always lead off.

A good floor is highly important. In private houses nothing is better than a good Holland floorcloth well stretched over the carpet. It is customary to provide three pieces for dancing: a piano and two violins or piano, cornet, and violin. Sometimes harp and violins are used.

The ladies' toilet room should be well supplied with mirrors, pins, needles and thread for repairing rents, and plenty of attendants to assist the fair ones at their toilets.

The supper hour is usually from twelve to one o'clock and the hour of departing from two to three A.M. The supper is regulated by the wealth of the host. A caterer may serve it up in good style with extra appliances of salads, oysters, fancy ices, coffees, wines, and fruits and cakes of every description. If supper be homemade, coffee and sandwiches with fruit and two or three kinds of ices and cake are all-sufficient.

No one sits down to a ball supper. If seats are ranged around the room for the ladies, the gentlemen stand.

Carpet should be laid from the edge of the pavement to the doorway, and if the evening be wet, a temporary covering should be erected for the protection of the ladies in passing from their carriages to the house.

A gentleman should not accept an invitation to a ball if he does not dance.

When your name is announced, look for the lady of the house and pay your respects to her. Good breeding demands that you do not present yourself at the beginning nor remain until the close of the evening.

Learn to Dance Without a Master! Articles, illustrated, and instructions for the Plain Waltz (as now danced), the Plain Polka, the Three-Slide Polka, the Polka Redowa, the Yorke, the Caprice, the Heel-and-Toe Polka, the Military Schottisch, the new Varsovianna, the Berlin, etc. In the February issue of Demorest's Family Magazine. —(old adv.)

Husband and wife should not enter the reception room arm-in-arm, as that is considered vulgar. The host introduces the guests to his wife if, as is frequently the case in official Washington, she is not acquainted with them.

It is well to throw open as many rooms as possible and to have tables scattered here and there, covered with choice engravings, photographic views, valuable scrapbooks, etc., for the entertainment of the guests.

Buffet for 1,000 People, White House Style, 1891

Cold Service

CONSOMMÉ EN TASSE

SANDWICHES   CAVIAR ON TOAST   RADISHES   CELERY

COLD SALMON MAYONNAISE   LOBSTER AND SHRIMP SALAD

WESTPHALIA HAM À LA GELÉE

BONED TURKEY   GALANTINE OF FAISON

COLD GAME IN SEASON

MAYONNAISE OF CHICKEN   COLD TURKEY   FILLET OF BEEF

GAME PIES   SADDLE OF VENISON, CURRANT JELLY

RUSSIAN SALAD

NEAPOLITAINE ICE CREAM   WATER ICES

NESSELRODE PUDDINGS

CLARET AND CHAMPAGNE JELLIES

BISCUITS GLACÉE   CHARLOTTES GLACÉE

ASSORTED CAKES   ASSORTED CANDIES

TEA   COFFEE   LEMONADE

The "German"

No lady's series of entertainments are complete without "the prime favorite." Young ladies now are much accustomed to forming social clubs with pretty, suggestive names which meet at the houses of the different members.

All must be formally introduced at the German, for no young lady can refuse to dance with a gentleman whom she may have received as a partner so long as she remain in the circle.

Favors are usually given.

O HARK, O HEAR—*no other music steals into your senses with the fine tinkling, tingling harmony that floats outward from the Paillard Gloria Interchangeable Music Box!* —*(old adv.)*

HOW TO RECEIVE AND ENTERTAIN

Friendly calls should be made in the forenoon, and require neatness without costliness of dress.

Calls to give invitations to dinner parties or balls should be very short and should be paid in the afternoon.

Visits of condolence require a grave style of dress.

A formal visit should never be made before noon. If a second visitor is announced, it will be proper for you to retire, unless you are very intimate both with the host and the visitor announced.

Visits after balls or parties should be made within a month. In the latter it is customary to enclose your card in an envelope bearing the address outside. This may be sent by post if you reside at a distance.

But, if living in the neighborhood, it is polite to send your servant or to call. In the latter case a corner should be turned down.

Scrape your shoes and use the mat. Never appear in a drawing room with mud on your boots.

When a new visitor enters a drawing room, if it be a gentleman, the ladies bow slightly; if a lady, the guests rise.

Hold your hat in your hand unless requested to place it down. Then lay it beside you.

The last arrival in a drawing room takes a seat left vacant near the mistress of the house.

A lady is not required to rise to receive a gentleman, nor accompany him to the door.

When your visitor retires, ring the bell for the servant. You may then accompany your guest as far toward the door as the circumstances of your friendship seem to demand.

Request the servant to be ready to attend to the door the moment the bell rings.

When you introduce a person, pronounce the name distinctly and say whatever you can to make the introduction agreeable. Such as "an old and valued friend," a "schoolfellow of mine" or "an old acquaintance of our family."

Never stare about you in a room as if you were taking stock.

The gloves should not be removed during a call.

Be hearty in your reception of guests, and where you see much diffidence, assist the stranger to throw it off.

A lady does not put her address on her visiting card.

A gentleman always and under any circumstances looks after his own hat, and a lady is not even supposed to know of its existence.

DINNER-GIVING
The Laying of the Table and the Treatment of Guests

In giving dinners, the apparently "trifling" details are of great importance when taken as a whole.

We gather around our board agreeable persons, and they pay us and our dinner the courtesy of dressing for the occasion. This reunion should be a time of profit as well as pleasure. There are certain established laws by which "dinner-giving" is regulated in polite society, and it may not be amiss to give a few observances in relation to them:

A guest should arrive at the house of his host at least a quarter of an hour before the time appointed for dinner.

All the linen throughout should be a spotless white, and underneath the linen tablecloth should be spread one of thick cotton flannel or baize, which gives the linen a finer appearance and deadens the sound of moving dishes.

Large and neatly folded napkins, ironed without starch, with pieces of bread three or four inches long, placed between the folds, but not to completely conceal it, are laid on each plate.

A vase filled with a few rare flowers is put on the center of the table in place of the large table castor, which has gone into disuse and is rarely seen now on well-appointed tables. The eye, in fact, should be gratified as much as the palate.

Each dish should be garnished sufficiently to be in good taste without looking absurd.

STATE DINING ROOM AT THE WHITE HOUSE, CA. 1890

Water bottles are now much in vogue with corresponding tumblers to cover them; these, accompanied with dishes of broken ice, may be arranged in suitable places.

If preferred, the dinner may all be served from the side table, thus relieving the host from the task of carving. If not served from the side table, the dishes are brought in ready-carved and placed before the host and hostess, then served and placed upon the waiter's salver, to be laid by that attendant before the guest. Jellies and sauces, when not to be eaten as a dessert, should be helped on the dinner plate, not on a small side dish as was the former usage. Butter is not served at the more elegant dinners.

All should have the opportunity of choice. The host will simply ask each one if he has any preference for a particular part of a dish; if the guest replies in the negative, you are not to repeat the question nor insist that he must have a preference.

Do not attempt to eulogize your dishes or apologize that you cannot

21

recommend them; this is extreme bad taste, as also is the vaunting of the excellence of your wines, etc., etc.

Do not insist upon your guests' partaking of particular dishes. Do not ask persons more than once, and never force a supply upon their plates. It is ill-bred, though common, to press anyone to eat, and moreover it is a great annoyance to many.

The hostess should retain her plate, knife, and fork until her guests have finished.

The crumb brush is not used until the preparation for bringing in the dessert.

Coffee and tea are served lastly, poured into tiny cups and served clear, passed around on a tray to each guest. Then the sugar and cream may be passed that each person can season his *café noir* to suit himself.

A Simple Family Dinner

A simple family dinner may be made quite attractive and satisfactory without much display or expense, consisting of good soup, then fish garnished with suitable additions, followed by a roast, then vegetables and some made dishes, a salad, crackers, cheese and olives, then dessert.

This sensible meal, well cooked and neatly served, is pleasing to almost anyone and is within the means of any housekeeper in ordinary circumstances.

FAMILY DINING ROOM AT THE WHITE HOUSE, CA. 1890

Soup or pudding is placed at the head of the table, meat at the lower end, vegetables on each side of the middle, and sauce boats in the middle, boiled meat at the top, roast meat at the bottom, soup in the middle, vegetables and sauce boats at cross-corners of the middle dish. Poultry or mutton is placed at the bottom, boiled poultry at the top, roast poultry or game at the bottom, vegetables and sauces so disposed as to give the appearance of the whole table being covered without being crowded.

SMALL POINTS ON TABLE ETIQUETTE

Delicacy of manner at table stamps both man and woman, for one can, at a glance, discern whether a person has been trained to eat well— i. e., to hold the knife and fork properly, to eat without the slightest sound of the lips, to drink quietly, to use the napkin rightly, to make no noise with any of the implements of the table, and last but not least, to eat slowly and masticate the food thoroughly. All these points should be most carefully taught to children, and then they will always feel at their ease at the grandest tables in the land. There is no position where the innate refinement of a person is more fully exhibited than at the table and nowhere that those who have not been trained in table etiquette feel more keenly their deficiencies.

The knife should never be used to carry food to the mouth.

Be careful to keep the mouth shut closely while masticating the food. It is the opening of the lips which causes the smacking which seems very disgusting. Chew your food well, but do it silently, and be careful to take small mouthfuls.

The knife can be used to cut the meat finely, as large pieces of meat are not healthful and appear very indelicate.

Be very careful not to clatter your knives and forks upon your plates, but use them without noise. When you are helped to anything, do not wait until the rest of the company are provided; it is not considered good breeding.

Soup is always served for the first course, and it should be eaten with dessert spoons and taken from the sides, not the tips of them, without any sound of the lips and not sucked into the mouth audibly from the end of the spoon.

Bread should not be broken into soup or gravy.

Never ask to be helped to soup a second time. The hostess may ask you to take a second plate, but you will politely decline. Fish chowder, which is served in soup plates, is said to be an exception which proves this rule, and when eating of that it is correct to take a second plateful if desired.

Bread is very frequently buttered in the air, bitten in gouges, and still held in the face and eyes of the table with the marks of the teeth on it. This is certainly not altogether pleasant, and it is better to cut it, a bit at a time, after buttering it, and put piece by piece in the mouth with one's finger and thumb.

Never help yourself to butter or any other food with your own knife and fork.

It is not considered good taste to mix food on the same plate.

Salt must be left on the side of the plate and never on the tablecloth.

Let us mention a few things concerning the eating of which there is sometimes doubt: A cream cake should be eaten with knife and fork, never bitten. Asparagus—which should be always served on bread or toast so as to absorb superfluous moisture—may be taken from the finger and thumb; if it is fit to be set before you, the whole of it may be eaten. Green corn should be eaten from the cob, but it must be held with a single hand.

Berries are to be eaten with a spoon. In England, they are many times the size of ours; there they take the berry by the stem, dip into powdered sugar, and eat it as we do the turnip radish.

It is not proper to drink with a spoon in the cup, nor should one, by the way, ever quite drain a cup or glass.

Don't, when you drink, elevate your glass as if you were going to stand it inverted on your nose. Bring the glass perpendicularly to the lips and then lift it to a slight angle. Do this easily.

Drink sparingly while eating. Drink gently and do not pour it down your throat like water turned out of a pitcher.

Unfold your napkin and lay it across your lap in such a manner that it will not slide off upon the floor; a gentleman should place it across his right knee. Do not tuck it into your neck like a child's bib. For an old person, however, it is well to attach the napkin to a napkin hook and slip it into the vest or dress buttonholes to protect the garments. Or a broad tape may be sewn at two places on the napkin so that it can be passed over the head.

Finger bowls are not a general institution, and yet they seem to be quite as needful as the napkin. They can be had quite cheaply and should be half filled with water and placed upon the side table or butler's tray with the dessert, bread, and cheese, etc. They are placed on a parti-colored napkin with a dessert plate underneath when the dessert is placed upon the table. A leaf or two of sweet verbena, an

CORRECT DINNER TABLE

INCORRECT DINNER TABLE

orange flower, or a small slice of lemon is usually put into each bowl. At dinner parties and luncheons they are indispensable.

A spoon should never be turned over in the mouth.

Ladies have frequently an affected way of holding the knife halfway down its length as if it were too big for their little hands, but this is as awkward a way as it is weak. The knife should be grasped freely by the handle only, the forefinger being the only one to touch the blade, and that only along the back of the blade at its root and no further down.

At the conclusion of a course, knife and fork should be laid side by side across the middle of the plate—never crossed; the old custom of crossing them was in obedience to an ancient religious formula.

One's teeth are not to be picked at table, but if it is impossible to hinder it, it should be done behind the napkin.

One may pick a bone at the table but, as with corn, only one hand is allowed to touch it. Yet one can usually get enough from it with knife and fork, which is certainly the more elegant way of doing, and to take her teeth to it gives a lady the look of caring a little too much for the pleasures of the table. One is, however, on no account, to suck one's finger after it.

There is a reason for everything in polite usage; thus the reason why one does not blow a thing to cool it is not only that it is an inelegant and vulgar action intrinsically but because it may be offensive to others —cannot help being so indeed—and it moreover implies haste which, whether from greediness or desire to get away, is equally objectionable. Everything else may be as easily traced to its origin in the fit and becoming thing to do.

CARVING

Carving is one important acquisition in the routine of daily living, and all should try to attain a knowledge or ability to do it well, and withal gracefully.

When carving use a chair slightly higher than the ordinary size, as it gives a better purchase on the meat and appears more graceful than when standing, as is often quite necessary when carving a very large joint. More depends on skill than strength. The platter should be placed opposite and sufficiently near to give perfect command of the article to be carved. Commence by cutting the slices thin, laying them carefully to one side of the platter, then afterwards placing the desired amount on each guest's plate, to be served in turn by the servant.

In carving fish, care should be taken to help it in perfect flakes; for if these are broken the beauty of the fish is lost. The carver should acquaint himself with the choicest parts and morsels, and to give each guest an equal share of those tidbits should be his maxim. In filling plates, avoid heaping one thing upon another, as it makes a bad appearance.

The root of the Beef Tongue is usually left on the platter.

In carving Neck of Veal, cut diagonally and separate small bones. To attempt to carve each chop and serve it, you would be compelled to exercise such a degree of strength that would make one's appearance very ungraceful and possibly, too, throwing gravy over your neighbor sitting next to you.

The modern way of serving a Pig is not to send it to the table whole but have it carved partially by the cook. The head may be divided and placed on the same platter.

A special sauce made with red wine and currant jelly is to accompany Venison.

Do not serve gravy before asking the guest if he pleases to have any.

Gravies should be sent to the table very hot, and in helping one to gravy or melted butter, place it on a vacant side of the plate—not *pour* it over their meat, fish, or fowl—that they may use only as much as they like.

Keep platter with meat over a hot-water dish or spirit lamp.

You may pin a white paper frill around the knucklebone.

An expert carver places the fork in the Turkey and does not remove it until the whole is divided.

Some are fond of Duck Feet, so when dressing the duck these should be neatly skinned and never removed.

The custom of cooking Partridges with their heads on is going into disuse somewhat.

In carving a Pheasant, pass the knife under the merrythought toward the neck.

Tame Pigeons should be cooked as soon as possible after they are killed, as they quickly lose their flavor. Wild Pigeons should hang a day or two in a cool place.

· GENERAL HINTS ON ETIQUETTE

There are a number of minor points of etiquette, not otherwise covered, which we propose touching upon here. Concerning gifts, one is never to be presented to anyone in hopes of a return.

If you present a book to a friend, do not write your name in it unless requested. By doing so you are taking for granted that your present will be accepted and also that a specimen of your penmanship will give additional value to the gift.

Never allude to a present you have given; do not even appear to see it if you are where it is.

Married ladies may occasionally accept a present from a gentleman who visits frequently at the house and desires to express his gratitude. An unmarried lady should not accept presents from any gentleman to whom she is not engaged or who is not a relative.

Never refuse a gift without good reason. Such deprecatory phrases as "I fear I rob you" or "I am really ashamed to take it" are in bad taste.

We should not neglect our young people in the drawing rooms. If we wish our children to have polished manners and to express themselves well, we must lead them to enter into the conversation.

In conversation the face must be pleasant, wearing something that almost approaches to a smile.

Never employ extravagance in conversation. It is absurd to say something is "immensely jolly" or "disgustingly mean."

No lady of breeding will sit sideways on her chair or with her legs crossed or stretched apart or hold her chin in her hands or twirl her watch chain, nor does a well-bred gentleman sit astride of his chair or bite his nails or nurse his leg. A man is always allowed more freedom than a woman, but both should be graceful and decorous in their deportment.

Never point; instead, move the head or wave the whole hand.

Sniffling and expectorating must not be indulged in in decent society.

Shyness may be overcome by determined mixing in society; nothing else will have an effect on it.

A foreigner should be addressed by his full name, as, *Monsieur de Montmorenci*. In speaking of him in his absence, you would say *Monsieur le Marquis de Montmorenci*.

To yawn, put your feet on a chair, stand with your back to the fire, take the most comfortable seat, etc., displays selfishness and a lack of respect.

Boasting is an ill-bred habit. Traveling is so universal a custom now that to mention the fact that you have been to Europe is to state nothing exceptional. Anybody with wealth, health, and leisure can travel.

Avoid any familiarity with a new acquaintance.

In walking on a public promenade, it is necessary to salute the same acquaintances only once in passing.

It is rude to examine the cards in a card basket unless you have an invitation to that effect.

When walking with a lady, give her the wall.

Long hair and a scrawling signature do not constitute genius. Be careful then how you draw upon yourself the ridicule of being a shallow pretender by adopting either or both.

Neither a gentleman nor a lady will boast of the conquests he or she has made. Such a course would have the effect of exciting the most profound contempt for the boasters in the breasts of all who heard them.

For one year after her debut the young lady is allowed to make calls only with her mother or other suitable chaperone.

MANAGEMENT AND DIRECTIONS OF DINNERS AND RECEPTIONS
ON STATE OCCASIONS AT THE WHITE HOUSE

Etiquette as observed in European courts is not known at the White House.

The President's secretary issues invitations by direction of the President to the distinguished guests.

The usher in charge of the cloakroom hands to the gentleman on arrival an envelope containing a diagram of the table whereon the

A STATE DINNER AT THE WHITE HOUSE, 1888

29

State Dinner at the White House, 1891

BLUE POINTS

HAUTE SAUTERNE

Potages

POTAGE TORTUE À L'ANGLAISE   CONSOMMÉ PRINTANIÈRE ROYALE

AMONTILLADO

Hors d'Oeuvres

CANAPÉ À LA RUSSE   TIMBALES À LA TALLEYRAND

RAUENTHALER BERG

Poissons

SAUMON, SAUCE HOLLANDAISE   GRENADINES DE BASS

POMMES DE TERRE DUCHESSE   CUCUMBER SALADE

ERNEST JEROY

Relevès

SELLE D'AGNEAU, SAUCE MENTHE   FILET DE BOEUF À LA RICHELIEU

CHATEAU MARGAUSE

Entrèes

RIS DE VEAU À LA PERIGNEUX   COTELETTES D'AGNEAU D'OR MAISON

TERRAPIN À LA MARYLAND

PUNCH CARDINAL

CLAS DE VOUGEOT

Rôti

CANVAS BACK DUCK

Entremets

GERMAN ASPARAGUS   PETITE POIS

GELÉE AU CHAMPAGNE   PLOMBIÈRE AUX FRAMBOISE

PUDDING DIPLOMATE

CAFÉ   LIQUEURS

FRUITS   FROMAGE

name and seat of the respective guest and the lady he is to escort to dinner are marked.

A card corresponding with his name is placed on the napkin belonging to the cover of the seat he will occupy.

The President's seat is in the middle of the table. The most distinguished guests sit on his right and left. If their wives are present, they will occupy these seats, and the gentlemen will be seated next to the President's wife, whose seat is directly opposite the President.

Official dinners all over the world are always served after the French fashion and are divided into three distinct parts. Two of them are served from the kitchen and the third from the pantry.

The first part of the dinner served French style includes from oysters on the shell to the sherbets.

The second service continues to the sweet dishes.

The third includes ice, cakes, fruits, cheeses, which are all understood as desserts and are dressed in the pantry.

All principal dishes, which are artistically decorated, are shown to the President first, then are carried around the table before being carved by the steward in the pantry.

Fancy folding of the napkins is considered out of fashion; the plain

THE EAST ROOM BEFORE A STATE DINNER, 1903

31

square folded, so as to show monogram in the middle, is much preferred.

Flower decorations on the table are to be in flat designs, so as not to obscure the view of the guests.

Corsage bouquets for ladies consist of not more than eight large roses tied together by silk ribbon with the name of the lady stamped on in gold letters.

Gentlemen's boutonnières consist of only one rosebud.

Bouquets for ladies are to be placed on the right side; for gentlemen, on the napkin next to card bearing his name.

Printed menus are never used on any official occasion.

The private dinner menus are either printed or written on a plain card and placed on each cover.

Liqueurs, cordials, cigars are served on a separate table after the ladies have retired to the parlor.

Recipes

She measured out the butter with a very solemn air,
The milk and sugar also; she took the greatest care
To count the eggs correctly and to add a little bit
Of baking powder which, you know, beginners oft omit,
Then she stirred it all together and she baked it full an hour,
But she never quite forgave herself for leaving out the flour.

A COOK

Is wanted for the family of the President of the United States. No one need apply who is not perfect in the business and can bring indubitable testimonials of sobriety, honesty, and attention to the duties of the station.—Advertisement in the New York Packet, *winter of 1789, by President George Washington*

"The most respected person in the house, other than the President's immediate family, is the cook! All administrations seem to be in awe of her. She is greeted pleasantly, and they really seem to be afraid to record complaints."—Irwin Hoover, former chief usher at the White House

Soups

FRESH UNCOOKED BEEF makes the best soup stock, with the addition of cracked bones, which are composed of an earthy substance, gelatin and a fatty fluid something like marrow. Put meat on to cook in *cold* water, in a covered pot, and simmer slowly. Never allow to boil fast. Never salt it before the meat is tender. Take off every particle of scum. For clear soups strain through a hair sieve or fold a clean towel in a colander set over an earthen bowl.

Stock is not as good when made entirely from cooked meats, but in a family where it requires a large joint roasted every day, the bones and bits of meat would furnish a family soup without buying fresh meat for the purpose; still, with the addition of a little fresh meat it would be more nutritious. In cold weather you can gather them up for several days and cook, then put aside till needed.

Coloring is used in some brown soups, the chief of which is brown burnt sugar, which is known as caramel by French cooks.

Pounded spinach leaves give a fine green color to soup. Pound a handful of spinach in a mortar, then tie it in a cloth and wring out all the juice; put this in the soup you wish to color green five minutes before taking it up.

To color soup red, skin six red tomatoes, squeeze out the seeds and put them into the soup with the other vegetables—or take the juice only, as directed for spinach.

Mock turtle soup, and sometimes veal and lamb soups, should be green. Okras give this color, or parsley or green leaves of celery will serve instead of spinach.

For white soups, which are of veal, lamb, or chicken, none but white vegetables are used: rice, pearl barley, vermicelli, or macaroni for thickening.

Grated carrot gives a fine amber color to soup. It must be put in as soon as the soup is free from scum.

Lemon peel and juice and orange peel and juice impart a fine, mild acid flavor to soup.

An agreeable flavor is sometimes imparted to soup by sticking some cloves into the meat used for making stock; a few slices of onions fried very brown in butter are nice; also, flour browned by simply putting it into a saucepan over the fire and stirring it constantly until it is a dark brown.

The meat from which soup has been made is good to serve cold thus: Take out all the bones; season with pepper and salt and catsup if liked; then chop it small, tie it in a cloth, and lay it between two plates with a weight on the upper one. Slice it thin for luncheon or supper, or make sandwiches of it or make a hash for breakfast, or make it into balls with the addition of a little wheat flour and an egg. Serve the balls fried in fat or boiled in the soup.

When soups and gravies are kept from day to day in hot weather, they should be warmed up every day and put into fresh-scalded pans and placed in a cool cellar. In temperate weather, every other day may be sufficient. [*Note:* Let's make it *every* day in the refrigerator!]

HERBS AND SPICES USED IN SOUPS

Basil—for bouillon or vegetable soup, also good in potato soup.

Marjoram—add a pinch to vegetable soup during last hour of cooking. Good in chicken soup.

Oregano—a pinch in tomato soup.

Rosemary—use ¼ teaspoon in chicken or pea soup.

Savory—a pinch in bean, pea, lentil or potato soup.

Thyme—a dash in fish chowder or vegetable soup.

Sage—use ¼ teaspoon in consommé and cream soups.

Allspice—tomato or pea soup.

Cloves—add ¼ teaspoon to borscht, split pea and potato soups.

Ginger—a pinch in bean soup.

Mace—for oyster stew or cream of chicken soup.

Mustard—add ¼ teaspoon to celery, mushroom, bean or lentil soup.

Nutmeg—chicken and cream soups.

Cayenne Pepper—vegetable juices and soups and oyster stew.

Chili Powder—add dash to vegetable soup just before serving.

TO MAKE A BOUQUET GARNI

Herb bags to season soups and stews may be made of pieces of heavy cheesecloth, four inches square. In the center of each square place about half a teaspoon each dried basil, marjoram, savory, thyme, parsley and a good pinch of sage, bay leaf, celery tops, etc. Tie the little bags securely and store in tightly covered jar until needed.

Meat Soups

BEEF VEGETABLE SOUP

Select a small shin of beef of moderate size, crack the bones in small pieces, wash and place it in a kettle to boil with five or six quarts of cold water. Let it boil about two hours or until it begins to get tender, then season it with a tablespoonful of salt and a teaspoonful of pepper; boil it one hour longer, then add to it one carrot, two turnips, two tablespoonfuls of rice or pearl barley, one head of celery, and a tea-spoonful of summer savory powdered fine, the vegetables to be minced up in small pieces like dice. After these have boiled a quarter of an hour, put in two potatoes cut up in small pieces. Let it boil half an hour longer, take the meat from the soup and, if intended to be served with it, take out the bones and lay it closely and neatly on a dish and garnish with sprigs of parsley.

Serve made mustard and catsup with it. It is very nice pressed and eaten cold. Four hours are required for making this soup. Should any remain over the first day, it may be heated with the addition of a little boiling water and served again. Some fancy a glass of brown sherry added just before being served.

[*Note:* Good old-fashioned vegetable soup, "like Grandma used to make," is one food modern cooks have not been able to improve!]

VEAL SOUP

Put a knuckle of veal into three quarts of cold water with a small quantity of salt and one small tablespoonful of uncooked rice. Boil slowly, hardly above simmering, four hours, when the liquor should be reduced to half the usual quantity. Remove from the fire. Into the tureen put the yolk of one egg and stir well into it a teacupful of cream or, in hot weather, new milk. Add a piece of butter the size of a hickory nut; on this strain the soup, boiling hot, stirring all the time. Just at the last, beat it well for a minute.

GAME SOUP

Two grouse or partridges (or, if you have neither, use a pair of rabbits), half a pound of lean ham, two medium-sized onions, one pound of lean beef, fried bread, butter for frying, pepper, salt, two stalks of white celery cut into inch lengths, three quarts of water.

Joint your game neatly, cut the ham and onions into small pieces and fry all in butter to a light brown. Put into a soup pot with the beef, cut into strips, and a little pepper. Pour on the water, heat slowly and stew gently two hours. Take out the pieces of bird and cover in a bowl. Cook the soup an hour longer, strain, cool, drop in the celery, and simmer ten minutes. Pour upon fried bread in the tureen.

Venison soup is made the same—with the addition of a tablespoonful of brown flour wet into a paste with cold water, adding a tablespoonful of catsup, Worcestershire, or other pungent sauce and a glass of Madeira or brown sherry.

CHICKEN CREAM SOUP

An old chicken is much the best for soup. Cut it up into quarters, put it into a soup kettle with half a pound of corned ham and an onion, add four quarts of cold water. Bring slowly to a gentle boil. Keep this up until the liquid has diminished one-third and the meat drops from the bones, then add half a cup of rice. Season with salt, pepper and a bunch of chopped parsley.

Cook slowly until the rice is tender, then the meat should be taken out. Now stir in two cups of rich milk thickened with a little flour. The chicken could be fried in a spoonful of butter and a gravy made, reserving some of the white part of the meat, chopping it and adding it to the soup.

[*Note:* Mrs. Gillette forgot one important step—did you notice? Take out the bones!]

PLAIN ECONOMICAL SOUP

Take a cold roast-beef bone, pieces of beefsteak, the rack of a cold turkey or chicken. Put them into a pot with three or four quarts of water, two carrots, three turnips, one onion, a few cloves, pepper, and salt. Boil the whole gently four hours, then strain it through a colander, mashing the vegetables so that they will all pass through. Skim off the fat and return the soup to the pot. Mix one tablespoonful of flour with two of water, stir it into the soup, and boil the whole ten minutes. Serve this soup with sippets of toast.

Sippets are bits of dry toast cut into a triangular form.

A seasonable dish about the holidays.

ARTICLES REQUIRED FOR THE KITCHEN, *Circa 1890*

The following list will show what articles are necessary for the kitchen and will be quite an aid to young housekeepers when about commencing to furnish the utensils needed in the kitchen department and may prove useful to many:

2 sweeping brooms and
  1 dustpan
1 whisk broom
1 breadbox
2 cake boxes
1 large flour box
1 large tin pepper box
1 dredging box
1 spice box containing smaller
  spice boxes
2 cake pans, two sizes
4 bread pans
2 square biscuit pans
1 dozen patty pans, and the
  same number of tartlet pans
1 large tin pail
  and 1 wooden pail
2 small tin pails
1 set of tin basins
1 set of tin measures
1 wooden butter ladle
1 tin skimmer
1 tin steamer
2 dippers, 2 sizes
2 funnels, 2 sizes
1 set of jelly cake tins
1 apple corer
1 lemon squeezer
1 meat cleaver
3 kitchen knives and forks
1 large kitchen fork
  and 4 kitchen spoons
1 wooden spoon for cake-making
1 large bread knife
1 griddle-cake turner,
  also 1 griddle
1 potato masher
1 meat board
1 meat saw
2 large earthen bowls
4 stone jars
1 coffee mill
1 candlestick
2 market baskets, 2 sizes
1 clock
1 ash bucket
1 gridiron
2 frying pans or spiders
4 flatirons, 2 No. 8 and 2 No. 6

4 pie pans
3 pudding molds, 1 for boiling,
  2 for baking
2 dishpans, 2 sizes
2 cake or biscuit cutters
2 graters, 1 large, 1 small
1 coffee canister
1 tea canister
1 tin or granite-ware teapot
1 tin or granite-ware coffeepot
1 griddle cake turner
4 milk pans, 1 milk strainer
1 dozen iron gem pans
1 coarse gravy strainer,
  1 fine strainer
1 colander
1 flour sifter
2 scoops, 1 for flour,
  1 for sugar
2 jelly molds
1 can opener, 1 egg beater
1 cork screw
1 chopping knife
2 wooden chopping bowls
1 clothes wringer
2 dripping pans, 2 sizes
3 iron kettles, porcelain-
  lined if possible
1 corn beef or fish kettle
1 tea kettle
2 granite-ware stew pans
1 wire toaster
1 double kettle for custards,
  grains, etc.
2 sugar boxes, 1 for coarse,
  1 for fine
1 waffle iron
1 stepladder
1 stove, 1 coal shovel
1 pair of scales
2 coal hods or buckets
1 kitchen table, 2 chairs
1 large clothes basket
1 wash boiler, 1 washboard
8 dozen clothespins
1 large nail hammer and
  1 small tack hammer
1 bean pot
a cake of sapolio always on hand

GREEN PEA SOUP

Wash a small quarter of lamb in cold water and put it into a soup pot with six quarts of cold water. Add to it two tablespoonfuls of salt and set it over a moderate fire—let it boil gently two hours, then skim it clear. Add a quart of shelled peas and a teaspoonful of pepper, cover it and let it boil for half an hour; then having scraped the skins from a quart of small young potatoes, add them to the soup. Cover the pot and let it boil for half an hour longer; work a quarter of a pound of butter and a dessert spoonful of flour together and add them to the soup ten or twelve minutes before taking it off the fire.

Serve the meat on a dish with parsley sauce over it and the soup in a tureen.

DRIED BEAN SOUP

Put two quarts of dried white beans to soak the night before you make the soup, which should be put on as early in the day as possible. Take two pounds of the lean of fresh beef—the coarse pieces will do. Cut them up and put them into your soup pot with the bones belonging to them (which should be broken in pieces) and a pound of lean bacon cut very small. If you have the remains of a piece of beef that has been roasted the day before and so much underdone that the juices remain in it, you may put it into the pot and its bones along with it. Season the meat with pepper only and pour on it six quarts of water. As soon as it boils, take off the scum and put in the beans (having first drained them) and a head of celery cut small or a tablespoonful of pounded celery seed. Boil it slowly till the meat is done to shreds and the beans all dissolved. Then strain it through a colander into the tureen and put into it small squares of toasted bread with the crust cut off.

[*Note:* This was the standard supper on a Monday washday. The bean soup boiled on the back of the wood-burning range, the "wash" bubbled at the front, and the housewife, stirring one with a wooden spoon and the other with a long stick, *steamed*. It was good for the complexion if not for the temper!]

Vose & Sons Pianos with the MOUSE-PROOF PEDAL. —(*old adv.*)

We've heard of a woman who said she'd walk five miles to get a bottle of Dr. Pierce's Favorite Prescription if she couldn't get it without. That woman had tried it! —(*old adv.*)

SQUIRREL SOUP

Wash and quarter three or four good-sized squirrels; put them on with a small tablespoonful of salt, directly after breakfast, in a gallon of cold water. Cover the pot close and set it on the back part of the stove to simmer gently, *not* boil. Add vegetables just the same as you do in case of other meat soups in the summer season, but especially good will you find corn, Irish potatoes, tomatoes, and Lima beans. Strain the soup through a coarse colander when the meat has boiled to shreds, so as to get rid of the squirrel's troublesome little bones. Then return to the pot and after boiling a while longer, thicken with a piece of butter rubbed in flour. Celery and parsley leaves chopped up are also considered an improvement by many. Pour over bread slices diced and fried in butter.

PHILADELPHIA PEPPER POT

Put two pounds of tripe and four calves' feet into the soup pot and cover them with cold water. Add a red pepper and boil closely until the calves' feet are very tender. Take out the meat, skim the liquid, stir it; cut the tripe into small pieces and put it back into the liquid. If there is not enough liquid, add boiling water. Add half a teaspoonful each of sweet marjoram, sweet basil, and thyme, two sliced onions, some sliced potatoes, salt. When the vegetables have boiled until almost tender, add a piece of butter rolled in flour. Serve hot.

[*Note:* Pepper Pot Soup is said to have been "invented" by General George Washington's cook at Valley Forge. Created out of desperation from the few kitchen scraps on hand, it won high praise from the ragged, hungry American soldiers and their commander. Perhaps this creative cook was the same one whom Washington lauded for his "sagacity" in discovering that apples would make tasty pies. Until that time *pyes* had been made of beef, veal, hens, and hares—seldom of fruit.]

OXTAIL SOUP

Two oxtails, two slices of ham, one ounce of butter, two carrots, two turnips, three onions, one leek, one head of celery, one bunch of savory herbs, pepper, one tablespoon salt, two tablespoons catsup, one-half glass port wine, three quarts of water.

Cut up the tails, separating them at the joints, wash them, and put them in a stewpan with butter. Slice the vegetables and add with herbs.

41

Add one-half pint water and stir over quick fire till the juices are drawn. Fill the pan with water, and when boiling, add the salt. Skim well and simmer very gently for four hours or until the tails are tender. Take them out, skim and strain the soup, thicken it with flour, and flavor it with the catsup and port wine. Put back the tails, simmer for five minutes more and serve.

MULLAGATAWNY SOUP

Cut four onions, one carrot, two turnips, and one head of celery into three quarts of liquor in which one or two fowls have been boiled. Keep it over a brisk fire till it boils, then place it on a corner of the fire and let it simmer twenty minutes. Add one tablespoon of curry powder and one tablespoon of flour. Mix the whole well together and let it boil three minutes. Pass it through a colander. Serve with pieces of roast chicken in it. Pass boiled rice in a separate dish. This soup must be of good yellow color and not too thick. If you find it too thick, add a little boiling water and a teaspoon of sugar. Half veal and half chicken will answer as well.

CALF'S HEAD SOUP

[*Note:* First catch your calf!] Scald a well-cleansed calf's head, remove the brain, tie the head up in a cloth and boil an hour or until the meat will easily slip from the bone; take out, save the broth, cut the meat in small, square pieces and throw them into cold water; when cool, put the meat in a stewpan and cover with some of the broth; let it boil until quite tender and set aside.

In another stewpan melt some butter and in it put a quarter of a pound of lean ham, cut small, with fine herbs to taste; also parsley and one onion; add about a pint of the broth, let it simmer for two hours and then dredge in a small quantity of flour; now add the remainder of the broth and a quarter bottle of Madeira or sherry. Let all stew quietly for ten minutes and rub it through a medium sieve. Add the calf's head, seasoned with cayenne pepper, salt, the juice of one lemon, a little pounded mace, and a dessert-spoon of sugar.

[*Note:* Calf's Head Soup was a delicacy featured in many an old cookbook. Mrs. Franklin D. Roosevelt served it at the White House May 17, 1939, to King George VI and Queen Elizabeth. It has always been considered a gourmet's delight.]

PORTABLE SOUP

Put on, in four gallons of water, ten pounds of a shin of beef, free from fat and skin, six pounds of a knuckle of veal, and two fowls. Break the bones and cut the meat into small pieces; season with one ounce of whole black pepper and a quarter of an ounce of Jamaica pepper and the same of mace. Cover the pot very closely and let it simmer twelve or fourteen hours and then strain it. The following day take off the fat and clear the jelly from any sediment adhering to it, boil it gently upon the stove without covering the saucepan and stir it frequently till it thickens to a strong glew. Pour it into broad tin pans and put it in a cool oven. When it will take the impression of a knife, score it in equal squares. Stand it in a south window or near a stove. When dry, break it at the scores. Wrap it in paper and put it closely up in boxes. There should always be a large supply of this soup, as with it and catsup no one will ever be at a loss for dressed dishes and soups.

[*Note:* Portable Soup, sometimes called "veal glew," was the forerunner of bouillon cubes. Hardened into a jelly, then cut into squares, it was easily carried on journeys. The traveler had only to add spring water and heat it over a campfire and he had nourishing "instant soup"!]

TURTLE SOUP

Kill the turtle at night in winter and in the morning in summer. Hang it up by the hind fins, cut off the head, and let it bleed well. In dressing, separate the bottom shell from the top with great care lest the gall bladder be broken. Put the liver in a bowl of water; empty the entrails and lay them in water; if there be eggs, lay them in water also. It is proper to have a different bowl of water for each. Cut the flesh from the bottom shell and lay it in water, then break the shell in two, put it in a pot, having washed it clean; pour on water enough to cover it, add one pound of middling [the coarser part of flour] with four onions chopped and set it on the fire to boil. Let it boil steadily three hours. If the water boils away too much, add more.

Wash the top shell nicely after taking out the flesh, cover it and set it by. Parboil the fins, clean them nicely, taking off all the black skin; put them in water. Cut the flesh taken from the bottom and top shell in small pieces; cut the fins in two, lay them with the flesh in a dish, sprinkle salt over and cover them up.

When the shell, etc., is done, take out the bacon, scrape the shell clean and strain the liquor, one-third of which put back in the pot;

43

reserve the rest for the soup. Take out all the nice bits, strain, and put them in the gravy; lay the fins, cut in small pieces, in with them and as much of the flesh as will be sufficient to fill the upper shell; add to it (if a large turtle) one bottle of wine, cayenne pepper, and salt to your taste, one gill of mushroom catsup, one gill of lemon pickle, mace, nutmeg, and cloves pounded, to season high.

Mix two large spoonfuls of flour in one pound and a quarter of butter, put it in with thyme, parsley, marjoram, and savory tied in bunches. Stew all these together till the flesh and fins are tender. Wash out the top shell, put a puff paste around the brim, sprinkle the shell over with pepper and salt, then take the herbs out of the stew. If the gravy is not thick enough, add more flour and fill the shell. If there are no eggs in the turtle, boil six new-laid eggs for ten minutes, put them in cold water a few minutes, peel and slice them and place them on the turtle. Make a rich forcemeat, fry the balls nicely, and put them also in the shell; set it in a dripping pan, with something under the sides to keep it steady; have the oven heated as for bread, and let it remain till nicely browned. Fry the liver and send it in hot.

To prepare the soup, commence early in the morning; put on eight pounds of coarse beef, some bacon, onions, sweet herbs, pepper, and salt. Make a rich soup, strain it and thicken with a bit of butter and brown flour; add to it the water left from boiling the bottom shell; season very high with wine, catsup, spice and cayenne; put in the flesh you reserved and if it is not enough, add the nicest parts of a well-boiled calf's head, but do not use the eyes or tongue; let it boil till tender, and serve it up with fried forcemeat balls in it. If you have curry powder it will give a higher flavor to both soup and turtle than spice.

BOULA ☆

1 can pea soup	Pepper
1 can green turtle soup	Whipped cream, slightly salted
Sherry, ½ to 1 cup	Parmesan cheese

Combine soups and bring to boiling point. Season to taste with sherry and freshly ground pepper. Fill individual bowls; top each with a spoonful of whipped cream and sprinkle with cheese. Place under broiler a moment to brown topping slightly. Serve immediately. Serves 4–6.

[*Note:* Boula soup is an old favorite which was served in President Martin Van Buren's day. President and Mrs. John F. Kennedy served it at the White House and, as sports enthusiasts, renamed it for the college song, "Boula-Boula!" A suggestion: try fresh green peas, pureed, in place of the canned pea soup.]

Soups Without Meat

ONION SOUP

This is a refreshing dish when one is fatigued:

One quart of milk, six large onions, yolks of four eggs, three table-spoonfuls of butter, a large one of flour, one cupful of cream, salt, pepper. Put the butter in a frying pan. Cut the onions into thin slices and drop in the butter. Stir until they begin to cook, then cover tight and set back where they will simmer, but not burn, for half an hour. Now put the milk on to boil and then add the dry flour to the onions and stir constantly for three minutes over the fire; then turn the mixture into the milk and cook fifteen minutes. Rub the soup through a strainer, return to the fire, season with salt and pepper. Beat the yolks of the eggs well, add the cream to them and stir into the soup. Cook three minutes, stirring constantly. If you have no cream, use milk, in which case add a tablespoonful of butter at the same time. Pour over fried croutons in a soup tureen.

WINTER VEGETABLE SOUP

Scrape and slice three turnips and three carrots and peel three onions and fry all with a little butter until a light yellow. Add a bunch of celery and three or four leeks cut in pieces. Stir and fry all the ingredients for six minutes. When fried, add one clove of garlic, two stalks of parsley, two cloves, salt, pepper, and a little grated nutmeg. Cover with three quarts of water and simmer three hours, taking off the scum carefully. Strain and use. Croutons, vermicelli, Italian pastes, or rice may be added.

> *Do you know that you can buy a chimney to fit your lamp that will last till some accident happens to it? Do you know that Macbeth's "pearl top" or "pearl glass" is that chimney? Your dealer will get it if you insist on it. He may tell you it costs him three times as much as some others. That is true. He may say that they are just as good. Don't you believe it—they may be better for him; he may like the breaking.—Macbeth's, Pittsburg. —(old adv.)*

45

MEASURES AND WEIGHTS IN ORDINARY USE

AMONG HOUSEKEEPERS, *Circa 1890*

4 teaspoonfuls equal 1 tablespoonful liquid
4 tablespoonfuls equal 1 wineglass or half a gill
2 wineglasses equal 1 gill or half a cup
2 gills equal 1 coffee-cupful or 16 tablespoonfuls
2 coffee-cupfuls equal 1 pint
2 pints equal 1 quart
4 quarts equal 1 gallon
2 tablespoonfuls equal 1 ounce, liquid
1 tablespoonful of salt equals 1 ounce
16 ounces equal 1 pound or a pint of liquid
4 coffee-cupfuls of sifted flour equal 1 pound
1 quart of unsifted flour equals 1 pound
8 or 10 ordinary-sized eggs equal 1 pound
1 pint of sugar equals 1 pound, white granulated
2 coffee-cupfuls of powdered sugar equal 1 pound
1 coffee-cupful of cold butter, pressed down, is one-half pound
1 tablespoonful of soft butter, well rounded, equals 1 ounce
An ordinary tumblerful equals 1 coffee-cupful or half a pint
About 25 drops of any thin liquid will fill a common-sized teaspoon
1 dash of pepper equals three good shakes
1 pint of finely chopped meat, packed solidly, equals 1 pound

A set of tin measures (with small spouts or lips) from a gallon down to half a gill will be found very convenient in every kitchen, though common pitchers, bowls, glasses, etc., may be substituted.

APOTHECARIES' WEIGHTS

20 grains	=	1 scruple
3 scruples	=	1 drachm
8 drachms	=	1 ounce
12 ounces	=	1 pound

OTHER WEIGHTS

14 pounds	=	1 stone of iron or lead
56 pounds	=	1 firkin of butter
100 pounds	=	1 quintal of fish
196 pounds	=	1 barrel of flour
200 pounds	=	1 barrel of beef or pork
250 pounds	=	1 pig of iron or lead

SPRING VEGETABLE SOUP

Half-pint green peas, two shredded lettuces, one onion, a small bunch of parsley, two ounces butter, the yolks of three eggs, one pint of water, one and a half quarts of soup stock. Put in a stewpan the lettuce, onion, parsley, and butter with one pint of water and let them simmer till tender. Season with salt and pepper. When done, strain off the vegetables and put two-thirds of the liquor with the stock. Beat up the yolks of the eggs with the other third, toss it over the fire, and at the moment of serving add this with the vegetables to the strained-off soup.

[*Note:* As good a spring tonic as a dose of bitters if you hadn't seen fresh vegetables all winter!]

IRISH POTATO SOUP

Peel and boil eight medium-sized potatoes with a large onion, sliced, some herbs, salt and pepper. Press all through a colander; then thin it with rich milk and add a lump of butter and more seasoning if necessary. Let it heat well and serve hot.

[*Note:* My "other grandfather" would have eaten this three times a day. Born in Belfast and brought up on tales of the terrible potato famine of 1845, he prized King Potato above all other foods.]

PEA SOUP

Put a quart of dried peas into five quarts of water, boil four hours, then add three or four large onions, two heads of celery, a carrot, two turnips, all cut up rather fine. Season with pepper and salt. Boil two hours longer; if the soup becomes too thick, add more water. Strain through a colander and stir in a tablespoonful of cold butter. Serve hot with small pieces of toasted bread placed in the bottom of the tureen.

TOMATO SOUP 1

Peel two quarts of tomatoes, boil them in a saucepan with an onion and other soup vegetables, strain and add a level tablespoonful of flour dissolved in a third of a cup of melted butter, add pepper and salt. Serve very hot over little squares of bread fried brown and crisp in butter. An excellent addition to a cold meat lunch.

47

TOMATO SOUP 2

Place over the fire a quart of peeled tomatoes, stew them soft with a pinch of soda. Strain it so that no seeds remain, set it over the fire again and add a quart of hot boiled milk; season with salt and pepper, a piece of butter the size of an egg, add three tablespoonfuls of rolled cracker and serve hot. Canned tomatoes may be substituted.

TURTLE SOUP FROM BEANS

Soak overnight one quart of black beans. Next day, boil them in the proper quantity of water, say a gallon, then dip the beans out of the pot and strain them through a colander. Then return the flour of the beans, thus pressed, into the pot in which they were boiled. Tie up in a thin cloth some thyme, a teaspoonful of summer savory and parsley and let it boil in the mixture. Add a tablespoonful of cold butter, salt and pepper. Have ready four hard-boiled yolks of eggs quartered and a few forcemeat balls; add them to the soup with a sliced lemon and half a glass of wine just before serving.

This approaches so near in flavor to the real turtle soup that few are able to distinguish the difference.

MARTHA WASHINGTON'S KITCHEN AT MOUNT VERNON

FISH SOUP

Select a large, fine fish and clean it thoroughly. Put it over the fire with a sufficient quantity of water, allowing for each pound of fish one quart of water. Add an onion cut fine and a bunch of sweet herbs. When the fish is cooked and is quite tasteless, strain all through a colander, return to the fire, add some butter, salt and pepper to taste. A small tablespoonful of Worcestershire sauce may be added.

OYSTER SOUP

Scald one gallon of oysters in their own liquor. Add one quart of rich milk to the liquor, and when it comes to a boil, skim out the oysters and set aside. Add the yolks of four eggs, two good tablespoonfuls of butter and one of flour, all mixed well together but in this order—first, the milk; then after beating the eggs add a little of the hot liquor to them gradually and stir them rapidly into the soup. Lastly, add the butter and whatever seasoning you fancy besides plain pepper and salt, which must both be put in to taste, with caution. Celery salt most persons like extremely; others would prefer a little marjoram and thyme; others, again, mace and a bit of onion. Use your own discretion in this regard. Serve with or without pieces of fried bread—called *croutons* in kitchen French.

Soup Garnishes

EGG DUMPLINGS FOR SOUP

To half a pint of milk put two well-beaten eggs and as much wheat flour as will make a smooth, rather thick batter free from lumps. Drop this batter, a tablespoonful at a time, into boiling soup.

NOODLES FOR SOUP

Beat up one egg light, add a pinch of salt and flour enough to make a *very* stiff dough; roll out very thin like thin pie crust, dredge with flour to keep from sticking. Let it remain on the bread board to dry for an hour or more; then roll it up into a tight scroll like a sheet of music. Begin at the end and slice it into slips as thin as straws. After all are cut,

49

mix them lightly together and, to prevent them sticking, keep them floured a little until you are ready to drop them into your soup, which should be done shortly before dinner, for if boiled too long they will go to pieces.

[*Note:* Did your grandmother make noodles this way? Mine did. The table-top was covered with drying noodles. They were delicious.]

FORCEMEAT BALLS FOR SOUP

One cupful of cooked veal or fowl meat, minced; mix with this a handful of fine bread crumbs, the yolks of four hard-boiled eggs rubbed smooth together with a tablespoon of milk. Season with pepper and salt. Add a half teaspoon of flour and bind all together with two beaten eggs, the hands to be well floured and the mixture to be made into little balls the size of a nutmeg. Drop into the soup about twenty minutes before the time planned for serving.

Fish

In selecting fish choose only those in which the eye is full and prominent, the flesh thick and firm, the scales bright and fins stiff.

Steaming fish is much superior to boiling, but the ordinary conveniences in private houses do not admit of the possibility of enjoying this delicate way of cooking it.

The heads of some fish, as the cod, halibut, etc., are considered tidbits by many. Small fish, or pan fish as they are usually called, are served without the heads, with the exception of brook-trouts and smelts; these are usually cooked whole with the head on. Bake fish slowly, basting often with butter and water. Salmon is considered the most nutritious of all fish. When boiling fish, adding a little vinegar and salt to the water seasons and prevents the nutriment from being drawn out; the vinegar acting on the water hardens the water.

Salt fish should be soaked in water before boiling, according to the time it has been in salt. When it is hard and dry, it will require thirty-six hours soaking before it is dressed, and the water must be changed three or four times. When fish is not very salty, twenty-four hours or even one night will suffice.

For Hooping-Cough Croup. Roche's Herbal Embrocation. —(*old adv.*)

PAN FISH

Place them in a thick-bottom frying pan with heads all one way. Fill spaces with smaller fish. When they are fried quite brown and ready to turn, put a dinner plate over them, drain off the fat; then invert the pan and they will be left unbroken on the plate. Put the lard back into the pan, and when *hot*, slip back the fish. When the other side is brown, drain, turn on a plate as before, and slip them on a warm platter to be sent to the table. Leaving the heads on and the fish a crispy-brown, in perfect shape, improves the appearance if not the flavor. Garnish with slices of lemon.—*Hotel Lafayette, Philadelphia*

FISH AND OYSTER PIE

Any remains of cold fish, such as cod or haddock, two dozen oysters, pepper and salt to taste, bread crumbs sufficient for the quantity of fish, one-half teaspoonful of grated nutmeg, one teaspoonful of finely chopped parsley.

Clear the fish from the bones and put a layer of it in a pie dish, which sprinkle with pepper and salt; then a layer of bread crumbs, oysters, nutmeg, and chopped parsley. Repeat this until the dish is quite full. You may form a covering either of bread crumbs, which should be browned, or puff paste, which should be cut off into long strips and laid in cross-bars over the fish, with a line of the paste first laid around the edge. Before putting on the top, pour in some made melted butter or a little thin white sauce and the oyster liquor and bake.

Time: If of cooked fish, one-quarter hour; if made of fresh fish and puff paste, three-quarters of an hour.

STEAMED FISH

Secure the tail of the fish in its mouth, the body in a circle. Pour over it half a pint of vinegar, seasoned with pepper and salt; let it stand an hour in a cool place; pour off the vinegar and put it in a steamer over boiling water and steam twenty minutes or longer for large fish. When the meat easily separates from the bone, it is done. Drain well and serve on a very clean white napkin, neatly folded and placed on the platter; decorate the napkin around the fish with sprigs of curled parsley or with fanciful beet cuttings or alternately with both.

51

FRICASSEE SALMON

This way of cooking fresh salmon is a pleasant change from the ordinary modes of cooking it. Cut one and one-half pounds of salmon into pieces one inch square. Put the pieces in a stewpan with half a cupful of water, a little salt, a little white pepper, one clove, one blade of mace, three pieces of sugar, one shallot, and a heaping teaspoonful of mustard mixed smoothly with half a teacupful of vinegar. Let this boil up once and add six tomatoes peeled and cut into tiny pieces, a few sprigs of parsley finely minced, and one wineglassful of sherry. Let all simmer gently for three-quarters of an hour. Serve very hot and garnish with dry toast cut in triangular pieces. This dish is good very cold for luncheon or breakfast.

TURBAN OF SALMON ☆

2½ cups cooked, flaked fish (salmon is best)
1½ cups milk
1 slice onion
Blade of mace (¼ teaspoon)
Sprig of parsley
¼ cup butter
¼ cup flour
½ teaspoon salt
⅛ teaspoon pepper
2 egg yolks, slightly beaten
Lemon juice
⅔ cup buttered cracker crumbs

Scald milk with onion, mace, and parsley; remove seasonings. Melt butter; add flour, salt, and pepper. Add milk gradually while stirring constantly. Bring to boiling point and add egg yolks (first putting a little of the white sauce into the eggs). Cook another minute. Put layer of fish on buttered dish; sprinkle with salt, pepper, and a few drops of lemon juice. Cover with sauce. Continue with fish and sauce in alternate layers. Cover with buttered cracker crumbs. Bake in hot oven (450°) until crumbs are brown. Cut in squares and garnish with crosses of pimiento. If you use three one-pound cans of salmon and double the amount of sauce, this will serve twelve.

BAKED WHITE FISH WITH BORDEAUX SAUCE

Clean and stuff the fish. Put it in a baking pan and add a liberal quantity of butter, previously rolled in flour, to the fish. Put in the pan half a pint of claret and bake for an hour and a quarter. Remove the fish and strain the gravy; add to the latter a gill more of claret, a teaspoonful of brown flour, and a pinch of cayenne and serve with the fish.—*Plankington House, Milwaukee*

FISH IN HOT WHITE SAUCE

Flake up cold boiled halibut or other fish and set the plate into the steamer that the fish may heat without drying. Boil the bones and skin of the fish with a slice of onion and a very small piece of red pepper (a bit of this the size of a kernel of coffee will make the sauce quite as hot as most persons like it). Boil this stock down to half a pint; thicken with one teaspoonful of butter and one teaspoonful of flour, mixed together. Add one drop of extract of almond. Pour this sauce over halibut and stick parsley over it.

FRESH STURGEON STEAK IN MARINADE

Take one slice of sturgeon two inches thick. Let it stand in hot water five minutes, drain, and put it in a bowl, to which add a gill of vinegar, two tablespoonfuls of melted butter, half a teaspoonful of salt, a salt-spoonful of black pepper, and the juice of half a lemon. Let it stand six hours, turning it occasionally, then drain and dry on a napkin. Dip fish in beaten egg, roll in bread crumbs, and fry in very hot fat. For sauce to serve with the fish, beat up the yolks of two raw eggs; add a teaspoonful of French mustard and, by degrees, half of the marinade, stirring till smooth.

PLANKED SHAD

Procure at a house-furnishing store a shad-board of oak. It is better to purchase one ready made, the cost being only about seventy-five cents. These boards are very strong and smooth, and are furnished with thick wires crossing the board diagonally. These secure the fish without nailing. The plank should be well seasoned. Cut off the head and tail of the finest shad you can get, split it down the back, and after a good washing, wipe it dry. Scatter upon it some salt and pepper.

Having placed the plank before the fire until it has become very hot and ready to char, place the shad (spread open) within the wires crossing the hot board, with the back next to the plank, the head end down. Roast, and in a little while turn the other end on the board, placing the tail end down. That the juice of the fish may be well absorbed, turn the board frequently up and down. When sufficiently roasted, add some fresh butter and send to the table on the board, under which place a large tray or dish.

Shad cooked in this way are greatly relished by parties, who in the shad-season frequently repair to the banks of our rivers where there are shad fisheries and purchase of the fisherman the shad fresh from the water.

FRIED EELS

After cleaning the eels well, cut them in pieces two inches long; wash them and wipe them dry; roll them in wheat flour or rolled cracker and fry, as directed for other fish, in hot lard or beef dripping, salted. They should be browned all over and thoroughly done.

BAKED SMELTS

Wash and dry them thoroughly in a cloth and arrange them nicely in a flat baking dish; the pan should be buttered, also the fish. Season with salt and pepper and cover with bread or cracker crumbs. Place a piece of butter over each. Bake for fifteen or twenty minutes. Garnish with fried parsley and cut lemon.

Shellfish

BOILED LOBSTER

Put a handful of salt into a large kettle of boiling water. When the water boils very hard, put in the lobster, having first brushed it and tied the claws together with a bit of twine. Keep it boiling from twenty minutes to half an hour, in proportion to its size. If boiled too long, the meat will be hard and stringy. When it is done, take it out, lay it on its claws to drain, and then wipe it dry.

It is scarcely necessary to mention that the head of a lobster and what are called the lady-fingers are not to be eaten.

The male is best for boiling; the hen lobsters are preferred for sauce or salad on account of their coral. The sand pouch near the throat should be removed. Care should be exercised that none of the feathery, tough, gill-like particles found under the body shell get mixed with the meat, as they are indigestible and have caused much trouble. They are supposed to be the cause of so-called poisoning from eating lobster.

LOBSTER NEWBURG

Take one whole lobster, cut up in pieces about as large as a hickory nut. Put in the same pan with a piece of butter the size of a walnut. Season with salt and pepper to taste, and thicken with heavy cream sauce; add the yolk of an egg and two ounces of sherry wine.

Cream Sauce for above is made as follows: one ounce of butter, melted in sauce pan, two ounces of flour mixed with butter, thin down to proper consistency with boiling cream. —*Rector's Oyster House, Chicago*
[*Note:*

THIS IS A HICKORY NUT   THIS IS A WALNUT

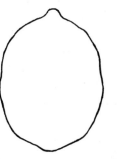

in case you haven't gone nutting recently—]

DEVILED CRABS

Half a dozen fresh crabs, boiled and minced; two ounces of butter; one small teaspoonful of mustard powder; cayenne pepper and salt to taste. Put the meat into a bowl and mix carefully with it an equal quantity of fine bread crumbs. Work the butter to a light cream, mix the mustard well with it, then stir in very carefully, a handful at a time, the mixed crabs, a tablespoonful of cream, and the crumbs. Season to taste with cayenne pepper and salt. Fill the crab shells with the mixture, sprinkle bread crumbs over the tops, put three small pieces of butter upon the top of each, and brown them quickly in a hot oven. They will puff in baking and will be found very nice. Half the quantity can be made. A crab shell will hold the meat of two crabs.

55

CRAB IMPERIAL ☆

⅓ green pepper, finely diced
1 pimiento, finely diced
⅓ tablespoon dry mustard
⅓ tablespoon salt

1 egg
⅓ cup mayonnaise
1 pound back-fin or
　lump crabmeat

Mix above ingredients gently, being careful not to break lumps of crabmeat. Fill crab shells or casserole. Top with thin coating of mayonnaise and sprinkle with paprika. Bake at 350° for fifteen minutes.

SHERRIED CRAB À LA SUNDAY BRUNCH ☆

3 cups milk
　Dash cayenne pepper
1 envelope potato soup mix
1 can crabmeat
2 tablespoons chopped parsley

2 hard-cooked eggs, chopped
2 tablespoons sherry
½ cup fine fresh bread crumbs
1 tablespoon butter, melted

Stir milk and cayenne pepper into soup mix, and heat to boiling point over medium heat. Add crabmeat, parsley, chopped eggs and sherry. Pour into a buttered one-quart casserole dish. Combine bread crumbs and melted butter and sprinkle over top of crabmeat mixture. Bake at 325° for fifteen minutes or until the topping is nicely browned. Serves five or six. You can make it ahead of time and pop it into the oven for a last-minute warming.

[*Note:* There wasn't a single shrimp recipe in the old *White House Cookbook.* Maybe they hadn't been invented yet. Here are some modern recipes which are very good, though for shrimp-lovers nothing beats a plain Shrimp Cocktail.]

SHRIMP COCKTAIL DIP ☆
[*for potato chips, crackers, celery, etc.*]

Chop one-half pound cooked shrimp (or one five-ounce can) and add to one cup large-curd cottage cheese. Mix in three tablespoons chili sauce, a half teaspoon onion juice, two teaspoons lemon juice, a quarter teaspoon Worcestershire sauce and about one-third cup milk or enough to make consistency right for dipping. Popular with the Crowd From the Office.

SHRIMP–LIMA CASSEROLE ☆

Make a cream sauce of three tablespoons butter, three tablespoons flour, three-fourths teaspoon salt and one and a half cups milk. Cook and stir over low heat till thickened; remove from heat; add a half cup finely minced American cheese, and stir till melted.

Add to cheese sauce one teaspoon grated onion, six chopped ripe olives, and a quarter teaspoon dry mustard or curry powder if you like it.

Combine sauce with two cups cooked dry limas or one package frozen green limas, cooked, and one cup cooked shrimp. Bake in one-quart casserole at 350° about twenty to thirty minutes till brown and bubbly on top. Serves four. Salmon, tuna or cooked meat may be used instead of shrimp.

This is our Christmas Eve casserole. Everybody likes it except the One Who Doesn't Care for Shrimp and the One Who Doesn't Care for Lima Beans.

SHRIMP-CRAB CASSEROLE ☆

2 four-and-one-half-ounce cans shrimp, deveined	½ teaspoon salt
1 can crabmeat, flaked (7 ounces)	1 tablespoon Worcestershire sauce
1 cup chopped celery	⅔ cup mayonnaise
½ cup chopped onion	⅓ cup dry bread crumbs
½ cup chopped green pepper	¼ cup melted butter
	Parsley for garnish

Toss together lightly shrimp, crabmeat, celery, onion, and green pepper. A few shrimp may be reserved for garnish. Blend salt and Worcestershire sauce into mayonnaise. Add to shrimp mixture and combine carefully. Put mixture in a greased one-and-a-half-quart casserole. Stir bread crumbs into melted butter and sprinkle on top of casserole. Bake in moderate oven (350°) about thirty minutes. Garnish with reserved shrimp and parsley for serving. Serves six.

HOUSEKEEPER'S TIMETABLE
1890

Food	Mode of Preparation	Time of Digestion H M
Apples, sour, hard	Raw	2 50
Apples, sweet, mellow	Raw	1 50
Asparagus	Boiled	2 30
Beans (pod)	Boiled	2 30
Beans with green corn	Boiled	3 45
Beef	Roasted	3 00
Beefsteak	Broiled	3 00
Beefsteak	Fried	4 00
Beef, salted	Boiled	4 15
Bass, fresh	Broiled	3 00
Beets, young	Boiled	3 45
Beets, old	Boiled	4 00
Bread, Corn	Baked	3 15
Bread, Wheat	Baked	3 30
Butter	Melted	3 30
Cabbage	Raw	2 30
Cabbage and vinegar	Raw	2 00
Cabbage	Boiled	4 30
Cauliflower	Boiled	2 30
Cake, sponge	Baked	2 30
Carrot, orange	Boiled	3 15
Cheese, old	Raw	3 30
Chicken	Fricasseed	3 45
Codfish, dry and whole	Boiled	2 00
Custard, one quart	Baked	2 45
Duck, tame	Roasted	4 00
Duck, wild	Roasted	4 50
Dumpling, apple	Boiled	3 00
Eggs, hard	Boiled	3 30
Eggs, soft	Boiled	3 00
Eggs	Fried	3 30
Eggs	Raw	2 00
Fowls, domestic, roasted or	Boiled	4 00
Gelatine	Boiled	2 30
Goose, wild	Roasted	2 30
Lamb	Boiled	2 30
Meat and vegetables	Hashed	2 30
Milk	Raw	2 15
Milk	Boiled	2 00
Mutton	Roast	3 15
Mutton	Broiled	3 00
Onions	Boiled	3 00
Oysters	Roasted	3 15
Oysters	Stewed	3 30
Parsnips	Boiled	3 00
Pig's Feet	Soused	1 00
Pork	Roast	5 15
Pork	Boiled	4 30
Pork	Fried	4 15
Potatoes	Boiled	3 30
Potatoes	Baked	3 30
Rice	Boiled	1 00
Salmon, fresh	Boiled	1 45
Sausage	Fried	4 00
Vegetable Soup	Boiled	4 00

[*Note:* Oysters were one of the most popular foods of the nineteenth century, and no really elegant dinner was complete without them. Many were spawned in contaminated waters, however, and were responsible for much of the then-prevalent typhoid fever. Today we enjoy pure-bred, pedigreed oysters! Following are a few of the oyster recipes which were most familiar to our great-grandparents, beginning with Pickled Oysters, which was the special favorite of a number of Presidents.]

PICKLED OYSTERS
[*President U. S. Grant loved them!*]

Put a hundred large oysters and their liquor over the fire, salt lightly, and let them just come to a boil. Draw to the back of the stove, skim off the top, take out the oysters with a skimmer, and set them aside in an earthen dish to cool. To the liquor in the kettle add a pint of vinegar, a red pepper broken into pieces (rejecting the seed), whole cinnamon, cloves, and pepper to the liking. Boil this liquor a bit and pour warm over the cooled oysters. Cover and set in a cool place. If they are to be kept longer than two or three days, put them in cans and keep cool. Before serving, add a few raw cranberries and thin slices of lemon if you prefer.

FRIED OYSTERS

Take large oysters from their own liquor into a thickly folded napkin to dry them; then make hot an ounce each of butter and lard in a thick-bottom frying pan. Season the oysters with pepper and salt, then dip each one into egg and cracker crumbs rolled fine until it will take up no more. Place them in the hot grease and fry them a delicate brown, turning them on both sides by sliding a broad-bladed knife under them. Serve them crisp and hot. Some prefer to roll oysters in corn meal and others use flour, but they are much more crisp with egg and cracker crumbs.—*Boston Oyster House*

Black watered silk is admirably combined with black camel's hair for dresses of middle-aged and elderly ladies. A suggestion of silver throughout an entire black costume gives a beautiful and uncommon effect to this somber dress. —The Elite News, 1887

59

DRY OYSTER STEW

Take six to twelve large oysters and cook them in half a pint of their own liquor; season with butter and white pepper; cook for five minutes, stirring constantly. Serve in hot soup plates or bowls.—*Fulton Fish Market, New York*

BOSTON FRY

Prepare the oysters in egg batter and fine cracker meal; fry in butter over a slow fire for about ten minutes; cover the hollow of a hot platter with tomato sauce; place the oysters in it but not covering; garnish with chopped parsley sprinkled over the oysters.—*Boston Oyster House*

BROILED OYSTERS

Dry a quart of oysters in a cloth. Dip each in melted butter well peppered, then in beaten egg or not, then in bread or cracker crumbs, also peppered. Broil on a wire broiler over live coals, three to five minutes. Dip over each a little melted butter. Serve hot.

[*Note:* Might be good on your outdoor grill this summer!]

PAN OYSTERS

Cut some stale bread in thin slices, taking off all the crust. Round the slices to fit pattypans; toast, butter, place them in the pans and moisten with three or four teaspoonfuls of oyster liquor. Place on the toast a layer of oysters, sprinkle with pepper, and put a small piece of butter on top of each pan; place all the pans in a baking pan and place in the oven, covering tightly. They will cook in seven or eight minutes if the oven is hot. Or cook till the beards are ruffled, remove the cover, sprinkle lightly with salt, replace and cook one minute longer. Serve in pattypans. They are delicious.—*New York Style*

MOCK OYSTERS

Grate the corn, while green and tender, with a coarse grater, into a deep dish. To two ears of corn allow one egg. Beat the whites and yolks separately and add them to the corn with one tablespoonful of wheat flour and one of butter, a teaspoonful of salt and pepper to taste. Drop spoonfuls of this batter into a frying pan with hot butter and lard mixed, and fry a light brown on both sides. In taste they have a singular resemblance to fried oysters. The corn *must* be *young*.

FROGS STEWED

Wash and skin the hind legs and quarters, parboil them about three minutes, drain them. Now put into a stewpan two ounces of butter. When it is melted, lay in the frogs and fry about two minutes, stirring them to prevent burning. Shake over them a tablespoonful of sifted flour and stir it into them. Add a sprig of parsley, a pinch of powdered summer savory, a bay leaf, three slices of onion, salt and pepper, a cup of hot water and one of cream. Boil gently until done. Remove the legs, strain and mix into the gravy the yolks of two eggs, well beaten to a cream; put the legs in a suitable dish, pour over the gravy and serve.

Meats

The oven should be the hottest when the meat is put into it, in order to quickly crisp the surface and close the pores of the meat. If the oven is too hot to hold the hand in for only a moment, then the oven is right to receive the meat.

To lard meats draw ribbons of fat pork through the upper surface of the meat, leaving both ends protruding. This is accomplished by the use of a larding needle which may be procured at house-furnishing stores.

If found frozen, remove ice from meat and put it in fresh, cold water, letting it lie till wanted for cooking. Do not put it into warm water or place it before the fire.

Potatoes are injured by being frozen. Other vegetables are not the worse for it, provided they are always thawed in cold water.

[*Note:* Though old-fashioned cooks just cooked meats "till they were done," today we like to be a bit more scientific about it. Following are general rules for roasting meats.]

61

MODERN TIMES AND TEMPERATURES FOR COOKING MEAT

		Oven Temp.	Time per Pound
Beef	rare	300° F.	18–20 min.
	medium		22–25
	well-done		27–30
Pork	always well done, never "pinkish"	350°	30–35
Smoked Pork		300°	25–30
Lamb		300°	30–35
Veal		300°	25–30

MEATS AND THEIR ACCOMPANIMENTS

Pickles are good with all roast meats, and in fact are suitable accompaniments to all kinds of meats in general.

Spinach is the proper accompaniment to veal, green peas to lamb.

Lemon juice makes a very grateful addition to nearly all the insipid members of the fish kingdom. Slices of lemon cut into very small dice and stirred into drawn butter and allowed to come to the boiling point, served with fowls, is a fine accompaniment.

Beef

SPICED BEEF

For a round of beef weighing twenty or twenty-four pounds, take one quarter of a pound of saltpeter, one quarter of a pound of coarse brown sugar, two pounds of salt, one ounce of cloves, one ounce of allspice, and half an ounce of mace. Pulverize these materials thoroughly, mix them well together, and with them rub the beef on every part. Let the beef lie for eight or ten days in the pickle thus made, turning and rubbing it every day; then tie it around with a broad tape to keep it in shape. Make a coarse paste of flour and water; lay a little suet finely chopped over and under the beef, and enclose the beef entirely in the paste and bake it six hours. When you take the beef from the oven, remove the paste, but do not remove the tape until you are ready to send it to the table. If you wish to eat the beef cold, keep it well covered that it may retain its moisture.

[*Note:* Very much like Thomas Jefferson's "Hunter's Beef." See *The Virginia Housewife* in The Presidents' Wives section.]

SPICED BEEF RELISH

Take two pounds of raw, tender beefsteak, chop it very fine, put into it salt, pepper, a little sage, and two tablespoonfuls of melted butter. Roll two crackers very fine; add these and two well-beaten eggs. Make it up into the shape of a roll and bake it. Baste with butter and water. Cut in slices when cold.

ROAST BEEF

One very essential point in roasting beef is to have the oven well heated when the beef is first put in; this causes the pores to close up quickly and prevents the escape of the juices.

Take a rib piece or loin roast of seven or eight pounds. Wipe it thoroughly all over with a clean wet towel. Lay it in a dripping pan, and baste it well with butter or suet fat. Set it in the oven. Baste it frequently with its own drippings, which will make it brown and tender. When partly done, season with salt and pepper, as it hardens any meat to salt it when raw, and draws out its juices; then dredge with sifted flour to give it a frothy appearance. It will take a roast of this size about two hours time to be properly done, leaving the inside a little rare or red—half an hour less would make the inside quite rare. Remove the beef to a heated dish, set where it will keep hot; then skim the drippings from all fat, and add a tablespoonful of sifted flour, a little pepper, and a teacupful of boiling water. Boil up once and serve hot in a gravy boat.

Some prefer the clear gravy without the thickening. Serve with mustard or grated horse-radish and vinegar.

YORKSHIRE PUDDING

This is a very nice accompaniment to a roast of beef; the ingredients are, one pint of milk, four eggs, white and yolks beaten separately, one teaspoonful of salt, and two teaspoonfuls of baking powder sifted through two cups of flour. It should be mixed very smooth, about the consistency of cream. Regulate your time when you put in your roast, so that it will be done half an hour or forty minutes before dishing up. Take it from the oven, set it where it will keep hot. In the meantime, have this pudding prepared. Take two common biscuit tins, dip some of the drippings from the dripping pan into these tins, pour half of the pudding into each, set them into the hot oven, and keep them in until the dinner is dished up; take these puddings out at the last moment and send to the table hot. This is considered much better than the old way of baking the pudding under the meat.

BEEFSTEAK 1

The first consideration in broiling is to have a clear, glowing bed of coals. The steak should be about three-quarters of an inch in thickness, and should be pounded only in extreme cases, i.e., when it is cut *too* thick and is "stringy." Lay it on a buttered gridiron, turning it often, as it begins to drip, attempting nothing else while cooking it. Have everything else ready for the table; the potatoes and vegetables dished and in the warming closet. Do not season it until it is done, which will be in about ten to twelve minutes. Remove it to a warm platter, pepper and salt it on both sides and spread a liberal lump of butter over it. Serve at once while hot. No definite rule can be given as to the *time* of cooking steak, individual tastes differ so widely in regard to it, some only liking it when well done, others so rare that the blood runs out of it. The best pieces for broiling are the porterhouse and sirloin.

BEEFSTEAK 2

Take a smooth, thick-bottomed frying pan, scald it out with hot water, and wipe it dry; set it on the stove or range, and when *very* hot, rub it over the bottom with a rag dipped in butter; then place your steak or chops in it, turn often until cooked through, take up on a warm platter, and season both sides with salt, pepper, and butter. Serve hot.

Many prefer this manner of cooking steak rather than broiling or frying in a quantity of grease.

BEEFSTEAK AND ONIONS

Prepare the steak in the usual way. Have ready in a frying pan a dozen onions cut in slices and fried brown in a little beef drippings or butter. Dish your steak, and lay the onions thickly over the top. Cover and let stand five minutes, then send to the table hot.

The Two Winners—The Jersey Lily and Hard-to-Beat Flour For Sale by Scott's —(old adv.)

HELEN RUTH'S STEAK MARINADE ☆

¼ cup soy sauce
¼ cup salad oil
Juice of ½ lemon

1 tablespoon brown sugar
¼ teaspoon garlic salt
Oregano, a sprinkle

Marinate your steak—sirloin, chuck, any kind—in this for several hours, turning it a few times. Then grill the steak and sit back and wait for compliments!

[*Note:* This is the best of my sister-in-law's many good recipes. With the steak she serves Rice Pilaf; her recipe is on page 109. I offer them to you as a package deal, because the steak marinade should be served that way.]

POT ROAST

This is an old-fashioned dish, often cooked in our grandmothers' time. Take a piece of fresh beef weighing about five or six pounds. It must not be *too fat*. Wash it and put it into a pot with barely sufficient water to cover it. Set it over a slow fire, and after it has stewed an hour, salt and pepper it. Then stew it slowly until tender, adding a little onion if liked. Do not replenish the water at the last, but let all nearly boil away. When tender all through, take the meat from the pot and pour the gravy in a bowl. Put a large lump of butter in the bottom of the pot, then dredge the piece of meat with flour and return it to the pot to brown, turning it often to prevent its burning. Take the gravy that you have poured from the meat into the bowl and skim off all the fat; pour this gravy in with the meat and stir in a large spoonful of flour; wet with a little water; let it boil up ten or fifteen minutes and pour into a gravy dish. Serve both hot, the meat on a platter. Some are very fond of this way of cooking a piece of beef which has been previously placed in spiced pickle for two or three days.

[*Note:* This was an "old-fashioned" recipe in 1887; probably it was pre-Civil War.]

You can have the ELITE NEWS *delivered at your office or residence for ten cents a month.*—(*old adv.*)

"*I find* FAIRY *Soap in every way most satisfactory.*"—*Mary Garfield Stanley-Brown.*

We want to convince you as we have the popular daughter of the late President Garfield that FAIRY *Soap is purer, whiter and more delicate than any other.*—(*old adv.*)

SAUERBRATEN ☆

4 pounds boneless rump or sirloin tip roast	4 bay leaves
2 onions, peeled and sliced	4 cups water
10 whole black peppers	2 cups vinegar
10 whole cloves	4 tablespoons sugar
	1½ teaspoons salt

Place meat in deep bowl. Add onions and spices. Bring water, vinegar, sugar, and salt to boil and pour over meat. Cover dish and let stand in refrigerator about four days. Remove meat from bowl and reserve vinegar marinade. Pat meat dry; coat with flour. *Slowly* brown meat on both sides in a small amount of shortening. Use a dutch oven for this. Add one cup marinade (strained to eliminate bay leaves and pepper), including the onions. Cover. Cook in moderate oven (350°) about three hours or until meat is tender. Add more marinade if necessary. Remove meat to plate. Strain drippings; let stand a minute until fat rises to surface. Skim off fat. Add enough reserved marinade to drippings. Cook until thickened. Add a little flour if necessary.

[*Note:* There are no ginger snaps in this Cincinnati sauerbraten! But see below.]

MILWAUKEE SAUERBRATEN ☆

4 pounds beef (rump, chuck, or sirloin)	1 teaspoon salt
1 cup vinegar	2½ tablespoons shortening
1 quart water	2 tablespoons flour
1 onion, sliced	2 ginger snaps
3 bay leaves	½ tablespoon sugar
3 cloves	½ glass red wine

Mix liquids, onions, spices; let meat stand in it four days. Turn meat over now and then. Brown meat in hot shortening, then set aside. Brown flour in the shortening and add the vinegar bath. Add ginger snaps and sugar and boil until thick. Put in meat, cover pan, and bake at 325° two and one-half to three hours, turning and basting frequently. Add red wine about one-half hour before done. When meat is tender, skim grease from gravy and strain.

SIGMA CHI CORNED BEEF CASSEROLE ☆
[*courtesy of Toledo, Ohio, alumni*]

1 eight-ounce package of
    noodles, cooked
1 twelve-ounce can of corned
    beef, diced
¼ pound American cheese,
    diced small

½ cup chopped onion
1 ten and one-half ounce can
    cream of chicken soup
1 cup milk
¾ cup buttered bread crumbs
    sprinkled on top

Mix ingredients together lightly. Bake forty-five minutes at 350° in greased casserole dish.

[*Note:* Sigma Chi husbands liked this. I don't know about Betas, Phi Delts, etc.]

STEWED BEEF KIDNEY

Cut the kidney into slices, season highly with pepper and salt, fry it a light brown, take out the slices, then pour a little warm water into the pan, dredge in some flour, put in slices of kidney again; let them stew very gently; add some parsley if liked. Sheep's kidneys may be split open, broiled over a clear fire, and served with a piece of butter placed on each half.

BOILED BEEF TONGUE

Wash a fresh tongue and just cover it with water in the pot; put in a pint of salt and a small red pepper; add more water as it evaporates, so as to keep the tongue nearly covered until done—when it can be easily pierced with a fork; take it out, and if wanted soon, take off the skin and set it away to cool. If wanted for future use, do not peel until it is required. A cupful of salt will do for three tongues, if you have that number to boil; but do not fail to keep water enough in the pot to keep them covered while boiling. If salt tongues are used, soak them overnight, of course omitting the salt when boiling. Or, after peeling a tongue, place it in a saucepan with one cup of water, half a cup vinegar, four tablespoonfuls sugar, and cook until the liquor is evaporated.

Parker's Beautiful Cut Glass Aids Digestion —(*old adv.*)

HAMBURGER STEAK

Take a pound of round steak. Chop it until a perfect mince; it cannot be chopped too fine. Also chop a small onion quite fine and mix well with the meat. Season with salt and pepper and make into cakes as large as a biscuit but quite flat. Have ready a frying pan with butter and lard mixed; when boiling hot, put in steak and fry brown. Serve with brown gravy made from the grease the steak was fried in.

BEEFSTEAK PIE

Cut up rump or flank steak into strips two inches long and about an inch wide. Stew them with the bone in just enough water to cover them until partly cooked; have half a dozen of cold boiled potatoes sliced. Line a baking dish with pie paste, put in a layer of the meat with salt, pepper, and a little of thinly sliced onion, then one of the sliced potatoes with bits of butter dotted over them. Then the steak, alternated with layers of potato, until the dish is full. Add the gravy or broth, having first thickened it with brown flour. Cover with a top crust, making a slit in the middle; brush a little beaten egg over it and bake until quite brown.

BEEF CROQUETTES

Take cold roast beef. Put it into a wooden bowl and chop it fine. Mix with it about twice the quantity of hot mashed potatoes well seasoned with butter and salt. Beat up an egg and work it into the potato and meat, then form the mixture into little cakes the size of fish balls. Flatten them a little, roll in flour or egg and cracker crumbs, fry in butter and lard mixed, browning on both sides. Serve piping hot.

ROAST BEEF HEART

Wash it carefully and open it sufficiently to remove the ventricles, then soak it in cold water until the blood is discharged. Wipe it dry and stuff it nicely with dressing as for turkey; roast it about an hour and a half. Serve it with the gravy, which should be thickened with some of the stuffing and a glass of wine. It is very nice hashed, served with currant jelly.—*Palmer House, Chicago*

RED FLANNEL HASH ☆

[*Note:* This is an Old New England dish that traveled west with many a homesteader.]

6 medium whole beets, cooked
4–6 medium potatoes, cooked
1½ cups chopped cooked meat
    (beef, corned beef, etc.)
½ teaspoon salt
⅛ teaspoon pepper

1 tablespoon onion, minced
4 tablespoons butter
   or drippings
1 tablespoon water
2 tablespoons cream or milk

Coarsely chop beets and potatoes and mix with meat and seasonings. Melt fat in skillet and spread out meat mixture in skillet and sprinkle with water. Cook over medium heat twenty-five minutes or until brown crust begins to form on bottom. Pour milk over and cook five minutes longer. May be cut down the middle and folded as omelet.

ANNABELLE'S BURGUNDY BEEF STEW ☆

¼ pound salt pork, finely diced
2 pounds round steak
    cut in two-inch pieces
2 tablespoons flour
  Salt, pepper, thyme,
    marjoram

1 cup Burgundy wine
1 cup beef bouillon
½ pound sliced fresh mushrooms
12 small white onions
12 small potato balls
6 carrots cut in half-inch slices

Fry out salt pork until browned; remove from fat. Brown steak in fat and sprinkle with flour and spices. Put steak and salt pork in casserole and pour on wine and bouillon. Cover closely and bake at 275° for four hours or until meat is very tender. Let this dish "mellow" for a few hours or overnight in refrigerator or freezer. For final preparation before serving, add mushrooms, onions, potatoes, and carrots (all uncooked). Bake for one hour in 325° oven until vegetables are tender. Serves six to eight.

NEE BAN TEAS. *Fresh invoice received monthly. Formosa Flowery Oolong, $2 a pound. Mikado (mixed), 5 pounds for $3. Royal Copenhagen cups and saucers 75¢ to $2. "A delicious cup of tea free." W. Fitz-Hugh Smith—late of Nee Ban—(old adv.)*

HUNGARIAN GOULASH ☆

Brown two pounds of chuck or rump, cut into one-inch pieces, in four tablespoons of hot fat. Add and brown lightly one cup sliced onions and one small clove of garlic, minced. Mix together and stir in: three-fourths cup catsup, three-eighths cup Worcestershire sauce, one teaspoon vinegar, one tablespoon brown sugar, two and a half teaspoons Hungarian paprika, two teaspoons salt, one teaspoon dry mustard, dash of red pepper. Add three cups water, cover and simmer two to two and a half hours. Serve over noodles.

SKILLET MEAL ☆

1 cup dry rice	1½ cups canned tomatoes
¼ cup butter	2 teaspoons salt
1 cup sliced onions	2 tablespoons Worcestershire
1 pound ground beef	sauce
½ cup sliced peppers	1 teaspoon sugar
1 cup diced celery	

Wash rice and allow to stand while preparing other ingredients. Melt fat in skillet and add onion and meat. Brown. Add peppers, celery, tomatoes, and seasonings. Mix well. Sprinkle rice over top. Cover. Cook eight minutes on high heat, turn to low heat and cook forty-five minutes longer.

MEAT LOAF ☆

1½ lbs. ground chuck	1 cup milk, tomato juice,
1 egg	broth or gravy
1 cup bread crumbs	1 tablespoon parsley
½ cup chopped onion	1 teaspoon rosemary or marjoram
½ cup chopped green pepper	or mixture of both
½ cup chopped celery	

Mix all ingredients well. Mold into a loaf and bake in fry pan in 300° oven for one hour.

Black Grenadines for the Spring of 1893 are now ready and have been placed on exhibition in our Black Goods Department on the Second Floor. James McCreery & Co., Broadway and 11th, New York. —(old adv.)

Mutton and Lamb

BOILED LEG OF MUTTON

To prepare a leg of mutton for boiling, wash it clean, cut a small piece off the shank bone, and trim the knuckle. Put it into a pot with water enough to cover it, and boil gently from two to three hours, skimming well. Then take it from the fire, and keeping the pot well covered, let it finish by remaining in the steam for ten or fifteen minutes. Serve it up with a sauceboat of melted butter into which a teacupful of capers or nasturtiums has been stirred. If the broth is to be used for soup, put in a little salt while boiling; if not, salt it well when partly done and boil the meat in a cloth.

LEG OF MUTTON À LA VENISON

Remove all the rough fat from the mutton and lay it in a deep earthen dish. Rub into it thoroughly the following: one tablespoonful of salt, one each of celery salt, brown sugar, black pepper, English mustard, allspice, and some sweet herbs, all powdered and mixed; after which pour over it slowly a teacup of good vinegar, cover tightly, and set in a cool place four or five days, turning it and basting often with the liquid each day. To cook, put in a kettle a quart of boiling water, place over it an inverted shallow pan, and on it lay the meat just as removed from the pickle. Cover the kettle tightly and stew four hours. Do not let the water touch the meat. Add a cup of hot water to the pickle remaining and baste with it. When done, thicken the liquid with flour and strain through a fine sieve to serve with the meat; also a relish of currant jelly, the same as for venison.

This is a fine dish when the directions are faithfully followed.

[*Note:* I have followed the directions faithfully and am too tired to eat.]

BROILED MUTTON CHOPS

Loin of mutton, pepper and salt, a small piece of butter. Cut the chops from a tenderloin of mutton, remove a portion of the fat, and trim them into a nice shape; slightly beat and level them; place the gridiron over a bright, clear fire, rub the bars with a little fat, and lay on the chops. While broiling, frequently turn them, and in about eight minutes they

71

will be done. Season with pepper and salt, dish them on a very hot dish, rub a small piece of butter on each chop, and serve very hot and expeditiously. Nice with tomato sauce poured over them.

ROAST QUARTER OF LAMB

Procure a nice hindquarter, remove some of the fat that is around the kidney, skewer the lower joint up the fillet, place it in a moderate oven, let it heat through slowly, then dredge it with salt and flour. Quicken the fire. Put half a pint of water into the dripping pan with a teaspoonful of salt. With this liquor baste the meat occasionally. Serve with lettuce, green peas, and mint sauce.

A quarter of lamb weighing seven or eight pounds will require two hours to roast.

A breast of lamb roasted is very sweet, and is considered by many as preferable to hindquarter. It requires nearly as long a time to roast as the quarter, and should be served in the same manner.

Make the gravy from the drippings, thickened with flour.

The mint sauce is made as follows: Take fresh, young spearmint leaves stripped from stems; wash and drain them or dry on a cloth, chop very fine, put in a gravy tureen, and to three tablespoonfuls of mint add two of finely powdered cut-loaf sugar; mix, and let it stand a few minutes; then pour over it six tablespoonfuls good cider or white-wine vinegar. The sauce should be made some time before dinner, so that the flavor of the mint may be well extracted.

Veal

FRIED VEAL CHOPS

Sprinkle over them salt and pepper, then dip them in beaten egg and cracker crumbs, and fry in drippings or in hot lard and butter mixed. If you wish a gravy with them, add a tablespoonful of flour to the gravy they were fried in and turn in cream or milk. Season to taste with salt and pepper. Boil up and serve hot with the gravy in a separate dish. This dish is very fine accompanied with a few sound fresh tomatoes, sliced and fried in the same grease the cutlets were, and all dished on the same platter.

BRAIN CUTLETS

Well wash the brains and soak them in cold water till white. Parboil them till tender in a small saucepan for about a quarter of an hour; then thoroughly drain them and place them on a board. Divide them into small pieces with a knife. Dip each piece into flour and then roll them in egg and bread crumbs. Fry them in butter or well-clarified dripping. Serve very hot with gravy. Another way of doing brains is to prepare them as above, and then stew them gently in rich stock, like stewed sweetbreads. They are also plainly boiled and served with parsley and butter sauce.

CALF'S HEAD BOILED

Put the head into boiling water and let it remain about five minutes. Take it out, hold it by the ear, and with the back of the knife scrape off the hair (should it not come off easily, dip the head again in boiling water). When perfectly clean, take the eyes out, cut off the ears, and remove the brain, which soak for an hour in warm water. Put the head to soak in hot water a few minutes to make it look white, and then have ready a stewpan, into which lay the head; cover it with cold water, and bring it gradually to boil. Remove the scum and add a little salt, which increases it and causes it to rise to the top. Simmer it very gently from two and a half to three hours, or until the bones will slip out easily, and when nearly done, boil the brains fifteen or twenty minutes; skin and chop them (not too finely), and add a tablespoonful of minced parsley which has been previously scalded and a pinch of pepper, salt; then stir into this four tablespoonfuls of melted butter; set it on the back of the range to keep it hot. When the head is done, take it up, and drain very dry. Score the top and rub it over with melted butter; dredge it with flour, and set it in the oven to brown.

When you serve the head, have it accompanied with a gravy boat of melted butter and minced parsley.

KALV SYLTA or "KALV DANS" [*Calf Dance—Jellied Veal*] ☆

Take three or four pounds of young veal shoulder (and plenty of extra bone and knuckle to make jell) and boil, with onion and bay leaf, in water just to cover. Cook until veal is so tender that it falls from bone.

73

Drain meat well, saving broth. Cut meat into small pieces with scissors. Strain broth free of bone. To strained broth add cut-up veal; season with salt and pepper, and after bringing to rolling boil, add one envelope gelatin which has been dissolved in a quarter cup cold water. Take from fire and put into small loaf pans. Set aside to cool, then refrigerate. When jelled, slice and serve.

["Both my parents were born in Norway, and the above recipe was a favorite at our table. Kalv dans was quite a lot of work, so my father always helped my mother make it."—*Mrs. Otto Wernicke*]

Pork

ROAST PIG

Make dressing as for fowls. Take young pig about six weeks old, wash thoroughly inside and outside. In another water put a teaspoon of baking soda and rinse outside again. Wipe dry, salt inside and stuff with dressing, making it full and plump and giving it original size and shape. Sew it up, place it in kneeling posture in dripping pan, tying legs in proper position. Pour a little hot salted water into pan, baste with butter and water a few times as pig warms, afterwards with gravy from pan. When it begins to smoke, rub all over with rag dipped in melted butter. This will keep skin from cracking and it will still be crisp. It will take two to three hours to roast. Make gravy by skimming off most grease; add to that left in pan a good tablespoon of flour and water for right consistency; let all boil up once. Place pig on large, hot platter, surround with parsley or celery tops. Place a green wreath around the neck and a sprig of celery in its mouth. In carving, cut off head first; split down the back, take off hams and shoulders and separate ribs.

PORK TENDERLOINS

The tenderloins are unlike any other part of the pork in flavor. They may be fried or broiled; the latter way, being dryer, requires they be well buttered before serving, which should be done on a hot platter before the butter becomes oily. Fry them in a little lard, turning them to have them cooked through; when done, remove, and keep hot while making a gravy by dredging a little flour into the hot fat; if not enough, add a little butter or lard, stir until browned, and add a little milk or cream, stir briskly, and pour over the dish. A little Worcestershire sauce may be added to the gravy if desired.

PORK CHOPS AND FRIED APPLES

Season the chops with salt and pepper and a little powdered sage; dip them into bread crumbs. Fry slowly on both sides until they are done. Put them on a hot dish; pour off part of the fat into another pan to make a gravy to serve with them, if you choose. Then fry apples which you have sliced about two-thirds of an inch thick, cutting them around the apple so that the core is in the center of each piece; then cut out the core. When they are browned on one side and partly cooked, turn them carefully with a pancake turner, and finish cooking; dish around the chops or on a separate dish.

FRIED SALT PORK

Cut in thin slices and freshen in cold water; roll in flour and fry crisp. (If required quickly, pour boiling water over the slices, let stand a few minutes, drain and roll in flour as before.) Drain off most of the grease from the frying pan; stir in while hot one or two tablespoonfuls of flour, about half a pint of milk, a little pepper, and salt if overfreshened; let it boil, and pour into a gravy dish. A teaspoonful of finely chopped parsley will add pleasantly to the appearance of the gravy.

FRIED HAM AND EGGS

Cut slices of ham quite thin, cut off the rind or skin, put them into a hot frying pan, turning them often until crisp, taking care not to burn the slices; three minutes will cook them well. Dish them on a hot platter; then turn off the top of the grease, rinse out the pan, and put back the clear grease to fry the eggs. Break the eggs separately in a saucer, that in case a bad one should be among them it may not mix with the rest. Slip each egg gently into the frying pan. Do not turn them while they are frying, but keep pouring some of the hot lard over them with a kitchen spoon; this will do them sufficiently on the upper side. They will be done enough in about three minutes; the white must retain its transparency so that the yolk will be seen through it. When done, take them up with a tin slice, drain off the lard, and if any part of the white is discolored or ragged, trim it off. Lay a fried egg upon each slice of the ham, and send to table hot.

PIGS' FEET PICKLED

Take twelve pigs' feet, scrape and wash them clean, put them into a saucepan with enough hot (not boiling) water to cover them. When partly done, salt them. It requires four to five hours to boil them soft. Pack them in a stone crock, and pour over them spiced vinegar made hot. They will be ready to use in a day or two. If you wish them for breakfast, split them, make a batter of two eggs, a cup of milk, salt, a teaspoonful of butter, with flour enough to make a thick batter; dip each piece in this and fry in hot lard. Or, dip them in beaten egg and flour and fry. Souse is good eaten cold or warm.

COUNTRY PORK SAUSAGES

Six pounds lean fresh pork, three pounds of chine fat, three tablespoonfuls of salt, two of black pepper, four tablespoonfuls of pounded and sifted sage, two of summer savory. Chop the lean and fat pork finely, mix the seasoning in with your hands, taste to see that it has the right flavor, then put them into cases, either the cleaned intestines of the hog, or make long, narrow bags of stout muslin, large enough to contain each enough sausage for a family dish. Fill these with the meat, dip in melted lard, and hang them in a cool, dry dark place. Some prefer to pack the meat in jars, pouring melted lard over it, covering the top, to be taken out as wanted and made into small round cakes with the hands, then fried brown. Many like spices added to the seasoning—cloves, mace, and nutmeg. This is a matter of taste.

SCRAPPEL

Scrappel is a most palatable dish. Take the head, heart and any lean scraps of pork, and boil until the flesh slips easily from the bones. Remove the fat, gristle and bones, then chop fine. Set the liquor in which the meat was boiled aside until cold, take the cake of fat from the surface, and return to the fire. When it boils, put in the chopped meat and season well with pepper and salt. Let it boil again, then thicken with corn meal as you would in making ordinary corn meal mush, by letting it slip through the fingers slowly to prevent lumps. Cook an hour, stirring constantly at first, afterwards putting back on the range in a position to boil gently. When done, pour into a long, square pan, not too deep, and mold. In cold weather this can be kept several weeks. Cut into slices when cold, and fried brown, as you do mush. It is a cheap and delicious breakfast dish.

[*Note:* I thought this was spelled "Scrapple." Sometimes it is called "Ponhoss," or "Ponhaus" maybe. No matter. It is delicious. It's an old Pennsylvania-Dutch recipe, and it was one of my German grandfather's specialties. He made it with meticulous care, the way he did everything, sifting the meal carefully through his fingers so it wouldn't get lumpy, stirring tirelessly. He made it just before bedtime. In the morning it was firm and cold, ready to be sliced, fried, and eaten hot with butter or syrup. A hearty breakfast for winter mornings! What an aggravation to him were two teen-age granddaughters who often were too rushed to eat decently, who would bolt a glass of orange juice and a piece of toast and dash off to school. A fine way to court "consumption," he said grumpily. He would be 100 years old this year. I wish now I had taken time *every* morning to eat his Scrapple. Following is the way I make it for my family.]

SAUSAGE SCRAPPLE ☆

¾ pound sausage meat	1 teaspoon poultry seasoning
5 cups cold water	⅛ teaspoon pepper
1½ cups yellow cornmeal	1 teaspoon celery seeds
1 tablespoon salt	

This recipe also suggests one or two onions, minced, and half a teaspoon of curry powder. I don't use them, but you may want to. I don't like it too spicy.

Simmer sausage in water (and onions) uncovered ten minutes. Sift in cornmeal gradually, and add seasonings, stirring constantly. Simmer ten minutes, stirring occasionally. Pour into greased loaf pan. Chill till firm. Slice one-quarter inch thick. Fry in hot fat till golden brown on both sides. Slices may be floured before frying to make them crispier.

Would you rather buy lamp-chimneys, one a week the year around, or one that lasts till some accident breaks it? Macbeth's "pearl glass" almost never breaks from heat. Your dealer knows where you can get it and how much it costs. It costs more than common glass, and maybe he thinks tough glass isn't good for his business. Macbeth's, Pittsburg. —(old adv.)

For the new Empire Costumes, wear Empire Stays. Made in harmony with Butterick Patterns. —(old adv.)

HEAD CHEESE

Boil the forehead, ears, and feet, and nice scraps trimmed from the hams of the fresh pig, until the meat will almost drop from the bones. Then separate the meat from the bones, put it in a large chopping bowl, and season with pepper, salt, sage, and summer savory. Chop it rather coarsely; put it back into the same kettle it was boiled in, with just enough of the liquor in which it was boiled to prevent its burning; warm it through thoroughly, mixing it well together. Now pour it into a strong muslin bag, press the bag between two flat surfaces, with a heavy weight on top; when cold and solid it can be cut in slices. Good cold, or warmed up in vinegar.

TO CURE HAMS AND BACON

For each hundred pounds of hams, make a pickle of ten pounds of salt, two pounds of brown sugar, two ounces of saltpeter, and one ounce of red pepper, and from four to four and a half gallons of water, or just enough to cover the hams, after being packed in a watertight vessel, or enough salt to make a brine to float a fresh egg high enough, that is to say, out of water. First rub the hams with common salt, and lay them into a tub. Take the above ingredients, put them into a vessel over the fire, and heat it hot, stirring it frequently. Remove all the scum, allow it to boil ten minutes, let it cool, and pour over the meat. After laying in this brine five or six weeks, take out, drain and wipe, and smoke from two to three weeks. Small pieces of bacon may remain in this pickle two weeks, which would be sufficient.

TO SMOKE HAMS AND FISH AT HOME

Take an old hogshead, stop up all the crevices, and fix a place to put a cross-stick near the bottom, to hang the articles to be smoked on. Next, in the side, cut a hole near the top, to introduce an iron pan filled with hickory wood sawdust and small pieces of green wood. Having turned the hogshead upside down, hang the articles upon the cross-stick, introduce the iron pan in the opening, and place a piece of red-hot iron in the pan, cover it with sawdust, and all will be complete. Let a large ham remain ten days, and keep up a good smoke. The best way for keeping hams is to sew them in coarse cloths, whitewashed on the outside.

TO CURE ENGLISH BACON

In smoking this bacon, the sweetest flavor is derived from black birch chips, but if these are not to be had, the next best wood is hickory; the smoking with corn-cobs imparts a rank flavor to this bacon, which is very distasteful to English people visiting this country. It requires three weeks or a month to smoke this bacon properly.

TOAD IN THE HOLE [*Old English Recipe*] ☆

Mix one cup flour, one teaspoon baking powder, one-half teaspoon salt. Beat two eggs, three-fourths cup milk and one-fourth cup water. Add liquid ingredients to the dry, and beat with egg beater until bubbly. Place one pound link sausages in pan, prick them with fork and bake them in hot oven [400°] until fat running out has greased pan—about ten minutes. Pour batter over sausages and bake about thirty-five minutes until light brown and puffy. Serves four.

ORANGE PORK CHOPS ☆

Brown four center-cut pork chops in a heavy skillet. Then place them in flat, uncovered baking dish and pour over them: one six-ounce can of frozen orange juice concentrate, thawed, six ounces dry white wine, and one teaspoon each dried oregano and dried sweet basil. Put chops covered with sauce in a 350° oven and cook thirty minutes. Sprinkle top of chops generously with slivered almonds; spoon sauce up over almonds and cook thirty minutes longer or until sauce thickens slightly. Serve with sauce on chops to *two people*—like Bride and Bridegroom, or Newly Retired Couple Whose Children Have Grown-Up and Married, or Couple Whose Children Have Gone to Camp and Now They Can Eat What They Like Instead of Setting a Good Example.

> *A maiden's wishes are but three,*
> *O'er all the world whoe'er she be,*
> *To handsome grow,*
> *To have a beau,*
> *And to the bridal altar go,*
> *All these fruitions of her hope*
> *Come quickly if she'll* USE PEAR'S SOAP. —(*old adv.*)

EVELYN'S CHINESE PORK CHOPS ☆

Brown four pork chops thoroughly without added fat. Salt. Add one-fourth cup water, cover and simmer thirty minutes. Remove chops; pour off excess fat. Melt one chicken bouillon cube in one cup hot water in skillet and add:

½ teaspoon Worcestershire
   sauce
1 teaspoon soy sauce
1 tablespoon vinegar

⅓ cup pineapple juice from
   canned, cubed pineapple
¼ teaspoon prepared mustard

Combine two tablespoons cornstarch and two tablespoons cold water. Stir into skillet mixture and cook until thick, stirring constantly. Add pork chops and these ingredients:

1 nine-ounce can cubed
   pineapple, drained
1 tomato, cubed

½ green pepper cut in
   thin strips
½ cup chopped celery

Simmer only five minutes. Serve over four cups hot rice.

POMPEY'S HEAD ☆

[*Note:* This recipe was popular before automatic ovens were invented, because it could be allowed to cook for hours without close attention.]

1 pound sausage meat
1 pound ground beef
1 teaspoon salt
   Sprinkle of pepper

2 cups or No. 2 can tomatoes
1 cup finely chopped celery
1 tablespoon chopped onion
½ cup sliced green pepper

Combine meats and seasoning; make into a roll. Flour the outside well and put into a pan and brown in a hot oven (450°). When nicely browned, add the vegetables over and around the meat roll. Bake covered in 350° oven for one and a half hours. Baste the meat with the mixture several times during cooking period. When roll is finished, pour sauce over. [Remove cover from pan during last ten minutes of baking so roll will brown.]

Children Cry for Pitcher's Castoria. —(*old adv.*)

CROQUETTES OF ODDS AND ENDS

These are made from scraps that happen to be left from one or more meals and in such quantities that they cannot be warmed up separately, such as a couple of spoonfuls of frizzled beef and cream, the lean meat of one mutton chop, one spoonful of minced beef, two cold hard-boiled eggs, a little cold chopped potato, mashed potato seasoned and mixed with one raw egg, a little flour and butter and boiling water. Make into round cakes, and brown well with butter in frying pan. Most housekeepers would be surprised at the result.

Poultry and Game

Poultry should never be cooked until six or eight hours after it has been killed, but it should be picked and drawn as soon as possible. Plunge it in a pot of scalding hot water; then pluck off the feathers, taking care not to tear the skin. When it is picked clean, roll up a piece of white paper, set fire to it and singe off all the hairs. The head, neck and feet should be cut off and the ends of the legs skewered to the body and string tied around the body tightly.

Fowls and game when bought at our city markets require a more thorough cleansing than those sold in country places, where as a general thing the meat is wholly dressed. In large cities they lay for some length of time with the intestines undrawn, until the flavor of them diffuses itself all through the meat, rendering it distasteful. In this case it is safe after taking out the intestines to rinse out in several waters, and in next to the last water add a teaspoonful of baking soda, say to a quart of water. This process neutralizes all sourness and helps to destroy all unpleasant taste in the meat.

Poultry may be baked so that its wings and legs are soft and tender by being placed in a deep roasting pan with closed cover, thereby retaining the aroma and essences by absorption while confined. These pans are a recent innovation, and are made double, with a small opening in the top for giving vent to the accumulation of steam and gases when required. Roast meats of any kind can also be cooked in the same manner, and it is a great improvement on the old plan.

81

MODERN TIMES AND TEMPERATURES FOR ROASTING POULTRY AND GAME

Fowl or Game	Oven Temp.	Time per Pound
Chicken	300° F.	30–45 min.
Duck	325°	20–30
Goose	325°	20–25
Goose, wild	325°	15–20
Grouse or Prairie Chicken	350°	60–75 total
Guinea Hen	350°	20–22
Partridge	350°	30–35 total
Pheasant	350°	15–20
Quail	350°	25–30 total
Rabbit, Squirrel, Hare	325°	1½–2 hr. total
Squab or Pigeon	325°	45–60 min. total
Turkey		
10 pounds or less	325°	20–25
10–16 pounds	325°	18–20
18–25 pounds	300°	13–15
Turkey, wild	325°	20–25
Wild duck	325°	10–12 rare
		15–20 well-done
Venison	325°	25 rare

The above chart is for meat at room temperature. Birds should be weighed before being dressed and drawn or after being stuffed. Use lower figure for large birds, higher figure for small ones, and add fifteen to thirty minutes total cooking time for cold meat.

DRESSING OR STUFFING FOR FOWLS

For an eight- or ten-pound turkey cut the brown crust from slices or pieces of stale bread until you have as much as the inside of a pound loaf; put it into a suitable dish and pour tepid water (not warm, for that makes it heavy) over it; let it stand one minute as it soaks very quickly. Now take up a handful at a time and squeeze it hard and dry with both hands, placing it as you go along in another dish; this process makes it very light. When all is pressed dry, toss it all up lightly through your fingers; now add pepper, salt—about a teaspoonful—also a teaspoonful of powdered summer savory, the same amount of sage or the green herb, minced fine; add half a cup of butter and a beaten egg or not. Work thoroughly all together, and it is ready for dressing either fowls, fish, or meats. A little chopped sausage in turkey dressing is considered by some an improvement, when well incorporated with the other ingredients. For geese and ducks the stuffing may be made the same as for turkey with the addition of a few slices of onion chopped fine.

This recipe was obtained from an old colored cook who was famous for his fine dressings for fowls, fish, and meats, and his advice was *always* soak stale bread in *cold* liquid, either milk or water, when used for stuffing or for puddings, as they were much lighter. Hot liquid makes them heavy.

[*Note: Cold* liquid for light dressings—this is a "new departure" worth trying!]

ROAST TURKEY

Select a young turkey; remove all the feathers carefully, singe it over a burning newspaper on the top of the stove, then "draw" it nicely, being very careful not to break any of the internal organs. Remove the crop carefully, cut off the head and tie the neck close to the body by drawing the skin over it. Now rinse and wash, as above, dry inside and out, rub the inside with some salt, then stuff the breast and body with "Dressing for Fowls." Then sew up the turkey with a strong thread, tie the legs and wings to the body, rub it over with a little soft butter, sprinkle some salt and pepper over, dredge with a little flour, place it in a dripping pan, pour in a cup of boiling water, and set it in the oven.

Baste the turkey often, turning it around occasionally so that every part will be uniformly baked. When pierced with a fork and the liquid runs out perfectly clear, the bird is done. If any part is likely to scorch, pin over it a piece of buttered white paper. A fifteen-pound turkey requires between three and four hours to bake. Serve with cranberry sauce.

TURKEY SCALLOP

Pick the meat from the bones of cold turkey and chop it fine. Put a layer of bread crumbs on the bottom of a buttered dish, moisten them with a little milk, then put in a layer of turkey with some of the filling, and cut small pieces of butter over the top, sprinkle with pepper and salt, then another layer of bread crumbs, and so on until the dish is nearly full. Add a little hot water to the gravy left from the turkey and pour over it; then take two eggs, two tablespoonfuls of milk, one of

83

melted butter, a little salt and cracker crumbs, as much as will make it thick enough to spread on with a knife, put bits of butter over it, and cover with a plate. Bake three-quarters of an hour. Ten minutes before serving, remove the plate and let it brown.

[*Note:* Could be a quick company-dish with canned turkey or chicken and canned gravy or dried gravy-mix.]

CHICKEN PIE

Stew chicken tender, season and thicken gravy, take it from the fire. Take out the largest bones, scrape the meat from the neck and backbone, throw the bones away. Line the sides of a four- or six-quart pudding-dish with a rich baking-powder or soda-biscuit dough, a quarter of an inch thick. Put in part of the chicken, a few lumps of butter, pepper and salt (if needed), some cold boiled eggs cut in slices. Add the rest of the chicken and season as before; a few new potatoes in their season might be added. Pour over the gravy, being sure to have enough to fill the dish, and cover with a crust a quarter of an inch thick made with a hole in the center the size of a teacup. Brush over the top with beaten white of egg, and bake for half to three-quarters of an hour. Garnish the top with small bright celery leaves, neatly arranged in a circle.

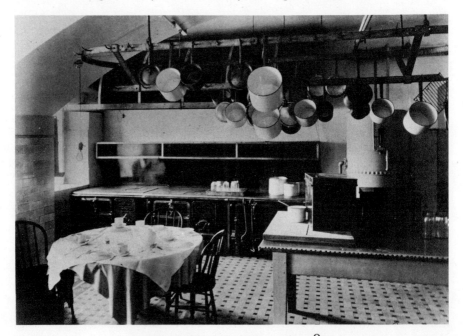

WHITE HOUSE KITCHEN, CIRCA 1895

FRIED CHICKEN

Wash and cut up a young chicken, wipe it dry, season with salt and pepper, dredge it with flour or dip each piece in beaten egg and then in cracker crumbs. Have in a frying pan one ounce each of butter and sweet lard made boiling hot. Lay in the chicken and fry brown on both sides. Take up, drain them, and set aside in a covered dish. Stir into the gravy left, if not too much, a large tablespoonful of flour, make it smooth, add a cup of cream or milk, season with salt and pepper, boil up and pour over the chicken. Some like chopped parsley added to the gravy. Serve hot.

If the chicken is old, put it into a stewpan with a little water and simmer gently till tender; season with salt and pepper, dip in coating as above and fry. Use the broth the chicken was cooked in to make the gravy.

DUMPLING FOR CHICKEN [1879]

One pint of flour, one pinch of salt, one heaping teaspoonful of baking powder, milk for stiff batter. Cut off in small lumps from the spoon, boil twenty minutes. Do not uncover the pot until done.—*Mrs. Lew Wallace* [wife of General Lew Wallace, Civil War leader and author of *Ben Hur*.]

FRIED CHICKEN À LA ITALIENNE

Make common batter and mix into it a cupful of chopped tomatoes, one onion chopped, some minced parsley, and salt and pepper. Cut up young tender chickens, dry them well, and dip each piece in the batter, then fry brown in plenty of butter in a thick-bottom frying pan. Serve with tomato sauce.

Batter: Two cups flour and two teaspoons baking powder, sifted together, to which add one-half teaspoon salt, two beaten eggs, and one and one-half cups milk. Stir well, then add chopped tomatoes, onion, and parsley.

CURRY CHICKEN

Cut up a young chicken as for fricassee, wash well and put it into a stew pan with water to cover it. Boil closely covered until tender, then add a large teaspoonful of salt and cook a few minutes longer. Remove chicken; pour liquor into bowl and set it to one side. Now cut up into the stewpan two small onions and fry them with a piece of butter as large as an egg. When brown, skim out onions and put in the chicken. Fry for three or four minutes, then sprinkle over two teaspoonfuls of curry powder. Now pour in the liquor in which the chicken was stewed, stir all well together, and stew five minutes longer. Stir into this a tablespoonful of sifted flour made thin with a little water. Lastly, stir in a beaten yolk of egg, and it is done. Serve with hot boiled rice laid round on the edge of a platter and the chicken curry in the center. This makes a handsome side dish and a fine relish accompanying a full dinner of roast beef or any roast. All first-class grocers and druggists keep India Curry Powder put up in bottles. Beef, veal, mutton, duck, pigeons, partridges, rabbits, or fresh fish may be substituted for the chicken if preferred.

CHICKEN AND MACARONI

Boil a chicken until very tender, take out all the bones and pick up the meat quite fine. Boil half a pound of macaroni until tender, first breaking it up into pieces an inch long. Butter a deep pudding dish, put on the bottom a layer of the cooked macaroni, then a layer of the minced chicken, bits of butter, pepper and salt, then some of the chicken liquor, over this put another layer of macaroni, and so on until the dish is filled. Pour a cup of cream over the whole and bake half an hour. Serve on a platter.

Chicken With a Difference

LIME CHICKEN MARINADE ☆

¼ cup lime juice (bottled or fresh)
½ cup salad oil
½ teaspoon sugar
1 teaspoon dry mustard

¼ teaspoon each rosemary, thyme, and basil
1 bay leaf
1 teaspoon salt
¼ teaspoon Tabasco

Marinate chicken four hours or longer (cut-up, halved, or quartered chicken). Baste while broiling with the marinade, and also sprinkle pieces with Accent and paprika.

86

MANDARIN CHICKEN ☆

2 eleven-ounce cans
   mandarin oranges
½ cup white wine
½ cup melted butter
2 tablespoons soy sauce

Broiler chickens, quartered
1 can tomato sauce
1 clove garlic, minced,
   or garlic powder
½ teaspoon ginger

Drain oranges, reserving syrup. Combine wine, butter, and soy sauce. Marinate chicken in this mixture three hours in refrigerator. Drain chicken, saving marinade. Season and broil. To marinade add orange syrup, tomato sauce, garlic, and ginger. Heat and use to baste chicken while broiling. Five minutes before serving add orange pieces to sauce. Spoon sauce over each piece of chicken.

BAKED CHICKEN SALAD WITH WHITE SAUCE ☆

2 cups cut-up cooked chicken
1 cup diced celery
2 teaspoons minced onion
½ cup coarsely chopped pecans
2 hard-cooked eggs, sliced thin

½ teaspoon salt
¼ teaspoon black pepper
1 tablespoon lemon juice
¾ cup mayonnaise
1 cup crushed potato chips

Mix all ingredients except potato chips and cover with a white sauce; top with potato chips and bake in greased casserole thirty minutes at 350°. Serves six to eight.

CHICKEN PACIFIC ☆

Dip six chicken breasts or other pieces in the following mixture:

2 cups sour cream
1 teaspoon each tarragon,
   thyme, and paprika

½ teaspoon garlic powder
2½ teaspoons salt

Then dip chicken in cornflake crumbs (about one and a half cups), rolling to coat well. Place half a stick of butter in a baking dish and melt

87

in preheated 350° oven. Add chicken to dish and bake forty-five minutes on one side; turn and bake about twenty minutes longer.

Serve with this sauce, which may be passed separately or spooned over chicken, which is then baked ten additional minutes:

1 cup cooked, cleaned prawns or tiny canned shrimp	¼ cup diced ripe olives

Add shrimp and olives to sour-cream mixture in which chicken was dipped. Heat if sauce is to be passed separately.

Chicken Pacific may be baked and frozen. To serve, thaw completely and reheat.

CHICKEN BAKED IN SOUR CREAM ☆

Pour over cut-up chicken pieces (breasts are best): One carton sour cream, one and a half or two cans cream of chicken soup, a half cup sherry, one can mushrooms with liquid. Bake at 350° for an hour and a half, turning the chicken or basting.

ASPARACHICK AU GRATIN ☆

4 cups bread cubes	⅓ cup flour
1 cup grated, sharp cheese	1 teaspoon salt
¼ cup butter, melted	¼ teaspoon pepper
1 package frozen asparagus pieces, cooked, and drained	3 cups milk, scalded
	3 cups diced, cooked chicken
¼ cup butter	

Mix bread cubes, cheese and melted butter lightly. Line a 9 by 12 baking dish with half of the mixture. Add a layer of asparagus. Blend one-fourth cup butter (melted), flour, salt, and pepper and add milk, cooking and stirring constantly till thick. Add the chicken to this white sauce and pour over the asparagus. Top with remaining bread-cube mixture. Bake at 350° for thirty minutes. White sauce is improved if one and a half cups chicken broth and one and a half cups milk are used instead of three cups milk. Serves about six at a ladies' luncheon.

BRAISED DUCKS

Prepare a pair of fine young ducks, place them in a stewpan together with two or three slices of bacon, a carrot, an onion stuck with two cloves, and a little thyme and parsley. Season with pepper and cover the whole with a broth, adding to the broth a gill of white wine. Place the pan over a gentle fire and allow the ducks to simmer until done, basting them frequently. When done, remove them from the pan and place them where they will keep hot. A turnip should then be cut up and fried in some butter. When nicely browned, drain the pieces and cook them until tender in the liquor in which the ducks were braised. Now strain and thicken the gravy, and after dishing up the ducks, pour it over them, garnishing with the pieces of turnip.—*Palmer House, Chicago*

WILD DUCKS

Most wild ducks are apt to have the flavor of fish, and in the hands of inexperienced cooks are sometimes unpalatable on this account. Before roasting them, parboil them with a small peeled carrot put within each duck. This absorbs the unpleasant taste. An onion will have the same effect, but unless you use onions in the stuffing, the carrot is preferable. Roast the same as a tame duck. Or put into the duck a whole onion peeled, plenty of salt and pepper, and a glass of claret. Bake in a hot oven twenty minutes. Serve hot with the gravy it yields in cooking and a dish of currant jelly.

CANVASBACK DUCK

The epicurean taste declares that this special kind of bird requires no spices or flavors to make it perfect, as the meat partakes of the flavor of the food that the bird feeds upon, being mostly wild celery. The delicious flavor is best preserved when roasted quickly with a hot fire. After dressing the duck in the usual way by plucking, singeing, and drawing, wipe it with a wet towel, truss the head under the wing, place it in a dripping pan, put it in the oven (basting often), and roast it half an hour. It is generally preferred a little underdone. Place it when done on a hot dish, season well with salt and pepper, pour over it the gravy it has yielded in baking, and serve it immediately while hot. It will generally be conceded that the best ducks are to be found along the Potomac River.—*Delmonico's, New York*

PIGEON PIE

Take half a dozen pigeons; stuff each one with a dressing the same as for turkey; loosen the joints with a knife, but do not separate them. Put them in a stewpan with water enough to cover them; let them cook until nearly tender, then season them with salt and pepper and butter. Thicken the gravy with flour, then remove and cool. Butter a pudding dish, line the sides with a rich crust. Have ready some hard-boiled eggs cut in slices. Put in a layer of egg and birds and gravy until the dish is full. Cover with a crust and bake.

ROAST GOOSE (ENGLISH STYLE)

The bird should not be more than eight months old, and the fatter, the more tender and juicy the meat. Stuff with the following mixture: three pints of bread crumbs, six ounces of butter (or part butter and part salt pork), one teaspoonful each of sage, black pepper, and salt, and one chopped onion. Do not stuff very full, and stitch openings firmly together to keep flavor in and fat out. Place in a baking pan with a little water and baste frequently with salt and water (some add vinegar) and turn often so that the sides and back may be nicely browned. Bake two hours or more. When done, take from the pan and pour off the fat. To the brown gravy left, add the chopped giblets which have previously been stewed until tender; also, add the water they were boiled in. Thicken this gravy with a little flour and butter rubbed together, bring to a boil and serve.

[*Note:* Very likely the same "English-style" recipe which inspired the Cratchit family to shout, "There never was such a goose!" in *A Christmas Carol*. The youngest Cratchits, you may recall, "were steeped in sage and onion to the eyebrows."]

WIDGEON AND TEAL

A widgeon is a waterfowl of the duck persuasion, as is also the teal, although smaller than the common duck. They are dressed precisely like the duck, only less time in cooking is required for the widgeon and still less for the teal.

Every old-style bonnet ribbon seems to have been revived by the French and American manufacturers. —*The Elite News, 1887*

ROAST PARTRIDGE

Pluck, singe, draw, and truss them; roast about twenty minutes; baste them well with butter. When the gravy begins to run from them, they are done. Put them on dishes, three in each dish, with some bread crumbs fried a nice brown and arranged in small heaps. The gravy should be served in a tureen separately. Orange sauce is a nice accompaniment. If these birds have a bitter taste when cooked, do not eat them. It is produced by their feeding on laurel berries in winter, when their food is scarce. Laurel berries are poisonous, and people have died from eating birds that have fed on them.

ROAST LARKS

These are considered the most delicate of the small birds. When cleaned and prepared for roasting, brush them with the yolk of an egg and roll them in bread crumbs. Spit them on a small bird-spit, and tie that on a larger spit. Ten or fifteen minutes at a quick fire will cook them; baste them with fresh butter and sprinkle them with bread crumbs till they are quite covered while roasting. Sauce with grated bread fried in butter, which set to drain before the fire that it may harden. Serve the crumbs under the larks when you dish them, and garnish them with slices of lemon.

ROAST WOODCOCK

Skin the head and neck of the bird, pluck the feathers, and truss it by bringing the beak of the bird under the wing and fastening the pinion to the thigh; twist the legs at the knuckles and press the feet upon the thigh. Put a piece of bread under each bird to catch the drippings, baste with butter, dredge with flour, and roast fifteen or twenty minutes with a sharp fire. When done, cut the bread in diamond shape, each piece large enough to stand one bird upon, place them aslant on your dish, and serve with gravy enough to moisten the bread. Serve some in the dish and some in the tureen; garnish with slices of lemon.

SNIPE

Snipes are similar to woodcocks and may be served in the same manner; they will require less time to roast.

REED BIRDS

Pick and draw them very carefully, salt and dredge with flour, and roast with a quick fire ten or fifteen minutes. Serve on toast with butter and pepper. You can put in each one an oyster dipped in butter and then in bread crumbs before roasting. They are also very nice broiled.

ROAST QUAIL

Rinse well and steam over boiling water until tender, then dredge with flour and smother in butter; season with salt and pepper and roast inside the stove. Thicken the gravy. Serve with green grape jelly and garnish with parsley.

SNOW BIRDS

One dozen thoroughly cleaned birds; stuff each with an oyster, put them into a yellow dish, and add two ounces of boiled salt pork and three raw potatoes cut into slices. Add a pint of oyster liquor, an ounce of butter, salt, and pepper. Cover the dish with a crust and bake in a moderate oven.

[*Note:* What does a yellow dish have that a green dish doesn't have?]

TO ROAST PARTRIDGES, PHEASANTS, QUAILS, OR GROUSE

Carefully cut out all the shot, wash thoroughly but quickly, using soda in the water; rinse again and dry with a clean cloth. Stuff them and sew them up. Skewer the legs and wings to the body, larder the breast with very thin slices of fat salt pork, place them in the oven, and baste with butter and water before taking up, having seasoned them with salt and pepper, or you can leave out the pork and use only butter or cook them without stuffing. Make a gravy of the drippings thickened with browned flour. Boil up and serve in a boat.

These are all very fine broiled, first splitting down the back, placing on the gridiron the inside down; cover them with a baking tin and broil slowly at first. Serve with cream gravy.

ROAST HARE OR RABBIT

A very close relationship exists between the hare and the rabbit, the chief difference being in the smaller size and shorter legs and ears of the latter. The manner of dressing and preparing each for the table is, therefore, pretty nearly the same. To prepare them for roasting, first skin, wash well in cold water, and rinse thoroughly in lukewarm water. If a little musty from being emptied before they were hung up and afterward neglected, rub the insides with vinegar and afterward remove all taint of the acid by a thorough washing in lukewarm water. After being well wiped with a soft cloth, put in a dressing as usual, sew the animal up, truss it and roast for a half or three-quarters of an hour, until well-browned, basting it constantly with butter and dredging with flour just before taking up.

To make a gravy after the rabbits are roasted, pour nearly all the fat out of the pan, but do not pour the bottom or brown part of the drippings. Put the pan over the fire, stir into it a heaping teaspoonful of flour, and stir until the flour browns. Then stir in a pint of boiling water. Season the gravy with salt and pepper; let it boil for a moment. Send hot to the table in a tureen with the hot rabbits. Serve with currant jelly.

SQUIRREL

They are cooked similar to rabbits, are excellent when broiled or made into a stew, and, in fact, are very good in all the different styles of cooking similar to rabbit.

There are many species common to this country, among them the black, red, gray, and fox. Gophers and chipmunks may also be classed as another but smaller variety.

SALMI OF GAME

This is a nice mode of serving the remains of roasted game, but when a superlative salmi is desired, the birds must be scarcely more than half roasted for it. In either case, carve them very neatly and strip every particle of skin and fat from the legs, wings, and breasts. Bruise the bodies well and put them with the skin and other trimmings into a very clean stewpan. If for a simple and inexpensive dinner, merely add to them two sliced onions, a bay leaf, a small blade of mace, and a few

93

peppercorns; then pour in a pint or more of good veal gravy or strong broth, and boil it briskly until reduced by nearly half; strain the gravy, pressing the bones well to obtain all the flavor. Skim off the fat, add a little cayenne and lemon juice, heat the game very gradually in it, but do not on any account allow it to boil. Place pieces of fried bread round a dish, arrange birds in good form in the center; give the sauce a boil and pour it on them.

ROAST HAUNCH OF VENISON

To prepare a haunch of venison for roasting, wash it slightly in tepid water and dry it thoroughly by rubbing it with a clean, soft cloth. Lay over the fat side a large sheet of thickly buttered paper and next a paste of flour and water about three-quarters of an inch thick. Cover this again with two or three sheets of stout paper, secure the whole well with twine, and put down to roast, with a little water, in the dripping pan. Let the fire be clear and strong; baste the paper immediately with butter or clarified drippings. Roast the joint from three to four hours, according to its weight and quality. Doe venison will require half an hour less time than buck venison. About twenty minutes before the joint is done, remove the paste and paper, baste the meat in every part with butter, and dredge it very lightly with flour. Let it take a pale brown color, and serve hot with unflavored gravy made with a thickening in a tureen and good currant jelly. Venison is much better when the deer has been killed in the autumn, when wild berries are plentiful, and it has had abundant opportunities to fatten upon this and other fresh food.—*Windsor Hotel, Montreal*

VENISON HASHED

Cut the meat in nice, small slices, and put the trimmings and bones into a saucepan with barely water enough to cover them. Let them stew for an hour. Then strain the liquid into a stewpan; add to it some bits of butter, rolled in flour, and whatever gravy was left of the venison the day before. Stir in some currant jelly and give it a boil-up. Then put in the meat, and keep it over the fire just long enough to warm it through; but do not allow it to boil, as it has been once cooked already.

Try it with your Thanksgiving Dinner. Sparkling Manitou Ginger Champagne. Non-Alcoholic. Strictly a Temperance Drink.—(old adv.)

Eggs

There are so many ways of cooking and dressing eggs that it seems unnecessary for the ordinary family to use only those that are the most practical.

To ascertain the freshness of an egg, hold it between your thumb and forefinger in a horizontal position, with a strong light in front of you. The fresh egg will have a clear appearance, both upper and lower sides being the same. The stale egg will have a clear appearance at the lower side while the upper side will exhibit a dark or cloudy appearance.

Another test is to put them in a pan of cold water; those that are the first to sink are the freshest; the stale will rise and float on top; or, if the large end turns up in the water, they are not fresh. The best time for preserving eggs is from July to September.

TO PRESERVE EGGS

There are several recipes for preserving eggs, and we give first one which we know to be effectual, keeping them fresh from August until spring. Take a piece of quicklime as large as a good-sized lemon and two teacupfuls of salt; put it into a large vessel and slake it with a gallon of boiling water. It will boil and bubble until thick as cream; when it is cold, pour off the top, which will be perfectly clear. Drain off this liquor and pour it over your eggs; see that the liquor more than covers them. A stone jar is the most convenient—one that holds about six quarts.

Another manner of preserving eggs is to pack them in a jar with layers of salt between, the large end of the egg downward, with a thick layer of salt at the top; cover tightly and set in a cool place.

FRIED EGGS

Break the eggs, one at a time, into a saucer, and then slide them carefully off into a frying pan of lard and butter mixed, dipping over the eggs the hot grease in spoonfuls, or turn them over—frying both sides without breaking them. They require about three minutes' cooking.

Eggs can be fried round like balls by dropping one at a time into a quantity of hot lard, the same as for fried cakes, first stirring the hot

95

lard with a stick until it runs round like a whirlpool; this will make the eggs look like balls. Take out with a skimmer. Eggs can be poached the same in boiling water.

EGGS AUX FINES HERBES

Roll an ounce of butter in a good teaspoonful of flour; season with pepper, salt, and nutmeg; put it into a coffeecupful of fresh milk, together with two teaspoonfuls of chopped parsley; stir and simmer it for fifteen minutes; add a teacupful of thick cream. Hard-boil five eggs and halve them; arrange them in a dish with the ends upwards, pour the sauce over them, and decorate with little heaps of fried bread crumbs round the margin of the dish.

EGGS IN CASES

Make little paper cases of buttered writing paper; put a small piece of butter in each, and a little chopped parsley or onion; pepper and salt. Place the cases upon a gridiron over a moderate fire of bright coals, and when the butter melts, break a fresh egg into each case. Strew in upon them a few seasoned bread crumbs, and when nearly done, glaze the tops with a hot shovel. Serve in the paper cases.

OMELET OF HERBS

Parsley, thyme, and sweet marjoram mixed makes the famous *Omelette aux Fines Herbes* so popular at every wayside inn in the most remote corner of sunny France. An omelet "jardiniere" is two tablespoonfuls of mixed parsley, onion, chives, shallots, and a few leaves each of sorrel and chervil, minced fine and stirred into the beaten eggs before cooking. It will take a little more butter to fry it than a plain one.

BAKED OMELET

Beat the whites and yolks of four or six eggs separately; add to the yolks a small cup of milk, a tablespoonful of flour or cornstarch, a teaspoonful of baking powder, one-half teaspoonful of salt, and, lastly, the stiff-beaten whites. Bake in a well-buttered pie-tin or plate about half an hour in a steady oven. It should be served the moment it is taken from the oven, as it is liable to fall.

RUM OMELET

Put a small quantity of lard into the pan; let it simmer a few minutes and remove it; wipe the pan dry with a towel, and put in a little fresh lard in which the omelet may be fried. Care should be taken that the lard does not burn, which would spoil the color of the omelet. Break three eggs separately; put them into a bowl and whisk them thoroughly with a fork. The longer they are beaten, the lighter will the omelet be. Beat up a teaspoonful of milk with the eggs and continue to beat until the last moment before pouring into the pan, which should be over a hot fire. As soon as the omelet sets, remove the pan from the hottest part of the fire. Slip a knife under it to prevent sticking to the pan. When the center is almost firm, slant the pan, work the omelet in shape to fold easily and neatly, and when slightly browned, hold a platter against the edge of the pan and deftly turn it out onto the hot dish. Dust a liberal quantity of powdered sugar over it and singe the sugar into neat stripes with a hot iron rod heated in the coals; pour a glass of warm Jamaica rum around it, and when it is placed on the table set fire to the rum. With a tablespoon dash the burning rum over the omelet, put out the fire and serve. Salt *mixed* with the eggs prevents them from rising, and when it is so used the omelet will look flabby, yet without salt it will taste insipid. Add a little salt to it just before folding it and turning it out on the dish.

APPLE OMELET

Apple omelet, to be served with broiled spare-rib or roast pork, is very delicate. Take nine large tart apples, four eggs, one cup of sugar, one tablespoonful of butter; add cinnamon or other spices to suit your taste. Stew the apples till they are very soft; mash them so that there will be no lumps; add the butter and sugar while they are still warm; but let them cool before putting in the beaten eggs; bake this till it is brown; you may put it all in a shallow pudding dish or in two tin plates to bake. Very good.

OX EYES

Take slices one inch thick from good light bread, cut rounds with a three-inch cutter, cut a smaller ring one and one-half inch, scoop out to take in an egg, brush with butter and crisp in quick oven. Break a

97

fresh egg in each. Season with salt and pepper, then put in oven to set.

[*Note:* I don't quite understand how to arrange the "rings" to look like an ox eye. I'm not even sure I want them staring up at me from the breakfast table, but I'll bet a child would be intrigued by this idea.]

Butter and Cheese

TO MAKE BUTTER

Thoroughly scald the churn, then cool well with ice or spring water. Now pour in the thick cream. Churn fast at first, then, as the butter forms, more slowly, always with perfect regularity. In warm weather pour a little cold water into the churn should the butter form slowly; in winter, if the cream is too cold, add a little warm water to bring it to the proper temperature. When the butter has come, rinse the sides of the churn down with cold water and take the butter up with the dasher or a wooden ladle, turning it dexterously just below the surface of the buttermilk to catch every stray bit.

When you have collected all the butter, gather it behind the ladle and drain off the water, working the butter to get the milk out. Work in a tablespoon of salt to the pound and set it in a cool place to harden. Knead it until not another drop of water exudes. Then with the ladle make the butter up into rolls, balls, stamped pats, etc.

TO MAKE BUTTER QUICKLY

Immediately after the cow is milked strain milk into clean pans and set over moderate fire until scalding hot. Set aside, and when cold, skim off cream. Put it into clean earthen basin and beat it with a wooden spoon until butter is made, which will not be long. Take it from the milk and work it with a little cold water. Drain off water, put a small tablespoonful of fine salt to each pound, and work it in. A small teaspoonful of fine white sugar worked in will be found an improvement—sugar is a great preservative. Make the butter in a roll; cover with a bit of muslin; keep in a cool place. A reliable recipe.

99

PUTTING UP BUTTER TO KEEP

Take of the best pure, common salt two quarts, and one ounce of white sugar and one of saltpeter; pulverize them together completely. Work the butter well, then thoroughly work in an ounce of this mixture to every pound of butter. The butter to be made into half-pound rolls and put into the following brine—to three gallons of brine strong enough to bear an egg, add a quarter of a pound of white sugar.

CURDS AND CREAM

One gallon of milk will make a moderate dish. Put one spoonful of prepared rennet to each quart of milk, and when you find that it has become curd, tie it loosely in a thin cloth and hang it to drain; do not wring or press the cloth. When drained, put the curd into a mug and set in cool water, which must be frequently changed (an icebox saves this trouble). When you dish it, if there is whey in the mug, ladle it gently out without pressing the curd; lay it on a deep dish and pour fresh cream over it; have powdered loaf sugar to eat with it; also hand around the nutmeg grater.

Prepared rennet can be had at almost any druggist's, and at a reasonable price. Call for Crosse & Blackwell's Prepared Rennet.

NEW JERSEY CREAM CHEESE

First scald the quantity of milk desired; let it cool a little, then add the rennet; the directions for quantity are given on the packages of "Prepared Rennet." When the curd is formed, take it out on a ladle without breaking it; lay it on a thin cloth held by two persons; dash a ladleful of water over each ladleful of curd, to separate the curd; hang it up to drain the water off; and then put it under a light press for one hour. Cut the curd with a thread into small pieces, lay a cloth between each two, and press for an hour. Take them out, rub them with fine salt, let them lie on a board for an hour, and wash them in cold water. Let them lie to drain, and in a day or two the skin will look dry. Put some sweet grass under and over them, and they will soon ripen.

The safest colors for cheap portieres are olive green and brick red.

Packages delivered, ten cents; trunks, twenty-five cents.—(old adv.)

COTTAGE CHEESE

Put a pan of sour or loppered milk on the stove or range where it is not too hot; let it scald until the whey rises to the top (be careful that it does not boil, or the curd will become hard and tough). Place a clean cloth or towel over a sieve, and pour this whey and curd into it, leaving it covered to drain two to three hours; then put it into a dish and chop it fine with a spoon, adding a teaspoonful of salt, a tablespoonful of butter, and enough sweet cream to make the cheese the consistency of putty. With your hands make it into little balls flattened. Keep it in a cool place. Many like it made rather thin with cream, serving it in a deep dish. You may make this cheese of sweet milk by forming the curd with prepared rennet.

SLIP

Slip is bonnyclabber without its acidity, and so delicate is its flavor that many persons like it just as well as ice cream. It is prepared thus: Make a quart of milk moderately warm; then stir into it one large spoonful of the preparation called rennet; set it by, and when cool again it will be as stiff as jelly. It should be made only a few hours before it is to be used, or it will be tough and watery; in summer set the dish on ice after it has jellied. It must be served with powdered sugar, nutmeg, and cream.

CHEESE FONDUE

Melt an ounce of butter, and whisk into it a pint of boiled milk. Dissolve two tablespoonfuls of flour in a gill of cold milk, add it to the boiled milk, and let it cool. Beat the yolks of four eggs with a heaping teaspoonful of salt, half a teaspoonful of pepper, and five ounces of grated cheese. Whip the whites of the eggs and add them; pour the mixture into a deep tin lined with buttered paper, and allow for the rising, say four inches. Bake twenty minutes and serve the moment it leaves the oven.

SCALLOPED CHEESE

Any person at all fond of cheese could not fail to favor this recipe: Take three slices of bread, well buttered, first cutting off the brown

101

outside crust. Grate fine a quarter of a pound of any kind of good cheese. Lay the bread in layers in a buttered baking dish, sprinkle over it the grated cheese, some salt and pepper to taste. Mix four well-beaten eggs with three cups of milk; pour it over the bread and cheese. Bake it in a hot oven as you would cook a bread pudding. This makes an ample dish for four people.

CAYENNE CHEESE STRAWS

A quarter of a pound of flour, two ounces butter, two ounces grated parmesan cheese, a pinch of salt, and a few grains of cayenne pepper. Mix into a paste with the yolk of an egg. Roll out to the thickness of a silver quarter, about four or five inches long; cut into strips about a third of an inch wide, twist them as you would a paper spill, and lay them on a baking-sheet slightly floured. Bake in a moderate oven until crisp, but they must not be the least brown. If put away in a tin, these cheese straws will keep a long time. Serve cold, piled tastefully on a glass dish. You can make the straws of remnants of puff pastry, rolling in the grated cheese.

WELSH RAREBIT

Grate three ounces of dry cheese and mix it with the yolks of two eggs, four ounces of grated bread, and three of butter. Beat the whole together in a mortar with a dessertspoonful of made mustard, a little salt, and some pepper. Toast some slices of bread. Cut off the outside crust, cut it in shapes, and spread the paste thick upon them. Put them in the oven, let them become hot and slightly browned, serve hot as possible.

[*Note:* Some called it "rarebit" even in 1891, but it began much earlier than that, in England, as "rabbit." Following is a gourmet version that is very close to the original.]

WELSH RABBIT FOR SIX

Melt one tablespoon of butter; add two heaping cups sharp cheese, grated. Melt cheese, then pour in one-quarter bottle of beer; mix well. As cheese and beer are heating, add quickly one beaten egg, stirring constantly. Add one teaspoon Worcestershire sauce, salt, pepper, and one-quarter to one-half teaspoon dry mustard. Serve over toast or crackers. For tomato-cheese rabbit, omit beer and egg; add one eight-ounce can tomato sauce.

BOYS' FAVORITE CHEESE SOUFFLÉ ☆

Make a white sauce with four tablespoons melted butter, four table-spoons flour, one and one-half cups milk, one teaspoon salt, and a dash of cayenne. Cook, stirring until thick and smooth; add one-half pound pasteurized process cheese, diced, and stir until cheese is melted. Remove from heat and add six beaten yolks of eggs (pour a little hot cheese sauce into the eggs and stir before adding eggs to sauce—prevents curdling). Cool mixture slightly, then pour it slowly over six stiffly beaten egg whites, cutting and folding the mixture together thoroughly. Pour into ungreased two-quart casserole. Run tip of spoon around in mixture, one inch from edge of casserole to make "track" which will form "top hat" as soufflé bakes. Bake one hour in slow oven, 300°. Serve at once!

PARTY CHEESE ☆

Scoop out center of baby Gouda cheese; mix it with spicy deviled ham, a little Tabasco sauce, and onion. Refill cheese shell. Serve with crackers.

Vegetables

Every sort of culinary vegetable is much better when freshly gathered and cooked as soon as possible. Most vegetables, when peeled, are better when laid in cold water a short time before cooking. Onions, cabbage, carrots, and turnips should be cooked in a great deal of water. Potatoes rank first in importance and consequently should be properly served. It requires some little intelligence to cook even so simple and common a dish as boiled potatoes. They should be made uniform in size by cutting. The best part of a potato is next to the skin, therefore they should be pared very thinly, if at all.

[*Note:* Potatoes were, indeed, the most important vegetable on Victorian tables. Others ranked far below them. Since three-quarters of the population lived on farms or in villages, fresh vegetables were not accessible the year around. From autumn till spring, country folk ate whatever "kept" in the root cellar. How good the first rhubarb and dandelion greens must have tasted! City people who lived near the big markets were luckier. They could buy, if they could afford it, a wider variety of "imported" vegetables, thereby cultivating more sophisticated and expensive tastes. At family reunions you could tell the Country Cousins from the City Cousins; the latter dropped such impressive names as "French artichokes" and "Brussels sprouts" and, possibly, were never invited back to the old homestead.

According to the old *White House Cookbook*, these vegetables were available in Washington markets in the winter of 1891:

White potatoes, sweet potatoes, cabbage, onions, parsnips, oyster plant, okra, celery, chicory, carrots, turnips, Jerusalem artichokes, French artichokes, Brussels sprouts, beets, mushrooms raised in hot-houses, pumpkin, winter squash, dry shallots, and garden herbs for seasoning put up in the dry state.]

TO BOIL NEW POTATOES

Do not have the potatoes dug long before they are dressed, as they are never good when they have been out of the ground some time. Well wash them, rub off the skins with a coarse cloth, and put them in *boiling* salted water. Let them boil until tender; try them with a fork, and when done, pour the water away from them; let them stand by the side of the fire with the lid of the saucepan partially removed, and when the potatoes are thoroughly dry, put them in a hot vegetable dish with a piece of butter the size of a walnut; pile the potatoes over this, and serve. If the potatoes are too old to have the skins rubbed off, boil them in their jackets; drain, peel, and serve them as above, with a piece of butter placed in the midst of them. They require twenty to thirty minutes to cook. Serve them hot and plain or with melted butter over them.

MASHED POTATOES

Take the quantity needed, pare off the skins, and lay them in cold water half an hour; then put them into a saucepan with a little salt; cover with water and boil them until done. Drain off the water and mash them fine with a potato masher. Have ready a piece of butter the size of an egg, melted in half a cup of boiling hot milk, and a good pinch of salt; mix it well with the mashed potatoes until they are a smooth paste, taking care that they are not too wet. Put them into a vegetable dish, heap them up and smooth over the top, put a small piece of butter on the top in the center, and have dots of pepper here and there on the surface as large as a half-dime.

Some prefer using a heavy fork or wire beater, instead of a potato masher, beating the potatoes quite light, and heaping them up in the dish without smoothing over the top.

BROWNED POTATOES

Mash them the same as above, put them into the dish that they are to be served in, smooth over the top, and brush over with the yolk of an egg, or spread on a bountiful supply of butter and dust well with flour. Set in the oven to brown; it will brown in fifteen minutes when the oven is set to a quick fire.

POTATO PUFFS

Prepare the potatoes as directed for mashed potato. While *hot*, shape in balls about the size of an egg. Have a tin sheet well buttered, and place the balls on it. As soon as all are done, brush over with beaten egg. Brown in the oven. When done, slip a knife under them and slide them upon a hot platter. Garnish with parsley and serve immediately.

POTATOES À LA CRÊME

Heat a cupful of milk; stir in a heaping tablespoonful of butter cut up in as much flour. Stir until smooth and thick; pepper and salt, and add two cupfuls of cold boiled potatoes, sliced, and a little very finely chopped parsley. Shake over the fire until the potatoes are hot all through, and pour into a deep dish.

SARATOGA CHIPS [*the Original "Potato Chip"*]

Peel good-sized potatoes and slice them as evenly as possible. Drop them into ice water. Have a kettle of very hot lard, as for cakes; put a few at a time into a towel and shake, to dry the moisture out of them, and then drop them into the boiling lard. Stir them occasionally, and when of a light brown take them out with a skimmer, and they will be crisp and not greasy. Sprinkle salt over them while hot.

FRIED RAW POTATOES

Peel half a dozen medium-sized potatoes very evenly, cut them in slices as thin as an eggshell, and be sure to cut them for the *breadth*, not the length, of the potato. Put a tablespoonful each of butter and sweet lard into the frying pan, and as soon as it boils, add the sliced potatoes, sprinkling over them salt and pepper to season them. Cover them with a tight-fitting lid, let the steam partly cook them, then remove the lid and let them fry a bright gold color, shaking and turning them carefully, so as to brown equally. Serve very hot.

Fried, cold, cooked potatoes may be fried by the same recipe, only slice them a little thicker.

Remark—Boiled or steamed potatoes chopped up or sliced while they are yet warm never fry so successfully as when cold.

SCALLOPED POTATOES [KENTUCKY STYLE]

Peel and slice raw potatoes thin, the same as for frying. Butter an earthen dish, put in a layer of potatoes, and season with salt, pepper, butter, a bit of onion chopped fine, if liked; sprinkle a little flour. Now put another layer of potatoes and the seasoning. Continue in this way till the dish is filled. Just before putting into the oven, pour a quart of *hot* milk over. Bake three-quarters of an hour.

BROWNED POTATOES WITH A ROAST

About three-quarters of an hour before taking up your roast, peel middling-sized potatoes, boil them until partly done, then arrange them in the roasting pan around the roast, basting them with the drippings at the same time you do the meat, browning them evenly. Serve hot with the meat. Many cooks partly boil the potatoes before putting around the roast. New potatoes are very good cooked around a roast.

Fill Your Own Teeth with CRYSTALINE. *Stop Pain and Decay. Lasts a lifetime. Circular free. T. F. Truman, M. D., Wells Bridge, N.Y.* —(old adv.)

SWEET POTATOES

Boiled, steamed, and baked the same as Irish potatoes; generally cooked with their jackets on. Cold sweet potatoes may be cut in slices across lengthwise and fried as common potatoes, or may be cut in half and served cold.

Boiled sweet potatoes are very nice. Boil until partly done, peel them and bake brown, basting them with butter or beef drippings several times. Serve hot. They should be a nice brown.

SCALLOPED ONIONS

Take eight or ten onions of good size, slice them, and boil until tender. Lay them in a baking dish; put bread crumbs, butter in small bits, pepper and salt, between each layer until the dish is full, putting bread crumbs last; add milk or cream until full. Bake twenty minutes or half an hour.

A little onion is not an injurious article of food, as many believe. A judicious use of plants of the onion family is quite as important a factor in successful cookery as salt and pepper. When carefully concealed by manipulation in food, it affords zest and enjoyment. Many successful compounds derive their excellence from the partly concealed flavor of the onion, which imparts a delicate appetizing aroma highly prized by epicures.

KARTOFFEL KLOSSE [*Potato Dumplings*] ☆

5 medium-sized potatoes	2 eggs
Salt	2 slices diced white bread
1 cup dry bread crumbs	browned in butter (croutons)

Boil potatoes a day before using; this is *important*. Skin potatoes and put through food chopper on second day. Add salt, the dry bread crumbs, eggs and croutons. Mix well. Form into balls about two to three inches in diameter (larger than golf balls, smaller than tennis balls!). Roll in flour and drop in boiling, salted water, and let cook until they come to top of water.

"When Mother was a young girl in Germany—about seventy years ago—her father was a cobbler who made shoes for the richest people in Osnabruck. He had about sixteen apprentices and other men working for him. Mother and her mother and sisters had to feed the men three

107

meals a day with a big dinner at noon, and this was the dinner they often served. Incidentally, the men worked from 7 A.M. until 8 P.M. with one hour off for dinner, then the apprentices went to school three nights a week!"—*Mrs. Edward Aldwiger*

TO BOIL RICE

Pick over the rice carefully; wash it in warm water, rubbing it between the hands, rinsing it in several waters; then let it remain in cold water until ready to be cooked. Have a saucepan of water slightly salted; when it is boiling hard, pour off the cold water from the rice and sprinkle it in the boiling water by degrees, so as to keep the particles separated. Boil it steadily for twenty minutes, then take it off from the fire and drain off all the water. Place the saucepan with the lid partly off on the back part of the stove, where it is only moderately warm, to allow the rice to dry. The moisture will pass off and each grain of rice will be separated, so that if shaken the grains will fall apart. This is the true way of serving rice as a vegetable, and is the mode of cooking it in the southern states where it is raised.

GEORGIA BOILED RICE

This is a very easy way to prepare rice for the table, used by Negro cooks before the Civil War. Have over the fire three quarts boiling salted water. Throw one cup of rice into it after the rice is washed and drained. Boil ten minutes as rapidly as possible. Then drain off the water; put a clean folded towel into the saucepan over the rice; set the saucepan where it will not burn, allow it to steam for ten minutes. It is then ready to serve.

BLUE
Blue is the Dyspeptic
Blue is the Bottle

*Rosy is the man after taking
from the Blue bottle of*
JOHNSON'S DIGESTIVE
TABLETS
—(old adv.)

RICE PILAF ☆

1 medium onion, sliced
1 cup rice, uncooked
2 cans beef consommé

¼ pound butter
1 can mushrooms

Brown onion in butter lightly, then mix all ingredients together and bake one hour at 350°. Nice change from baked potatoes. Good with French bread and garlic butter [and Steak Marinade—see page 65].

FRIED CAULIFLOWER

Boil the cauliflowers till about half done. Mix two tablespoonfuls of flour with two yolks of eggs, then add water enough to make a rather thin paste; add salt to taste. The two whites are beaten till stiff, and then mixed with the yolks, flour, and water. Dip each branch of the cauliflowers into the mixture and fry them in hot fat. When done, take them off with a skimmer, turn into a colander, dust salt all over, and serve warm. Asparagus, celery, eggplant, oyster plant are all fine when fried in this manner.

STEAMED CABBAGE

Take a sound, solid cabbage, and with a large sharp knife shave it *very finely*. Put it in a saucepan; pour in half a teacupful of water or just enough to keep it from burning; cover it very tightly, so as to confine the steam; watch it closely, add a little water now and then, until it begins to be tender; then put into it a large tablespoonful of butter, and salt and pepper to taste; dish it hot. If you prefer to give it a tart taste, just before taking from the fire add a third of a cup of good vinegar.

LADIES' CABBAGE

Boil a firm white cabbage fifteen minutes, changing the water then for more from the boiling teakettle. When tender, drain and set aside until perfectly cold. Chop fine and add two beaten eggs, tablespoonful of butter, pepper, salt, three tablespoonfuls of rich milk or cream. Stir all well together and bake in a buttered pudding dish until brown. Serve very hot. This dish resembles cauliflower and is found by most to be very digestible and palatable.

109

SOURCROUT

Barrels having held wine or vinegar are used to prepare sourcrout in. It is better, however, to have a special barrel for the purpose. Strassburg, as well as all Alsace, has a well-acquired fame for preparing the cabbages. They slice very white and firm cabbages in fine shreds with a machine made for the purpose. At the bottom of a small barrel they place a layer of coarse salt, and alternately layers of cabbage and salt, being careful to have one of salt on the top. As each layer of cabbage is added, it must be pressed down by a large and heavy pestle, and fresh layers are added as soon as the juice floats on the surface. The cabbage must be seasoned with a few grains of coriander, juniper berries, etc. When the barrel is full it must be put in a dry cellar, covered with a cloth and under a plank, and on this heavy weights are placed. At the end of a few days it will begin to ferment, during which time the pickle must be drawn off and replaced by fresh, until the liquor becomes clear. This should be done every day. Renew the cloth and wash the cover, put the weights back, and let stand for a month. By that time the sourcrout will be ready for use. Care must be taken to let the least possible air enter the sourcrout and to have the cover perfectly clean. These precautions must not be neglected.

This is often fried in the same manner as fried cabbage, excepting it is first boiled until soft in just enough water to cook it, then fry and add vinegar.

STEWED TOMATOES

Pour boiling water over a dozen sound ripe tomatoes; let them remain for a few moments; then peel off the skins, slice them, and put them over the fire in a well-lined tin or graniteware saucepan. Stew them about twenty minutes, then add a tablespoonful of butter; salt and pepper to taste; let them stew fifteen minutes longer; and serve hot. Some prefer to thicken tomatoes with a little grated bread, adding a teaspoonful of sugar; others who like the flavor of onion chop one up and add while stewing; then again, some other cooks prefer to add as much green corn as there are tomatoes.

SCALLOPED TOMATOES

Butter the sides and bottom of a pudding dish. Put a layer of bread crumbs in the bottom; on them put a layer of sliced tomatoes; sprinkle with salt, pepper, and some bits of butter, and a very *little* white sugar.

Then repeat with another layer of crumbs, another of tomato, and seasoning until full, having the top layer of slices of tomato, with bits of butter on each. Bake covered until well cooked through; remove the cover and brown quickly.

STUFFED BAKED TOMATOES

From the blossom-end of a dozen tomatoes—smooth, ripe, and solid— cut a thin slice, and with a small spoon scoop out the pulp without breaking the rind surrounding it. Chop a small head of cabbage and a good-sized onion finely, and mix with them fine bread crumbs and the pulp. Season with pepper, salt and sugar, and add a cup of sweet cream. When all is well mixed, fill the tomato shells, replace the slices, and place the tomatoes in a buttered baking dish, cut ends up, and put in the pan just enough water to keep from burning. Drop a small lump of butter on each tomato, and bake half an hour or so, till well done; place another bit of butter on each, and serve in same dish. Very fine.

Another stuffing which is considered quite fine. Cut a slice from the stem of each and scoop out the soft pulp. Mince one small onion and fry it slightly; add a gill of hot water, the tomato pulp, and two ounces of cold veal or chicken chopped fine, simmer slowly, and season with salt and pepper. Stir into the pan cracker dust or bread crumbs enough to absorb the moisture; take off from the fire and let it cool. Stuff the tomatoes with this mass; sprinkle dry crumbs over the top; add a small piece of butter to the top of each and bake until slightly browned on top.

SCRAMBLED TOMATOES

Remove the skins from a dozen tomatoes; cut them up in a saucepan; add a little butter, pepper and salt. When sufficiently boiled, beat up five or six eggs, and just before you serve, turn them into the saucepan with the tomatoes, and stir one way for two minutes, allowing them time to be done thoroughly.

TOMATOES ALFRED LUNT ☆

[*Note:* Someone once told me—I wish it had been the great actor himself—that this was Alfred Lunt's original concoction. Anything the Lunts like, I like.]

In deep dish slice a layer of tomatoes thin; sprinkle them with ground pepper, salt, sugar, chives and finely chopped parsley. Make a second and also a third layer, each time sprinkling the same condiments on the tomatoes. Mix olive oil and about half a cup of wine vinegar (twice as much oil as vinegar) and add a little grated onion. Taste for flavor. Pour over tomatoes, let stand at least two hours in ice box.

GREEN CORN, BOILED

This should be cooked on the same day it is gathered; it loses its sweetness in a few hours and must be artificially supplied. Strip off the husks, pick out all the silk, and put the corn in boiling water; if not entirely fresh, add a tablespoonful of sugar to the water, but *no salt*. Boil twenty minutes (fast) and serve; or you may cut it from the cob, put in plenty of butter and a little salt, and serve in a covered vegetable dish. The corn is much sweeter when cooked with the husks on, but requires longer time to boil.

Green corn left over from dinner makes a nice breakfast dish, prepared as follows: Cut the corn from the cob, and put into a bowl with a cup of milk to every cup of corn, a half cup of flour, one egg, a pinch of salt, and a little butter. Mix well into a thick batter and fry in small cakes in very hot butter. Serve with plenty of butter and powdered sugar sprinkled generously on top.

CORN PUDDING

This is a Virginia dish. Scrape the substance out of twelve ears of tender, green, uncooked corn (it is better scraped than grated, as you do not get those husky particles which you cannot avoid with a grater); add yolks and whites, beaten separately, of four eggs, a teaspoonful of sugar, the same of flour mixed in a tablespoonful of butter, a small quantity of salt and pepper, and one pint of milk. Bake about half or three-quarters of an hour.

BOURBON BEANS ON THE BIG BOARD ☆

Stir into ten and one half cups of canned baked beans one half cup bourbon, one half cup strong black coffee, two and one half cups canned sliced pineapple. Let stand, covered, in bean pot or baking dish, at room temperature one and one half hours. Remove cover; bake at 375° one and one half hours. Top with halved pineapple rings. Return to oven for another fifteen minutes. Serves twelve.

GREEN BEANS (SICILIAN) ☆

One pound (or two cans)
whole green beans
1 cup sliced onion rings
1 cup sliced pitted ripe olives
½ cup diced pimiento
5 to 6 tablespoons olive oil

½ teaspoon or less oregano (depends on how much you like oregano)
Salt and coarse black pepper to taste

Drain green beans. Sauté beans, onion rings, ripe olive slices, and pimiento in olive oil until onion is golden but still firm and other ingredients are heated through, stirring only when necessary. Season with oregano, salt, and pepper. May be prepared in chafing dish or electric skillet at the table. Serves eight to ten.

GLAZED LIMAS ☆

1 package frozen lima beans
1 small red onion, sliced
1 medium-size tart apple,
cored and sliced

2 tablespoons butter
3 tablespoons brown sugar

Cook beans as directed on package; drain well. In skillet sauté onion and apple in butter until tender. Add brown sugar and beans. Toss lightly and heat through. Serves six.

STEWED PARSNIPS

After washing and scraping the parsnips, slice them about half of an inch thick. Put them in a saucepan of boiling water containing just enough to barely cook them; add a tablespoonful of butter, season with salt and pepper, then cover closely. Stew them until the water has cooked away, watching carefully and stirring often to prevent burning, until they are soft. When they are done they will be of a creamy light straw color and deliciously sweet, retaining all the goodness of the vegetable.

There's no disagreeable stickiness, no permeating scent, no irritation from Wool Soap using—it gives the skin the clean freshness of a "dip in purity." (old adv.)

113

FRIED EGGPLANT

Take fresh, purple eggplants of a middling size. Cut them in slices a quarter of an inch thick and soak them for half an hour in cold water with a teaspoonful of salt in it. Have ready some cracker or bread crumbs and one beaten egg; drain off the water from the slices, lay them on a napkin, dip them in the crumbs and then in the egg, put another coat of crumbs on them, and fry them in butter to a light brown. The frying pan must be hot before the slices are put in—they will fry in ten minutes.

You may pare them before you put them into the frying pan, or you may pull the skins off when you take them up. You must not remove them from the water until you are ready to cook them, as the air will turn them black.

STUFFED EGGPLANT

Cut the eggplant in two; scrape out all the inside and put it in a saucepan with a little minced ham; cover with water and boil until soft. Drain off the water. Add two tablespoonfuls of grated crumbs, a tablespoonful of butter, half a minced onion, salt and pepper. Stuff each half of the hull with the mixture, add a small lump of butter to each, and bake fifteen minutes.

Minced veal or chicken in the place of ham is equally good, and many prefer it.

STEWED SALSIFY OR OYSTER PLANT

Wash the roots and scrape off their skins, throwing them, as you do so, into cold water, for exposure to the air causes them to immediately turn dark. Then cut crosswise into little thin slices; throw into fresh water, enough to cover; add a little salt, and stew in a covered vessel until tender, or about one hour. Pour off a little of the water, add a small lump of butter, a little pepper, a gill of sweet cream, and a teaspoonful of flour stirred to a paste. Boil up and serve hot.

Salsify may be simply boiled, and melted butter turned over it.

ASPARAGUS WITH EGGS

Boil a bunch of asparagus twenty minutes; cut off the tender tops and lay them in a deep pie plate, buttering, salting, and peppering well.

Beat up four eggs, the yolks and whites separately, to a stiff froth; add two tablespoonfuls of milk or cream, a tablespoonful of warm butter, pepper and salt to taste. Pour evenly over the asparagus mixture. Bake eight minutes or until the eggs are set. Very good.

STEWED GREEN PEA PODS

The Germans prepare a very palatable dish of sweet young pods alone by boiling them till tender, then draining and stirring in a little butter with some savory herbs.

GREENS

About a peck of greens is enough for a mess for a family of six, such as dandelions, cowslips, burdock, chicory, and others. All should be examined carefully, the tough ones thrown out, the rest thoroughly washed till free of sand. Adding a handful of salt to the water will free greens from insects. Put greens into a large pot half full of boiling water, with a handful of salt, and boil steadily till stalks are tender—five to twenty minutes according to the maturity of the greens. Drain, chop them a little, season with salt, pepper, and butter. Vinegar may be added if liked.

MUSHROOMS FOR WINTER USE

Wash and wipe clean with a wet flannel small button mushrooms. (The best grow on uplands or in high, open fields, where the air is pure.) Melt a quarter of a pound of the very best butter in a frying pan. Add two whole cloves, a saltspoonful of salt, and a tablespoonful of lemon juice. When hot, add a quart of mushrooms, toss them about in the butter for a moment only, then put them in jars. Fill the top of each jar with an inch or two of the butter and let it cool. Keep the jars in a cool place, and when the butter is quite firm, add a top layer of salt. Cover to keep out dust.

TRUFFLES AU NATUREL

The truffle belongs to the family of the mushrooms. They are used in this country as a condiment for boned turkey and chicken, scrambled eggs, fillets of beef, game, and fish. They add a peculiar zest and flavor

115

to sauces that cannot be found in any other plant in the vegetable kingdom. Select fine truffles; wash them in several waters with a brush; wrap each in buttered paper and bake in a hot oven for quite an hour. Take off the paper, wipe the truffle and serve hot in a napkin.

Salads

Everything in the makeup of a salad should be of the freshest material, the vegetables crisp and fresh, the oil or butter the very best; meats, fowl, and fish well cooked, pure cider or white-wine vinegar—in fact, every ingredient first-class, to insure success.

To destroy the small snails and other insects which cluster in the leaves of cabbage, cauliflower, lettuce, and similar plants, put them in a pan of strong brine, with the stalk ends uppermost, and in about twenty or thirty minutes the insects will fall out and sink to the bottom. A pound and a half of salt to the gallon of water will answer for this purpose, and if strained daily, it will last for some time.

The vegetables used in salad are: beetroot, onions, potatoes, cabbage, lettuce, celery, cucumbers, lentils, haricots, winter cress, peas, French beans, radish, cauliflower—all these may be used judiciously in salad, if properly seasoned.

Chervil is a delicious salad herb, invariably found in all salads prepared by a French gourmet. No man can be a true epicure who is unfamiliar with this excellent herb. It may be procured from the vegetable stands at Fulton and Washington markets the year round. Its leaves resemble parsley, but are more divided, and a few of them added to a breakfast salad give a delightful flavor.

Chervil vinegar—A few drops of this vinegar added to fish sauces or salads is excellent and well repays the little trouble taken in its preparation. Half fill a bottle with fresh or dry chervil leaves; fill the bottle with good vinegar and heat it gently by placing it in warm water, which bring to boiling point; remove from the fire; when cool, cork, and in two weeks it will be ready for use.

[*Note:* "Salads are a lady's dish—seldom enjoyed by men," said one old cookbook. With citrus fruits scarce, salads practically nonexistent and vegetables "cooked to death" in large quantities of water, where did they get their Vitamins A, B, C, G, and K? Well, they ate tomatoes from their gardens in 1891, though old-timers could remember when tomatoes were called "love apples" and were considered highly poisonous.]

PEPPERGRASS AND CRESS

These are used mostly as an appetizer, served simply with salt. Cresses are occasionally used in making salad.

MIXED SUMMER SALAD

Three heads of lettuce, two teaspoonfuls of green mustard leaves, a handful of watercresses, five tender radishes, one cucumber, three hard-boiled eggs, two teaspoonfuls of white sugar, one teaspoonful salt; one teaspoonful of pepper, one teaspoonful of made mustard, one teacupful of vinegar, half a teacupful of oil.

Mix all well together and serve with a lump of ice in the middle. —*Common Sense in the Household*

ENDIVE

This ought to be nicely blanched and crisp, and is the most wholesome of all salads. Take two, cut away the root, remove the dark-green leaves, and pick off all the rest; wash and drain well, add a few chives. Dress with mayonnaise dressing.

Endive is extensively cultivated for the adulteration of coffee, is also a fine relish, and has broad leaves. Endive is of the same nature as chicory, the leaves being curly.

CELERY UNDRESSED

To crisp celery, let it lie in ice water two hours before serving. To fringe the stalks, stick several coarse needles into a cork and draw the stalk halfway from the top through the needles several times and lay in the refrigerator to curl and crisp. Or serve plain in goblet-shaped salad glasses.

117

GREEN BEAN SALAD

String young beans; break into half-inch pieces; wash, cook soft in salt water, and drain well. Add finely chopped onions, pepper, salt, and a little olive oil or melted butter and vinegar. Cool.

POTATO SALAD, HOT

Pare six or eight large potatoes and boil till done, and slice thin while hot. Peel and cut up three large onions into small bits and mix with the potatoes. Cut up some breakfast bacon into small bits, sufficient to fill a teacup, and fry it a light brown; remove the meat, and into the grease stir three tablespoonfuls of vinegar, making a sour gravy, which with the bacon pour over the potato and onion. Mix lightly. To be eaten when hot.

TO DRESS CUCUMBERS RAW

They should be as fresh from the vine as possible, few vegetables being more unwholesome when long gathered. As soon as they are brought in, lay them in cold water. Just before they are to go to table take them out, pare them, and slice them into a pan of fresh cold water. When they are all sliced, transfer them to a deep dish; season them with a little salt and black pepper, and pour over them some of the best vinegar. You may mix with them a small quantity of sliced onions, not to be eaten, but to communicate a slight flavor of onion to the vinegar.

DUTCH SALAD

A dozen anchovies; one herring, diced; an equal quantity of diced Bologna or Lyons sausage or smoked ham and sausages; an equal quantity of diced breast of cold roast fowl or veal; an equal quantity of diced beetroots and pickled cucumbers. Add thrice the quantity of cold boiled potatoes, cut in larger dice. Add a tablespoonful of capers, yolks and whites of some hard-boiled eggs, minced separately, and a dozen stoned olives. Mix all well together, reserving some olives and anchovies to ornament the top of the bowl. Beat up together oil and Tarragon vinegar with white pepper and French mustard to taste; pour over salad and it is ready to be served.

[*Note:* I have tried to envision this salad, to imagine the mingled tastes,

118

but the mind boggles. . . . I hope to hear from some reader that she has tried it and loved it. Incidentally, home economics teachers must wince at "hard-boiled eggs." Eggs may have been hard-boiled in 1887, but they are never anything but "hard-cooked" today.]

SALAD OF MIXED FRUITS

Put in the center of a dish a pineapple properly pared, cored, and sliced, yet retaining as near as practicable its original shape. Peel, quarter, and remove the seeds from four sweet oranges; arrange them in a border around the pineapple. Select four fine bananas, peel and cut into slices lengthwise; arrange these zigzag-fence fashion around the border of the dish. In the V-shaped spaces around the dish put tiny mounds of grapes of mixed colors. When complete, the dish should look very appetizing. To half a pint of clear sugar syrup add half an ounce of good brandy; pour over the fruit and serve.

ORANGE COCONUT SALAD

Peel and slice a dozen oranges, grate a coconut, and slice a pineapple. Put alternate layers of each until the dish is full. Then pour over them sweetened wine. Served with small cakes.

When oranges are served whole, they should be peeled and prettily arranged in a fruit dish. A small knife is best for this purpose. Break the skin from the stem into six or eight even parts, peel each section down half way, and tuck the point in next to the orange.

CAPER SALAD ☆

1 box gelatin	1 small can pimientos
1½ cups sugar	½ cup pecans
1 large can pineapple	1 bottle capers
1 quart boiling water	

Soak gelatin and sugar in pineapple juice. Add one quart boiling water. Cool. Add pineapple and other ingredients, including caper juice.

[*Note:* My mother served this salad at many bridge parties; I have served it, too. Capers always seem like a party to me. Two cans of pineapple chunks may be substituted for the rings.]

119

SHERRY AMBROSIA SALAD [*To Serve Ten*] ☆

1 pineapple	1 quart grated coconut
1 pint strawberries	4 bananas
6 oranges	1 cup sherry wine
Sugar	

Peel and cut pineapple into slices, then thin strips. Hull berries and cut in halves. Peel oranges, divide into natural segments, then cut in halves. Sprinkle all ingredients with sugar and set on ice. When ready to serve, sprinkle bottom of a deep salad bowl with grated coconut. Cover with layer of pineapple and sprinkle again with coconut. Add layers of strawberries, oranges, and sliced bananas, putting a layer of coconut between each two layers of fruit and on top. Pour over all the sherry combined with the juices that have drained from the fruits. Garnish with whole strawberries and thin slices of orange, and serve very cold in punch cups.

["This is from my mother's 1905 recipe book, and it is very good." —*Oca Hupp Ratcliff*]

MAYONNAISE DRESSING

Put the yolks of four fresh raw eggs with two hard-boiled ones into a cold bowl. Rub these as smooth as possible before introducing the oil; a good measure of oil is a tablespoonful to each yolk of raw egg. All the art consists in introducing the oil by degrees, a few drops at a time. You can never make a good salad without taking plenty of time. When the oil is well mixed, and assumes the appearance of jelly, put in two heaping teaspoonfuls of dry table salt, one of pepper, and one of made mustard. Never put in salt and pepper before this stage of the process, because the salt and pepper would coagulate the albumen of the eggs, and you could not get the dressing smooth. Two tablespoonfuls of vinegar added gradually.

CREAM DRESSING

Two tablespoonfuls of whipped sweet cream, two of sugar, and four of vinegar. Beat well and pour over the cabbage, previously cut very fine and seasoned with salt.

SYDNEY SMITH'S SALAD DRESSING

Sydney Smith, 1771–1845, was an English clergyman, author, and wit who apparently was as famed for his salad recipe as for any of his more intellectual works; it appeared in many a nineteenth-century cookbook.

> Two boiled potatoes strained through a kitchen sieve,
> Softness and smoothness to the salad give;
> Of mordant mustard take a single spoon,
> Distrust the condiment that bites too soon!
> Yet deem it not, thou man of taste, a fault
> To add a double quantity of salt.
> Four times the spoon with oil of Lucca crown,
> And twice with vinegar procured from town;
> True taste requires it and your poet begs
> The pounded yellow of two well-boiled eggs.
> Let onion's atoms lurk within the bowl
> And, scarce suspected, animate the whole,
> And lastly in the flavored compound toss
> A magic spoonful of anchovy sauce,
> Oh, great and glorious! Oh, herbaceous meat!
> 'Twould tempt the dying Anchorite to eat,
> Back to the world he'd turn his weary soul
> And plunge his fingers in the salad bowl.

Some old cookbooks report the Reverend Mr. Smith's final stanza this way:

> Then though green turtle fail, though venison's tough,
> And ham and turkey are not boiled enough,
> Serenely full, the epicure may say:
> "Fate cannot harm me; I have dined today!"

When the ladies of Waupun, Wisconsin, compiled their cookbook in 1905, however, they did not use Mr. Smith's famous recipe at all. They merely remarked succinctly under Salads:

> Our salads are good, delicious and cool
> Though not patterned after Sydney Smith's rule,
> For not boring you with that stupid dressing,
> We claim you should give us, at least, your blessing.

121

DRESSING FOR COLE SLAW

Beat up two eggs with two tablespoons of sugar and a piece of butter the size of half an egg, a teaspoonful of mustard, a little pepper, and lastly, a teacup of vinegar. Put all these ingredients into a dish over the fire and cook like a soft custard. Some think it improved by adding half a cupful of thick sweet cream to this dressing; in that case use less vinegar. Either way is very fine.

FRENCH SALAD DRESSING

Mix one saltspoon of pepper with one of salt; add three tablespoonfuls of olive oil, and one even tablespoonful of onion, scraped fine, then one tablespoonful of vinegar. When well mixed, pour the mixture over your salad and stir all till well mingled.

Macaroni and Noodles

MACARONI AND CHEESE

Break half a pound of macaroni into pieces an inch or two long; cook it in boiling water enough to cover it well; put in a good teaspoonful of salt; let it boil about twenty minutes. Drain it well, and then put a layer in the bottom of a well-buttered pudding dish, upon this some grated cheese, and small pieces of butter, a bit of salt, then more macaroni, and so on, filling the dish. Sprinkle the top layer with a thick layer of cracker crumbs. Pour over the whole a teacupful of cream or milk. Set it in the oven and bake half an hour. It should be nicely browned on top. Serve in the same dish in which it was baked, with a clean napkin pinned around it.

MACARONI À LA CRÊME

Boil one-quarter of a pound of macaroni in plenty of hot water, salted, until tender. Put half a pint of milk in a double boiler, and when it boils, stir into it a mixture of two tablespoonfuls of butter and one of flour. Add two tablespoonfuls of cream, a little white and cayenne pepper, salt to taste, and from one-quarter to one-half a pound of grated cheese according to taste. Drain and dish the macaroni. Pour the boiling sauce over it and serve immediately.

HOMEMADE NOODLES ☆

Beat two egg yolks, add a quarter-teaspoon salt and enough flour (about one cup) to make a stiff dough. Roll out very thin on floured board and let stand for twenty minutes. Then roll up and slice about an eighth-inch thick. Separate strips; spread them out to dry for several hours.

[*Note:* These are wonderful in homemade vegetable soup!—that's the way I use them. Or they may be added to any boiling soup or cooked in salted water. In any case, cook about 10 minutes.]

Breads

GENERAL REMARKS

The importance of this branch of the intelligent, painstaking house-keeper's duties can scarcely be overestimated. As there is no one article of food that enters so largely into our daily fare as bread, so no degree of skill in preparing other articles can compensate for lack of knowledge in the art of making good, palatable, and nutritious bread. Many a case of chronic dyspepsia is attributable primarily to the habitual eating of heavy, sour, or ill-baked bread, and in almost every case this is caused by the ignorance or negligence of the maker or baker.

Salt is always used in bread-making; it makes dough rise better.

The milk should be boiled, not simply scalded.

Yeast must be good and fresh.

An almost certain way of spoiling dough is to leave it half-made.

As a general rule, the oven for baking bread should be rather quick. Dough should rise and bread begin to brown slightly after about

123

fifteen minutes. Bake from fifty to sixty minutes to have it brown, not black or whitey brown.

Never leave the bread on a pine table to absorb the odor of the wood.

A yard and a half square of coarse table linen makes the best bread-cloth.

Compressed yeast, as now sold in most grocery stores, makes fine, light, sweet bread and is a much quicker process.

[*Note:* If you would like to try some of these interesting old bread recipes, here are some tips which may help:

Substitute yeast cakes for liquid yeast. For one pint liquid in recipe, use ¼ yeast cake to raise bread overnight, one yeast cake to prepare in five hours, two yeast cakes to prepare in three hours. Mixtures containing eggs or large amounts of shortening require more yeast or a longer time for rising. Dissolve yeast in a little lukewarm liquid.

MODERN OVEN TEMPERATURES FOR BREAD

Slow oven	250 to 325°
Moderate	325 to 400°
Quick or hot oven	400 to 450°
Very hot oven	450 to 550°

Perhaps you test your oven temperature as the ladies of 1891 did, by sprinkling flour on a pan and placing it in the heated oven:

If it turns a delicate brown in five minutes, the oven is *slow*.

If it turns a medium golden brown in five minutes, the oven is *moderate*.

If it turns a deep dark brown in five minutes, the oven is *hot*.

If it turns a deep dark brown in three minutes, the oven is *very hot*.

You may use white tissue paper instead of flour or—go ahead, pamper yourself—use your nice, automatic oven-thermometer.]

Yeast Breads

HOMEMADE YEAST

Boil six large potatoes in three pints of water. Tie a handful of hops in a small muslin bag and boil with the potatoes; when thoroughly cooked, drain the water on enough flour to make a thin batter; set this on the stove or range and scald it enough to cook the flour (this makes the yeast keep longer); remove it from the fire, and when cool enough, add the potatoes mashed, also half a cup of sugar, half a tablespoonful of ginger, two of salt, and a teacupful of yeast. Let it stand in a warm place until it has thoroughly risen, then put it in a large-mouthed jug and cork tightly; set away in a cool place. The jug should be scalded before putting in the yeast.

Two-thirds of a coffeecupful of this yeast will make four loaves.

When it is convenient to get compressed yeast, it is much better and cheaper than to make your own, a saving of time and trouble. Almost all groceries keep it, delivered to them fresh-made daily.

WHEAT BREAD

Sift the flour into a large bread pan or bowl; make a hole in the middle of it, and pour in the yeast in the ratio of half a teacupful of yeast to two quarts of flour. Stir the yeast lightly, then pour in your "wetting," either milk or water, as you choose—which use warm in winter and cold in summer. (If you use water as "wetting," dissolve in it a bit of butter of the size of an egg; if you use milk, no butter is necessary.) Stir in the "wetting" very lightly, but do not mix all the flour into it; then cover the pan with a thick blanket or towel and set it, in winter, in a warm place to rise—this is called "putting the bread in sponge." In summer the bread should not be wet overnight. In the morning add a teaspoonful of salt and mix all the flour in the pan with the sponge, kneading it well; then let it stand two hours or more until it has risen quite light; then remove the dough to the molding-board and mold it for a long time, cutting it in pieces and molding them together again and again until the dough is elastic under the pressure of your hand, using as little flour as possible; then make it into loaves and put the loaves into baking-tins. The loaves should come halfway up the pan, and they should be allowed to rise until the bulk is doubled. When the loaves are ready to be put into the oven, the oven should be ready to receive them. It should be hot enough to brown a teaspoonful of flour in five minutes. The heat should be greater at the bottom than at the top of the oven, and the fire so arranged as to give sufficient strength of heat through the baking without being replenished. Let them stand ten or fifteen minutes, prick them three or four times with a fork and bake in a quick oven from forty-five to sixty minutes.

If these directions are followed, you will obtain sweet, tender, and wholesome bread. If by any mistake the dough becomes sour before you are ready to bake it, you can rectify it by adding a little dry super-

125

carbonate of soda, molding the dough a long time to distribute the soda equally throughout the mass. All bread is better, if naturally sweet, without the soda; but *sour bread* you should never eat, if you desire good health.

Keep well covered in a tin box or large stone crock, which should be wiped out every day or two and scalded and dried thoroughly in the sun once a week.

SALT-RISING BREAD

While getting breakfast in the morning, as soon as the teakettle has boiled, take a quart tin cup or an earthen quart milk pitcher, scald it, then fill one-third full of water about as warm as the finger could be held in; then to this add a teaspoonful of salt, a pinch of brown sugar, and coarse flour enough to make a batter of about the right consistency for griddlecakes. Set the cup, with the spoon in it, in a closed vessel half-filled with water, moderately hot, but not scalding. Keep the temperature as nearly even as possible, and add a teaspoonful of flour once or twice during the process of fermentation. The yeast ought to reach to the top of the bowl in about five hours. Sift your flour into a pan, make an opening in the center, and pour in your yeast. Have ready a pitcher of warm milk, salted, or milk and water (not too hot, or you will scald the yeast germs) and stir rapidly into a pulpy mass with a spoon. Cover this sponge closely and keep warm for an hour, then knead into loaves, adding flour to make the proper consistency. Place in warm, well-greased pans, cover closely, and leave till it is light. Bake in a steady oven, and when done, let all the hot steam escape. Wrap closely in damp towels and keep in closed earthen jars until it is wanted.

This in our grandmothers' time used to be considered the prize bread, on account of its being sweet and wholesome and requiring no prepared yeast to make it. Nowadays yeast bread is made with very little trouble, as the yeast can be procured at almost any grocery.

RYE AND CORN BREAD

One quart of rye meal or rye flour, two quarts of Indian meal, scalded (by placing in a pan and pouring over it just enough *boiling* water to merely wet it, but not enough to make it into a batter, stirring constantly with a spoon), one-half cup of molasses, two teaspoonfuls salt, one teacup yeast. Make it as stiff as can be stirred with a spoon, mixing with warm water, and let rise all night. In the morning add a level teaspoonful of soda dissolved in a little water; then put it in a large pan and smooth the top with the hand dipped in cold water; let it stand a short time and bake five or six hours. If put in the oven late in the day, let it remain all night.

Graham may be used instead of rye, and baked as above.

This is similar to the "Rye and Injun" of our grandmothers' days, but that was placed in a kettle, allowed to rise, then placed in a covered iron pan upon the hearth before the fire, with coals heaped upon the lid, to bake all night.

GRAHAM BREAD

One teacupful of wheat flour, one-half teacupful of Puerto Rico molasses, one-half cupful of good yeast (or three-quarters of a cake), one teaspoon salt, one pint warm water. Add sufficient graham flour to make the dough as stiff as can be stirred with a strong spoon. This is to be mixed at night. In the morning add one teaspoonful of soda dissolved in a little water. Mix well and pour into two medium-sized pans. They will be about half-full. Let it stand in a warm place until it rises to the top of the pans, then bake in a pretty hot oven [350°] one hour. This should be covered about twenty minutes when first put into the oven with a thick brown paper or an old tin cover; it prevents the upper crust hardening before the loaf is well-risen. If these directions are correctly followed, the bread will not be heavy or sodden, as it has been tried for years and never failed.

GERMAN BREAD

One pint of milk well boiled, one teacupful of sugar, two tablespoonfuls of nice lard or butter, two-thirds of a teacupful of baker's yeast. Make a rising with the milk and yeast; when light, mix in the sugar and shortening with flour enough to make as soft a dough as can be handled. Flour the pasteboard well; roll out about one-half inch thick; put this quantity into two large, greased pans. Make about a dozen indentures with the finger on the top; put a small piece of butter in each and sift over the whole one tablespoonful of sugar mixed with one teaspoonful of cinnamon. Let this stand for a second rising; when perfectly light, bake in a quick oven fifteen or twenty minutes.

127

RAISED POTATO CAKE

Potato cakes, to be served with roast lamb or with game, are made of equal quantities of mashed potatoes and of flour, say one pint of each, one tablespoon of butter, a little salt, and milk enough to make·a batter as for griddlecakes. To this allow a fourth of a teacupful of fresh yeast. Let it rise till it is light and bubbles of air form; then dissolve a quarter of a teaspoonful of soda in a spoonful of warm water and add to the batter. Bake in greased muffin tins. These are good with fricasseed chicken. Take them from the tins and drop in the gravy just before sending to the table.

PARKER HOUSE ROLLS
[the original recipe from the Parker House]

One pint of milk, boiled and cooled; a piece of butter the size of an egg; one-half cupful of fresh yeast; one tablespoonful of sugar; one pinch of salt; two quarts of sifted flour.

Melt the butter in the warm milk; then add the sugar, salt, and flour and let it rise overnight. Mix rather soft. In the morning add to this half a teaspoonful of soda dissolved in a spoonful of water. Mix in enough flour to make the same stiffness as any biscuit dough. Roll out not more than a quarter of an inch thick. Cut with a large round cutter; spread soft butter over the tops and fold one half over the other by doubling it. Place them apart a little so that there will be room to rise. Cover and place them near the fire for fifteen or twenty minutes before baking. Bake in rather a quick oven.

PARKER HOUSE ROLLS (UNFERMENTED)

These rolls are made with baking powder and are much sooner made, although the preceding recipe is the old original one. Stir into a quart of sifted flour three large teaspoonfuls of baking powder, a tablespoonful of cold butter, a teaspoonful of salt and one of sugar, and a well-beaten egg. Rub all well into the flour. Pour in a pint of cold milk, mix up quickly into a smooth dough. Roll it out less than half an inch thick, cut with a large biscuit cutter, spread soft butter over the top of each. Fold one half over the other by doubling it; lay them a little apart on greased tins. Set them immediately in a pretty hot oven. Rub over the tops with sweet milk before putting in the oven to give them a glaze.

128

SALLY LUNN
[Frequently seen on Southern tables]

Warm one-half cupful of butter in a pint of milk. Add a teaspoonful of salt, a tablespoonful of sugar, and seven cupfuls of sifted flour. Beat thoroughly, and when the mixture is blood-warm, add four beaten eggs and, last of all, half a cup of good lively yeast. Beat hard until the batter breaks in blisters. Set it to rise overnight. In the morning dissolve half a teaspoonful of soda, stir it into the batter and turn it into a well-buttered, shallow dish to rise again about fifteen or twenty minutes. Bake about fifteen to twenty minutes.

The cake should be torn apart, not cut. Cutting with a knife makes warm bread heavy. Bake a light brown.

SALLY LUNN [UNFERMENTED]

Rub a piece of butter as large as an egg into a quart of flour. Add a tumbler of milk, two eggs, three tablespoonfuls of sugar, three teaspoonfuls of baking powder, and a teaspoonful of salt. Scatter the baking powder, salt, and sugar into the flour. Add the eggs, the butter (melted), and the milk. Stir all together and bake in well-greased round pans. Eat warm with butter.

LONDON HOT CROSS BUNS

Three cups of milk, one cup of yeast (or one cake of compressed yeast dissolved in a cup of tepid water), and flour enough to make a thick batter. Set this as a sponge overnight. In the morning add half a cup of melted butter, one cup of sugar, half a nutmeg grated, one saltspoonful of salt, half a teaspoonful of soda, and flour enough to roll out like biscuits. Knead well and set to rise for five hours. Roll the dough half an inch thick. Cut in round cakes and lay in rows in a buttered baking pan. Let the cakes stand half an hour or until light, then put them in the oven, having first made a deep cross on each with a knife. Bake a light brown, and brush over with white of egg beaten stiff with powdered sugar.

129

ENGLISH CRUMPETS

One quart of warm milk, half a cup of yeast, one teaspoonful of salt, flour enough to make a stiff batter. When light, add half a cupful of melted butter, a teaspoonful of soda dissolved in a little water, and a very little more flour. Let it stand twenty minutes or until light. Grease some muffin rings, place them on a hot griddle and fill them half full of the batter. When done on one side, turn and bake the other side. Butter them while hot. Pile one on another and serve immediately.

COFFEE CAKE

One cup of brown sugar, one cup of butter, two eggs, one-half cup of molasses, one cup of strong, cold coffee, one teaspoonful of soda, two teaspoonfuls of cinnamon, one teaspoonful of cloves, one cup of raisins or currants, and five of sifted flour. Add the fruit last, rubbed in a little of the flour. Bake about one hour.

GRAM'S COFFEE CAKE ☆

1 yeast cake	1 tablespoon salt
¼ cup warm water	2 tablespoons sugar
1 pint potato water	1 egg yolk
2 large tablespoons butter	5 cups sifted flour
(or chicken fat)	½ cup chopped pecans
Grated rind of 1 small lemon	½ cup chopped candied cherries
and 1 small orange	

Dissolve yeast cake in one-quarter cup warm water. Put in potato water, shortening, grated rind, salt, sugar, and egg yolk. Add flour and knead well. Let rise until twice original bulk. Add pecans and cherries. Roll like stollen. Spread dough with butter. Bake at 400° till golden brown.

"My grandmother, who is now ninety-six, used to supply the church with six of these coffee cakes weekly for *kaffee klatsch*. Her home always had a delicious yeasty smell; bowls of dough were set to rise over every register! The above recipe is like a holiday stollen."—*Mrs. Byron Hawkins*

$75.00 a Month can be made Working for us. Persons preferred who can furnish a horse. B. F. Johnson Co., Richmond, Va. —(old adv.)

SOMETHING-FOR-THE-GIRLS COFFEE CAKE ☆

Mix two cups prepared biscuit mix, one egg, one-quarter cup sugar, and two-thirds cup syrup from canned, crushed pineapple. Pour into greased 8- or 9-inch square pan. Sprinkle with one-quarter cup brown sugar and a little nutmeg or cinnamon. Bake at 400° twenty-five to thirty minutes.

MRS. RODDY'S COFFEE CAKE ☆

Scald one cup milk, and add three tablespoons shortening, one-half cup sugar, and one teaspoon salt. Let cool and add one cake yeast (dissolved according to instructions on wrapper). Add two beaten eggs and three and a half to four cups flour. Mix well. Put in greased pan, cover, and let rise till doubled in bulk. Then knead and roll out long and narrow. Spread with butter, cinnamon, raisins, and nuts. Form into tea rings, let rise again, and bake thirty minutes at 350°. This can also be baked over fruit or with fruit on top. If made into tea ring, it can be iced with butter icing. This recipe makes two large rings or three small ones.

"My friend's mother made this coffee cake for her six children every Saturday for years and, at seventy-six, is still making it weekly. I have been making it for at least twenty years, and it never fails."—*Mrs. George Meyer*

MARYLAND SPOON BREAD ☆

½ cup fine yellow cornmeal	½ cup boiling water
1 teaspoon bacon drippings	1 egg, beaten
1 teaspoon sugar	1 cup sour milk or buttermilk
½ teaspoon salt	¼ teaspoon soda

Put cornmeal, drippings, sugar and salt into a baking dish. Pour the boiling water over them gradually and beat well. When the mixture is cool, add the beaten egg and the milk and the soda and one teaspoon of cold water. Beat the whole mixture well. Bake in deep dish 20 minutes in medium oven [350°].

McLaughlin's Roasted Coffee—Best Value for Your Money
It costs the grocer more than any other package coffee, but to the consumer is worth at least five cents a pound more. The glazing on this Coffee settles it and is made of Corn Starch and Reclarified Sugar, therefore perfectly healthful. This saves you the Cost of Eggs, equal to from 5 to 10 cents a pound. —(old adv.)

Quick Breads

CORN BREAD

Two cups of sifted meal, half a cup of flour, two cups of sour milk, two well-beaten eggs, half a cup of molasses or sugar, a teaspoonful of salt, two tablespoonfuls of melted butter. Mix the meal and flour smoothly and gradually with the milk, then the butter, molasses, and salt, then the beaten eggs, and lastly dissolve a level teaspoonful of baking soda in a little milk and beat thoroughly all together. Bake nearly an hour in well-buttered tins, not very shallow. This recipe can be made with sweet milk by using baking powder in place of soda.—*St. Charles Hotel, New Orleans*

JOHNNIE CAKE

Sift one quart of Indian meal into a pan; make a hole in the middle and pour in a pint of warm water, adding one teaspoonful of salt. With a spoon mix the meal and water gradually into a soft dough; stir it very briskly for a quarter of an hour or more, till it becomes light and spongy; then spread the dough smooth and even on a straight, flat board (a piece of the head of a flour barrel will serve for this purpose); place the board nearly upright before an open fire, and put an iron against the back to support it. Bake it well. When done, cut it in squares. Send it hot to table, split and buttered.—*Old Plantation Style*

BANANA BREAD ☆

1 cup sugar	½ cup sour milk (or sweet)
½ cup shortening	2 cups flour sifted with:
2 well-beaten eggs	1 teaspoon baking soda
3 crushed bananas	½ teaspoon salt

Mix first four ingredients. Add milk and flour alternately. Bake in greased pan fifty to sixty minutes or longer (till toothpick inserted in center comes out clean) at 375°. In glass pan, reduce heat to 350°. Remove from pan after five minutes; keep turning loaf so that air circulates around it until it is cool.

DATE-NUT BREAD ☆

2 cups boiling water
½ pound dates, cut up

2 teaspoons baking soda

Pour water over dates and soda. Let stand while mixing the next six ingredients:

2 tablespoons butter, creamed
2 cups sugar
2 eggs, beaten
2 teaspoons vanilla

4 cups sifted flour
1 teaspoon salt
½ cup walnuts cut up

Add to this the date-mixture and walnuts. Bake at 350° for forty-five minutes. If baked in 5 greased #2 tin cans, these loaves make nice gifts for neighbors at Christmas.

BOSTON BROWN BREAD (UNFERMENTED)

One cupful of rye flour, two cupfuls of cornmeal, one cupful of white flour, half a teacupful of molasses, a teaspoonful of salt. Stir all together thoroughly and wet up with sour milk (about two cups or more). Add a level teaspoonful of soda dissolved in a tablespoonful of water. The same can be made of sweet milk, using less, and substituting baking powder for soda. The batter to be stirred as thick as can be with a spoon and turned into well-greased pans and steamed three and one-half hours, covered closely. If put into small cans, baking-powder size, it may be steamed one and one-half to two hours. Dry in slow oven [300°] fifteen minutes. Most excellent.

BAKING POWDER BISCUITS 1

2 cups flour
1 tablespoon baking powder
½ teaspoon baking soda

½ teaspoon salt
4–5 tablespoons lard
¾ cup buttermilk or sour milk

Sift dry ingredients. Cut in lard with knives or pastry blender. Add buttermilk gradually to make a soft dough. Toss on floured board. Knead gently. Roll or press to half-inch thickness. Cut with cutter or glass dipped in flour. Bake on ungreased baking sheet at 450° twelve to fifteen minutes.

133

BAKING POWDER BISCUITS 2

Two pints of flour, butter the size of an egg, three heaping teaspoonfuls of baking powder, and one teaspoonful of salt. Make a soft dough of sweet milk or water, knead as little as possible, cut out with the usual biscuit cutter, and bake in rather a quick oven.

BISCUITS ☆

2 cups flour
1 teaspoon cream of tartar
½ teaspoon soda
1 teaspoon salt (or less)

4 tablespoons (or more) of shortening
1 egg
⅓ cup (or more) of milk

Sift dry ingredients together. Cut in the shortening. Add the egg, slightly beaten, and one-third cup milk, then add more milk if too dry. Roll or drop from spoon on greased baking sheet. Bake in hot oven (450°) twelve to fifteen minutes.

BEATEN BISCUITS 1 ☆

1 quart sifted winter
    wheat flour
2 teaspoons salt

⅔ cup lard
1 cup or less water-and-milk
    combined

Sift flour and salt together. Cut in lard until mixture resembles fine meal. Add liquid to make a stiff dough. Knead until smooth, then beat on wooden block, using old-fashioned rolling pin or wooden potato masher, about one-half hour. When dough is beaten out flat, it is folded again and again and beaten until the dough snaps and crackles and blisters. Roll one-third inch thick; cut with very small biscuit cutter. Place on baking sheet; prick biscuits with a fork. Bake at 350°, about thirty minutes.

"This is one recipe I have never made, and I doubt if many people will because of all the work! But I have seen Beaten Biscuits made and have eaten them, and they are delicious. When I was a child and visited on farms around this section, many people had wooden blocks or old tree stumps on which they "beat the biscuits." —*Mrs. Thomas G. Gordon*

BEATEN BISCUITS 2
[*an old Southern favorite*]

Two quarts of sifted flour, a teaspoonful of salt, a tablespoonful of sweet
lard, one egg. Make up with half a pint of milk, or if milk is not to be
had, plain water will answer. Beat well until the dough blisters and
cracks. Pull off a two-inch square of the dough; roll it into a ball with
the hand; flatten, stick with a fork, and bake in a quick oven.

It is not beating hard that makes the biscuit nice but the regularity
of the motion. Beating hard, the old cooks say, kills the dough. (These
were beaten about thirty minutes.)

VINEGAR BISCUITS

Take two quarts of flour, one large tablespoonful of lard or butter, one
tablespoonful and a half of vinegar, and one teaspoonful of soda. Put
the soda in the vinegar and stir well. Stir in the flour; beat two eggs
very light and add to it. Make a dough with warm water stiff enough to
roll out, and cut with a biscuit cutter one inch thick, and bake in a
quick oven.

SCOTCH SCONES

Thoroughly mix, while dry, one quart of sifted flour, loosely measured,
with two heaping teaspoonfuls of baking powder. Rub into it a tablespoonful of cold butter and a teaspoonful of salt. Be sure that the butter
is well worked in. Add sweet milk enough to make a very soft paste.
Roll out the paste about a quarter of an inch thick, using plenty of flour
on the pasteboard and rolling pin. Cut it into triangular pieces, each
side about four inches long. Flour the sides and bottom of a biscuit tin
and place the pieces on it. Bake immediately in a quick oven from
twenty to thirty minutes. When half-done, brush over with sweet milk.
Some cooks prefer to bake them on a floured griddle and cut them a
round shape the size of a saucer, then scar them across to form four
quarters.

*The National Bank, old enough to be careful, young enough to be obliging,
strong enough to be safe.* —(*old adv.*)

135

RAISED MUFFINS

Three pints of flour, three eggs, a piece of butter the size of an egg, two heaping teaspoonfuls of white sugar, one-half cake compressed yeast, and a quart of milk. Warm the milk with the butter in it. Cool a little, stir in the sugar, and add a little salt. Stir this gradually into the flour, then add the eggs well beaten. Dissolve the yeast in half a cup of luke-warm water and add to the other ingredients.

Breakfast Dishes

GRANDMA'S PANCAKES ☆

Make batter for a double batch of buttermilk pancakes. [I use a mix.] Bake 8-inch pancakes on greased griddle and, as they are made, place them in a pie pan and set in preheated 250° oven. Stack them, buttering each one liberally (much more than you ordinarily would butter a pancake) and sprinkling on top of each several teaspoons of granulated sugar. Butter and sugar will melt and make their own syrup. Keep stacking until you have several layers hot in the oven. Now cut down through them, as you would cut a cake, and serve in wedges.

This will call for seconds all around and keep you busy for some time! Served this way, however, everyone can be eating at one time.

"When we used to visit my grandmother on the farm, one of the great treats was her pancakes, served as only she served them. I often make them; we call them Grandma's Pancakes."—*Mrs. John E. Smith*

FLANNEL CAKES (FROM THE SOUTH)

Heat a pint of sweet milk, and into it put two heaping tablespoonfuls of butter. Let it melt, then add a pint of cold milk and the well-beaten yolks of four eggs, placing the whites in a cool place; also, a teaspoonful of salt, four tablespoonfuls of homemade yeast, and sufficient flour to make a stiff batter. Set it in a warm place to rise. Let it stand three hours or overnight. Before baking, add the beaten whites. Bake like any other griddlecake. Be sure to make the batter stiff enough, for flour must not be added after it has risen unless it is allowed to rise again. These, half corn meal and half wheat, are very nice.

GREEN CORN GRIDDLECAKES

One pint of milk, two cups grated green corn, a little salt, two eggs, a teaspoonful of baking powder, flour sufficient to make a batter. Fry on the griddle. Butter them hot and serve.

To grease griddle: Heat griddle. Take a small stick like a good-sized skewer, wind a bit of cloth around the end of it and fasten it by winding a piece of thread around that and tying it firm. Grease the griddle with this.

HASTY PUDDING OR CORN MEAL MUSH

>Father and I went down to camp
>Along with Captain Gooden,
>And there we saw the men and boys
>As thick as hasty puddin'
>   —Yankee Doodle

Put two quarts of water into a clean dinner pot or stewpan, cover it, and let it become boiling hot over the fire. Then add a tablespoonful of salt; take off the light scum from the top; have sweet, fresh yellow or white corn meal ready. Take a handful of the meal with the left hand and a pudding-stick in the right, then with the stick stir the water around and, by degrees, let fall the meal. When one handful is exhausted, refill it. Continue to stir and add meal until it is as thick as you can stir easily or until the stick will stand in it. Stir it a while longer. Let the fire be gentle. When it is sufficiently cooked, which will be in half an hour, it will bubble or puff up. Turn it into a deep basin. This is eaten cold or hot with milk or with butter and syrup or sugar or with meat and gravy, the same as potatoes and rice.

WARM DISHES FOR BREAKFAST

The following of hot breakfast dishes may be of assistance in knowing what to provide for the comfortable meal called breakfast:

Broiled beef steak, broiled chops, broiled chicken, broiled fish, broiled quail on toast, fried pork tenderloins, fried pigs' feet, fried oysters, fried clams, fried liver and bacon, fried chops, fried pork, ham and eggs fried, veal cutlets breaded, sausages, fricasseed tripe, fricasseed kidneys, turkey or chicken hash, corn beef hash, beef croquettes, codfish balls, creamed codfish, stewed meats on toast, poached eggs on toast, omelettes, eggs boiled plain, and eggs cooked in any of the various styles.

137

Potatoes in any of the various modes of cooking, also stewed tomatoes, stewed corn, raw radishes, cucumbers sliced, tomatoes sliced raw, watercress, lettuce.

To be included with the breakfast dishes: oatmeal mush, cracked wheat, hominy or corn-meal mush, these with cream, milk, and sugar or syrup.

Then numberless varieties of bread can be selected, in form of rolls, fritters, muffins, waffles, corncakes, griddlecakes, etc.

When obtainable, always have a vase of choice flowers on the breakfast table; also some fresh fruit, if convenient.

FRIED MUSH

Make it like Hasty Pudding, turn it into bread tins, and when cold, slice it. Dip each piece in flour and fry it in lard and butter mixed in the frying pan, turning to brown well both sides. Must be served hot.

HOMINY

This form of cereal is very little known and consequently little appreciated in most Northern households. Big Hominy and Little Hominy, as they are called in the South, are staple dishes there and generally take the place of oatmeal, which is apt to be too heating for the climate. The former is called "samp" here. It must be boiled for at least eight hours to be properly cooked and may then be kept on hand for two or three days and warmed over, made into croquettes or balls or fried in cakes. The fine hominy takes two or three hours for proper cooking and should be cooked in a dish set into another of boiling water and kept steadily boiling until thoroughly soft.

SAMP OR HULLED CORN

An old-fashioned way of preparing hulled corn was to put a peck of old, dry, ripe corn into a pot filled with water and with it a bag of hardwood ashes, say a quart. After soaking awhile, it was boiled until the skins or hulls came off easily. The corn was then washed in cold water to get rid of the taste of potash and then boiled until the kernels were soft. Another way was to take the lye from the leaches where potash was made, dilute it, and boil the corn in this until the skin or hull came off. It makes a delicious dish eaten with milk or cream.

Toast Dishes

AMERICAN TOAST

To one egg thoroughly beaten, put one cup of sweet milk and a little salt. Slice light bread and dip into the mixture, allowing each slice to absorb some of the milk, then brown on a hot, buttered griddle or thick-bottom frying pan. Spread with butter and serve hot.

NUNS' TOAST

Cut four or five hard-boiled eggs into slices. Put a piece of butter half the size of an egg into a saucepan, and when it begins to bubble, add a finely chopped onion. Let the onion cook a little without taking color, then stir in a teaspoonful of flour. Add a cupful of milk and stir until it becomes smooth, then put in the slices of eggs and let them get hot. Pour over neatly trimmed slices of hot buttered toast. The sauce must be seasoned to taste with pepper and salt.

CHEESE TOAST

Put half an ounce of butter in a frying pan. When hot, add gradually four ounces of mild American cheese. Whisk it thoroughly until melted. Beat together half a pint of cream and two eggs; whisk into the cheese; add a little salt; pour over the crisp toast and serve. The above recipe is usually called Welsh Rarebit.

MUSHROOMS ON TOAST

Peel a quart of mushrooms and cut off a little of the root end. Melt an ounce of butter in the frying pan and fry in it half a pound of raw minced steak. Add two saltspoonfuls of salt, a pinch of cayenne, and a gill of hot water. Fry until the juices are extracted from the meat. Add the mushrooms, toss them about until lightly cooked, and pour out on hot toast. Some add a little sherry to the dish before removing from the fire.

CODFISH ON TOAST (CUBAN)

Take a teacupful of freshened codfish, picked up fine. Fry a sliced onion in a tablespoonful of butter. When it has turned a light brown, put in the fish with water enough to cover it. Add half a can of tomatoes or half a dozen fresh ones. Cook an hour. Serve on toast, hot.

BAKED EGGS ON TOAST

Toast six slices of bread, dip them in hot salted water, and butter them lightly. After arranging them on a platter, break enough eggs to cover them, breaking one at a time, and slip them over the toast so that they do not break. Sprinkle over them salt and pepper and turn over all some kind of thickened gravy—either chicken or lamb, cream or a cream sauce [see White Sauce]. Turn this over the toast and eggs and bake in a hot oven until the eggs are set or about five minutes. Serve at once.

REED BIRDS ON TOAST

Remove the feathers and legs of a dozen reed birds. Split them down the back, remove the entrails, and place them on a double broiler. Brush a little melted butter over them and broil the inner side thoroughly first, then lightly broil the other side. Melt one-quarter of a pound of butter, season it nicely with salt and pepper, dip the birds in it, and arrange them nicely on slices of toast.

[*Note:* Reedbirds, or bobolinks, were popular table fare and were easily found within walking distance of the White House in 1887. They sold for seventy-five cents a dozen in markets.]

CHICKEN HASH WITH RICE TOAST

Boil a cup of rice the night before; put it into a square, narrow bread pan; set it in the icebox. Next morning, cut it into half-inch slices, rub over each slice a little warm butter, and toast them on a broiler to a delicate brown. Arrange the toast on a warm platter and turn over the whole a chicken hash made from the remains of cold fowl, the meat picked from the bones, chopped fine, put into the frying pan, and heated through with butter, salt, pepper, and a little water to moisten.

Doughnuts

DOUGHNUTS OR FRIEDCAKES

Success in making good friedcakes depends as much on the *cooking* as the mixing. In the first place, there should be boiling lard enough to free them from the bottom of the kettle, so that they swim on the top, and the lard should never be so hot as to smoke or so cool as not to be at the boiling point; if it is, they soak grease and are spoiled. If it is at the right heat, the doughnuts will in about ten minutes be of a delicate brown outside and nicely cooked inside. Five or six minutes will cook a cruller. Try the fat by dropping a bit of the dough in first; if it is right, the fat will boil up when it is dropped in. They should be turned over almost constantly, which causes them to rise and brown evenly. When they are sufficiently cooked, raise them from the hot fat and drain them until every drop ceases dripping.

CRULLERS OR FRIEDCAKES

One and a half cupfuls of sugar, one cupful of sour milk, two eggs, two scant tablespoonfuls of melted butter, half a nutmeg grated, a large teaspoonful of cinnamon, a teaspoonful of salt and one of soda. Make a little stiffer than biscuit dough, roll out a quarter of an inch thick, and cut with a friedcake cutter, with a hole in the center. Fry in hot lard.

These can be made with sweet milk and baking powder, using two heaping teaspoonfuls of the baking powder in place of soda.

RAISED DOUGHNUTS

Old-fashioned "raised doughnuts" are seldom seen nowadays, but are easily made. Make a sponge as for bread, using a pint of warm water or milk and a large half cupful of yeast; when the sponge is very light, add half a cupful of butter or sweet lard, a coffeecupful of sugar, a teaspoonful of salt, one small teaspoonful of soda dissolved in a little

141

water, one tablespoonful of cinnamon, a little grated nutmeg. Stir in now two well-beaten eggs, add sifted flour until it is the consistency of biscuit dough, knead it well, cover and let rise. Then roll the dough out onto a sheet half an inch thick, cut out with a very small biscuit cutter, or in strips half an inch wide and three inches long, place them on greased tins, cover them well, and let them rise before frying them. Drop them in very hot lard. Raised cakes require longer time than cakes made with baking powder. Sift powdered sugar over them as fast as they are fried, while warm. Our grandmothers put allspice into these cakes; that, however, is a matter of taste.

CRULLERS OR WONDERS

Three eggs, three tablespoonfuls of melted lard or butter, three table-spoonfuls of sugar. Mix very hard with sifted flour, as hard as can be rolled, and roll very thin like piecrust. Cut in squares three inches long and two wide, then cut several slits or lines lengthwise, to within a quarter of an inch of the edges of the ends; run your two forefingers through every other slit; lay them down on the board edgewise, and dent them. These are very dainty when fried. Fry in hot lard till a light brown.

FASTNACHTS [*Doughnuts*] ☆

2 cups milk	3 eggs, beaten
6–7 cups flour	½ teaspoon nutmeg
1 yeast cake dissolved in	¼ cup melted butter
1 cup warm water	¼ teaspoon salt
1 cup sugar	

Scald milk and set aside to cool. Add one-half cup flour to dissolved yeast and mix to a batter, then add to scalded milk, which is now lukewarm. Stir in one teaspoon sugar and about three cups flour. Let rise overnight in warm place. In the morning add beaten eggs, nutmeg, butter, sugar, and salt. Mix thoroughly. Stir in enough flour until batter cannot be stirred with a spoon. Set aside to rise until light. Roll on floured board and cut with doughnut cutter. Let rise again. Fry in hot fat till golden brown.

"Fred's mother made doughnuts every Shrove Tuesday and, though she was not Dutch, she used this Pennsylvania-Dutch recipe. Lots of the doughnuts consumed in New Orleans on Shrove Tuesday now come from the corner bakery or French Market!"—*Mrs. Frederick Mohr*

Sandwiches

HAM SANDWICHES

Make a dressing of half a cup of butter, one tablespoonful of mixed mustard, one of salad oil, a little red or white pepper, a pinch of salt, and the yolk of an egg. Rub the butter to a cream, add the other ingredients, and mix thoroughly; then stir in as much chopped ham as will make it consistent, and spread between thin slices of bread. Omit salad oil and substitute melted butter, if preferred.

WATERCRESS SANDWICHES

Wash well some watercress, and then dry it in a cloth, pressing out every atom of moisture, as far as possible; then mix with the cresses hard-boiled eggs chopped fine and seasoned with salt and pepper. Have a stale loaf and some fresh butter, and with a sharp knife, cut as many thin slices as will be required for two dozen sandwiches; then cut the cress into small pieces, removing the stems; place it between each slice of bread and butter, with a light sprinkling of lemon juice. Press down the slices hard, and cut them sharply on a board into small squares, leaving no crust.

CHEESE SANDWICHES

These are extremely nice, and are very easily made. Take one hard-boiled egg, a quarter of a pound of common cheese grated, half a teaspoonful of salt, half a teaspoonful of pepper, half a teaspoonful mustard, one tablespoonful of melted butter, and one tablespoonful of vinegar or cold water. Take the yolk of the egg and put it into a small bowl and

143

crumble it down, put into it the butter and mix it smooth with a spoon, then add the salt, pepper, mustard, and the cheese, mixing each well. Then put in the tablespoonful of vinegar, which will make it the proper thickness. If vinegar is not relished, then use cold water instead. Spread this between two biscuits or pieces of oatcake, and you could not require a better sandwich. Some people will prefer the sandwiches less highly seasoned. In that case, season to taste.

[*Note:* This was it for Sandwiches according to the 1891 edition of *The White House Cookbook*. They certainly didn't play the large part in daily diets that they do now. Sandwiches were "invented" by the Earl of Sandwich in the eighteenth century (he didn't want to take time out from his card games for a lengthy meal). Peanut butter was developed about 1890, but apparently the news did not travel fast to the White House when this cookbook was written. The children of Presidents Cleveland and Harrison, therefore, were denied that noontime classic— the Peanut Butter Sandwich.]

Cakes

SUGGESTIONS IN REGARD TO CAKE-MAKING

Eggs beat up much lighter and sooner by being placed in a cold place some time before using them; a small pinch of soda sometimes has the same effect.

Flour should always be sifted before using it.

Cream of tartar or baking powder should be thoroughly mixed with the flour.

Butter should be placed where it will become moderately soft but not melted in the least, or the cake will be sodden and heavy.

Sugar should be rolled and sifted, spices ground or pounded, raisins or any other fruit looked over and prepared. Currants especially should be nicely washed, picked, dried in a cloth, and then carefully examined that no pieces of grit may be left amongst them. They should then be laid on a dish before the fire to become thoroughly dry.

Eggs should be well beaten, the whites and yolks separately, the yolks to a thick cream, the whites until they are a stiff froth. Always stir the butter and sugar to a cream, then add the beaten yolks, then the milk, the flavoring, then the beaten whites and, lastly, the flour. If fruit is used, dredge with a little sifted flour.

Pour all in well-buttered cakepans. While the cake is baking, care should be taken that no cold air enters the oven, only when necessary to see that the cake is baking properly. The oven should be an even, moderate heat, not too cold or too hot; much depends on this for success.

Cake is often spoiled by being looked at too often. The heat should be tested before the cake is put in, which can be done by throwing on the floor of the oven a tablespoonful of new flour. If the flour takes fire or assumes a dark brown color, the temperature is too high and must be allowed to cool. If the flour remains white after the lapse of a few seconds, the temperature is too low. When the oven is of the proper temperature, the flour will slightly brown and look slightly scorched.

Another good way to test the heat is to drop a few spoonfuls of the cake batter on a small piece of buttered letter paper and place it in the oven during the finishing of the cake, so that the piece will be baked before putting in the whole cake. If the little drop of cake batter bakes evenly without burning around the edge, it will be safe to put the whole cake in. If the oven seems too hot, fold a thick brown paper double and lay it on the bottom of the oven; then after the cake has risen, put a thick brown paper over the top or butter well a thick white paper and lay it carefully over the top.

If, after the cake is put in, it seems to bake too fast, put a brown paper loosely over the top of the pan, care being taken that it does not touch the cake. Do not open the door for five minutes; the cake should then be carefully examined and the door shut carefully or the rush of cold air will cause it to fall. Setting a small dish of hot water in the oven will also prevent scorching.

To ascertain when the cake is done, run a broom straw into the middle of it; if it comes out clean and smooth, the cake will do.

When the recipe calls for baking powder and you have none, you can use cream of tartar and soda—one level teaspoonful of soda to two heaping teaspoonfuls of cream tartar. When sour milk is called for in the recipe, use only soda. Cakes made with molasses burn much more easily than those made with sugar.

Never stir the cake after butter and sugar are creamed, but beat it down from the bottom, up and over.

When making most cakes, especially sponge, the flour should be added by degrees, stirred very slowly and lightly, for if stirred hard and fast it will make it porous and tough.

145

Cookies, jumbles, gingersnaps, etc., require a quick oven.

To remove a cake from a tin after it is baked so that it will not crack, break, or fall, first butter the tin well all around the sides and bottom; then cut a piece of letter paper to exactly fit the tin, butter that on both sides, placing it smoothly on the bottom and sides of the tin. When the cake is baked, let it remain in the tin till it is cold, then set it in the oven a minute, or just long enough to warm the tin through. Remove it from the oven, turn it upside down on your hand, tap the edge of the tin on the table, and it will slip out with ease, leaving it whole.

If a cake pan is too shallow for holding the quantity of cake to be baked, for fear of its being so light as to rise above the pan, that can be remedied by thoroughly greasing a piece of thick glazed letter paper with soft butter. Place or fit it around the sides of the buttered tin, allowing it to reach an inch or more above the top. If the oven heat is moderate, the butter will preserve the paper from burning.

Frosting: In the first place the eggs should be cold and the platter on which they are to be beaten also cold. Allow, for the white of one egg, one small teacupful of powdered sugar. Break the eggs and throw a small handful of the sugar on them as soon as you begin beating; keep adding it at intervals until it is all used up. The eggs must not be beaten until the sugar has been added in this way, which gives a smooth tender frosting and one that will dry much sooner than the old way.

[*Note:* With no "automatic" oven regulators or timers, you can see how resourceful nineteenth-century cooks had to be! They learned to bake by trial and error and were expected to make not too many errors. No wonder grandmothers found it hard to explain exactly how long or at what temperatures they baked their prize cakes.

"Powdered sugar," often called for in these old recipes, was not confectioner's sugar. Sugar sometimes was sold in hard cones. It was necessary for the cook to chip it, then roll or powder it before she used it.

Below are approximate oven temperatures for the following cake recipes. Results cannot be guaranteed. To be sure of "doneness" you had better heed the advice of Mrs. 1887—test with a broomstraw until the straw comes out clean and touch the center of the cake lightly with your finger; if the cake springs back, it is done.]

Slow oven (fruit cake or thick loaf cake) 200°–300°

Moderate (medium-size cakes 1″–2½″ thick) 300°–375°

Hot (biscuits, cookies, pastry) 375°–425°

Very hot (puff paste) 425°–500°

146

EQUIVALENTS

Butter............1 pound = 2 cups
Butter............"the size of an egg" = ¼ cup
Flour.............1 pound = 4 cups bread flour, or
4½ cups cake flour, sifted
Sugar.............1 pound = 2 cups granulated, or
2¼ cups brown, firmly packed, or
3½ cups confectioner's, sifted, or
50–70 lumps of loaf sugar
Saleratus: Baking soda.

ELECTION CAKE

5 gills new milk
½ pint yeast
3 pounds (3 quarts sifted
and well heaped) flour
1¼ pounds (a rounded pint)
soft butter
1¾ pounds (one quart) sugar

3 eggs
2 pounds raisins
1 teaspoonful soda
1 gill brandy or wine or
¼ pint molasses
2 teaspoonfuls cinnamon and
2 of nutmeg

Scald milk, cool till blood-warm; add yeast, then the flour in which all the butter and one-half the sugar have been added. Then mix and let rise overnight. In the morning add other ingredients, let rise again. When light, fill pans, let rise again. Bake in a moderate oven. Makes three large loaves.

PIONEER CAKE

One and a half cupfuls of sugar, a half cupful of butter, three cupfuls of flour, three eggs, one teaspoonful of cream of tartar, a half teaspoonful of soda, half pound of dried cherries and spice to taste.

9x9x2   350°   35-40min.

ANCIENT MAIDEN'S CAKE

Quarter of a pound each of fresh sweet butter and pulverized loaf sugar; cream together; a few drops of extract of lemon, vanilla, rose, peach or other flavor to taste; whites of five eggs beaten as light as possible and, lastly, a quarter of a pound of flour gently stirred in. Bake in scalloped pans. If the A. M.'s matrimonial prospects are good, frost or ice with icing of proper flavor, otherwise, serve plain.

HICKORY NUT OR WALNUT CAKE

Two cups of fine, white sugar, creamed with half a cup of butter; three eggs; two-thirds of a cup of sweet milk; three cups of sifted flour; one heaping teaspoonful of baking powder sifted through the flour. A tablespoonful (level) of powdered mace, a coffeecup of hickory nut or walnut meats, chopped a little. Fill the cake pans with a layer of the cake, then a layer of raisins upon that, then strew over these a handful of nuts, and so on, until the pan is two-thirds full. Line the tins with well-buttered paper and bake in a steady but not quick oven. This is most excellent.

SOFT GINGER CAKE

Stir to a cream one cupful of butter and half a cupful of brown sugar; add to this two cupfuls of cooking molasses, a cupful of sweet milk, a tablespoonful of ginger, a teaspoonful of ground cinnamon. Beat all thoroughly together, then add three eggs, the whites and yolks beaten separately. Beat into this two cups of sifted flour, then a teaspoonful of soda dissolved in a spoonful of water, and, last, two more cupfuls of sifted flour. Butter and paper two common square bread pans; divide the mixture and pour half into each. Bake in a moderate oven. This cake requires long and slow baking, from forty to sixty minutes. If sour milk is used, the cakes are much lighter, but either sweet or sour is most excellent.

MEXICAN WEDDING CAKES ☆

½ pound butter   1 cup ground pecans
2 cups flour   1 teaspoon vanilla
4 tablespoons sugar

Mix butter, flour, and sugar as pie crust. Add nuts and vanilla. Take small bit, roll between palms, flatten to size of a quarter, one-quarter inch thick. Bake eighteen to twenty minutes in moderate oven (350°) on greased sheet. Don't brown. Roll in powdered sugar while warm. Nice for teas or as a Christmas cookie.

148

BERRY TEACAKES

Nice little teacakes to be baked in greased muffin rings are made of one cup of sugar, two eggs, one and a half cups of milk, one heaping teaspoonful of baking powder, a piece of butter the size of an egg, and flour sufficient to make a stiff batter. In this batter stir a pint bowl of fruit—any fresh are nice or canned berries with the juice poured off—lightly dredged with flour. Serve while warm and they are a dainty addition to the tea table, eaten with butter.

GALETTES—FRENCH CAKES [1879]

1 pound butter	5 eggs
1 pound brown sugar	1 teaspoon vanilla
2 pounds flour	1 teaspoon cinnamon

Make a stiff dough. Shape it into oblong pieces. Cook each piece, one at a time, on a French iron. Place piece on one side of iron; press down with other side of iron. When one side of cake is golden brown, turn and brown other side. Four ounces of whisky or brandy may be added along with one teaspoon soda, in which case a little more flour will be needed to make dough stiff.

[*Note:* This makes a large quantity. You may want to try half the recipe.]

"This recipe has been in our family for at least five generations. It belonged to my great-grandmother and then to my grandmother who came to this country from Jumet, Belgium, in 1879, when she was four. The iron that my mother uses to make these cakes was brought over at that time. There are a few of them around, but they are hard to find. You can buy aluminum ones, but they don't work as well."—*Mrs. William E. Ervin (and her mother, Mrs. Renée Barenbrugge)*

LEMON GINGERBREAD

Squeeze out the juice of two or three lemons into half a pint of brandy; grate the peel and mix with one pound of flour in a good-sized bowl; depress the flour in center and pour in a pint of sugar-house molasses, a pint of melted butter, and the brandy. Add quarter of an ounce of cayenne pepper and ginger to taste, and mix thoroughly. Bake in a *moderate* oven.

149

MOUNTAIN GINGERBREAD

Six cups of flour, two cups of butter, two cups of sugar, two cups of molasses, four eggs, one teacup of ginger, one teaspoonful of soda, two teaspoonsful of tartaric acid. This is a batter, and if baked in a Turk's head or bread pan, keeps a long time, and is very nice.

HARD GINGERBREAD

Made the same as Soft Ginger Cake, omitting the eggs, and mixing hard enough to roll out like biscuit. Roll nearly half an inch thick and cut out like small biscuits. Or it can be baked on a sheet or on a biscuit-tin; cut slits a quarter of an inch deep across the top of the tin from side to side. When baked and while hot, rub over the top with molasses, and let it dry on.

These two above recipes are the best of a large variety tried, the ingredients giving the best proportion for flavor and excellence.

HOT MILK CAKE ☆

½ cup hot milk
2 tablespoons butter
2 eggs
1 cup sugar

1 cup flour
1 teaspoon baking powder
1 teaspoon vanilla

Let milk come to boil, then add butter. Beat eggs well; add sugar, flour and baking powder, hot milk, and one teaspoon vanilla. (Beat egg-sugar mixture very well, then fold in flour quickly, and add milk quickly without beating.) Bake twenty minutes in 350° oven in a pan about 7 by 11. After cake is baked, spread it with this mixture: three tablespoons butter, three tablespoons cream, half a cup brown sugar, half a cup cocoanut. Slide under broiler to brown, but watch closely, for it burns easily.

SNOW CAKE

One pound of arrowroot, quarter of a pound of pounded white sugar, half a pound of butter, the whites of six eggs, flavoring to taste of essence of almonds or vanilla, or lemon. Beat the butter to a cream; stir in the sugar and arrowroot gradually, at the same time beating the mixture; whisk the whites of the eggs to a stiff froth; add them to the other ingredients, and beat well for twenty minutes; put in whichever of the above flavorings may be preferred; pour the cake into a buttered mold or tin, and bake it in a *moderate* oven from one to one and a half hours. *This is a genuine Scotch recipe.*

PLAIN POUND CAKE

This is the old-fashioned recipe that our mothers used to make, and it can be kept for weeks in an earthen jar, closely covered, first dipping letter paper in brandy and placing over the top of the cake before covering the jar.

Beat to a cream one pound of butter with one pound of sugar; after mixing well with the beaten yolks of twelve eggs, add one grated nutmeg, one glass of wine, one glass of rose water. Then stir in one pound of sifted flour and the well-beaten whites of the eggs. Bake a nice light brown.

FEATHER CAKE

One egg, one cup of sugar, one tablespoonful of cold butter, half a cup of milk, one and one-half cups of flour, one teaspoonful of cream tartar, half a teaspoonful of soda. A nice plain cake—to be eaten while it is fresh. A spoonful of dried applesauce or of peach sauce, a spoonful of jelly, the same of lemon extract, nutmeg, cinnamon, cloves, and spice —ground—or half a cupful of raisins might be added for a change.

GRANDMA'S DARK CAKE ☆

2 cups brown sugar	1 cup buttermilk
¼ cup butter or other shortening	1 egg
	1 teaspoon vanilla
3 tablespoons cocoa	Raisins and nuts if desired
Boiling water	2 cups sifted cake flour
1 teaspoon soda	1 teaspoon baking powder

Cream sugar and butter together till fluffy. Cover cocoa with boiling water to make half a cupful. Put soda into buttermilk and pour into cocoa mixture. Beat egg and add to sugar mixture, then put in vanilla, raisins and nuts and add all this to cocoa. Add sifted flour with baking powder gradually, beating well. Bake in two greased nine-inch pans at 350°–375° thirty-five minutes or till done.

[*Note:* My grandmother often made this dark cake for us, and we loved it. When she was eighty, I begged her for the recipe.

"I don't know—" she said reluctantly. "I could make it for you easier than I can tell you—"

Finally she agreed to try to dictate the ingredients and instructions.

"Mercy, I hope that's right," she worried. "If it isn't, just keep tasting and adding till it's the way you want it."

I'm not that kind of creative cook, so I made it just the way she told me. It never has turned out as perfect as hers, but it's still very good. Perhaps the one she made is, for me, flavored with nostalgia.

Good cooks require "good eaters" to inspire them. After my grandfather died, Grandmother lost interest in cooking. No more dark cake or dumplings, fried chicken, apple pie, or Floating Island. When the three girls at home asked her why, she replied simply, "There isn't anybody to cook for anymore."]

ONE-TWO-THREE-FOUR CAKE

One cupful of butter, two cupfuls of sugar, three cupfuls of flour, four eggs. Rub well together and add one cupful of sweet milk or cream, nutmeg to taste, and three teaspoonfuls baking powder or one teaspoonful of soda with two teaspoonfuls cream of tartar. Bake carefully in a quick oven.

[*Note:* An easy-to-remember recipe and one that is older than the original *White House Cookbook.*]

ONE-EGG CAKE

Cream a half cup sugar, one tablespoon butter and one egg. Beat till very light. Add a half cup milk, one heaping cup flour, one teaspoon baking powder, one teaspoon vanilla and one-quarter teaspoon salt. Beat well and pour into shallow greased pan. Bake at 375° about twenty-five minutes. Use as shortcake for strawberries and other fruits.

Ask some questions about PEARLINE *of any woman who uses it. Ask her how the clothes look and last when they're not rubbed over the washboard. Ask her how it would seem to go back to that eternal rub, rub, rub. She'll probably ask you, "How in the world do you manage without it?"* —(old adv.)

OATMEAL-APPLE CAKE ☆

2 cups flour	5 large apples, peeled
½ cup rolled oats	and sliced
¾ cup brown sugar	1 cup water
¾ cup butter or margarine	¾ cup granulated sugar
1 teaspoon vanilla	1 tablespoon cornstarch

Mix flour, rolled oats, brown sugar, and butter until crumbly. Remove a half cup for topping, and line greased eight-inch pan with remainder. Press sliced apples into dough. Mix water, sugar, cornstarch and vanilla together and cook until thick. Pour cornstarch mixture over apples and top with remaining half cup of crumbs. Bake in a moderate oven (350°) twenty to twenty-five minutes. Top with whipped cream if desired.

FARMER'S FRUIT LOAF

Soak three cupfuls of dried apples overnight in cold water enough to swell them; chop them in the morning and put them on the fire with three cups of molasses. Stew until almost soft; add a cupful of nice raisins (seedless if possible) and stew a few moments. When cold, add three cupfuls of flour, one cupful of butter, three eggs, and a teaspoonful of soda. Bake in a steady oven. This will make two good-sized panfuls of splendid cake. The apples will cook like citron and taste delicious. Raisins may be omitted; also, spices to taste may be added. This is not a dear but a delicious cake.

NILA'S APPLE-DATE-NUT CAKE ☆

1 cup boiling water	1 stick butter or margarine
1 cup chopped dates (full cup)	1 egg
1 cup chopped apples	1 cup sugar
1 teaspoon soda	1½ cups flour
1 teaspoon salt	1 cup broken pecans

Pour water over dates, apples, soda, and salt and let cool. Beat margarine or butter and egg and sugar until fluffy. Add date-apple mixture to butter-mixture. Mix well, then add flour and pecans. Mix well. Bake in 9 by 13 pan (greased) at 350° for fifty-five minutes. For

153

cookie squares, bake in two pans at 350° for forty to forty-five minutes. Sprinkle with powdered sugar or ice.

FRUIT CAKE BY MEASURE

Two scant teacupfuls of butter, three cupfuls of dark-brown sugar, six eggs (whites and yolks beaten separately), one pound of raisins (seeded), one of currants (washed and dried), half a pound of citron cut in thin strips, half a cupful of cooking molasses, and half a cupful of sour milk. Stir the butter and sugar to a cream. Add to that half a grated nutmeg, one tablespoonful of ground cinnamon, one teaspoonful of cloves, one teaspoonful of mace. Add the molasses and sour milk. Stir all well; then put in the beaten yolks of egg, a wineglass of brandy. Stir again all thoroughly, and then add four cupfuls of sifted flour, alternately with the beaten whites of egg. Now dissolve a level teaspoonful of soda and stir in thoroughly. Mix the fruit together and stir into it two heaping tablespoonfuls of flour; then stir it in the cake. Butter two common-sized baking tins carefully, line them with letter paper well buttered, and bake in a moderate oven two hours. After it is baked, let it cool in the pan. Afterward put it into a tight can, or let it remain in the pans and cover tightly. Best recipe of all.

SPONGE CAKE

Separate the whites and yolks of six eggs. Beat the yolks to a cream, to which add two teacupfuls of powdered sugar, beating again from five to ten minutes, then add two tablespoonfuls of milk or water, a pinch of salt, and flavoring. Now add part of the beaten whites; then two cups of flour in which you have sifted two teaspoonfuls of baking powder; mix gradually into the above ingredients, stirring slowly and lightly, only enough to mix them well; lastly, add the remainder of the whites of the eggs. Line the tins with buttered paper and fill two-thirds full.

ROLLED JELLY CAKE

Three eggs, one teacup of fine sugar, one teacup of flour. Beat the yolks until light, then add the sugar, then add two tablespoonfuls of water, a pinch of salt. Lastly, stir in the flour, in which there should be a heaping teaspoonful of baking powder (the flour to be added gradually). Bake in long, shallow biscuit tins well greased. Turn out on a damp towel on a breadboard, cover the top with jelly, and roll up while warm.

EASY SPONGE CAKE WITH FRUIT ☆

Sift one cup sugar, one cup flour and two teaspoons baking powder. Add one-half cup water and two egg yolks. Stir well. Beat two egg whites and fold in. Pour batter over hot cooked fruit—this can be cherries, blueberries, etc. Cook fruit right in the cake pan, adding a little butter and sugar if necessary. (Don't grease pan.) Bake at 325° about thirty-five to forty minutes. You can use canned cherries or blueberries, but fresh, tart red cherries right off the tree (sweetened) are superb! Good with whipped cream or without.

KRUM KAKE ☆

3 eggs slightly beaten
1 cup rich cream
½ cup butter, melted
About 2 cups flour

¾ cup sugar
A little salt and cardamom seed

Bake on small waffle-like iron. Roll the cakes as soon as you take them out of the iron.

FATTIGMANN [*Poor Man*] ☆

10 egg yolks
3 rounded tablespoons sugar
5 tablespoons cream

1 tablespoon brandy
A little cardamom, if desired

Beat all together a half-hour. Add enough flour till mixture is thick dough. Chill till the next day. Roll out as thin as possible on floured board. Cut in diamonds with pastry cutter and fry in deep fat, a few at a time. Drain on absorbent paper, cool, and store in airtight can.

99-44/100% Pure!
The owner of a celebrated ostrich farm uses IVORY SOAP *exclusively in the delicate process of cleaning ostrich plumes when taken from his birds and when they become soiled by wear.* —(old adv.)

155

POOR MAN'S CAKE

Two cupfuls of flour, one cupful each sweet cream and sugar, one egg, one teaspoonful of soda, and two teaspoonfuls dry cream of tartar. Bake carefully and a very nice cake will result.

BRANDY-WINE CHEESECAKE

Half a pound each of butter and sugar, eight eggs, one pint of milk, quarter of a pound of currants, four ounces of bread, one tablespoonful each of brandy, wine, and rose water, one small nutmeg grated, half a teaspoonful of cinnamon. Put the milk on to boil, beat up four eggs and stir into it; when it is a thick curd, take if off, and when cool, mash it very fine. Crumb the bread and mix with the curd; beat the butter and sugar to a cream; add the curd and bread to it. Whisk other four eggs thick and light and pour them into the mixture, then add gradually the brandy, wine, rose water and spice, and lastly the currants. Line square tin pan, put in the filling, and bake in a quick oven.

Always pour a little hot milk into the eggs first before adding them to hot mixture. This will prevent curdling.

LEMON CHEESECAKE ☆

Combine and stir well:

1 package lemon-flavored
    gelatin
1 cup boiling water
3 tablespoons lemon juice

Combine and whip together:

1 eight-ounce package soft
    cream cheese
1 stick soft butter
    or margarine
1 cup sugar

Whip one large can chilled evaporated milk.

Combine all ingredients and whip. Pour into 9 by 13 pan, and sprinkle top lightly with graham cracker crumbs. Chill. Serves twelve to sixteen.

Dr. Sage's Catarrh Remedy! This is what we offer: $500 reward for a case of Catarrh which we cannot cure. No matter how bad your case or of how long standing, you can be cured! You're sure of that—or of $500. You can't have both, but you'll be have one or the other! —(old adv.)

Cake Frostings

ICING

Boil one-half cup sugar and one-fourth cup water until it forms a soft ball when a little is dropped in water. Pour over one stiffly beaten egg white, stirring constantly. A few cut-up marshmallows may be added to egg white first.

PLAIN CHOCOLATE ICING

Put into a shallow pan four tablespoonfuls of scraped chocolate, and place it where it will melt gradually, but not scorch. When melted, stir in three tablespoonfuls of milk or cream and one of water; mix all well together and add one scant teacupful of sugar. Boil about five minutes, and while hot (and when the cakes are nearly cold), spread some evenly over the surface of one of the cakes; put a second one on top, alternating the mixture and cakes; then cover top and sides and set in a warm oven to harden. All who have tried recipe after recipe, vainly hoping to find one where the chocolate sticks to the cake and not to the fingers, will appreciate the above. In icing many of the most palatable of cakes, the recipe just given here will be found very satisfactory.

FANCY FROSTING

The flavors mostly used are lemon, vanilla, almond, rose, chocolate, and orange. If you wish to ornament with figures or flowers, make up rather more icing, keep about one-third out until that on the cake is dried; then, with a clean glass syringe, apply it in such forms as you desire and dry as before. What you keep out to ornament with may be tinted pink with cochineal, blue with indigo, yellow with saffron or the grated rind of an orange strained through a cloth, green with spinach juice, and brown with chocolate, purple with cochineal and indigo. Strawberry juice, or currant and cranberry juices, color a delicate pink.

Set the cake in a cool oven with the door open to dry, or in a draught in an open window.

157

PLAIN FROSTING

For the white of one egg take nine heaping teaspoonfuls of white sugar and one teaspoonful of cornstarch. Beat the egg to a stiff froth, so that the plate can be turned upside down without the egg falling off; stir in the sugar and the starch slowly with a wooden spoon, ten or fifteen minutes constantly. To frost a common-sized cake one and one-half eggs will suffice.

BOILED FROSTING

To one pound of finest pulverized sugar, add three wineglassfuls of clear water. Let it stand until it dissolves; then boil it until it is perfectly clear and threads from the spoon. Beat well the whites of four eggs. Pour the sugar into the dish with the eggs, but do not mix them until the syrup is lukewarm; then beat all well together for one half hour.

Season to your taste with vanilla, rose water, or lemon juice. The first coating may be put on the cake as soon as it is well mixed. Rub the cake with a little flour before you apply the icing. While the first coat is drying, continue to beat the remainder; you will not have to wait long if the cake is set in a warm place near the fire. This is said to be a most excellent recipe for icing.

GOLDEN FROSTING

A very delicious and handsome frosting can be made by using the yolks of eggs instead of the whites. Proceed exactly as for ordinary frosting. It will harden just as nicely as that does. That is particularly good for orange cake, harmonizing with the color of the cake in a way to please those who love rich coloring.

> *Bostonians grate radishes into an intellectual sort of sauce for breakfast fish.*
>
> *Modern gastronomic authority says we must eat strawberries with a fork, and never with a spoon.*
>
> *It was Mrs. Parvenue who, served with artichokes at a dinnery party, asked the servant for a nut-cracker.*
>
> *Sam Ward used to say he shivered to see anyone cut lettuce. The wonder is he escaped a perpetual chill.— The Elite News, 1887*

Cookies

WINE JUMBLES

One cup of butter, two of sugar, three eggs, one wineglass of wine, one spoonful of vanilla, and flour enough to roll out. Roll as thin as the blade of a knife and cut with an oval cutter or a jagging iron. Bake on tin sheets, in a quick oven, until a dark brown. These will keep a year if kept in a tin box and in a dry place.

ALMOND JUMBLES

Three cupfuls of soft sugar, two cupfuls of flour, half a cupful of butter, one teacupful of loppered milk, five eggs separated, two tablespoonfuls of rose water, three-quarters of a pound of almonds blanched and chopped *very* fine, one teaspoonful of soda dissolved in boiling water.

Cream the butter and sugar; stir in the beaten yolks, the milk, flour, rose water, almonds, and, lastly, the beaten whites very lightly and quickly; drop, in rings, on buttered paper and bake at once.

CRISP COOKIES

One cup of butter, two cups of sugar, three eggs well beaten, a teaspoonful of soda and two of cream of tartar, a spoonful of milk, one teaspoonful of nutmeg and one of cinnamon, flour enough to make a soft dough just stiff enough to roll out. Try a pint of sifted flour to begin with, working it in gradually. Spread a little sweet milk over each, and sprinkle with sugar. Bake in a quick oven a light brown.

SELF-DIGESTERS

Two pounds and a half of unbolted flour, half a pound of butter, one tablespoonful of ginger, one teaspoonful of allspice and cloves mixed, one tablespoonful of saleratus. Mix all the ingredients with as much molasses as will make a stiff dough. Knead it well, then roll in thin sheets and cut with a round cutter. Place on buttered tins, then wash them over with thin molasses and water and bake in a moderate oven.

159

PRESS COOKIES ☆

1 cup shortening (2 sticks
   butter or margarine)
⅔ cup sugar
1 egg
½ teaspoon baking powder

2½ cups sifted,
   all-purpose flour
⅛ teaspoon salt
1 teaspoon vanilla

Cream shortening (which is room temperature) and sugar well. Add egg, beaten, and gradually add rest of ingredients. Mix well. Bake at 400° about five minutes, then turn down to 375° and bake till light brown. You can roll out the dough and cut the cookies in shapes instead of using a cooky press.

BUTTERSCOTCH COOKIES ☆

1 heaping cup shortening
1 cup brown sugar,
   packed down
1 teaspoon cream of tartar

1 teaspoon soda
1 teaspoon vanilla
1 cup nuts
4 cups flour

Mix well. Make into a long roll, chill, and slice. (Will keep in ice box several days.) Bake on a greased sheet at 400° about ten minutes.

GINGER SNAPS

One cup brown sugar, two cups molasses, one large cup butter, two teaspoonfuls soda, two teaspoonfuls ginger, three pints flour to commence with. Rub shortening and sugar together into the flour; add enough more flour to roll very smooth, very thin, and bake in a quick oven. (The dough can be kept for days by putting it in the flour barrel under the flour.) The more flour that can be worked in and the smoother they can be rolled, the better and more brittle they will be. Should be rolled out to waferlike thinness. Bake quickly without burning. They should become perfectly cold before putting aside.

Fancy cakes for afternoon teas now come in the form of tennis racquets, whips, Alpine sticks and mallets.

New peas from the South are tender and delicious—too nice to be conveyed on a knife blade to any mouth.—The Elite News, 1887

GINGER COOKIES ☆

1 cup sorghum molasses	1 tablespoon ginger
1 cup sugar	A pinch of salt
1 cup lard	3 cups of flour or enough to
1 cup boiling water	make dough stiff enough
1 tablespoon soda	to roll

Roll, cut with cookie cutter, and bake on greased sheet at 350° about 10 minutes.

OUR LITTLE ONES

Two pounds and a half of flour, half a pound of butter, two table-spoonfuls of ginger, one and a half tablespoonfuls of saleratus. Rub the flour, butter, and ginger together, then add the saleratus, with sufficient molasses to make a dough. Knead well. After remaining a short time in a cool place, roll it into thin sheets, cut with a round cutter, place them on slightly buttered tins, then wash them over with thin molasses and water, and bake in a *moderate* oven. This is specially recommended as wholesome for children.

GENEVA WAFERS

Two eggs, three ounces of butter, three ounces of flour, three ounces of pounded sugar. Well whisk the eggs, put them into a basin, and stir into them the butter, which should be beaten to a cream; add the flour and sifted sugar gradually, and then mix all well together. Butter a baking sheet, and drop on it a teaspoonful of the mixture at a time, leaving a space between each. Bake in a cool oven; watch the pieces of paste, and when half done, roll them up like wafers, and put in a small wedge of bread or piece of wood to keep them in shape. Return them to the oven until crisp. Before serving, remove the bread, put a spoonful of preserves in the widest end, and fill up with whipped cream. This is a very pretty and ornamental dish for the supper table, and is very nice, and very easily made.

It does not yet do to broil the alleged spring chicken too long, otherwise it will shrivel up into a "suspicion." — The Elite News, 1887

CHOCOLATE MACAROONS

Put three ounces of plain chocolate in a pan and melt on a slow fire; then work it to a thick paste with one pound of powdered sugar and the whites of three eggs; roll the mixture down to the thickness of about one-quarter of an inch; cut it in small, round pieces with a paste cutter, either plain or scalloped; butter a pan slightly and dust it with flour and sugar in equal quantities; place in the pan the pieces of mixture and bake in a hot but not too quick oven.

Pastries, Pies, and Tarts

GENERAL REMARKS

Use the very best materials in making pastry: the shortening should be fresh, sweet, and hard; the water cold (ice water is best); the paste rolled on a cold board; and all handled as little as possible.

When the crust is made, it makes it much more flakey and puff much more to place it in a dish covered with a cloth, and set in a very cold place for half an hour, or even an hour; in summer, it could be placed in the icebox.

A great improvement is made in pie crust by the addition of about a heaping teaspoonful of baking powder to a quart of flour; also brushing the paste as often as rolled out, and the pieces of butter placed thereon, with the white of an egg, assists it to rise in *leaves* or *flakes*. As this is the great beauty of puff paste, it is as well to try this method.

If currants are to be used in pies, they should be carefully picked over and washed in several waters, dried in a towel, and dredged with flour before they are suitable for use.

Raisins, and all dried fruits for pies and cakes, should be seeded, stoned, and dredged with flour before using.

Almonds should be blanched by pouring boiling water upon them and then slipping the skin off with the fingers. In pounding them, always add a little rose or orange water, with fine sugar, to prevent their becoming oily.

Great care is requisite in heating an oven for baking pastry. If you can hold your hand in the heated oven while you count twenty, the oven has just the proper temperature, and it should be kept at this temperature as long as the pastry is in: this heat will bake to a light brown and will give the pastry a fresh and flakey appearance. If you suffer the heat to abate, the undercrust will become heavy and clammy, and the upper crust will fall in.

Another good way to ascertain when the oven is heated to the proper degree for puff paste: Put a small piece of the paste in previous to baking the whole, and then the heat can thus be judged of.

Piecrust can be kept a week, and the last be better than the first, if put in a tightly covered dish and set in the ice chest in summer, and in a cool place in winter, and thus you can make a fresh pie every day with little trouble.

In baking custard, pumpkin, or squash pies, it is well, in order that the mixture may not be absorbed by the paste, to first partly bake the paste before adding it, and when stewed fruit is used, the filling should be perfectly cool when put in, or it will make the bottom crust sodden.

MODERN BAKING TIMES AND TEMPERATURES

Fruit pies, two-crust	450° for 10 minutes, then 350° for 35 minutes or longer till browned
Open fruit pies	450° for 20 minutes
Custard, pumpkin, etc.	450° for 15 minutes, then 325° for 30 minutes.
Previously cooked fillings, such as mince	450° for 30 minutes
Deep fruit pies	450° for 10 minutes, then 350° for 40 minutes
Pie shells without filling	500° for 12 minutes
Dumplings	350° for 30 minutes
Dumplings with cooked filling	450° for 15 minutes
Meringue	300° for 15 to 20 minutes

How To Make a Pie

After making the crust, take a portion of it, roll it out, and fit it to a buttered pie plate by cutting it off evenly around the edge. Gather up the scraps left from cutting and make into another sheet for the top crust; roll it a little thinner than the undercrust. Lap one half over the other and cut three or four slits about a quarter of an inch from the folded edge (this prevents the steam from escaping through the rim of the pie and causing the juices to run out from the edges). Now fill your pie plate with your prepared filling, wet the top edge of the rim, lay the upper crust across the center of the pie, turn back the half that is lapped over, seal the two edges together by slightly pressing down with your thumb, then notch evenly and regularly with a three-tined fork, dipping occasionally in flour to prevent sticking. Bake in a rather quick oven until a light brown and the filling boils up through the slits in the upper crust.

To prevent the juice soaking through into the crust, making it soggy, wet the undercrust with the white of an egg just before you put in the pie mixture. If the top of the pie is brushed over with the egg, it gives it a beautiful glaze.

Rule for Undercrust

A good rule for piecrust for a pie requiring only an undercrust—as a custard or pumpkin pie—is: three *large* tablespoonfuls of flour sifted; rubbing into it a *large* tablespoonful of cold butter (or part butter and part lard) and a pinch of salt; mixing with *cold* water enough to form a smooth, stiff paste, rolled quite thin.

PLAIN PIECRUST

Two and a half cupfuls of sifted flour; one cupful of shortening, half butter and half lard, cold; a pinch of salt; a heaping teaspoonful of baking powder, sifted through the flour. Rub thoroughly the shortening into the flour. Mix together with half a teacupful of *cold* water, or enough to form a rather stiff dough; mix as little as possible, just enough to get it into shape to roll out; it must be handled very lightly. This rule is for two pies.

When you have a little piecrust left, do not throw it away; roll it thin, cut it in small squares, and bake. Just before tea, put a spoonful of raspberry jelly on each square.

FINE PUFF PASTE

Into one quart of sifted flour, mix two teaspoonfuls of baking powder and a teaspoonful of salt; *then sift again*. Measure out one teacupful of butter and one of lard, hard and cold. Take the lard and rub into the flour until a very fine, smooth paste. Then put in just enough *ice water*, say half a cupful, containing a beaten white of egg, to mix a very stiff dough. Roll it out into a thin sheet, spread with one-fourth of the butter, sprinkle over with a little flour, then roll up closely in a long roll, like a scroll; double the ends towards the center, flatten and reroll, then spread again with another quarter of the butter. Repeat this operation until the butter is used up. Put it on an earthen dish, cover it with a cloth, and set it in a cold place (in the icebox in summer); let it remain until *cold*—an hour or more—before making out the crust. Tarts made with this paste cannot be cut with a knife when fresh; they go into flakes at the touch.

You may roll this pastry in any direction, from you, towards you, sideways, anyway, it matters not, but you must have nice flour, *ice water*, and very *little* of it, and strength to roll it, if you would succeed.

This recipe was purchased from a cook on one of the Lake Michigan steamers many years ago, and it is, without exception, the finest puff paste ever seen.

PUFF PASTE OF SUET

Two cupfuls of flour, one-half teaspoonful of salt, one teaspoonful of baking powder, one cup of suet freed of skin and chopped very fine, one cupful of water. Place the flour, sifted with the powder, in a bowl; add suet and water; mix into smooth, rather firm dough.

This paste is excellent for fruit puddings, and dumplings, that are boiled; if it is well made, it will be light and flaky, and the suet imperceptible. It is also excellent for meat pies, baked or boiled. All the ingredients should be very cold when mixing, and the suet dredged with flour after it is chopped, to prevent the particles from adhering to each other.

FOR ICING PASTRY

To ice pastry, which is the usual method adopted for fruit tarts and sweet dishes of pastry, put the white of an egg on a plate, and with the blade of a knife beat it to a stiff froth. When the pastry is nearly baked, brush it over with this, and sift over some pounded sugar; put it back into the oven to set the glaze, and in a few minutes it will be done. Great care should be taken that the paste does not catch or burn in the oven, which it is very liable to do after the icing is laid on.

Or make a meringue by adding a tablespoonful of white sugar to the beaten white of one egg. Spread over the top and slightly brown in the oven.

GREEN APPLE PIE

Peel, core, and slice tart apples enough for a pie; sprinkle over about three tablespoonfuls of sugar, a teaspoonful of cinnamon, a small level tablespoonful of sifted flour, two tablespoonfuls of water, a few bits of butter. Stir all together with a spoon. Put it into a pie-tin lined with pie paste. Cover with a top crust and bake about forty minutes.

The result will be a delicious, juicy pie.

APPLE CUSTARD PIE 1

Three cupfuls of milk, four eggs, one cupful of sugar, two cupfuls of thick stewed apples strained through a colander. Beat the whites and yolks of the eggs lightly and mix the yolks well with the apples, flavoring with nutmeg. Then beat into this the milk and, lastly, the whites. Let the crust partly bake before turning in this filling. To be baked with only the one crust, like all custard pies.

APPLE CUSTARD PIE 2

Select fair sweet apples, pare and grate them, and to every teacupful of the apple, add two eggs well beaten, two tablespoonfuls of fine sugar, one of melted butter, the grated rind and half the juice of one lemon, half a wineglass of brandy, and one teacupful of milk. Mix all well and pour into a deep plate lined with paste. Put a strip of the paste around the edge of the dish and bake thirty minutes.

APPLE CUSTARD PIE 3

Lay a crust in your plates. Slice apples thin and half fill your plates. Pour over them a custard made of four eggs and one quart of milk, sweetened and seasoned to your taste.

IRISH APPLE PIE

Pare and take out the cores of the apples, cutting each apple into four or eight pieces, according to their size. Lay them neatly in a baking dish, seasoning them with brown sugar, and any spice, such as pounded cloves and cinnamon, or grated lemon peel. A little quince marmalade gives a fine flavor to the pie. Add a little water and cover with puff paste. Bake for an hour.

COCONUT PIE

Cut off the brown part of the cocoanut, grate the white part, mix it with milk, and set it on the fire and let it boil slowly eight or ten minutes. To a pound of the grated coconut, allow a quart of milk, eight eggs, four tablespoonfuls of sifted white sugar, a glass of wine, a small cracker (pounded fine), two spoonfuls of melted butter, and half a nutmeg. The eggs and sugar should be beaten together to a froth, then the wine stirred in. Put them into the milk and coconut, which should be first allowed to get quite cool; add the cracker and nutmeg; turn the whole into a deep pie plate with a lining and rim of puff paste. Bake them as soon as turned into the plates.

CHOCOLATE CUSTARD PIE

One-quarter cake unsweetened chocolate, grated; one pint of boiling water; six eggs; one quart of milk; one-half cupful of white sugar; two teaspoonfuls of vanilla. Dissolve the chocolate in a very little milk, stir into the boiling water, and boil three minutes. When nearly cold, beat up with this the yolks of all the eggs and the whites of three. Stir this mixture into the milk, season, and pour into shells of good paste. When the custard is "set"—but not more than half done—spread over it the whites whipped to a froth, with two tablespoonfuls of sugar. You may bake these custards without paste in a pudding dish or cups set in boiling water.

LEMON PIE 1

Take a deep dish, grate into it the outside of the rind of two lemons; add to that a cup and a half of white sugar, two heaping tablespoonfuls of unsifted flour, or one of cornstarch; stir it well together, then add the yolks of three well-beaten eggs; beat this thoroughly; then add the juice of the lemons, two cups of water, and a piece of butter the size of a walnut. Set this on the fire in another dish containing boiling water and cook it until it thickens and will dip up on the spoon like cold honey. Remove it from the fire, and when cooled, pour it into a deep pie tin lined with pastry; bake, and when done, have ready the whites, beaten stiff, with three small tablespoonfuls of sugar. Spread this over the top and return to the oven to set and brown slightly. This makes a deep, large-sized pie, and very superior.

LEMON PIE 2

Moisten a heaping tablespoonful of cornstarch with a little cold water, then add a cupful of boiling water. Stir over the fire till it boils and cooks the cornstarch, say two or three minutes. Add a teaspoonful of butter and a cupful of sugar. Take off the fire, and when slightly cooled, add an egg well beaten and the juice and grated rind of a fresh lemon. Bake with a crust. This makes one small pie.

ORANGE PIE

Grate the rind of one and use the juice of two large oranges. Stir together a large cupful of sugar and a heaping tablespoonful of flour; add to this the well-beaten yolks of three eggs and two tablespoonfuls of melted butter. Reserve the whites for frosting. Turn this into a pie pan lined with pie paste, and bake in a quick oven. When done so as to resemble a finely baked custard, spread on the top of it the beaten whites, which must be sweetened with two tablespoonfuls of sugar; spread evenly, and return to the oven and brown slightly.

The addition of the juice of half a lemon improves it, if convenient to have it.

BAKERS' CUSTARD PIE

Beat up the yolks of three eggs to a cream. Stir thoroughly a tablespoonful of sifted flour into three tablespoonfuls of sugar. (This separates the particles of flour so that there will be no lumps.) Then add it to the beaten yolks, put in a pinch of salt, a teaspoonful of vanilla, and a little grated nutmeg; next the well-beaten whites of the eggs; and, lastly, a pint of scalded milk (not boiled) which has been cooled; mix this in by degrees, turn all into a deep pie pan lined with puff paste, and bake from twenty-five to thirty minutes.

This recipe came from a celebrated cook in one of the best New York bakeries. He was asked "why it was that their custard pies had that look of solidity and smoothness that our homemade pies have not." He replied, "The secret is the addition of this *bit of flour*—not that it thickens the custard any to speak of, but prevents the custard from breaking or wheying, and gives that smooth appearance when cut."

BOSTON CREAM PIE

Cream Part—Put on a pint of milk to boil. Break two eggs into a dish and add one cup of sugar and half a cup of flour previously mixed. After beating well, stir it into the milk just as the milk commences to boil; add an ounce of butter and keep on stirring one way until it thickens. Flavor with vanilla or lemon.

Crust Part—Three eggs, beaten separately; one cup of granulated sugar; one and a half cups of sifted flour; one large teaspoonful of baking powder; and two tablespoonfuls of milk or water. Divide the batter in half and bake on two medium-sized pie tins. Bake in a rather quick oven to a straw color. When done and cool, split each one in half with a sharp broad-bladed knife and spread half the cream between each. Serve cold.

The cake part should be flavored the same as the custard.

CHERRY PIE

Line your pie plate with good crust; fill half full with ripe cherries; sprinkle over them about a cupful of sugar and a teaspoonful of sifted flour; dot a few bits of butter over them. Now fill the crust full to the top. Cover with the upper crust and bake.

This is one of the best of pies, if made correctly, and the cherries in any case should be stoned. Those who have not time or are too lazy to remove the stones should never attempt to make cherry pies.

CURRANT PIE

Make in just the same way as the Cherry Pie, unless they are somewhat green, then they should be stewed a little.

169

GREEN TOMATO PIE

Take medium-sized tomatoes, pare, and cut out the stem end. Having your pie pan lined with paste made as biscuit dough, slice the tomatoes *very thin*, filling the pan somewhat heaping, then grate over it a nutmeg and put in half a cup of butter and a medium cup of sugar, if the pan is rather deep. Sprinkle a small handful of flour over all, pouring in half a cup of vinegar before adding the top crust. Bake half an hour in a moderately hot oven, serving hot. Good. Try it.

PECAN PIE ☆

Cream one tablespoon butter with one cup brown sugar. Add one cup white corn syrup and stir until well blended. Add three well-beaten eggs, a pinch of salt, one tablespoon vanilla, and one cup pecan nut-meats, broken. Pour mixture into unbaked pie shell and bake in hot oven (450°) for ten minutes, then reduce heat to 300° and bake thirty-five minutes longer. May be served with whipped cream.

RHUBARB PIE 1

Cut the large stalks off where the leaves commence, strip off the outside skin, then cut the stalks in pieces half an inch long. Line a pie dish with paste rolled rather thicker than a dollar piece; put in a layer of the rhubarb nearly an inch deep. To a quart bowl of cut rhubarb, put a large teacupful of sugar; strew it over with a saltspoonful of salt and a little nutmeg grated; shake over a little flour; cover with a rich piecrust, cut a slit in the center, trim off the edge with a sharp knife, and bake in a quick oven until the pie loosens from the dish. Rhubarb pies made in this way are altogether superior to those made of the fruit stewed.

RHUBARB PIE 2 ☆

3 cups diced rhubarb	2 eggs
1 cup sugar	1 tablespoon lemon juice
3 tablespoons flour	(optional)

Arrange rhubarb in an unbaked pastry shell. Blend sugar and flour, and add to them eggs and lemon juice. Stir until thick. Pour over

170

rhubarb and cover with lattice or top crust. (Cut slits in top crust). Bake at 400° twenty minutes, then reduce temperature to 350° and bake twenty minutes longer. This pie may be made with egg yolks alone and topped with meringue made of the two egg whites.

[*Note:* This recipe was heavily spotted with rhubarb, sugar, egg, etc., which is always a good testimonial—used often, well-liked!]

MOLASSES PIE

Two teacupfuls of molasses, one of sugar, three eggs, one tablespoonful of melted butter, one lemon, nutmeg. Beat and bake in pastry.

LEMON RAISIN PIE

One cup of chopped raisins, seeded; the juice and grated rind of one lemon; one cupful of cold water; one tablespoonful of flour; one cupful of sugar; two tablespoonfuls of butter. Stir lightly together and bake with upper crust and undercrust.

FINGER PIE ☆

1 heaping tablespoon flour	Milk
⅔ cup granulated sugar	Butter

Mix flour and sugar with finger in bottom of an eight-inch uncooked pie crust. Add milk to almost fill crust, and stir. Top with bits of butter and sprinkle with cinnamon. Bake at 425° for about one-half hour. Cool before cutting.

This pie can be made with light cream or "half-and-half."

SUGAR CREAM PIE ☆

2 tablespoons-plus flour (about one-fourth cup)	¼ teaspoon salt
1 cup brown sugar	1½ cups light cream

Mix flour and sugar and salt; add cream and stir well. Pour into unbaked pie shell. Bake at 450° ten minutes, then reduce heat to 325° and bake forty-five minutes, or till an inserted knife comes out clean.

SWEET POTATO PIE

One pound of steamed sweet potatoes finely mashed, two cups sugar, one cup cream, one-half cup butter, three well-beaten eggs. Flavor with lemon or nutmeg and bake in pastry shell. Fine.

COOKED MEAT FOR MINCE PIES

In order to succeed in having a good mince pie, it is quite essential to cook the meat properly, so as to retain its juices and strength of flavor.

Select four pounds of lean beef, the neck piece is as good as any; wash it, and put it into a kettle with just water enough to cover it; take off the scum as it reaches the boiling point; add hot water from time to time, until it is tender, then season with salt and pepper; take off the cover and let it boil until almost dry, or until the juice has boiled back into the meat. When it looks as though it was beginning to fry in its own juice, it is time to take up, and set aside to get cold, which should be done the day before needed. Next day, when making the mincemeat, the bones, gristle and stringy bits should be well picked out before chopping.

MINCE PIES

The Astor House, some years ago, was *famous* for its mince pies. The chief pastry cook at that time, by request, published the recipe. Those who partake of it never fail to speak in laudable terms of the superior excellence of this recipe, when strictly followed.

Four pounds of lean boiled beef, chopped fine; twice as much of chopped green tart apples; one pound of chopped suet, three pounds of raisins, seeded; two pounds of currants picked over, washed, and dried; half a pound of citron cut up fine; one pound of brown sugar; one quart of cooking molasses; two quarts of sweet cider; one pint of boiled cider; one tablespoonful of salt; one tablespoonful of pepper; one tablespoonful of mace; one tablespoonful of allspice; and four tablespoonfuls of cinnamon; two grated nutmegs; one tablespoonful of cloves. Mix thoroughly and warm it on the range until heated through. Remove from the fire, and when nearly cool, stir in a pint of good brandy and one pint of Madeira wine. Put into a crock, cover it tightly, and set it in a cold place where it will not freeze, but keep perfectly cold. Will keep good all winter.—*Chef de Cuisine, Astor House, New York*

MINCEMEAT CRESCENTS ☆

1 large jar mincemeat	¼ teaspoon ground cloves
2 apples, grated	⅛ teaspoon allspice
½ cup currants or raisins	¼ teaspoon nutmeg
½ cup brown sugar	1 teaspoon salt
1 tablespoon cornstarch	1 teaspoon brandy
½ teaspoon cinnamon	1 teaspoon rum

Mix dry ingredients, then add all ingredients and mix well. Prepare pastry dough, roll and cut into small circles with cooky cutter or tumbler. Fill one-half of each pastry circle with mincemeat mixture; fold other half over filling. Press edges together with fork. Bake at 350° thirty to thirty-five minutes. May be frosted immediately with powdered sugar frosting; use melted butter and a little brandy in the frosting.

TARTLETS

Tartlets are nice made in this manner: Roll some good puff paste out thin and cut it into two and a half inch squares; brush each square over with the white of an egg, then fold down the corners, so that they all meet in the middle of each piece of paste; slightly press the two pieces together; brush them over with the egg; sift over sugar, and bake in a nice quick oven for about a quarter of an hour. When they are done, make a little hole in the middle of the paste and fill it up with apricot jam, marmalade, or red-currant jelly. Pile them high in the center of a dish, on a napkin, and garnish with the same preserve the tartlets are filled with.

FUNERAL PIE ☆
[*Did you ever eat Funeral Pie?*]

This Pennsylvania-Dutch dessert can be made well in advance of serving; it's a good "keeper." Years ago, when a death in the family seemed inevitable, the pies were baked several days ahead. When the sad event finally occurred, mourning relatives and friends were sustained, if not consoled, by the popular delicacy.

The story is told of a Pennsylvania-Dutch father who had been given up by his physician. Mother and the daughters sadly began to bake Funeral Pies. When the delicious aroma drifted into Father's bedroom, he called his wife to his bedside.

173

"Mama, I thought I was a goner," he said, "but now I think I get well."

"Papa, you can't!" exclaimed Mama. "The Funeral Pies is made!"

[The pie tastes even better on happy occasions.]

Soak one cup of raisins in two cups of warm water about two hours.

In a double-boiler top combine one and a half cups sugar and four level tablespoons flour, mixed. Add one well-beaten egg, juice of one lemon, a bit of grated lemon rind and one-fourth teaspoon salt. Add raisins and soaking water. Cook about fifteen minutes, then cool.

Pour into unbaked pie shell. Top with lattice-strips of dough. Bake at 375° about three-quarters of an hour, or until well browned.

[Who has a recipe for Methodist pie, described in this old jingle?

A Methodist I was born,
A Methodist I shall die,
I was baptized in the Methodist faith
And ate of the Methodist Pie.]

PLUM CUSTARD TARTLETS

One pint of greengage plums, after being rubbed through a sieve; one large cup of sugar; the yolks of two eggs well beaten. Whisk all together until light and foamy; then bake in small pattypan shells of puff paste, a light brown. Then fill with the plum paste. Beat the two whites until stiff and add two tablespoonfuls of powdered sugar; spread over the plum paste and set the shells into a moderate oven for a few moments.

These are much more easily handled than pieces of pie or even pies whole, and can be packed nicely for carrying.

LEMON TARTS ☆

2 cups sugar	4 eggs, well beaten
½ cup lemon juice	Miniature tart shells,
2 teaspoons grated lemon rind	baked and cooled
1 cup butter	

In double boiler combine sugar, lemon juice, and rind. Mix well, then stir in butter and heat over boiling water, stirring until butter is melted. Add well-beaten eggs (add a little of the hot mixture to the eggs before pouring them in). Continue stirring until mixture is thick enough to pile slightly. Cool thoroughly, then spoon filling into tart shells.

CARAMEL TARTS ☆

Fill baked tart shells with the following caramel mixture which has been cooked till thickened:

2 cups light brown sugar	2 egg yolks
4 tablespoons flour	2 tablespoons butter
1 cup top milk	1 teaspoon vanilla

Top with meringue made of the two egg whites and ¼ cup sugar. Bake at 300°, fifteen to twenty minutes. (Highly caloric but good!)

Puddings and Other Desserts

DELICATE INDIAN PUDDING

One quart milk, two heaping tablespoonfuls of Indian meal, four of sugar, one of butter, three eggs, one teaspoonful of salt. Boil milk in double boiler; sprinkle the meal into it, stirring all the while; cook twelve minutes, stirring often. Beat together the eggs, salt, sugar, and one-half teaspoonful of ginger. Stir the butter into the meal and milk. Pour this gradually over the egg mixture. Bake slowly one hour. Serve with sauce of heated syrup and butter.

CORN PUDDING

Barely cut the kernels from two ears of fresh corn. Then turn knife blade and scrape all the watery pulp from the ears. Meanwhile, bring to a boil, and let boil about thirty seconds, one cup of milk. Let milk cool. Have ready three eggs, beaten, salt to taste, and one tablespoon sugar. Mix cooled milk with egg mixture and pour over the corn. Stir well. Bake at 350° for an hour or until the pudding is "set."

COTTAGE PUDDING

One heaping pint of flour, half a cupful of sugar, one cupful of milk, one teaspoonful of soda dissolved in the milk, one tablespoonful of butter, two teaspoonfuls of cream of tartar rubbed dry in the flour. Flavor with nutmeg. Bake in a *moderate* oven. Cut in slices and serve warm with wine or brandy sauce or sweet sugar sauce.

FRENCH COCONUT PUDDING

One quart of milk, three tablespoonfuls of cornstarch, the yolks of four eggs, half a cupful of sugar, and a little salt. Put part of the milk, salt, and sugar on the stove and let it boil. Dissolve the cornstarch in the rest of the milk. Stir into the milk, and while boiling, add the yolks and a cupful of grated chocolate. Flavor with vanilla.

Frosting—The whites of four eggs beaten to a stiff froth, half a cupful of sugar. Flavor with lemon. Spread it on the pudding and put it into the oven to brown, saving a little of the frosting to moisten the top; then put on grated coconut to give it the appearance of snowflake.

THUN PUDDING

Chop very small two ounces of almonds and some lemon peel; put them in a saucepan with one pint of milk and sugar to taste; when this begins to boil, stir in slowly one large cupful of ground rice, and let it boil ten minutes, stirring the whole time. Pour in a mold, and when cold, turn out. Put two ounces of white sugar in a pan, with a little water; stir until melted and become a light golden brown. Add one pint of milk; bring this to a boil, then strain it, and add the yolks of four eggs. Put the latter mixture on the fire and stir until it thickens. When cold, pour it round the pudding.

ENGLISH PLUM PUDDING [*the Genuine*]

Soak one pound of stale bread in a pint of hot milk, and let it stand and cool. When cold, add to it one-half pound of sugar and the yolks of eight eggs beaten to a cream, one pound of raisins stoned and floured, one pound of Zante currants washed and floured, a quarter of a pound of citron cut in slips and dredged with flour, one pound of beef suet

176

chopped finely and *salted*, one glass of wine, one glass of brandy, one nutmeg, and a tablespoonful of mace, cinnamon, and cloves mixed. Beat the whole well together and, as the last thing, add the white of the eight eggs beaten to a stiff froth. Pour into a cloth previously scalded and dredged with flour; tie the cloth firmly, leaving room for the pudding to swell, and boil six hours. Serve with wine or brandy sauce.

It is best to prepare the ingredients the day before and cover closely.

OLD ENGLISH PLUM PUDDING

To make what is termed a pound pudding, take of raisins well stoned, currants thoroughly washed, one pound each; chop one pound of suet very fine and mix with them; add quarter of a pound of flour or bread very finely crumbed, three ounces of sugar, one ounce and a half of grated lemon peel, a blade of mace, half a small nutmeg, half a dozen eggs well beaten. Work it well together, put it into a cloth, tie it firmly (allowing room to swell), and boil not less than five hours. It should not be suffered to stop boiling till done.

BAKED PLUM PUDDING

It will be found best to prepare the ingredients the day before and cover closely. Grate a stale loaf of bread, or enough for a pint of crumbs; boil one quart of milk and turn boiling hot over the grated bread; cover and let steep an hour. In the meantime pick, soak, and dry half a pound of currants, half a pound of raisins, a quarter of a pound of citron cut in large slips, one nutmeg, one tablespoonful of mace and cinnamon mixed, one cupful of sugar, with half of a cupful of butter. When the bread is ready, mix with it the butter, sugar, spice, and citron, adding a glassful of white wine. Beat eight eggs very light, and when the mixture is quite cold, stir them gradually in; then add by degrees the raisins and currants dredged with flour. Stir the whole very hard. Put it into a buttered dish, bake two hours, and send to the table warm. Eat with wine sauce or wine and sugar. Most excellent.

THE BEST BREAD PUDDING

Take the inside of a small loaf of baker's bread and put it into a deep pan with two ounces of butter; pour over it one pint of boiling milk. After remaining a sufficient length of time to become completely saturated, with a spoon mash it until very smooth and fine; whisk six eggs until thick and light, which stir in gradually, then add one quart of milk. Mix all well together and sweeten to taste. Pour the mixture into a pudding dish, sift a little cinnamon over the top, and bake in a *quick* oven. When done and cold, have some fine ripe peaches, which pare, slice, and sugar; just before sending the pudding to table, place as many on the top as the dish will conveniently hold, and sift over white sugar. This is second to none, especially with cream sauce.

ROYAL SAGO PUDDING

Three-quarters of a cupful of sago, washed and put into one quart of milk; put it into a saucepan, let it stand in boiling water on the stove or range until the sago has well swelled. While hot, put in two tablespoon-fuls of butter with one cupful of white sugar and flavoring. When cool, add the well-beaten yolks of four eggs, put in a buttered pudding dish, and bake from half to three-quarters of an hour; then remove it from the oven and place it to cool. Beat the whites of the eggs with three tablespoonfuls of powdered white sugar till they are a mass of froth; spread the pudding with either raspberry or strawberry jam, and then spread on the frosting; put in the oven for two minutes to slightly brown. If made in summer, be sure and keep the whites of the eggs on ice until ready for use, and beat them in the coldest place you can find, as it will make a much richer frosting.

The small white sago called pearl is the best. The large kind has an earthy taste. It should always be kept in a covered jar or box.

This pudding, made with tapioca, is equally good. Serve with any sweet sauce.

[*Note:* Sago: a kind of starch produced from the stem of several palms of the East Indies, forming light, wholesome, nutritious food. I don't know where present occupants of the White House obtain their sago. Unfortunately, George Washington's sago palm was among the plants destroyed by the $20,000 fire in the White House conservatory during Andrew Johnson's administration, 1867.]

SAGO APPLE PUDDING

One cupful of sago in a quart of tepid water with a pinch of salt, soaked for one hour; six or eight apples, pared and cored or quartered, and steamed tender and put in the pudding dish. Boil and stir the sago until clear, adding water to make it thin, and pour it over the apples. Bake one hour. This is good hot with butter and sugar or cold with cream and sugar.

BROWN BETTY 1

Go gather the apples that red, ripe are lying
And cut all the cores and the peelings away,
Then slice them just as one would slice them for frying,
And we'll have Brown Betty for dinner today.

Then get a deep pan with a close-fitting cover,
Alternately apples and crumbs in it lay,
With sugar and cinnamon sprinkle them over,
Oh, we'll bake Brown Betty for dinner today.

Now go fill the pitcher with milk that is creaming,
And carry Brown Betty along on a tray,
An odor deliciously spicy comes steaming,
We'll have a grand feast on Miss Betty today!
—*Rose Langtry, Crawfordsville, Ind., Cookbook, 1879*

Time changes most things but not——

BROWN BETTY 2 ☆

2 cups bread crumbs	½ teaspoon nutmeg or mace
¼ cup melted butter	¼ teaspoon cinnamon
6 cups apples (sliced, pared, and cored)	1½ tablespoons lemon rind (or use juice)
½ cup sugar, white or brown, firmly packed	½ cup water

Combine bread crumbs and melted butter, and arrange one-third mixture in bottom of greased casserole. Cover with half the apples and half the sugar-spice-lemon-water mixture. Alternate layers of crumbs, apples, and sugar; top with crumbs. Cover and bake at 375° one-half hour. Remove cover and bake one-half hour longer or until apples are tender. Serves six. Serve warm with cream or hard sauce.

179

HARD SAUCE ☆

⅓ cup butter or margarine   1 teaspoon vanilla extract
1 cup confectioner's sugar   Pinch of salt

Work butter with spoon or beater until light and creamy. Add sugar gradually while continuing to beat. Add vanilla a little at a time and salt. Chill until needed.

PLAIN RICE PUDDING

Pick over, wash, and boil a teacupful of rice. When soft, drain off the water. While warm, add to the rice a tablespoonful of cold butter. When cool, mix with it a cupful of sugar, a teaspoonful of grated nutmeg, and one of ground cinnamon. Beat up four eggs very light, whites and yolks separately. Add them to the rice, then stir in a quart of sweet milk gradually. Butter a pudding dish, turn in the mixture, and bake one hour in a moderate oven. Serve warm with sweet wine sauce.

If you have cold cooked rice, first soak it in the milk and proceed as above.

APPLE DUMPLINGS

Make a rich biscuit dough, the same as soda or baking-powder biscuit, only adding a little more shortening. Take a piece of dough out on the molding board, roll out almost as thin as piecrust; then cut into square pieces large enough to cover an apple. Put into the middle of each piece two apple halves that have been pared and cored; sprinkle on a spoonful of sugar and a pinch of ground cinnamon; turn the ends of the dough over the apple and lap them tight. Lay the dumplings in a dripping pan well buttered, the smooth side upward. When the pans are filled, put a small piece of butter on the top of each, sprinkle over a large handful of sugar, turn in a cupful of boiling water, then place in a moderate oven for three-quarters of an hour. Baste with the liquor once while baking. Serve with pudding sauce or cream and sugar.

BOILED APPLE DUMPLINGS

The same recipe as the above, with the exception that they are put into a small coarse cloth well floured after being dipped in hot water, each cloth to be tied securely, but leaving room enough for the dumpling to swell. Put them in a pot of boiling water and boil three-quarters of an hour. Serve with sweet sauce. Peaches and other fruits are used in the same manner.

BOILED APPLE PUFFETS

Three eggs, one pint of milk, a little salt, sufficient flour to thicken as waffle batter, one and one-half teaspoonfuls of baking powder. Fill cups alternately with a layer of batter and then of apples chopped fine. Steam one hour. Serve hot with flavored cream and sugar. You can substitute any fresh fruit or jams your taste prefers.

APPLE FRITTERS

Make a batter in the proportion of one cup sweet milk to two cups flour, a heaping teaspoonful of baking powder, two eggs beaten separately, one tablespoonful of sugar, and a saltspoon of salt. Heat the milk a little more than milk-warm; add it slowly to the beaten yolks and sugar, then add flour and whites of the eggs. Stir all together and throw in thin slices of good sour apples, dipping the batter up over them. Drop into boiling hot lard in large spoonfuls with pieces of apple in each and fry to a light brown. Serve with maple syrup or a nice syrup made with clarified sugar.

HUCKLEBERRIES WITH CRACKERS AND CREAM

Pick over carefully one quart of blueberries and keep them on ice until wanted. Put into each bowl for each guest two soda crackers broken in not too small pieces. Add a few tablespoonfuls of berries, a teaspoonful of powdered sugar, and fill the bowl with the richest of cold, sweet cream. This is an old-fashioned New England breakfast dish. It also answers for a dessert.

STEWED APPLES

Apples cooked in the following way look very pretty on a tea table and are appreciated by the palate. Select firm round greenings; pare neatly and cut in halves; place in a shallow stewpan with sufficient boiling

181

water to cover them and a cup of sugar to every six apples. Each half should cook on the bottom of the pan and be removed from the others so as not to injure its shape. Stew slowly until the pieces are very tender, remove to a glass dish carefully, boil the syrup a half hour longer, pour it over the apples and eat cold. A few pieces of lemon boiled in the syrup adds to the flavor.

BAKED PEARS

Pare and core the pears, without dividing; place them in a pan and fill up the orifice with brown sugar; add a little water and let them bake until perfectly tender. Nice with sweet cream or boiled custard.

SOFT CARAMEL CUSTARD

One quart of milk, half a cupful of sugar, six eggs, half a teaspoonful of salt. Put the milk on to boil, reserving a cupful. Beat the eggs and add the cold milk to them. Stir the sugar in a small frying pan until it becomes liquid and just begins to smoke. Stir it into the boiling milk; then add the beaten eggs and cold milk, and stir constantly until the mixture begins to thicken. Set away to cool. Serve in glasses.

BAKED CUSTARD

Beat five fresh eggs, the whites and yolks separately, the yolks with half a cup of sugar, the whites to a stiff froth; then stir them gradually into a quart of sweet, rich milk previously boiled and cooled; flavor with extract of lemon or vanilla and half a teaspoonful of salt. Rub butter over the bottom and sides of a baking dish or tin basin; pour in the custard, grate a little nutmeg over, and bake in a quick oven. It is better to set the dish in a shallow pan of hot water, reaching nearly to the top, the water to be kept boiling until the custard is baked; three-quarters of an hour is generally enough. Run a teaspoon handle into the middle of it; if it comes out clean it is baked sufficiently.

A Solomon in all his glory never conjured up "weskits" to compare with what a broker's clerk can show today. He not only wears a vest of gay and flowery pattern but adorns its extremely low opening with a false collar of white Marseilles or pique. This is a revival of a very old style and first took away our unprepared breath last summer.—"Fashions for Gentlemen," The Elite News, 1887

CUP CUSTARD

Six eggs, half a cupful of sugar, one quart of new milk. Beat the eggs, and the sugar and milk, and any extract or flavoring you like. Fill your custard cups, sift a little nutmeg or cinnamon over the tops, set them in a moderate oven in a shallow pan half filled with hot water. In about twenty minutes try them with the handle of a teaspoon to see if they are firm. Judgment and great care are needed to attain skill in baking custard; for if left in the oven a minute too long or if the fire is too hot, the milk will certainly whey.

Serve cold, with fresh fruit sugared and placed on top of each—strawberries, peaches or raspberries, as preferred.

BOILED CUSTARD

Beat seven eggs very light, omitting the whites of two; mix them gradually with a quart of milk and half a cupful of sugar; boil in a dish set into another of boiling water; add flavoring. As soon as it comes to the boiling point, remove it or it will be liable to curdle and become lumpy. Whip the whites of the two eggs that remain, adding two heaping tablespoonfuls of sugar. When the custard is cold, heap this on top; if in cups, put on a strawberry, or a bit of red jelly on each. Set in a cold place till wanted.

GERMAN CUSTARD

Add to a pint of good, rich, boiled custard an ounce of sweet almonds blanched, roasted, and pounded; also a small quantity of candied citron cut into the thinnest possible slips. Cook the custard as usual, and set it on the ice for some hours before using.

BAKED COCONUT CUSTARD

Grate as much coconut as will weigh a pound. Mix half a pound of powdered white sugar with the milk of the coconut, or with a pint of cream, adding two tablespoonfuls of rose water. Then stir in gradually a pint of rich milk. Beat to a stiff froth the whites of eight eggs and stir them into the milk and sugar, a little at a time, alternately with the grated coconut; add a teaspoonful of powdered nutmeg and cinnamon. Then put the mixture into cups and bake them twenty minutes in a moderate oven, set in a pan half filled with boiling water. When cold, grate loaf sugar over them.

SPANISH CREAM

Take one quart of milk and soak half a box of gelatin in it for an hour; place it on the fire and stir often. Beat the yolks of three eggs very light with a cupful of sugar, stir into the scalding milk, and heat until it begins to thicken (it should not boil, or it will curdle); remove from the fire and strain through thin muslin or tarlatan, and when nearly cold, flavor with vanilla or lemon; then wet a dish or mold in cold water, fill with the mixture and set aside to stiffen.

BAVARIAN CREAM

One quart of sweet cream, the yolks of four eggs, beaten together with a cupful of sugar. Dissolve half an ounce of gelatin or isinglass in half a teacupful of warm water; when it is dissolved, stir in a pint of boiling hot cream; add the beaten yolks and sugar; cook all together until it begins to thicken, then remove from the fire and add the other pint of cold cream, whipped to a stiff froth, adding a little at a time, and beating hard. Season with vanilla or lemon. Whip the whites of the eggs for the top. Dip the mold in cold water before filling; set it in a cold place. To this could be added almonds (pounded), grated chocolate, peaches, pineapples, strawberries, raspberries, or any other seasonable fruit.

CREAM FOR FRUIT

This recipe is an excellent substitute for pure cream, to be eaten on fresh berries and fruit.

One cupful of sweet milk; heat it until boiling. Beat together the whites of two eggs, a tablespoonful of white sugar, and a piece of butter the size of a nutmeg. Now add half a cupful of cold milk and a teaspoonful of cornstarch; stir well together until very light and smooth, then add it to the boiling milk; cook it until it thickens; it must not boil. Set it aside to cool. It should be of the consistency of real fresh cream. Serve in a creamer.

184

STRAWBERRY SPONGE

One quart of strawberries, half a package of gelatin, one cupful and a half of water, one cupful of sugar, the juice of a lemon, the whites of four eggs. Soak the gelatin for two hours in half a cupful of the water. Mash the strawberries and add half the sugar to them. Boil the remainder of the sugar and the water gently twenty minutes. Rub the strawberries through a sieve. Add the gelatin to the boiling syrup and take from the fire immediately; then add the strawberries. Place in a pan of ice water and beat five minutes. Add the whites of eggs and beat until the mixture begins to thicken. Pour in the molds and set away to harden. Serve with sugar and cream. Raspberry and blackberry sponges are made in the same way.

APPLE SNOW

Stew some fine-flavored sour apples tender, sweeten to taste, strain them through a fine wire sieve, and break into one pint of strained apples the white of an egg; whisk the apple and egg very briskly till quite stiff, and it will be as white as snow. Eaten with a nice boiled custard it makes a very desirable dessert. More eggs may be used, if liked.

ORANGE TRIFLE

Take the thin parings from the outside of a dozen oranges and put to steep in a wide-mouthed bottle; cover them with good cognac and let them stand twenty-four hours. Skin and seed the oranges and reduce them to a pulp; press this through a sieve, sugar to taste, arrange in a dish, and heap with whipped cream flavored with the orange brandy. Ice two hours before serving.

LEMON TRIFLE

The juice of two lemons and grated peel of one; one pint of cream, well sweetened and whipped stiff; one cupful of sherry; a little nutmeg. Let sugar, lemon juice, and peel lie together two hours before you add wine and nutmeg. Strain through double tarlatan, and whip gradually into the frothed cream. Serve very soon heaped in small glasses. Nice with cake.

185

GOOSEBERRY TRIFLE

One quart of gooseberries, sugar to taste, one pint of custard, a plateful of whipped cream.

Put the gooseberries into a jar, with sufficient moist sugar to sweeten them, and boil them until reduced to a pulp. Put this pulp at the bottom of a trifle dish; pour over it a pint of custard, and when cold, cover with whipped cream. The cream should be whipped the day before it is wanted for table, as it will then be so much firmer and more solid. This dish may be garnished as fancy dictates.

STRAWBERRY CHARLOTTE

Make a boiled custard of one quart of milk, the yolks of six eggs, and three-quarters of a cupful of sugar. Flavor to taste. Line a glass fruit dish with slices of sponge cake dipped in sweet cream; lay upon this ripe strawberries sweetened to taste, then a layer of cake and strawberries as before. When the custard is cold, pour over the whole. Now beat the whites of the eggs to a stiff froth, add a tablespoonful of sugar to each egg, and put over the top. Decorate the top with the largest berries saved out at the commencement.

Raspberry Charlotte may be made the same way.

COUNTRY PLUM CHARLOTTE

Stone a quart of ripe plums; first stew and then sweeten them. Cut slices of bread and butter and lay them in the bottom and around the sides of a large bowl or deep dish. Pour in the plums boiling hot; cover the bowl and set it away to cool gradually. When quite cold, send it to table and eat it with cream.

CHARLOTTE RUSSE

Whip one quart of rich cream to a stiff froth, and drain well on a nice sieve. To one scant pint of milk add six eggs beaten very light; make very sweet; flavor high with vanilla. Cook over hot water till it is a thick custard. Soak one full ounce of gelatin in a very little water, and warm it over hot water. When the custard is very cold, beat in lightly the gelatin and the whipped cream. Line the bottom of your mold with buttered paper, the side with sponge cake or ladyfingers fastened together with the white of an egg. Fill with the cream, put in a cold place or, in summer, on ice. To turn out, dip the mold for a moment in hot water. In draining the whipped cream, all that drips through can be rewhipped.

ORANGE CHARLOTTE

One-third each a box of gelatin, a cup of cold water, a cup of boiling water, and one cup sugar, the juice of one lemon, and one cup of orange juice and pulp, a little grated orange peel and the whites of four eggs. Soak the gelatin in the cold water one hour. Pour the boiling water over the lemon and orange juice, cover it and let stand half an hour; then add the sugar, let it come to a boil on the fire, stir in the gelatin, and when it is thoroughly dissolved, take from the fire. When cool enough, beat into it the four beaten whites of egg, turn into the mold and set in a cold place to stiffen, first placing pieces of sponge cake all around the mold.

BLANC MANGE

In one-half teacupful of water boil until dissolved one-half ounce of clarified isinglass (or patent gelatin, which is better) and stir it continually while boiling. Then squeeze the juice of one-half lemon upon one-half cupful of fine, white sugar. Stir the sugar into a pint of rich cream and one-quarter pint of Madeira or Sherry wine. When it is well mixed, add the dissolved isinglass or gelatin; stir all well together and pour into molds previously wet with cold water. Set the molds upon ice and let them stand until contents are hard and cold, then serve with sugar and cream or custard sauce.

HOLIDAY SNOW PUDDING WITH HOLLY SAUCE ☆

One package lime-flavored gelatin dissolved in three-fourths cup hot water. Add one cup canned pineapple juice. Chill until it begins to thicken, then fold in three stiffly beaten egg whites. Chill until set. Serve in individual dishes with the following sauce:

HOLLY SAUCE

Three egg yolks beaten with one-half cup sugar. Add slowly one-half cup scalded milk. Place in double boiler and, beating constantly, cook

187

over hot (not boiling) water until mixture coats spoon. Remove at once and add one-half teaspoon vanilla, one-fourth teaspoon orange extract and one-half cup chopped maraschino cherries. Chill thoroughly before serving. This dessert can be made a day or so in advance to avoid the Christmas rush. Serves four.

"For years my mother, back home in Ohio, has served Holiday Snow Pudding on Christmas Day. In my mind's eye, it *is* Christmas—light and refreshing after a heavy meal—and it looks festive."—*Mrs. John E. Smith*

Ice Cream and Ices

ICE CREAM

One pint of milk, the yolks of two eggs, six ounces of sugar, and one tablespoonful of cornstarch. Scald, but do not boil. Then put the whites of the two eggs into a pint of cream; whip it. Mix the milk and cream, flavor and freeze. One teaspoonful of vanilla or lemon is sufficient.

The quantity, of course, can be increased to any amount desired, so long as the relative proportions of the different ingredients are observed.

PURE ICE CREAM

Genuine ice cream is made of the pure sweet cream in this proportion: two quarts of cream, one pound of sugar. Beat up, flavor, and freeze.

For family use, select one of the new patent freezers, as being more rapid and less laborious for small quantities than the old style turned entirely by hand. All conditions being perfect, those with crank and revolving dashers effect freezing in eight to fifteen minutes.

FRUIT ICE CREAM

Ingredients—To every pint of fruit juice allow one pint of cream; add sugar to taste.

Let the fruit be well ripened; pick it off the stalks and put it into a large earthen pan. Stir it about with a wooden spoon, breaking it until it is well mashed; then, with the back of the spoon, rub it through a hair sieve. Sweeten it nicely with pounded sugar; whip the cream for a few minutes, add it to the fruit, and whisk the whole again for another five minutes. Put the mixture into the freezer and freeze. Raspberry, strawberry, currant, and all fruit ice creams are made in the same manner. A little pounded sugar sprinkled over the fruit before it is mashed assists to extract the juice. In winter, when fresh fruit is not obtainable, a little jam may be substituted for it; it should be melted and worked through a sieve before being added to the whipped cream; and if the color should not be good, a little prepared cochineal may be put in to improve its appearance.

In making berry flavoring for ice cream, the milk should never be heated; the juice of the berries added to *cold* cream, or fresh, rich milk, mixed with *cold* cream, the juice put in just before freezing, or when partly frozen.

CHOCOLATE ICE CREAM

Add four ounces of grated chocolate to a cupful of sweet milk, then mix it thoroughly to a quart of thick, sweet cream; no flavoring is required but vanilla. Sweeten with a cupful of sugar; beat again and freeze.

CUSTARD ICE CREAM

Sweeten one quart of cream or rich milk with half a pound of sugar, and flavor to taste. Put it over the fire in a farina kettle. As soon as it begins to boil, stir into it a tablespoonful of cornstarch or rice flour which has been previously mixed smooth with a little milk. After it has boiled a few minutes, take it off the fire and stir in very gradually six eggs which have been beaten until thick. When quite cold, freeze the mixture as you would freeze ice cream.

STRAWBERRY ICE CREAM

Mix a cupful of sugar with a quart of ripe strawberries, let them stand half a day, then mash and strain them through a coarse towel, then add to the juice a full cupful of sugar, and when dissolved, beat in a quart of fresh, thick cream. Raspberries, pineapple and other fruits are made the same way.

189

FRUIT CREAM

Make a rich, boiled custard; flavor with wine and vanilla; pour into a freezer. When half frozen, add pounded almonds, chopped citron and brandy, peaches or chopped raisins. Have the freezer half full of custard and fill up with the fruit. Mix well, and freeze again. Almost any kind of fruit that is preferred may be substituted for the above.

TUTTI FRUTTI ICE CREAM

Take two quarts of the richest cream and add to it one pound of pulverized sugar and four whole eggs. Mix well together. Place on the fire, stirring constantly, and just bring to boiling point; now remove immediately and continue to stir until nearly cold. Flavor with a tablespoonful of extract of vanilla. Place in freezer, and when half frozen, mix thoroughly into it one pound of preserved fruits, in equal parts of peaches, apricots, gages, cherries, pineapples, etc.; all of these fruits are to be cut up into small pieces, and mixed well with the frozen cream. If you desire to *mold* this ice, sprinkle it with a little carmine dissolved in a teaspoonful of water with two drops of spirits of ammonia; mix in this color, so that it will be streaky, or in veins like marble.

ICE CREAM WITHOUT A FREEZER

Beat the yolks of eight eggs very light, and add thereto four cupfuls of sugar, and stir well. Add to this, little by little, one quart of rich milk that has been heated almost to boiling, beating all the while; then put in the whites of eight eggs beaten to a stiff froth. Then boil the mixture in a pail set inside another containing hot water. Boil about fifteen minutes, or until it is as thick as a boiled custard, stirring steadily meanwhile. Pour into a bowl to cool. When quite cold, beat into it three pints of rich sweet cream and five teaspoonfuls of vanilla, or such other flavoring as you prefer. Put it into a pail having a close-fitting cover and pack in pounded ice and salt—*rock salt*, not the common kind—about three-fourths ice and one-fourth salt. When packed, before putting the ice on top of the cover, beat the custard as you would batter, for five minutes steady; then put on the cover and put the ice and salt over it, and cover the whole with a thick mat, blanket, or carpet, and let it stand for an hour. Then carefully uncover and scrape from the bottom and sides of the pail the thick coating of frozen custard, making every particle clear, and beat again very hard, until the custard is smooth, half-congealed paste. Do this thoroughly. Put on the cover, ice, salt, and blanket, and leave it for five or six hours, replenishing the ice and salt if necessary.—*Common Sense in the Household*

DOUGLAS LAKE RED RASPBERRY ICE CREAM ☆

Cook one pint red raspberries and one-fourth cup water till berries are tender. Add one and a quarter cups sugar; stir in one envelope plain gelatin which has been dissolved in one-fourth cup cold water. Cool. Chill till solid. Whip a half pint whipping cream till stiff. Beat raspberries till light and frothy; fold whipped cream into raspberries. Freeze; stir occasionally while freezing. (Raspberries may be rubbed through a sieve.)

BLACK CHERRY SAUCE FOR ICE CREAM ☆

Boil syrup from canned dark, sweet cherries with a strip of lemon peel and a dash of cinnamon until reduced to one-half cup. Remove peel, and add one-third cup port wine and the cherries which have been pitted. Serve warm over vanilla ice cream.

Preserves

In the old way of preserving we used pound for pound when fruits were kept in stone jars or crocks. Now, as most preserves are put up in sealed jars or cans, less sugar seems sufficient. Three-quarters of a pound is generally all that is required for a pound of fruit.

Fruit should be boiled in a porcelain-lined or graniteware dish if possible; other utensils, copper or metal, if made bright and clean, may answer as well.

There cannot be too much care taken in selecting fruit for jellies, for if the fruit is overripe, any amount of time in boiling will never make it jell. This is where so many fail in making good jelly. Another important matter is overlooked—that of carefully skimming off the juice after it begins to boil and a scum rises from the bottom to the top. The juice should not be stirred but the scum carefully taken off. If allowed to boil under, the jelly will not be clear.

When preserves or canned fruits show any indications of fermentation, they should be immediately reboiled with more sugar to save them. It is much better to be generous with the sugar at first than to have any losses afterwards. Keep all preserves in a cool, dry closet.

TO CLARIFY JELLY

The white of eggs is perhaps the best substance that can be employed in clarifying jelly, as well as some other fluids, for the reason that when albumen (and the white of eggs is nearly pure albumen) is put into a liquid that is muddy from substances suspended in it, on boiling the liquid the albumen coagulates in a flocculent manner and, entangling with the impurities, rises with them to the surface as a scum or sinks to the bottom, according to their weight.

PRESERVED CHERRIES

Take large, ripe Morella cherries. Weigh them and to each pound allow a pound of loaf sugar. Stone the cherries (opening them with a sharp quill) and save the juice that comes from them in the process. As you stone them, throw them into a large pan or tureen and strew about half the sugar over them; let them lie in it an hour or two after they are all stoned. Then put them into a preserving kettle with the remainder of the sugar and boil and skim them till the fruit is clear and the syrup thick.

TO PRESERVE BERRIES WHOLE

Buy the fruit when not too ripe, pick over immediately, wash if absolutely necessary, and put in glass jars, filling each one about two-thirds full.

Put in the preserving kettle a pound of sugar and one cupful of water for every two pounds of fruit, and let it come slowly to a boil. Pour this syrup into the jars over the berries, filling them up to the brim, then set the jars in a pot of cold water on the stove and let the water boil and the fruit become scalding hot. Now take them out and seal perfectly tight. If this process is followed thoroughly, the fruit will keep for several years.

PRESERVED GREEN TOMATOES

Take one peck of green tomatoes. Slice six fresh lemons without removing the skins, but taking out the seeds; put to this quantity six pounds of sugar, common white, and boil until transparent and the syrup thick. Ginger root may be added, if liked.

PRESERVED APPLES (WHOLE)

Peel and core large firm apples (pippins are best). Throw them into water as you pare them. Boil the parings in water for fifteen minutes, allowing a pint to one pound of fruit. Then strain, and adding three-quarters of a pound of sugar to each pint of water, as measured at first, with enough lemon peel, orange peel, or mace to impart a pleasant flavor, return to the kettle. When the syrup has been well skimmed and is clear, pour it boiling hot over the apples, which must be drained from the water in which they have hitherto stood. Let them remain in the syrup until both are perfectly cold. Then, covering closely, let them simmer over a slow fire until transparent. When all the minutiae of these directions are attended to, the fruit will remain unbroken, and present a beautiful and inviting appearance.

PRESERVING FRUIT—NEW MODE [*in 1887*]

Housekeepers who dislike the tedious, old-time fashion of clarifying sugar and boiling the fruit will appreciate the following recipes, no fire being needed in their preparation. The first is for "tutti frutti," and has been repeatedly tested with unvarying success.

Put one quart of white, preserving, fine Batavia brandy into a two-gallon stone jar that has a tightly fitting top. Then for every pound of fruit, in prime condition and perfectly dry, which you put in the brandy, use three-quarters of a pound of granulated sugar. Stir every day so that the sugar will be dissolved, using a clean, wooden spoon kept for the purpose. Every sort of fruit may be used, beginning with strawberries and ending with plums. Be sure and have at least one pound of black cherries, as they make the color of the preserve very rich. Strawberries, raspberries, blackberries, apricots, cherries (sweet and sour), peaches, plums, are all used, and, if you like, currants and grapes. Plums and grapes should be peeled and seeded, apricots and peaches peeled and cut in quarters or eighths or diced; cherries also must be seeded; quinces may be steamed until tender. The jar must be kept in a cool, dry place, and the daily stirring must never be forgotten, for that is the secret of success. You may use as much of one sort of fruit as you like, and it may be put in from day to day, just as you happen to have it. Half the quantity of spirits may be used. The preserve will be ready for use within a week after the last fruit is put in, and will keep for a number of months. We have found it good eight months after making.

NEW METHOD OF PRESERVING FRUIT [*in 1887*]

A new method of preserving fruit is practiced in England. Pears, apples, and other fruits are reduced to a paste by jamming, which is then pressed into cakes and gently dried. When required for use, it is only necessary to pour four times their weight of boiling water over them, and allow them to soak for twenty minutes, and then add sugar to suit the taste. The fine flavor of the fruit is said to be retained to perfection. The cost of the prepared product is scarcely greater than that of the original fruit, differing with the supply and price of the latter; the keeping qualities are excellent, so that it may be had at any time of the year, and bears long sea voyages without detriment. No peeling or coring is required, so there is no waste.

APPLE JELLY

Select apples that are rather tart and highly flavored; slice them without paring; place them in a porcelain preserving kettle, cover them with water, and let them cook slowly until the apples look red. Pour into a colander, drain off the juice, and let this run through a jelly bag. Return to the kettle, which must be carefully washed, and boil half an hour. Measure it and allow to every pint of juice a pound of sugar and half the juice of a lemon; boil quickly for ten minutes.

The juice of apples, boiled in shallow vessels without a particle of sugar, makes the most sparkling, delicious jelly imaginable. Red apples will give jelly the color and clearness of claret, while that from light fruit is like amber. Take the cider just as it is made, not allowing it to ferment at all, and, if possible, boil it in a pan, flat, very large, and shallow.

> "*Give a husband what he likes*
> *And save a thousand household strikes.*"

194

CALF'S FOOT JELLY

Wash and prepare four calf's feet, place them in four quarts of water, and let them simmer gently five hours. At the expiration of this time take them out and pour the liquid into a vessel to cool; there should be nearly a quart. When cold, remove every particle of fat, replace the jelly into the preserving kettle, and add one pound of loaf sugar, the rind and juice of two lemons; when the sugar has dissolved, beat two eggs with their shells in one gill of water, which pour into the kettle, and boil five minutes, or until perfectly clear; then add one gill of Madeira wine and strain through a flannel bag into any form you like.

WINE JELLY

One package of gelatin and one cupful of cold water soaked together two hours. Add to this three cupfuls of sugar, the juice of three lemons, and the grated rind of one. Now pour over this a quart of boiling water and stir until dissolved, then add a pint of sherry wine. Strain through a napkin, turn into molds dipped in cold water and place in the ice box for several hours.

One good way to mold this jelly is to pour some of it into the mold, harden it a little, put in a layer of strawberries or raspberries, or any fresh fruit in season, pour in jelly to set them; after they have set, another layer of jelly, then another of berries, and so fill each mold, alternating with jelly and berries.

STRAWBERRY JAM

To each pound of fine and not too ripe berries, allow three-quarters of a pound of sugar. Put them into a preserving pan, and stir gently, not to break up the fruit; simmer for one-half hour, and put into pots air-tight. An excellent way to seal jellies and jams is as the German women do: Cut round covers from writing paper a half inch too large for the tops, smear the inside with the unbeaten white of an egg, tie over with a cord, and it will dry quickly and be absolutely preservative. A circular paper dipped in brandy, and laid over the toothsome contents before covering, will prevent any dampness from affecting the flavor. These covers heavy with mold have been removed, to find the preserve intact.

195

BRANDIED PEACHES OR PEARS

Four pounds of fruit, four pounds of sugar, one pint of best white brandy. Make a syrup of the sugar and enough water to dissolve it. Let this come to a boil; put the fruit in and boil five minutes. Having removed the fruit carefully, let the syrup boil fifteen minutes longer, or until it thickens well; add the brandy, and take the kettle at once from the fire; pour the hot syrup over the fruit, and seal. If, after the fruit is taken from the fire, a reddish liquor oozes from it, drain this off before adding the clear syrup. Put up in glass jars. Peaches and pears should be peeled for brandying. Plums should be pricked and watched carefully for fear of bursting.

A NEW WAY OF KEEPING FRUIT

It is stated that experiments have been made in keeping fruit in jars covered only with cotton batting, and that at the end of two years the fruit was sound. The following directions are given for the process: Use crocks, stone butter jars, or any other convenient dishes. Prepare and cook the fruit precisely as for canning in glass jars; fill your dishes with fruit while hot; and immediately cover with cotton batting, securely tied on. Remember that all putrefaction is caused by the invisible creatures in the air. Cooking the fruit expels all these, and they cannot pass through the cotton batting. The fruit thus protected will keep an indefinite period. It will be remembered that Tyndall has proved that the atmospheric germs cannot pass through a layer of cotton.

[*Note:* I don't know who Tyndall was, but I hope not many 1887 readers tried this canning method!]

MACEDOINES

Suspend in the center of the jelly mold a bunch of grapes, cherries, berries, or currants on their stems, sections of oranges, pineapples, or brandied fruits, and pour in a little jelly when quite cold, but not set. It makes a very agreeable effect. By a little ingenuity you can imbed first one fruit and then another, arranging in circles, and pour a little jelly successively over each. Do not reheat the jelly, but keep it in a warm place while the mold is on ice and the first layers are hardening.

Use it up, wear it out, make it do or do without.

CANNED BOILED CIDER

Boiled cider, in our grandmother's time, was indispensable to the making of good "mince pie," adding the proper flavor and richness, which cannot be substituted by any other ingredient, and a gill of which being added to a rule of "fruit cake" makes it more moist, keeps longer, and is far superior to fruit cake made without it. Boiled cider is an article rarely found in the market nowadays, but can be made by anyone, with but little trouble and expense, using *sweet* cider, shortly after it is made, and before fermentation takes place. Place five quarts of *sweet* cider in a porcelain-lined kettle over the fire, boil it slowly until reduced to one quart, carefully watching that it does not burn; turn into glass jars while hot, and seal tightly, the same as canned fruit. It is then ready to use any time of the year.

PEACH BUTTER

Pare ripe peaches and put them in a preserving kettle with sufficient water to boil them soft, then sift through a colander, removing the stones. To each quart of peaches put one and one-half pounds of sugar, and boil very slowly one hour. Stir often, and do not let them burn. Put in stone or glass jars, and keep in a cool place.

STRAWBERRY CONSERVE

Prepare the fruit as for preserving, allowing half a pound of loaf sugar to one pound of fruit. Sprinkle the sugar over the fruit at night; in the morning, put it on the fire in a kettle and boil until the berries are clear. Spread on dishes and put in the sun until dry; after which, roll the fruit in sugar and pack it in jars.

PEACH CONSERVE

Halve the peaches and take out the stones. Pare them. Have ready some powdered white sugar on a plate or dish. Roll the peaches in it several times, until they will not take up any more. Place them singly on a plate, with the cup or hollow side up, that the juices may not run out. Lay them in the sun. The next morning roll them again. As soon as the juice seems set in the peaches, turn the other side to the sun.

197

When they are thoroughly dry, pack them in glass jars, or, what is still nicer, fig drums. They make an excellent sweetmeat just as they are; or if wanted for table use, put over the fire in porcelain, with a very little water, and stew a few minutes.

PEACH LEATHER

Stew as many peaches as you choose, allowing a quarter of a pound of sugar to one of fruit. Mash it up smooth as it cooks, and when it is dry enough to spread in a thin sheet on a board greased with butter, set it out in the sun to dry; when dry, it can be rolled up like leather, wrapped up in a cloth, and will keep perfectly from season to season. School children regard it as a delightful addition to their lunch of biscuit or cold bread. Apple and quince leather are made in the same fashion, only a little flavoring or spice is added to them.

CRYSTALLIZED FRUIT

Pick out the finest of any kind of fruit; leave on their stalks; beat the whites of three eggs to a stiff froth; lay the fruit in the beaten egg with the stalks upward; drain them. (Beat the egg that drips off again.) Select fruit out, one by one, and dip into a cup of finely powdered sugar; cover a pan with a sheet of fine paper; place fruit inside it, and put it in an oven that is cooling. When icing on fruit becomes firm, pile them on a dish and set them in a cool place. For this purpose, oranges or lemons should be carefully pared, and all the white inner skin removed that is possible to prevent bitterness; then cut lemons in thin, horizontal slices and oranges in quarters. Choose largest and finest cherries, strawberries, currants, etc., leaving stems out. Peaches should be pared and cut in halves, and sweet, juicy pears may be treated in the same way, or they look nicely when pared, leaving on the stems. Pineapples should be cut in thin slices and these, again, divided into quarters.

[*Note:* Remember, "powdered sugar" did not necessarily mean confectioner's sugar. Probably granulated sugar was used here, as we use it today to frost grapes.]

There should be a law to fine the man at hotels who uses a slice of bread to collect the last drop of soup.—The Elite News, 1887

Seasonings

KITCHEN PEPPER

Mix one ounce ginger, half an ounce each of black pepper, ground cinnamon, nutmeg and allspice, one teaspoonful of ground cloves, and six ounces of salt. Keep in a tightly corked bottle.

HERBS FOR WINTER

To prepare herbs for winter use, such as sage, summer savory, thyme, mint, or any of the sweet herbs, they should be gathered fresh in their season, or procured from the market. Examine them well, throwing out all poor sprigs; then wash and shake them; tie into small bundles, and tie over the bundles a piece of netting or old lace (to keep off the dust); hang up in a warm, dry place, the leaves downward. In a few days the herb will be thoroughly dry and brittle. Or you may place them in a cool oven and let them remain in it until perfectly dry. Then pick off all the leaves, and the tender tops of the stems; put them in a clean, large-mouthed bottle that is perfectly dry. When wanted for use, rub fine and sift through a sieve. It is much better to put them in bottles as soon as dried, as long exposure to the air causes them to lose strength and flavor.

HOMEMADE TABLE VINEGAR

Put in an open cask four gallons of warm rain water, one gallon of common molasses, and two quarts of yeast. Cover the top with thin muslin and leave it in the sun, covering it up at night and when it rains. In three or four weeks it will be good vinegar. If cider can be used in place of rain water, the vinegar will make much sooner—will not take more than a week to make a very sharp vinegar. Excellent for pickling purposes.

VERY STRONG TABLE VINEGAR

Take two gallons of good cider and thoroughly mix it with two pounds of new honey. Pour into your cask or bottle and let it stand from four to

199

six months, when you will have vinegar so strong that it cannot be used at table without diluting with water. It is the best ever procured for pickling purposes.

FLAVORED VINEGARS

Almost all the flavorings used for meats and salads may be prepared in vinegar with little trouble and expense, and will be found useful to impart an acid to flavors when lemons are not at hand.

Tarragon, sweet basil, burnet, green mint, sage, thyme, sweet marjoram, etc., may be prepared by putting three ounces of either of these herbs, when in blossom, into one gallon of sharp vinegar; let stand ten days, strain off clear, and bottle for use.

Celery and cayenne may be prepared, using three ounces of the seed as above.

HORSE-RADISH

Horse-radish is an agreeable relish and has a particularly fresh taste in spring. Scrape fine or grate and set on the table, providing hard-boiled eggs cut in halves or slices, oil, and other ingredients, to be mixed at table to individual taste.

CURRY POWDER

To make curry powder, take one ounce of ginger, one ounce of mustard, one ounce of pepper, three ounces of coriander seed, three ounces of turmeric, half an ounce of cardamoms, one-quarter ounce of cummin seed. Pound all these ingredients very fine in a mortar; sift them and cork tight in a bottle.

This can be had already prepared at most druggists, and it is much less trouble to purchase it than to make it at home.

TO BROWN BUTTER

Put a lump of butter into a hot frying pan, and toss it about until it browns. Stir brown flour into it until it is smooth and begins to boil. Use it for coloring gravies, and sauces for meats.

TO BROWN FLOUR

Spread flour upon a tin pie plate, set it upon the stove or in a *very* hot oven, and stir continually after it begins to color, until it is brown all through.

Keep it always on hand; put away in glass jars covered closely. It is excellent for coloring and thickening many dishes.

FRENCH MUSTARD

Three tablespoonfuls of dry mustard, one tablespoonful of granulated sugar, well worked together, then beat in an egg until it is smooth, add one teacupful of vinegar, a little at a time, working it all smooth; then set on the stove and cook three or four minutes, stirring all the time; when cool, add one tablespoonful of the best olive oil, taking care to get it all thoroughly worked in and smooth. You will find this very nice.

PREPARED COCONUT [*for Pies, Puddings, etc.*]

To prepare coconut for future use: first cut a hole through the meat at one of the holes in the end, draw off the milk, then loosen the meat by pounding the nut well on all sides. Crack the nut and take out the meat, and place the pieces of meat in a cool open oven overnight, or, for a few hours, to dry; then grate it. If there is more grated than is needed for present use, sprinkle it with sugar, and spread out in a cool dry place. When dry enough, put away in dry cans or bottles. Will keep for weeks.

TO CLARIFY BEEF DRIPPINGS

Drippings accumulated from different cooked meats of beef or veal can be clarified by putting it into a basin and slicing into it a raw potato, allowing it to boil long enough for the potato to brown, which causes all impurities to disappear. Remove from the fire, and when cool, drain it off from the sediment that settles at the bottom. Turn it into basins or small jars and set it in a cool place for future use. When mixed with an equal amount of butter, it answers the same purpose as clear butter for frying and basting any meats excepting game and poultry.

Mutton drippings impart an unpleasant flavor to anything cooked outside of its kind.

Sauces

In making a good sauce but little merit can be claimed when the house-keeper or cook has plenty of good and proper materials on hand; but it is when a fine flavor has been produced from an inadequate supply that praise is justly due; as, for instance, giving a rich flavor of meat to a mess of potatoes or some other plain dish when no meat has been employed. But to do this it is necessary to know the qualities of the various vegetables, and how these may be made to resemble the juice of animal food. The vegetable products of which by far the most can be made by a skillful housekeeper are onions, mushrooms and carrots, which may be dressed so exquisitely as hardly to be distinguished from the gravy of beef.

MUSHROOM SAUCE .

Wash a pint of small button mushrooms, remove the stems and outside skins, stew them slowly in veal gravy or milk or cream, adding an onion and seasoning with pepper, salt, and a little butter rolled in flour. Their flavor will be heightened by salting a few the night before, to extract the juice. In dressing mushrooms, only those of a dull pearl color on the outside and the under part tinged with pale pink should be selected. If there is a poisonous one among them, the onion in the sauce will turn black. In such a case throw the whole away.

DRAWN BUTTER

Melted butter is the foundation of most of the common sauces. Have a covered saucepan for this purpose. One lined with porcelain will be best. Take a quarter of a pound of the best fresh butter, cut it up, and mix with it about one tablespoonful of flour. When it is thoroughly mixed, put it into the saucepan, and add to it half a teacupful of hot water. Cover the saucepan and set it in a large tin of boiling water. Shake it round continually (always moving it the same way) till it is entirely melted and begins to simmer. Then let it rest till it boils up.

If you set it on too hot a fire, it will be oily.

If the butter and flour are not well mixed, it will be lumpy.

202

If you put too much water, it will be thin and poor. All these defects are to be carefully avoided.

In melting butter for sweet or pudding sauce, you may use milk instead of water.

TARTARE SAUCE

The raw yolks of two eggs, half a teacupful of pure olive oil, three tablespoonfuls of vinegar, one of made mustard, one teaspoonful of sugar, a quarter of a teaspoonful of pepper, one teaspoonful of salt, one of onion juice, one tablespoonful of chopped capers, one of chopped cucumber pickle. Put together the same as mayonnaise dressing, adding the chopped ingredients the last thing.

This sauce is good for fried or boiled fish, boiled tongue, fish salad, and may be used with fried and broiled meats.

WHITE SAUCE

Melt two tablespoons butter; blend in two tablespoons flour over low heat. Add salt. Add milk gradually, stirring continually until white sauce is thickened and smooth.

EGG SAUCE, OR WHITE SAUCE

Mix two tablespoonfuls of sifted flour with half a teacup of warm butter. Place over the fire a saucepan containing a pint of sweet milk and a saltspoon of salt, and a dash of white pepper; when it reaches the boiling point, add the butter and flour, stirring briskly until it thickens and becomes like cream. Have ready three cold, hard-boiled eggs, sliced and chopped; add them to the sauce; let them heat through thoroughly, and serve in a boat. If you have plenty of cream, use it and omit the butter. By omitting the eggs, you have the same as White Sauce.

FISH SAUCE

Make a pint of drawn butter. Add one tablespoonful of pepper sauce or Worcestershire sauce, a little salt, and six hard-boiled eggs, chopped fine. Pour over boiled fish and garnish with sliced lemon. Very nice.

203

CAPER SAUCE

Chop the capers a very little, unless quite small. Make half a pint of drawn butter, to which add the capers, with a large spoonful of the juice from the bottle in which they are sold. Let it just simmer, and serve in a tureen. Nasturtiums much resemble capers in taste, though larger, and may be used, and, in fact, are preferred by many. They are grown on a climbing vine and are cultivated for their blossom and for pickling. When used as capers they should be chopped more. If neither capers nor nasturtiums are at hand, some pickles chopped up form a very good substitute in the sauce.

BREAD SAUCE

One cup of stale bread crumbs, one onion, two ounces of butter, pepper and salt, a little mace. Cut the onion fine and boil it in milk till quite soft; then strain the milk on to the stale bread crumbs, and let it stand an hour. Put it in a saucepan with the boiled onion, pepper, salt, and mace. Give it a boil and serve in a sauce tureen. This sauce can also be used for grouse, and is very nice. Roast partridges are nice served with bread crumbs fried brown in butter, with cranberry or currant jelly laid beside them in the platter.

CHILI SAUCE

Boil together two dozen ripe tomatoes, three small green peppers, or a half teaspoonful of cayenne pepper, one onion cut fine, half a cup of sugar. Boil until thick; then add two cups of vinegar; then strain the whole, set back on the fire, and add a tablespoonful of salt and a teaspoonful each of ginger, allspice, cloves, and cinnamon. Boil all five minutes, remove, and seal in glass bottles. This is very nice.

MINT SAUCE

Take fresh young spearmint leaves, stripped from the stems; wash and drain them, or dry on a cloth. Chop very fine, put in a gravy boat, and to three tablespoonfuls of mint put two of white sugar; mix and let it stand a few minutes, then pour over it six tablespoonfuls of good cider or white-wine vinegar. The sauce should be made some time before it is to be used, so that the flavor of the mint may be well extracted. Fine with roast lamb.

SHARP BROWN SAUCE

Put in a saucepan one tablespoonful of chopped onion, three tablespoonfuls of good cider vinegar, six tablespoonfuls of water, three of tomato catsup, a little pepper and salt, half a cup of melted butter, in which stir a tablespoonful of sifted flour. Put all together and boil until it thickens. This is most excellent with boiled meats, fish, and poultry.

BÉCHAMEL SAUCE

Put three tablespoonfuls of butter in a saucepan; add three tablespoonfuls of sifted flour, a quarter of a teaspoonful of nutmeg, ten peppercorns, a teaspoonful of salt; beat all well together; then add to this, three slices of onion, two slices of carrot, two sprigs of parsley, two of thyme, a bay leaf, and half a dozen mushrooms cut up. Moisten the whole with a pint of stock or water and a cup of sweet cream. Set it on the stove and cook slowly for half an hour, watching closely that it does not burn; then strain through a sieve. Most excellent with roast veal, meats, and fish.—*St. Charles Hotel, New Orleans*

MAÎTRE D'HÔTEL

Make a teacupful of drawn butter; add to it the juice of a lemon, two tablespoonfuls of minced onion, three tablespoonfuls of chopped parsley, a teaspoonful of powdered thyme or summer savory, a pinch of cayenne and salt. Simmer over the fire, and stir well. Excellent with all kinds of fish.

WINE SAUCE FOR GAME

Half a glass of currant jelly, half a glass of port wine, half a glass of water, a tablespoonful of cold butter, a teaspoonful of salt, the juice of half a lemon, a pinch of cayenne pepper, and three cloves. Simmer all together a few minutes, adding the wine after it is strained. A few spoonfuls of the gravy from the game may be added to it. This sauce is especially nice with venison.

205

HOLLANDAISE SAUCE

Half a teacupful of butter, the juice of half a lemon, the yolks of two eggs, a speck of cayenne pepper, half a cupful of boiling water, half a teaspoonful of salt. Beat the butter to a cream, add the yolks of eggs one by one, then the lemon juice, pepper, and salt, beating all thoroughly. Place the bowl in which is the mixture in a saucepan of boiling water. Beat with an egg beater until it begins to thicken, which will be in about a minute; then add the boiling water, beating all the time; stir until it begins to thicken like soft custard; stir a few minutes after taking from the fire. Be careful not to cook it too long. This is very nice with baked fish.

OLD-FASHIONED APPLE SAUCE

Pare and chop a dozen medium-sized apples, put them in a deep pudding dish, sprinkle over them a heaping coffee cupful of sugar and one of water. Place them in the oven and bake slowly two hours or more, or until they are a deep red-brown. Quite as nice as preserves.

RAISIN-NUT SAUCE ☆
[*served on baked ham or tongue*]

Mix one tablespoon flour with a quarter of a cup of firmly packed brown sugar. Add one cup water. Bring to boiling point. Add a quarter teaspoon salt, three tablespoons lemon juice, and half a cup of seedless raisins. Simmer five minutes. Then add a quarter of a cup of chopped nut meats and one tablespoon butter. Heat until butter melts.

"I grew up on this kind of Old Kentucky cookery and have served it myself to members of the armed forces all over the United States and Germany in the past eleven years. From airmen first class to at least one rear admiral, there has been never a complaint but usually requests for seconds."—*Mrs. Kenneth S. Mann*

Sweet Sauces

TEMPERANCE FOAM SAUCE

Beat up, as for hard sauce, white sugar with butter, until very light, in the proportion of half a cupful of butter to one cupful of sugar;

flavor with essence of lemon or bitter almonds. Fifteen minutes before serving, set the bowl in a pan of hot water and stir it till hot. It will rise in a white foam to the top of the bowl.

NUN BUTTER

Four ounces of butter, six ounces of sugar, as much wine as the butter will take. Beat the butter and sugar together, and gradually add the wine and a little nutmeg.

WINE SAUCE

Two ounces of butter, two teaspoonfuls of flour, half a pint of boiling water, one gill of Madeira wine, quarter of a pound of sugar, half a grated nutmeg. Mix the flour and butter together, pour in the boiling water, let it boil a few minutes; then add the sugar and wine. Just before going to table add the nutmeg. Serve hot.

BRANDY SAUCE, COLD

Two cupfuls of powdered sugar, half a cupful of butter, one wineglassful of brandy, cinnamon and nutmeg, a teaspoonful of each. Warm the butter slightly and work it to a light cream with the sugar, then add the brandy and spices, beat it hard and set aside until wanted. Should be put into a mold to look nicely and served on a flat dish.

BRANDY OR WINE SAUCE

Take one cupful of butter, two of powdered sugar, the whites of two eggs, five tablespoonfuls of sherry wine or brandy, and a quarter of a cupful of boiling water. Beat butter and sugar to a cream, add the whites of the eggs, one at a time, unbeaten, and then wine or brandy. Place the bowl in hot water and stir till smooth and frothy.

SAUCE FOR PLUM PUDDING

Cream together a cupful of sugar and half a cupful of butter; when light and creamy, add the well-beaten yolks of four eggs. Stir into this one wineglass of wine or one of brandy, a pinch of salt, and one large cupful of hot cream or rich milk. Beat this mixture well. Place it in a saucepan over the fire; stir it until it cooks sufficiently to thicken like cream. Be sure and not let it boil. Delicious.

LIQUID BRANDY SAUCE

Brown over the fire three tablespoonfuls of sugar; add a cupful of water, six whole cloves, a piece of stick cinnamon, the yellow rind of a lemon cut very thin. Let the sauce boil, strain while hot, then pour it into a sauce bowl containing the juice of the lemon and a cup of brandy. Serve warm.

GRANDMOTHER'S SAUCE

Cream together a cupful of sifted sugar and half a cupful of butter; add a teaspoonful of ground cinnamon and an egg well beaten. Boil a teacupful of milk and turn it, boiling hot, over the mixture slowly, stirring all the time; this will cook the egg smoothly. It may be served cold or hot.

CARAMEL SAUCE

Place over the fire a saucepan; when it begins to be hot, put into it four tablespoonfuls of white sugar and one tablespoonful of water. Stir it continually for three or four minutes until all the water evaporates; then watch it carefully until it becomes a delicate brown color. Have ready a pint of cold water and cup of sugar mixed with some flavoring; turn it into the saucepan with the browned sugar and let it simmer for ten minutes; then add half a glass of brandy or a glass of wine. The wine or brandy may be omitted if preferred.

ROSE BRANDY [*for cakes and puddings*]

Gather the leaves of roses while the dew is on them, and as soon as they open, put them into a wide-mouthed bottle, and when the bottle is full, pour in the best of fourth-proof French brandy.

It will be fit for use in three or four weeks, and may be frequently replenished. It is sometimes considered preferable to wine as a flavoring for pastries and pudding sauces.

LEMON BRANDY [*for cakes and puddings*]

When you use lemons for punch or lemonade, do not throw away the peels, but cut them in small pieces—the thin yellow outside (the thick part is not good)—and put them in a glass jar or bottle of brandy. You will find this brandy useful for many purposes.

In the same way keep for use the kernels of peach and plum stones, pounding them slightly before you put them into the brandy.

ORANGE SAUCE FOR WHITE CAKE ☆

¾ cup sugar
2 tablespoons flour
¼ teaspoon salt

1 teaspoon nutmeg
1 cup boiling water
1 tablespoon butter

Mix dry ingredients; slowly add water, then butter, stirring constantly. Simmer over low heat for five minutes until clear and thick, stirring all the while. Top slices of white cake with sliced fresh oranges (or canned mandarin oranges) and pour sauce over. Whipped cream may be used on each slice, too.

Pickles and Catsups

GENERAL REMARKS

Pickles should never be put into vessels of brass, copper, or tin, as the action of the acid on such metals often results in poisoning the pickles. Porcelain or graniteware is the best for such purposes.

Vinegar that is used for pickling should be the best cider or white-wine, and should never be boiled more than five or six minutes, as it reduces its strength. In putting away pickles, use stone or glass jars; the glazing of common earthenware is rendered injurious by the action of the vinegar. When the jar is nearly filled with the pickles, the vinegar should completely cover them, and if there is any appearance of their not doing well, turn off the vinegar and cover with fresh vinegar and spices. Alum in small quantities is useful when making pickles in strong ginger tea. Pickles should be kept closely covered, put into glass jars, and sealed tightly.

Turmeric is India ginger, and is used very much in pickling as a coloring.

A piece of horse-radish put into a jar of pickles will keep the vinegar from losing its strength, and the pickles will keep sound much longer, especially tomato pickles.

CUCUMBER PICKLES 1

Select the medium, small-sized cucumbers. For one bushel, make a brine that will bear up an egg; heat it boiling hot and pour it over the cucumbers; let them stand twenty-four hours, then wipe them dry; heat some vinegar boiling hot, and pour over them, standing again twenty-four hours. Now change the vinegar, putting on fresh vinegar, adding one quart of brown sugar, a pint of white mustard seed, a small handful of whole cloves, the same of cinnamon sticks, a piece of alum the size of an egg, half a cup of celery seed. Heat it all boiling hot and pour over the cucumbers.

CUCUMBER PICKLES 2 (FOR WINTER USE)

A good way to put down cucumbers, a few at a time:

When gathered from the vines, wash, and put in a firkin or half-barrel layers of cucumbers and rock salt alternately, enough salt to make sufficient brine to cover them, no water; cover with a cloth; keep them under the brine with a heavy board; take off the cloth, and rinse it every time you put in fresh cucumbers, as a scum will rise and settle upon it. Use plenty of salt and they will keep a year. To prepare pickles for use, soak them in hot water, and keep in a warm place until they are fresh enough, then pour spiced vinegar over them and let them stand overnight, then pour that off and put on fresh.

GREEN TOMATO PICKLES (SWEET)

One peck of green tomatoes, sliced the day before you are ready for pickling, sprinkling them through and through with salt, not *too* heavily. In the morning drain off the liquor that will drain from them. Have a dozen good-sized onions rather coarsely sliced; take a suitable kettle and put in a layer of the sliced tomatoes, then of onions, and between each layer sprinkle the following spices: six *red* peppers chopped coarsely, one cup of sugar, one tablespoonful of ground allspice, one tablespoonful of ground cinnamon, a teaspoonful of cloves, one tablespoonful of mustard. Turn over three pints of good vinegar, or enough to completely cover them; boil until tender. This is a choice recipe.

PICKLED WHITE CABBAGE

This recipe recommends itself as of a delightful flavor, yet easily made, and a convenient substitute for the old-fashioned, tedious method of pickling the same vegetable. Take a peck of quartered cabbage, put a layer of cabbage and one of salt, let it remain overnight; in the morning squeeze them and put them on the fire with four chopped onions covered with vinegar; boil for half an hour, then add one ounce of turmeric, one gill of black pepper, one gill of celery seed, a few cloves, one tablespoonful of allspice, a few pieces of ginger, half an ounce of mace, and two pounds of brown sugar. Let it boil half an hour longer, and when cold, it is fit for use. Four tablespoonfuls of made mustard should be added with the other ingredients.

PICKLED GREEN PEPPERS

Take two dozen large, green, bell peppers, extract the seeds by cutting a slit in the side (so as to leave them whole). Make a strong brine and pour over them; let them stand twenty-four hours. Take them out of the brine and soak them in water for a day and a night; now turn off this water and scald some vinegar, in which put a small piece of alum, and pour over them, letting them stand three days. Prepare a stuffing of two hard heads of white cabbage, chopped fine, seasoned slightly with salt and a cup of white mustard seed; mix it well and stuff the peppers hard and full; stitch up, place them in a stone jar, and pour over spiced vinegar scalding hot. Cover tightly.

GREEN PEPPER MANGOES

Select firm, sound, green peppers, and add a few red ones, as they are ornamental and look well upon the table. With a sharp knife remove

211

the top, take out the seed, soak overnight in salt water, then fill with chopped cabbage and green tomatoes, seasoned with salt, mustard seed, and ground cloves. Sew on the top. Boil vinegar sufficient to cover them with a cup of brown sugar, and pour over the mangoes. Do this three mornings, then seal.

CHOWCHOW (ENGLISH RECIPE)

This excellent pickle is seldom made at home, as we can get the imported article so much better than it can be made from the usual recipes. This we vouch for as being as near the genuine article as can be made: one quart of young, tiny cucumbers, not over two inches long; two quarts of *very* small white onions; two quarts of tender string beans, each one cut in halves; three quarts of green tomatoes, sliced and chopped very coarsely; two fresh heads of cauliflower, cut into small pieces, or two heads of white, hard cabbage.

After preparing these articles, put them in a stone jar, mix them together, sprinkling salt between them sparingly. Let them stand twenty-four hours, then drain off *all* the brine that has accumulated. Now put these vegetables in a preserving kettle over the fire, sprinkling through them an ounce of turmeric for coloring, six red peppers chopped coarsely, four tablespoonfuls of mustard, of sugar, and two-thirds of a teacup of best ground mixed mustard. Pour on enough of the best cider vinegar to cover the whole well; cover tightly and simmer all well until it is cooked all through and seems tender, watching and stirring it often. Put in bottles or glass jars. It grows better as it grows older, especially if sealed when hot.

PICKLE OF RIPE CUCUMBERS

This is a French recipe, and is the most excellent of all the high-flavored condiments; it is made by *sun-drying* thirty *old*, full-grown cucumbers, which have first been pared and split, had the seeds taken out, been salted, and let stand twenty-four hours. The sun should be permitted to *dry*, not simply drain them. When they are moderately dry, wash them with vinegar, and place them in layers in a jar, alternating them with a layer of horse-radish, mustard seed, garlic, and onions for each layer of cucumbers. Boil in one quart of vinegar, one ounce of race ginger, half an ounce of allspice, and the same of turmeric; when cool pour this over the cucumbers, tie up tightly, and set away. This pickle requires several months to mature it, but is delicious when old, keeps admirably, and only a little is needed as a relish.

PICCALILLI

One peck of green tomatoes; eight large onions, chopped fine, with one cup of salt well stirred in. Let it stand overnight; in the morning drain off all the liquor. Now take two quarts of water and one of vinegar, boil all together twenty minutes. Drain all through a sieve or colander. Put it back into the kettle again; turn over it two quarts of vinegar, one pound of sugar, half a pound of white mustard seed, two tablespoonfuls of ground pepper, two of cinnamon, one of cloves, two of ginger, one of allspice, and half a teaspoonful of cayenne pepper. Boil all together fifteen minutes, or until tender. Stir often to prevent scorching. Seal in glass jars.

A most delicious accompaniment for any kind of meat or fish.

AN ORNAMENTAL PICKLE

Boil fresh eggs half an hour, then put them in cold water. Boil red beets until tender, peel and cut in dice form, and cover with vinegar, spiced; shell the eggs and drop into the pickle jar.

[*Note:* "Pickled Eggs"—a *must* for Easter, I always thought.]

BLUEBERRY PICKLES

For blueberry pickles, old jars which have lost their covers, or whose edges have been broken so that the covers will not fit tightly, serve an excellent purpose, as these pickles *must not* be kept airtight.

Pick over your berries, using only sound ones; fill your jars or wide-mouthed bottles to within an inch of the top, then pour in molasses enough to settle down into *all* the spaces; this cannot be done in a moment, as molasses does not *run* very freely. Only lazy people will feel obliged to stand by and watch its progress. As it settles, pour in more until the berries are covered. Then tie over the top a piece of cotton cloth to keep the flies and other insects out, and set away in the preserve closet. Cheap molasses is good enough, and your pickles will soon be "sharp." Wild grapes may be pickled in the same manner.

213

WATERMELON PICKLE

Ten pounds of watermelon rind boiled in pure water until tender; drain the water off, and make a syrup of two pounds of white sugar, one quart of vinegar, half an ounce of cloves, one ounce of cinnamon. The syrup to be poured over the rind boiling hot three days in succession.

PICKLED BUTTERNUTS AND WALNUTS

These nuts are in the best state for pickling when the outside shell can be penetrated by the head of a pin. Scald them and rub off the outside skin, put them in a strong brine for six days, changing the water every other day, keeping them closely covered from the air. Then drain and wipe them (piercing each nut through in several places with a large needle) and prepare the pickle as follows: For a hundred large nuts, take of black pepper and ginger root each an ounce; and of cloves, mace, and nutmeg, each a half ounce. Pound all the spices to powder and mix them well together, adding two large spoonfuls of mustard seed. Put the nuts into jars, strewing the powdered seasoning between every layer of nuts. Boil for five minutes a gallon of the very best cider vinegar and pour it boiling hot upon the nuts. Secure the jars closely with corks. You may begin to eat the nuts in a fortnight.

POLITICAL POTPOURRI

One quart chopped cucumbers (ripe are best but green can be used), one pint chopped onions, one red pepper minced fine, one teaspoonful salt, twelve cinnamon buds. Mix. Pour over this one cupful malt vinegar. Put into pint cans, place a grape leaf or horseradish leaf on top. Screw on the cover and it will keep indefinitely. Fine to serve with fish or cold meats.

TOMATO CATSUP

Put into two quarts of tomato pulp (or two cans of canned tomatoes) one onion cut fine, two tablespoonfuls of salt, and three tablespoonfuls of brown sugar. Boil until quite thick; then take from the fire and strain it through a sieve, working it until it is all through but the seeds. Put it

214

back on the stove and add two tablespoonfuls of mustard, one of all-spice, one of black pepper, and one of cinnamon, one teaspoonful of ground cloves, half a teaspoonful of cayenne pepper, one grated nutmeg, one pint of good vinegar. Boil it until it will just run from the mouth of a bottle. It should be watched, stirred often, that it does not burn. If sealed tight while hot in large-mouthed bottles, it will keep good for years.

GREEN TOMATO CATSUP

One peck of green tomatoes and two large onions, sliced. Place them in layers, sprinkling salt between. Let them stand twenty-four hours and then drain them. Add a quarter of a pound of mustard seed, one ounce allspice, one ounce cloves, one ounce ground mustard, one ounce ground ginger, two tablespoonfuls black pepper, two teaspoonfuls celery seed, a quarter of a pound of brown sugar. Put all in preserving pan, cover with vinegar, and boil two hours. Strain through a sieve and bottle for use.

OYSTER CATSUP

One pint oyster meats, one teacupful sherry, a tablespoonful of salt, a teaspoonful of cayenne pepper, the same of powdered mace, a gill of cider vinegar.

Procure the oysters very fresh and open sufficient to fill a pint measure; save the liquor and scald the oysters in it with the sherry. Strain oysters and chop fine with spices until reduced to a pulp, then add pulp to the liquor. Boil again five minutes and skim well; rub the whole through a sieve, and when cold, bottle and cork closely. The corks should be sealed.

APPLE CATSUP

Peel and quarter a dozen sound, tart apples; stew them until soft in as little water as possible, then pass them through a sieve. To a quart of sieved apple, add a teacupful sugar, one teaspoonful each of pepper, cloves, and mustard, two teaspoonfuls cinnamon, and two medium onions chopped very fine. Stir all together, adding a tablespoonful of salt and a pint of vinegar. Place over the fire and boil one hour and

215

bottle while hot. Seal very tight. It should be about as thick as tomato catsup, so that it will just run from the bottle.

GOOSEBERRY OR GRAPE CATSUP

Five pounds of fruit gathered just before ripening, two and one-half pounds of sugar, one pint of vinegar, one tablespoonful each of ground black pepper, allspice, and cinnamon. Boil fruit in vinegar until reduced to a pulp, then add sugar and other seasoning. Seal it hot.

WALNUT CATSUP

One hundred walnuts, six ounces of shallots, one head of garlic, half a pound of salt, two quarts of vinegar, two ounces of anchovies, two ounces of pepper, a quarter of an ounce of mace, half an ounce of cloves. Beat in a large mortar a hundred green walnuts until they are thoroughly broken; then put them into a jar with six ounces of shallots cut into pieces, a head of garlic, two quarts of vinegar and the half pound of salt; let them stand for a fortnight, stirring them twice a day. Strain off the liquor, put into a stewpan with the anchovies, whole pepper, half an ounce of cloves, and a quarter of an ounce of mace. Boil it half an hour, skimming it well. Strain it off, and when cold, pour it clear from any sediment into small bottles, cork it down closely, and store it in a dry place. The sediment can be used for flavoring sauces.

SPICED VINEGAR

Take one quart of cider vinegar, put into it half an ounce of celery seed, one-third of an ounce of dried mint, one-third of an ounce of dried parsley, one garlic, three small onions, three whole cloves, a teaspoonful of whole peppercorns, a teaspoonful of grated nutmeg, salt to taste, and a tablespoonful of sugar; add a tablespoonful of good brandy. Put all into a jar and cover it well; let it stand for three weeks, then strain and bottle it well. Useful for flavoring salad and other dishes.

A NOVEL ENTERPRISE—$100. *There are in Chicago a great many animated advertisements in the form of mortals who are wearing watches which they found in cans of tea and coffee purchased at the Importers' Tea Company's branch stores.—(old adv.)*

Colorings

RED OR PINK COLORING

Take two cents' of cochineal. Lay it on a flat plate and bruise it with the blade of a knife. Put it into half a teacupful of alcohol. Let it stand a quarter of an hour and then filter it through fine muslin. Always ready for immediate use. Cork the bottle tight.

Strawberry or cranberry juice makes a fine coloring for frosting sweet puddings and confectionery.

DEEP RED COLORING

Take twenty grains of cochineal and fifteen grains of cream of tartar finely powdered; add to them a piece of alum the size of a cherrystone, and boil them with a gill of soft water in an earthen vessel, slowly, for half an hour. Then strain it through muslin and keep it tightly corked in a phial. If a little alcohol is added, it will keep any length of time.

YELLOW COLORING

Take a little saffron, put it into an earthen vessel with a very small quantity of cold, soft water, and let it steep till the color of the infusion is a bright yellow. Then strain it, add half alcohol to it. To color fruit yellow, boil the fruit with fresh lemons in water to cover them until it is tender; take it up, spread it on dishes to cool, and finish as may be directed.

To color icing, put the grated peel of a lemon or orange in a thin muslin bag, squeezing a little juice through it, then mixing with the sugar.

GREEN COLORING

Take fresh spinach or beet leaves and pound them in a marble mortar. If you want it for immediate use, take off the green froth as it rises and mix it with the article you intend to color. If you wish to keep it a few days, take the juice when you have pressed out a teacupful, and adding to it a piece of alum the size of a pea, give it a boil in a saucepan. Or make the juice very strong and add a quart of alcohol. Bottle it airtight.

217

SUGAR GRAINS

These are made by pounding white lump sugar in a mortar and shaking it through sieves of different degrees of coarseness, thus accumulating grains of different sizes. They are used in ornamenting cake.

SUGAR GRAINS, COLORED

Stir a little coloring—as the essence of spinach, prepared cochineal, liquid carmine, indigo, rouge, saffron, etc.—into the sugar grains made as above, until each grain is stained. Then spread them on a baking sheet and dry them in a warm place. They are used in ornamenting cake.

CARAMEL OR BURNT SUGAR

Put one cupful of sugar and two teaspoonfuls of water in a saucepan on the fire; stir constantly until it is quite a dark color, then add a half cupful of water and a pinch of salt. Let it boil a few minutes, and when cold, bottle.

For coloring soups, sauces, or gravies.

Confectionery

GENERAL REMARKS

In the making of confections, use the best granulated or loaf sugar. Beware of glucose mixed with sugar. Havana is the cheapest grade of white sugar and a shade or two lighter than the brown.

For common crack candies, the sugar can be kept from graining by adding a teaspoonful of vinegar or cream of tartar.

Essences and extracts should be bought at the druggist's, not the poor kind usually sold at the grocer's.

Grilled almonds are delicious and may alternate at dinner with the salted almonds now so fashionable.

PEPPERMINT DROPS

One cupful of sugar, crushed fine, and just moistened with boiling water, then boiled five minutes; then take from the fire and add cream of tartar the size of a pea. Mix well and add four or five drops of oil of peppermint. Beat briskly until the mixture whitens, then drop quickly upon white paper. Have the cream of tartar and oil of peppermint measured while the sugar is boiling. If it sugars before it is all dropped, add a little water and boil a minute or two.

LEMON DROPS

Upon a coffeecupful of finely powdered sugar, pour just enough lemon juice to dissolve it, and boil it to the consistency of thick syrup, and so that it appears brittle when dropped in cold water. Drop this on buttered plates in drops; set away to cool and harden.

ORANGE DROPS

Grate the rind of one orange and squeeze the juice, taking care to reject the seeds; add to this a pinch of tartaric acid; then stir in confectioners' sugar until it is stiff enough to form into small balls the size of a small marble. This is delicious candy.

The same process for lemon drops, using lemons in place of orange. Color a faint yellow.

BUTTERSCOTCH

Three cupfuls of white sugar, half a cupful of water, half a cupful of vinegar or half a teaspoonful of cream of tartar, a tablespoonful of butter, and eight drops of extract of lemon. Boil *without stirring* till it will snap and break. Just before taking from the fire, add a quarter of a teaspoonful of soda. Pour into well-buttered biscuit tins, a quarter of an inch thick. Mark off into inch squares.

EVERTON TAFFY, OR BUTTERSCOTCH

Two cupfuls of sugar, two cupfuls of dark molasses, one cupful of cold butter, grated rind of half a lemon. Boil over a slow fire until it hardens

219

when dropped in cold water. Pour thinly into tins well buttered, and mark into little inch squares before it cools.

POPCORN CANDY 1

Put into an iron kettle one tablespoonful of butter, three tablespoonfuls of water, and one cupful of white sugar. Boil until ready to candy, then throw in three quarts nicely popped corn. Stir vigorously until the sugar is evenly distributed over the corn; take the kettle from the fire and stir until it cools a little, and in this way you may have each kernel separate and all coated with the sugar. Of course, it must have your undivided attention from the first to prevent scorching. Almonds, English walnuts, or, in fact, any nuts are delicious prepared in this way.

POPCORN CANDY 2

Having popped your corn, salt it and keep it warm, sprinkle over with a whisk broom a mixture composed of an ounce of gum arabic and a half pound of sugar dissolved in two quarts of water. Boil all a few minutes. Stir the corn with the hands or large spoon thoroughly; then mold into balls with the hands.

POPCORN BALLS

Take three large ears of popcorn (rice is best). After popping, shake it down in pan so the unpopped corn will settle at the bottom; put the nice white popped in a greased pan. For the candy, take one cup of molasses, one cup of light brown or white sugar, one tablespoonful of vinegar. Boil until it will harden in water. Pour on the corn. Stir with a spoon until thoroughly mixed; then mold into balls with the hands.

No flavor should be added to this mixture, as the excellence of this commodity depends entirely upon the united flavor of the corn, salt, and the sugar or molasses.

HOARHOUND CANDY

Boil two ounces of dried hoarhound in a pint and a half of water for about half an hour. Strain, and add three and a half pounds of brown sugar. Boil over a hot fire until sufficiently hard. Pour out in flat, well-greased tins and marked into sticks or small squares with a knife as soon as cool enough to retain its shape.

JUJUBE PASTE

Two cupfuls of sugar, one-quarter of a pound of gum arabic, one pint of water. Flavor with the essence of lemon and a grain of cochineal. Let the mixture stand, until the gum is dissolved, in a warm place on the back of the stove, then draw forward and cook until thick. Try in cold water; it should be limber and bend when cold. Pour in buttered pans, an eighth of an inch thick. When cool, roll up in a scroll.

CANDIED ORANGES

Candied orange is a great delicacy, which is easily made: Peel and quarter the oranges. Make a syrup in the proportion of one pound of sugar to one pint of water; let it boil until it will harden in water; then take it from the fire and dip the quarters of orange in the syrup. Let them drain on a fine sieve placed over a platter, so that the syrup will not be wasted; let them drain this way until cool, when the sugar will crystallize. These are nice served with the last course of dinner. Any fruit the same.

CANDY ROLY-POLY

Take half a pint of citron, half a pint of raisins, half a pound of figs, a quarter of a pound of shelled almonds, one pint of peanuts before they are hulled. Cut up the citron, stone the raisins, blanch the almonds, and hull the peanuts; cut up the figs into small bits. Take two pounds of coffee-sugar and moisten with vinegar; put in a piece of butter as large as a walnut; stew till it hardens, but take off before it gets to the brittle stage; beat it with a spoon six or eight times; then stir in the mixed fruits and nuts. Pour into a wet cloth and roll it up like a pudding, twisting the ends of the cloth to mold it. Let it get cold, and slice off pieces as it may be wanted for eating.

Deafness and Head Noises Cured by Peck's Invisible Tubular Ear Cushions. Whispers Heard! —(old adv.)

221

MOLASSES CANDY

Put one quart of West India molasses, one cupful of brown sugar, and a piece of butter the size of half an egg into a six-quart kettle. Let it boil over a slack fire until it begins to look thick, stirring it often to prevent burning. Test it by taking some out and dropping a few drops in a cup of cold water. If it hardens quickly and breaks short between the teeth, it is boiled enough. Now put in half a teaspoonful of baking soda and stir it well; then pour it out into well-buttered, flat tins. When partly cooled, take up the candy with your hands well buttered, then pull and double, and so on, until the candy is a whitish yellow. It may be cut in strips and rolled or twisted.

If flavoring is desired, drop the flavoring on the top as it begins to cool, and when it is pulled, the whole will be flavored.

COCONUT CARAMELS

Two cupfuls of grated coconut, one cupful of sugar, two tablespoonfuls of flour, the whites of three eggs beaten stiff. Soak the coconut, if desiccated, in milk enough to cover it; then beat the whites of the eggs; add gradually the sugar, coconut, and flour. With your fingers make, by rolling the mixture, into cone shapes. Place them on buttered sheets of tin covered with buttered letter paper, and bake in a moderate heat about fifteen or twenty minutes. They should cool before removing from the tins.

FRENCH VANILLA CREAM

Break into a bowl the white of one or more eggs, as the quantity you wish to make will require; add to it an equal quantity of cold water, then stir in XXX powdered or confectioners' sugar until you have it stiff enough to mold into shape with the fingers. Flavor with vanilla to taste. After it is formed in balls, cubes, or lozenge shapes, lay them upon plates or waxed paper and set them aside to dry. This cream can be worked in candies similar to the French cooked cream.

The frock coat is getting to occupy a strangely unique position. When you must wear a frock coat, you must; but when there is no "must" about it, then there is no need of it.—"Fashions for Gentlemen," The Elite News, 1887

222

Beverages

Boiling water is a very important desideratum in the making of a good cup of coffee or tea, but the average housewife is very apt to overlook this fact. Do not boil the water more than three or four minutes; longer boiling ruins the water for coffee or teamaking, as most of its natural properties escape by evaporation, leaving a very insipid liquid, composed mostly of lime and iron, that would ruin the best coffee and give the tea a dark, dead look, which ought to be the reverse.

Water left in the teakettle over night *must never be used for preparing the breakfast coffee;* no matter how excellent your coffee or tea may be, it will be ruined by the addition of water that has been boiled more than once.

The Healing Properties of Tea and Coffee

The medical properties of these two beverages are considerable. Tea is used advantageously in inflammatory diseases and as a cure for the headache. Coffee is supposed to act as a preventive of gravel and gout, and to its influence is ascribed the rarity of those diseases in France and Turkey. Both tea and coffee powerfully counteract the effects of opium, and intoxicating liquors; though, when taken in excess, and without nourishing food, they themselves produce, temporarily at least, some of the more disagreeable consequences incident to the use of ardent spirits. In general, however, none but persons possessing great mobility of the nervous system, or enfeebled or effeminate constitutions, are injuriously affected by the moderate use of tea and coffee in connection with food.

COFFEE

One full coffeecupful of ground coffee, stirred with one egg and part of the shell, adding a half cupful of *cold* water. Put it into the coffee boiler, and pour on to it a quart of boiling water; as it rises and begins to boil, stir it down with a silver spoon or fork. Boil hard for ten or twelve minutes. Remove from the fire, and pour out a cupful of coffee, then pour back into the coffeepot. Place it on the back of the stove or range, where it will keep hot (and not boil); it will settle in about five minutes. Send to the table *hot.* Serve with good cream and lump sugar. Three-quarters of a pound of Java and a quarter of a pound of Mocha make the best mixture of coffee.

223

VIENNA COFFEE

Equal parts of Mocha and Java coffee. Allow one heaping tablespoonful of coffee to each person, and two extra to make good strength. Mix one egg with the grounds. Pour on coffee half as much boiling water as will be needed; let coffee froth, then stir down grounds, and let boil five minutes; then let coffee stand where it will keep hot, but not boil, for five or ten minutes; and add rest of water. To one pint of cream add the white of an egg well beaten; this is to be put in cups with sugar and hot coffee added.

FILTERED OR DRIP COFFEE

For each person allow a large tablespoonful of finely ground coffee, and to every tablespoonful allow a cupful of boiling water—the coffee to be one part Mocha to two of Java.

Have a small iron ring made to fit the top of the coffeepot inside, and to this ring sew a small muslin bag (the muslin for the purpose must not be too thin). Fit the bag into the pot, pour some boiling water in it, and when the pot is well warmed, put the ground coffee into the bag; pour over as much boiling water as is required, close the lid, and when all the water has filtered through, remove the bag and send the coffee to table. Making it in this manner prevents the necessity of pouring the coffee from one vessel to another, which cools and spoils it. The water should be poured on the coffee gradually so that the infusion may be stronger; and the bag must be well made that none of the grounds may escape through the seams and so make the coffee thick and muddy.

Patented coffeepots on this principle can be purchased at most house-furnishing stores.

ICED COFFEE

Make more coffee than usual at breakfast time—and stronger. When cold, put on ice. Serve with cracked ice in each tumbler.

SUBSTITUTE FOR CREAM IN COFFEE

Beat the white of an egg, put to it a small lump of butter, and pour the coffee into it gradually, stirring it so that it will not curdle. It is difficult to distinguish this from fresh cream.

224

Many drop a tiny piece of sweet butter into their cup of hot coffee as a substitute for cream.

SUBSTITUTES FOR COFFEE

Those who are not particular as to quality but only want something that looks like coffee will find the following among the best of many substitutes: roasted acorns, chick peas, beans, rye, cocoa shells, burned wheat bread, dried and roasted turnip, carrot, and dandelion root. We do not recommend any substitute.

TO MAKE TEA

Allow two teaspoonfuls of tea to one large cupful of boiling water. Scald the teapot, put in the tea, pour on about a cupful of boiling water, set it on the fire in a warm place where it will not boil but keep very hot; let it steep or "draw" ten or twelve minutes. Now fill up with as much boiling water as is required. Send hot to the table. It is better to use a china or porcelain teapot; but if you do use metal, let it be tin— new, bright and clean. Never use it when the tin is worn off and the iron exposed. If you do you are drinking tea-ate of iron.

Water which has been boiling more than five minutes or which has previously boiled should on no account be used. If the water does not boil or if it be allowed to overboil, the leaves of the tea will be only half-opened and the tea itself will be quite spoiled.

A Chinese being interviewed for "The Cook" says: "Drink your tea plain. Don't add milk or sugar. Tea-brokers and tea-tasters never do; epicures never do; the Chinese never do."

Milk contains fibrin, albumen, or some other stuff; and the tea, a delicate amount of tannin. Mixing the two makes the liquid turbid. This turbidity, if the cyclopedia is remembered aright, is tannate of fibrin or leather. People who put milk in tea are therefore drinking boots and shoes in mild disguise.

ICED TEA

Is now served to a considerable extent during the summer months. It is of course used without milk and the addition of sugar only serves to destroy the finer tea flavor. Use the black or green teas or both mixed, as fancied.

225

BUTTERMILK AS A DRINK

Buttermilk, so generally regarded as a waste product, has latterly been coming somewhat into vogue, not only as a nutrient but as a therapeutic agent; and in an editorial article the "Canada Lancet," some time ago, highly extolled its virtues. Experience has demonstrated it to be an agent of superior digestibility. It is, indeed, a true milk peptone—that is, milk already partially digested, not of that firm indigestible nature which is the result of the action of the gastric juice upon sweet cow's milk. It resembles koumiss in its nature and, with the exception of that article, it is the most grateful, refreshing, and digestible of the products of milk. It is a decided laxative to the bowels, a fact which must be borne in mind in the treatment of typhoid fever. It is a diuretic and may be prescribed with advantage in some kidney troubles. Owing to its acidity, it is believed to exercise a general impression on the liver. It is well adapted to many cases where it is customary to recommend lime-water and milk. It is invaluable in the treatment of diabetes, either exclusively or alternating with skimmed milk.

CURRANT WINE 1

The currants should be quite ripe. Stem, mash, and strain them, adding a half pint of water and less than a pound of sugar to a quart of the mashed fruit. Stir well up together and pour into a clean cask, leaving the bunghole open or covered with a piece of lace. It should stand for a month to ferment, when it will be ready for bottling. Just before bottling you may add a small quantity of brandy or whiskey.

CURRANT WINE 2

To each quart of currant juice add two quarts of soft water and three pounds of brown sugar. Put into a jug or small keg, leaving the top open until fermentation ceases and it looks clear. Draw off and cork tightly.
—*Long Island Recipe*

BLACKBERRY WINE

Cover your blackberries with cold water. Crush the berries well with a wooden masher; let them stand twenty-four hours. Strain, and to one gallon of juice put three pounds of common brown sugar. Put into wide-mouthed jars for several days, carefully skimming off the scum that will rise to the top. Put in several sheets of brown paper and let them remain in it three days. Skim again and pour through a funnel into your cask. There let it remain undisturbed until March, then strain again and bottle. These directions, if carefully followed out, will insure you excellent wine.

GRAPE WINE

Mash the grapes and strain them through a cloth. Put the skins in a tub after squeezing them with barely enough water to cover them. Strain the juice thus obtained into the first portion. Put three pounds of sugar to one gallon of the mixture. Let it stand in an open tub to ferment, covered with a cloth, for a period of from three to seven days. Skim off what rises every morning. Put the juice in a cask and leave it open for twenty-four hours, then bung it up and put clay over the bung to keep the air out. Let your wine remain in the cask until March, when it should be drawn off and bottled.

FLORIDA ORANGE WINE

Wipe oranges with wet cloth, peel off yellow rind very thin, squeeze and strain juice through a hair sieve. Measure juice. For each gallon add three pounds of granulated sugar, the white and shell of one egg, and one-third gallon cold water. Put sugar, egg white and shell (crushed small) and water over the fire and stir every two minutes until egg begins to harden. Boil syrup until it looks clear under the froth of egg which will form on the surface. Strain syrup, pour it upon the orange rind, and let it stand overnight. Next day, add the orange juice and again let it stand overnight. Strain it the second day and put it into a tight cask with a small cake of compressed yeast to about ten gallons of wine. Leave the bung out of the cask until the wine ceases to ferment (makes hissing noise). When fermentation ceases, close cask by driving in the bung, and let the wine stand about nine months before bottling it. Three months after it is bottled it can be used. A glass of brandy added to each gallon of wine after fermentation ceases is generally considered an improvement. There are seasons of the year when Florida oranges by the box are very cheap, and this fine wine can be made at a small expense.

RAISIN WINE

Take two pounds of raisins, seed and chop them, a lemon, a pound of white sugar, and about two gallons of boiling water. Pour into a stone jar and stir daily for six or eight days. Strain, bottle, and put in a cool place for ten days or so, when the wine will be ready for use.

CHERRY BOUNCE

To one gallon of wild cherries add enough good whiskey to cover the fruit. Let soak two or three weeks and then drain off the liquor. Mash the cherries without breaking the stones and strain through a jelly bag; add this liquor to that already drained off. Make a syrup with a gill of water and a pound of white sugar to every two quarts of liquor thus prepared; stir in well and bottle and tightly cork. A common way of making cherry bounce is to put wild cherries and whiskey together in a jug and use the liquor as wanted.

BLACKBERRY CORDIAL

Warm and squeeze the berries. Add to one pint of juice one pound of white sugar, one-half ounce of powdered cinnamon, one-fourth ounce of mace, two teaspoonfuls of cloves. Boil all together for one-fourth of an hour; strain the syrup and to each pint add a glass of French brandy. It will arrest dysentery if given in season and is a pleasant and safe remedy. (Two or three doses of a tablespoon each.) Excellent for children when teething.

[*Note:* Today, this is *not* considered excellent for children who are teething!]

GINGER BEER

Put into a kettle two ounces of powdered ginger root (or more if it is not very strong), half an ounce of cream of tartar, two large lemons cut in slices, two pounds of broken loaf sugar, and two gallons of soft boiling water. Simmer them over a slow fire for half an hour. When the liquor is nearly cold, stir into it a large tablespoonful of the best yeast. After it has fermented, which will be in about twenty-four hours, bottle for use.

The most exquisite epicure will be pleased by Knox's Sparkling Calvesfoot Gelatin. Received highest medal at the World's Fair. —(*old adv.*)

HOP BEER

Take five quarts of water and six ounces of hops; boil it three hours, then strain the liquor. Add to it five quarts of water, four ounces of bruised ginger root. Boil this again twenty minutes, strain, and add four pounds of sugar. When lukewarm, put in a pint of yeast. Let it ferment. In twenty-four hours it will be ready for bottling.

SPRUCE BEER

Allow an ounce of hops and a spoonful of ginger to a gallon of water. When well boiled, strain it and put in a pint of molasses or a pound of brown sugar and half an ounce or less of the essence of spruce. When cool, add a teacupful of yeast and put into a clean tight cask and let it ferment a day or two, then bottle it for use. You can boil the sprigs of spruce fir in place of the essence.

ROMAN PUNCH

Make two quarts of lemonade; add one tablespoonful extract of lemon. Work well and freeze. Just before serving add for each quart of ice half a pint of brandy and half a pint of Jamaica rum. Mix well and serve in high glasses, as this makes what is called a semi- or half-ice. It is usually served at dinners as a *coup de milieu*. In winter use snow to freeze.

RASPBERRY SHRUB

One quart of raspberry juice; half a pound of loaf sugar, dissolved; a pint of Jamaica rum or part rum and brandy. Mix thoroughly. Bottle for use.

WINE WHEY

Sweeten one pint of milk to taste, and when boiling, throw in two wine-glasses of sherry. When the curd forms, strain the whey through a muslin bag into tumblers.

Warner's Rust-Proof Corsets. Guaranteed! —(*old adv.*)

NOYAU CORDIAL

To one gallon of proof spirit add three pounds of loaf sugar and a tablespoonful of extract of almonds. Mix well together and allow to stand forty-eight hours covered closely. Now strain through thick flannel and bottle. This liquor will be much improved by adding half a pint of apricot or peach juice.

EGGNOG

Beat the yellows of twelve eggs very light; stir in as much white sugar as they will dissolve; pour in gradually one glass of brandy to cook the eggs, one glass of old whiskey, one grated nutmeg, and three pints of rich milk. Beat the whites to a froth and stir in last.

EGG FLIP OR MULLED ALE

Boil one quart of good ale with some nutmeg. Beat up six eggs and mix them with a little cold ale. Pour the hot ale to it; pour back and forth several times to prevent its curdling; warm and stir it till sufficiently thick. Add a piece of butter or a glass of brandy and serve it with dry toast.

MILK PUNCH

One pint of milk made very sweet; a wineglassful of brandy or rum. Stir well together. Grate a little nutmeg over the top of the glasses. Serve with a straw in each glass.

KOUMISS

Koumiss is prepared by dissolving four ounces of white sugar in one gallon of skimmed milk and placing in bottles of the capacity of one quart. Add two ounces of baker's yeast or a cake of compressed yeast to each bottle. Cork and tie securely, set in a warm place until fermentation is well underway, and lay the bottles on their sides in a cool cellar. In three days fermentation will have progressed sufficiently to permit the koumiss to be in good condition.

HOT PUNCH [OLD STYLE]

Half a pint of rum, half a pint of brandy, quarter of a pound of sugar, one large lemon, half a teaspoonful of nutmeg, one pint of boiling water. Rub the sugar over the lemon until it has absorbed all the yellow part of the skin, then put the sugar into a punch bowl. Add the lemon juice (free from pips) and mix these two together well. Pour over them the boiling water; stir well together; add the rum, brandy, and nutmeg; mix thoroughly and the punch will be ready to serve. It is very important in making good punch that all the ingredients are thoroughly incorporated. To insure success the processes of mixing must be diligently attended to.

LEMONADE

Three lemons to a pint of water makes strong lemonade. Sweeten to your taste.

STRAWBERRY OR RASPBERRY SYRUP

Mash the fresh fruit, express the juice, and to each quart add three and a half pounds of granulated sugar. The juice heated to 180° Fahrenheit and strained or filtered previous to dissolving the sugar will keep for an indefinite time canned hot in glass jars.

Many housekeepers, after the bottles and jars are thoroughly washed and dried, smoke them with sulphur in this way: Take a piece of wire and bend it around a small piece of brimstone the size of a bean; set the brimstone on fire, put it in the jar or bottle, bending the other end over the mouth of the vessel and cover with a cork. After the brimstone has burned away, fill the vessel with the syrup or preserves and cover tightly. There is no sulphurous taste left by the process.

PINEAPPLE ADE

Pare and slice very ripe pineapples; cut slices into small pieces. Put them with juice into a pitcher and sprinkle with plenty of powdered white sugar. Pour on boiling water, a small half pint to each pineapple. Cover pitcher and let it stand till quite cool, occasionally pressing down pineapple with a spoon. Then set pitcher in ice. Lastly, strain the

231

infusion into another vessel and transfer it to tumblers, putting into each glass some more sugar and a bit of ice. This beverage will be found delicious.

INEXPENSIVE DRINK

A very nice, cheap drink which may take the place of lemonade and be found fully as healthful is made with one cupful pure cider vinegar, half a cupful of good molasses, and one quart of ice water. A tablespoonful of ground ginger added makes a healthful beverage.

RASPBERRY VINEGAR

Turn over a quart of ripe raspberries, mashed, a quart of good cider vinegar. Add one pound of white sugar, mix well, then let stand in the sun four hours. Strain it, squeeze out the juice, and put in a pint of good brandy. Seal it up in bottles, airtight, and lay them on their sides in the cellar, covered with sawdust. When used, put two tablespoonfuls to a tumblerful of ice water. Fine.

SEIDLITZ POWDERS

Fold in a white paper a mixture of one drachm of Rochelle salts and twenty-five grains of carbonate of soda; in a blue paper, twenty grains of tartaric acid. They should all be pulverized quite finely. Put the contents of the white paper into a tumbler not quite half full of cold water and stir it till dissolved. Then put the mixture from the blue paper into another tumbler with the same quantity of water and stir that also. When the powders are dissolved in both tumblers, pour the first into the other, and it will effervesce immediately. Drink it quickly while foaming.

[*Note:* For Victorian "mornings-after."]

Menus for the Holidays

CIRCA 1887

NEW YEAR'S DAY

Breakfast

BAKED APPLES

HOMINY

BROILED WHITE FISH   HAM OMELET

POTATOES À LA CRÈME   PARKER HOUSE ROLLS

CRULLERS   TOAST

COFFEE

Dinner

OYSTERS ON THE HALF SHELL

JULIENNE SOUP

BAKED PICKEREL

ROAST TURKEY   OYSTER STUFFING

MASHED POTATOES   BOILED ONIONS

BAKED WINTER SQUASH

CRANBERRY SAUCE   CHICKEN PIE

PLAIN CELERY   LOBSTER SALAD

OLIVES   SPICED CURRANTS

ENGLISH PLUM PUDDING   WINE SAUCE

MINCE PIE   ORANGE WATER ICE

FANCY CAKES   CHEESE   FRUITS

NUTS   RAISINS   CONFECTIONERY

COFFEE

Supper

COLD ROAST TURKEY

BOSTON OYSTER PIE   CELERY SALAD

BAKED SWEET POTATOES

RUSKS   FRUIT CAKE

SLICED ORANGES

TEA

WASHINGTON'S BIRTHDAY

Breakfast

ORANGES

OATMEAL WITH CREAM

COUNTRY SAUSAGE   BAKED OMELET

LYONNAISE POTATOES   CLAM FRITTERS

EGG MUFFINS   WHEAT BREAD

COFFEE

Dinner

OYSTERS ON HALF SHELL

MOCK TURTLE SOUP

BAKED WHITE FISH   BÉCHAMEL SAUCE

BOILED TURKEY   OYSTER SAUCE

BOILED SWEET POTATOES

STEAMED POTATOES   STEWED TOMATOES

SCALLOPED ONIONS

SALMI OF GAME

OLIVES   CHICKEN SALAD

WASHINGTON PIE   BAVARIAN CREAM

VARIEGATED JELLY   MARBLE CAKE

CANDIED FRUITS   RAISINS AND NUTS

COFFEE

Supper

COLD BOILED TURKEY

POTATO CROQUETTES   LOBSTER SALAD

SODA BISCUITS

ENGLISH POUND CAKE

PINEAPPLE PRESERVES

TEA

FOURTH OF JULY

Breakfast

RED RASPBERRIES WITH CREAM

FRIED CHICKEN

SCRAMBLED TOMATOES

WARMED POTATOES   TENNESSEE MUFFINS

TOAST   COFFEE

Dinner

CLAM SOUP

BOILED COD WITH LOBSTER SAUCE

ROAST LAMB   MINT SAUCE

NEW POTATOES BOILED

GREEN PEAS   SPINACH WITH EGGS

CUCUMBERS SLICED

CHICKEN PATTIES

NAPLES BISCUITS   VANILLA ICE CREAM

CHOCOLATE MACAROONS   STRAWBERRIES

COFFEE

Supper

COLD SLICED LAMB

CRAB PIE WATERCRESS SALAD

CHEESE TOAST

GRAHAM BREAD SPONGE CAKE

BLACKBERRIES

TEA

THANKSGIVING DAY

Breakfast

GRAPES

OAT FLAKES

BROILED PORTERHOUSE STEAK

CODFISH BALLS BROWNED POTATOES

BUCKWHEAT CAKES MAPLE SYRUP

WHEAT BREAD

COFFEE

237

Dinner

OYSTERS ON HALF SHELL

CREAM OF CHICKEN SOUP

FRIED SMELTS — SAUCE TARTARE

ROAST TURKEY — CRANBERRY SAUCE

MASHED POTATOES — BAKED SQUASH

BOILED ONIONS — PARSNIP FRITTERS

OLIVES — CHICKEN SALAD

VENISON PASTRY

PUMPKIN PIE — MINCE PIE

CHARLOTTE RUSSE — ALMOND ICE CREAM

LEMON JELLY — HICKORY NUT CAKE

CHEESE — FRUITS

COFFEE

Supper

COLD ROAST TURKEY

SCALLOPED OYSTERS — POTATO SALAD

CREAM SHORT CAKE — ECLAIRS

PRESERVED EGG PLUMS

TEA

238

CHRISTMAS DAY

Breakfast

ORANGES

BOILED RICE

BROILED SALT MACKEREL

POACHED EGGS À LA CRÈME

POTATO FILLETS

FEATHER GRIDDLE CAKES

WHEAT BREAD

COFFEE

Dinner

OYSTERS ON HALF SHELL

GAME SOUP

BOILED WHITE FISH   SAUCE MAÎTRE D'HÔTEL

ROAST GOOSE   APPLE SAUCE

BOILED POTATOES   MASHED TURNIPS

CREAMED PARSNIPS   STEWED ONIONS

BOILED RICE   LOBSTER SALAD

CANVAS BACK DUCK

CHRISTMAS PLUM PUDDING   SAUCE

VANILLA ICE CREAM

MINCE PIE   ORANGE JELLY

DELICATE CAKE   SALTED ALMONDS

CONFECTIONERY   FRUITS

COFFEE

Supper

COLD ROAST GOOSE

OYSTER PATTIES

COLE SLAW   BUNS

CHARLOTTE RUSSE

PEACH JELLY

TEA

Food for the Sick

Dishes for invalids should be served in the daintiest and most attractive way; never send more than a supply for one meal. The same dish too frequently set before an invalid often causes a distaste, when perhaps a change would tempt the appetite.

The seasoning of food for the sick should be varied according to the condition of the patient. One recovering from illness can partake of a little piece of roast mutton; chicken, rabbit, game, fish, simply dressed, and simple puddings are all light food and easily digested. A mutton chop, nicely cut, trimmed, and broiled, is a dish that is often inviting to an invalid. As a rule, an invalid will be more likely to enjoy any preparation sent to him if it is served in small, delicate pieces. As there are so many small, dainty dishes that can be made for this purpose, it seems useless to try to more than give a small variety of them.

Pudding can be made of prepared barley or tapioca, well soaked before boiling, with an egg added, and a change can be made of light puddings by mixing up some stewed fruit with the puddings before baking; a bread pudding from stale bread crumbs and a tiny cup-custard, boiled in a small basin or cup; also various drinks, such as milk punch, wine, whey, apple toddy and various other nourishing drinks.

BEEFSTEAK AND MUTTON CHOPS

Select the tenderest cuts and broil over a clear, hot fire. Let the steak be rare, the chops well done. Salt and pepper. Lay between two *hot* plates three minutes and serve to your patient. If he is very weak, do not let him swallow anything except the juice, when he has chewed the meat well. The essence of rare beef, roasted or broiled, thus expressed, is considered by some physicians to be more strengthening than beef tea prepared in the usual manner.

BEEF TEA

One pound of lean beef, cut into small pieces. Put into a glass canning jar without a drop of water; cover tightly and set in a pot of cold water. Heat gradually to a boil and continue this steadily for three or four hours until the meat is like white rags and the juice all drawn out. Season with salt to taste, and when cold, skim.

241

CHICKEN BROTH

Make the same as mutton or beef broth. Boil chicken slowly, putting on just enough water to cover it well, watching it closely that it does not boil down too much. When the chicken is tender, season with salt and a very little pepper. The yolk of an egg beaten light and added is very nourishing.

OATMEAL GRUEL

Pour four tablespoonfuls of the best grits (oatmeal coarsely ground) into a pint of boiling water. Let it boil gently and stir it often till it becomes as thick as you wish it. Then strain it and add to it, while warm, butter, wine, nutmeg, or whatever is thought proper to flavor it. Salt to taste.

If you make the gruel of fine oatmeal, sift it, mix it first to a thick batter with a little cold water, and then put it into the saucepan of boiling water. Stir it all the time it is boiling, lifting the spoon gently up and down and letting the gruel fall slowly back again into the pan.

CORNMEAL GRUEL

Two tablespoonfuls of fine Indian meal, mixed smooth with cold water and a saltspoonful of salt. Add one quart of boiling water and cook twenty minutes. Stir it frequently, and if it becomes too thick, use boiling water to thin it. If the stomach is not too weak, a tablespoonful of cream may be used to cool it. Some like it sweetened and others like it plain. For very sick persons let it settle, pour off the top, and give without other seasoning. For convalescents, toast a piece of bread as nicely as possible and put it in the gruel with a tablespoonful of nice sweet cream and a little ginger and sugar. This should be used only when a laxative is allowed.

EGG GRUEL

Beat the yolk of an egg with one tablespoonful of sugar; pour one tea-cupful of boiling water on it; add the white of an egg, beaten to a froth, with any seasoning or spice desired. Take warm.

Do you have a little FAIRY *in your home? Use* FAIRY *Soap.* —(*old adv.*)

ARROWROOT MILK PORRIDGE

One large cupful of fresh milk, new if you can get it; one cupful of boiling water; one teaspoonful of arrowroot, wet to a paste with cold water; two teaspoonfuls of white sugar; a pinch of salt. Put the sugar into the milk, the salt into the boiling water, which should be poured into a farina kettle. Add the wet arrowroot and boil, stirring constantly until it is clear. Put in the milk and cook ten minutes, stirring often. Give while warm, adding hot milk should it be thicker than gruel.

ARROWROOT BLANC MANGE

One large cupful of boiling milk, one even tablespoonful of arrowroot rubbed to a paste with cold water, two teaspoonfuls of white sugar, a pinch of salt. Flavor with rose water. Proceed as in the foregoing recipes, boiling and stirring eight minutes. Turn into a wet mold, and when firm, serve with cream and powdered sugar.

SLIPPERY-ELM BARK TEA

Break the bark into bits, pour boiling water over it, cover and let it infuse until cold. Sweeten, ice, and take for summer disorders, or add lemon juice and drink for a bad cold.

FLAXSEED TEA

Upon an ounce of unbruised flaxseed and a little pulverized licorice root pour a pint of boiling (soft or rain) water; and place the vessel containing these ingredients near, but not on, the fire for four hours. Strain through a linen cloth. Make it fresh every day. An excellent drink in fever accompanied by a cough.

FLAXSEED LEMONADE

To a large tablespoonful of flaxseed, allow a tumbler and a half of cold water. Boil them together till the liquid becomes very sticky. Then strain it hot over a quarter of a pound of pulverized sugar and an ounce of pulverized gum arabic. Stir it till quite dissolved and squeeze into it the

243

juice of a lemon. This mixture has frequently been found an efficacious remedy for a cold, taking a wineglass of it as often as the cough is troublesome.

TAMARIND WATER

Put tamarinds into a pitcher or tumbler till it is one-third full; then fill up with cold water, cover it, and let it infuse for a quarter of an hour or more. Currant jelly or cranberry juice mixed with water also makes a pleasant drink for an invalid.

SAGO JELLY

Make the same as tapioca. If seasoning is not advisable, the sago may be boiled in milk instead of water and eaten plain. Rice jelly made the same, using only half as much rice as sago.

ARROWROOT WINE JELLY

One cupful of boiling water, one scant tablespoonful of arrowroot. Mix with a little cold water, one tablespoonful of sugar, a pinch of salt, and one tablespoonful of brandy or three tablespoonfuls of wine. Excellent for a sick person without fever.

TAPIOCA CUP PUDDING

This is very light and delicate for invalids. An even tablespoonful of tapioca, soaked for two hours in nearly a cup of new milk. Stir into this the yolk of a fresh egg, a little sugar, a grain of salt, and bake it in a cup for fifteen minutes. A little jelly may be eaten with it.

BAKED APPLES

Get nice fruit, a little tart and juicy but not sour; clean them nicely and bake in a moderate oven regulated so as to have them done in about an hour. When the skin cracks and the pulp breaks through in every direction, they are done and ready to take out. Serve with white sugar sprinkled over them.

SOFT TOAST

Toast well but not too brown two thin slices of stale bread. Put them on a warm plate, sprinkle with a pinch of salt, and pour upon them some boiling water; quickly cover with another dish of the same size and drain off the water. Put a very small bit of butter on the toast and serve at once while hot.

IRISH MOSS BLANC MANGE

A small handful of moss (to be purchased at any drug store). Wash it very carefully and put it in one quart of milk on the fire. Let the milk simmer for about twenty minutes or until the moss begins to dissolve. Then remove from the fire and strain through a fine sieve. Add two tablespoonfuls of sugar and half a teaspoonful of vanilla flavoring. Put away to harden in cups or molds, and serve with sugar and cream. A delicate dish for an invalid.

[*Note:* Particularly for one suffering from moss-deficiency!]

EGG TOAST

Brown a slice of bread nicely over the coals, dip it in hot water slightly salted, butter it, and lay it on the top of an egg that has been broken into boiling water and cooked until the white has hardened. Season the egg with a bit of butter and a crumb of salt.

The best way to cook eggs for an invalid is to drop them or else pour boiling water over the egg in the shell and let it stand for a few minutes on the back of the stove.

MULLED JELLY

Take one tablespoonful of currant or grape jelly; beat with it the white of one egg and a teaspoonful of sugar; pour on it a teacupful of boiling water and break in a slice of dry toast or two crackers.

CUP CUSTARD

Break into a coffeecup one egg. Put in two teaspoonfuls of sugar (beat it up thoroughly), a pinch of salt, and a pinch of grated nutmeg. Fill

245

up the cup with good sweet milk. Turn it into another cup, well buttered, and set it in a pan of boiling water reaching nearly to the top of the cup. Set it in the oven and when the custard is set, it is done. Eat cold.

[*Note:* An easy way to make one small custard for one small child!]

CLAM BROTH

Select twelve small, hardshell clams, drain them, and chop them fine. Add half a pint of clam juice or hot water, a pinch of cayenne, and a walnut of butter. Simmer thirty minutes. Add a gill of boiled milk, strain, and serve. This is an excellent broth for weak stomachs.

MILK OR CREAM CODFISH

This dish will often relish when a person is recovering from sickness when nothing else would. Pick up a large tablespoonful of salt codfish very fine; freshen it considerably by placing it over the fire in a basin, covering it with cold water as it comes to a boil; turn off the water and freshen again if very salty, then turn off the water until dry and pour over half a cupful of milk or thin cream; add a bit of butter, a sprinkle of pepper, and a thickening made of one teaspoonful of flour or corn-starch wet up with a little milk. When this boils up, turn over a slice of dipped toast.

CRACKER PANADA

Break in pieces three or four hard crackers that are baked quite brown and let them boil fifteen minutes in one quart of water. Remove from the fire, let them stand three or four minutes, strain off the liquor through a fine wire sieve, and season it with sugar.

This is a nourishing beverage for infants that are teething, and with the addition of a little wine and nutmeg is often prescribed for invalids recovering from a fever.

BREAD PANADA

Put three gills of water and one tablespoonful of white sugar on the fire, and just before it boils add two tablespoonfuls of the crumbs of stale white bread. Stir it well and let it boil three or four minutes; then add one glass of white wine, a grated lemon, and a little nutmeg. Let it boil up once, then remove it from the fire, and keep it closely covered until it is wanted for use.

SLIPPERY-ELM TEA

Put a teaspoonful of powdered slippery elm into a tumbler, pour cold water upon it, and season with lemon and sugar.

TOAST WATER OR CRUST COFFEE

Take stale pieces of crusts of bread, the end pieces of the loaf; toast them a nice, dark brown, care to be taken that they do not burn in the least, as that affects the flavor. Put the browned crusts into a large milk pitcher and pour enough boiling water over to cover them; cover the pitcher closely and let steep until cold. Strain and sweeten to taste; put a piece of ice in each glass. This is also good drunk warm with cream and sugar, similar to coffee.

[*Note:* If your husband has been complaining about the coffee, try this!]

PLAIN MILK TOAST

Cut a thin slice from a loaf of stale bread, toast it very quickly, sprinkle a little salt over it, and pour upon it three tablespoonfuls of boiling milk or cream. Crackers split and toasted in this manner are often very grateful to an invalid.

[*Note:* One of my grandmother's standard recipes for an "invalid." She buttered the toast, omitted the salt.]

LINSEED TEA

Put one tablespoonful of linseed into a stewpan with half a pint of cold water; place the stewpan over a moderate fire, and when the water is quite warm, pour it off, and add to the linseed half a pint of fresh cold water; then let the whole boil three or four minutes. Season it with lemon and sugar.

POWDERS FOR CHILDREN

A very excellent carminative powder for flatulent infants may be kept in the house and employed with advantage whenever the child is in pain or griped, dropping five grains of oil of anise seed and two of peppermint on half an ounce of lump sugar and rubbing it in a mortar with a drachm of magnesia into a fine powder. A small quantity of this may be given in a little water at any time and always with benefit.

Miscellany

TO CLEAN CURRANTS

Put them in a sieve or colander and sprinkle them thickly with flour. Rub them well until they are separated and the flour, grit, and fine stems have passed through the strainer. Place the strainer and currants in a pan of water and wash thoroughly; then lift the strainer and currants together, and change the water until it is clear. Dry the currants between clean towels. It hardens them to dry in an oven.

TO CHOP SUET

Break or cut in small pieces, sprinkle with sifted flour, and chop in a cold place to keep it from becoming sticky and soft.

ROAST CHESTNUTS

Peel the raw chestnuts and scald them to remove the inner skin; put them in a frying pan with a little butter and toss them about a few moments; add a sprinkle of salt and a suspicion of cayenne. Serve them after the cheese.

Peanuts may be blanched and roasted the same.

AFTER-DINNER CROUTONS

These crispy croutons answer as a substitute for hard-water crackers, and are also relished by most people.

Cut sandwich bread into slices one-quarter of an inch thick; cut each slice into four small triangles; dry them in the oven slowly until they assume a delicate brownish tint, then serve, either hot or cold. A nice way to serve them is to spread a paste of part butter and part rich, creamy cheese, to which may be added a very little minced parsley.

What Cooking Means to a Woman

It means the patience of Job and the persistence of the Pilgrim Fathers. It means the endurance, the long suffering, and the martyrdom of Joan of Arc. It means the steaming and the stewing and the baking and the broiling thrice daily, spring, summer, autumn, and winter, year after year, decade following decade. It means perspiration and desperation and resignation. It means a crown and a harp and a clear title to an estate in heaven. From her judgment and reason she must evolve triumphs that depend on salt and pepper and sugar and herbs. She must know how soon and how long and how much and how often. She must know quantity and quality and cost. She must serve the butcher, the baker, and the candlestick-maker. Then she must rise above it all and be a lady and a loaf-giver.

Prescriptions
Recipes
and Such

FOR

HEALTH

HOUSEHOLD

AND HAPPINESS

CIRCA 1887

RECIPE FOR A HAPPY DAY

Take a little dash of cold water,
A little leaven of prayer,
A little bit of sunshine gold
Dissolved in morning air,
Add to your meal some merriment,
Add thought for kith and kin
And then, as a prime ingredient,
Plenty of work thrown in,
Flavor it all with essence of love,
Add a dash of play,
Let the dear old Book and a glance above
Complete the well-spent day.

Great-Grandmother's Medicine Chest — KEEP OUT!

or

What Was Good Enough for Granny Is Not Good Enough for You!

IT IS THE HOPE of this author that no reader will be carried away by nostalgia for old-time nostrums that were "good enough for Grandma." All the following health recipes are ineffectual compared with modern miracle medicines and procedures. Fortunately, some of the ingredients are no longer available without prescription—the Pure Food and Drug Bill became law in 1906 and was strengthened in 1938 and thereafter—so you won't be able to make many of the recipes, anyway.

These Victorian concoctions for every ailment from toothache to melancholy are fun to read, however, although it is sobering to reflect that, in their gallant fight against disease—especially in the nursery— nineteenth-century wives and mothers had nothing better to rely on.

If you want to clean your windows with turkey wings, feel free. If you want to wash your horse in walnut-leaf tea, be my guest. Preserve your husband with kisses, by all means! But please don't take other "prescriptions" seriously. They were tested, approved, and/or recommended by *nobody* except Mrs. Gillette, the co-author of the original *White House Cookbook* of 1887, and that was more than seventy-five years ago.—*J.H.E.*

Health Suggestions

Use three Physicians,
First—Dr. Quiet,
Next—Dr. Merry-man
And Dr. Dyet.

A great many cannot see why it is they do not take a cold when exposed to cold winds and rain. The fact is, and ought to be more generally understood, that nearly every cold is contracted indoors and is not directly due to the cold outside but to the heat inside. A man will go

253

to bed at night feeling as well as usual and get up in the morning with a royal cold. He goes peeking around in search of cracks and keyholes and tiny drafts. Weather-strips are procured, and the house made as tight as a fruit-can. In a few days more the whole family has colds.

Let a man go home tired or exhausted, eat a full supper of starchy and vegetable food, occupy his mind intently for a while, go to bed in a warm, close room, and if he doesn't have a cold in the morning, it will be a wonder. A drink of whiskey or a glass or two of beer before supper will facilitate matters very much.

People swallow more colds down their throats than they inhale or receive from contact with the air, no matter how cold or chilly it may be. Plain, light suppers are good to go to bed on and are far more conducive to refreshing sleep than a glass of beer or a dose of chloral. In the estimation of a great many this statement is rank heresy, but in the light of science, common sense, and experience it is gospel truth.

Pure air is strictly essential to maintain perfect health. If a person is accustomed to sleeping with the windows open, there is but little danger of taking cold, winter or summer. Persons that shut up the windows to keep out the "night air" make a mistake, for at night the only air we breathe is "night air," and we need good air while asleep as much or even more than at any other time of day.

Ventilation can be accomplished by simply opening the window an inch at the bottom and also at the top, letting the pure air in, the bad air out. It is estimated that a grown person corrupts *one gallon of pure air every minute* or twenty-five barrels full in a single night in breathing alone.

Clothing that has been worn through the day should be changed for fresh ones to sleep in. Three pints of moisture, filled with the waste of the body, are given off every twenty-four hours, and this is mostly absorbed by the clothing.

Old and weak persons should avoid extreme changes of heat and cold. In passing from warm crowded rooms to the cold air, the mouth should be kept closed and all the breathing done through the nostrils only, that the cold air may be warmed before it reaches the lungs, causing no derangement.

WATER

Water is as necessary to health as pure air. Rain water, filtered, is probably the best attainable. Boiling the water destroys the vegetable and animal matter and leaves the mineral matter deposited on the bottom of the vessel; therefore, it leaves it clear from poisonous substances.

HOW TO USE HOT WATER

One of the simplest and most effectual means of relieving pain, externally and internally, is by the use of hot water.

For bruises, sprains, and such, apply immediately, as hot as can be borne, by means of a cloth or by immersion if convenient. If applied at once, the use of hot water will generally prevent nearly, if not entirely, the bruised flesh from turning black.

For pains resulting from indigestion and known as "wind colic," etc., a cupful of hot water, taken in sips, will often relieve at once. When that is insufficient, a flannel folded in several thicknesses, large enough to fully cover the painful place, should be wrung out of hot water and laid over the seat of the pain. It should be as hot as the skin can bear without injury and be renewed every ten minutes or oftener, if it feels cool, until the pain is gone. The remedy is simple, efficient, harmless, and within the reach of everyone, and should be more generally used than it is. If used along with common sense, it might save many a doctor's bill and many a course of drug treatment as well.

DRAUGHTS FOR THE FEET

Take a large leaf from the horse-radish plant and cut out the hard fibers that run through the leaf; place it on a hot shovel for a moment to soften it; fold it and fasten it closely in the hollow of the foot by a cloth bandage.

Burdock leaves, cabbage leaves, and mullen leaves are used in the same manner to alleviate pain and promote perspiration.

Garlics are also made for draughts by pounding them, placing them on a hot tin plate for a moment to sweat them, and binding them closely to the hollow of the foot by a cloth bandage.

Draughts of onions for infants are made by roasting onions in hot ashes and, when they are quite soft, peeling off the outside, mashing them, and applying them on a cloth as usual.

POULTICES

A Bread-and-Milk Poultice— Put a tablespoonful of the crumbs of stale bread into a gill of milk and give the whole one boil-up. Or take stale bread crumbs, pour over them boiling water, and boil till soft, stirring well; take from the fire and gradually stir in a little glycerine or sweet oil, so as to render the poultice pliable when applied.

255

Hop Poultice— Boil one handful of dried hops in half a pint of water until the half pint is reduced to a gill, then stir into it enough Indian meal to thicken it.

Mustard Poultice— Into one gill of boiling water stir one tablespoonful of Indian meal; spread the paste thus made upon a cloth and spread over the paste one teaspoonful of mustard flour. If you wish a mild poultice, use a teaspoonful of mustard as it is prepared for the table instead of the mustard flour. Equal parts of ground mustard and flour made into a paste with warm water and spread between two pieces of muslin form the indispensable mustard plaster.

Ginger Poultice— This is made like a mustard poultice, using ground ginger instead of mustard. A little vinegar is sometimes added to each of these poultices.

Stramonium Poultice— Stir one tablespoonful of Indian meal into a gill of boiling water, and add one tablespoonful of bruised stramonium seeds.

Wormwood and Arnica are sometimes applied in poultices. Steep the herbs in half a pint of cold water, and when all their virtue is extracted, stir in a little bran or rye meal to thicken the liquid. The herbs must not be removed from the liquid.

This is a useful application for sprains and bruises.

Linseed Poultice— Take four ounces of powdered linseed and gradually sprinkle it into a half pint of hot water.

A REMEDY FOR BOILS

An excellent remedy for boils is water of a temperature agreeable to the feelings of the patient. Apply wet linen to the part affected, and frequently renew or moisten it. It is said to be the most effectual remedy known. Take inwardly some good blood purifier.

CURE FOR RINGWORM

Yellow dock, root or leaves, steeped in vinegar, will cure the worst case of ringworm.

[*Note:* Ask your doctor how many times recently he has prescribed yellow dock steeped in vinegar for ringworm!]

There are fewer whole birds seen on hats and bonnets this spring.— The Elite News, 1887

How To Preserve Health

Adopt the plan of rising early and never sit up late at night.

Drink water generally and avoid taking spirits.

Keep the head cool by washing it with cold water; abate feverish symptoms when they arise by preserving stillness.

Symptoms of plethora and indigestion may be corrected by eating and drinking less per day for a short time.

Never indulge in luxuries; guard against intemperance. Never sit in a draught nor lie in a wet bed.

Walk one or two miles a day, regardless of weather unless very bad indeed. Even a lady with stout walking boots, a large thick cloak, and umbrella may defy bad weather.

In severe weather walk rapidly. Brisk walking throws the blood to the surface, thus keeping up a vigorous circulation, making a cold impossible if you do not get into a cold bed too quickly after reaching home. Neglect of these precautions brings sickness and death to multitudes every year.

The amount of exercise necessary depends upon constitution, education, sex, and age. For men twenty to fifty, eight or ten miles a day of walking exercise may be taken as the average; for women the same age, half this quantity will suffice. Less than this will go a great way, but for keeping up high health, the above amount, omitted only on thoroughly wet days, may be considered necessary.

By all means avoid a morbid desponding feeling, for scarcely anything is more injurious to health.

Mental as well as bodily exercise is essential; therefore, labor and study should succeed each other.

The plainest food is best, taken in quantities so small as not to oppress the stomach; a man should never know that he has a stomach except when he is hungry.

Fat is frequently a sign of disease. A race horse is brought to his prime condition by training. So man should restrict himself in diet and exhaust his fat by having a good sweating every day but not to take cold.

Lying too long in bed is injurious to health. The want of expansion of the chest through exercise will aggravate or create consumptive tendencies which all more or less have, and the constant heat of the back or one side, occasioned by cushioning, disturbs healthy action.

When food rises in the stomach, the stomach is speaking and we ought to listen to it.

Too little food has its symptoms as well. The body will flag for want

257

of stimulus. Everyone should endeavor to discover his own maximum and minimum allowance and adhere to it.

Those who think most require the most sleep. The time "saved" from necessary sleep is destruction to mind, body, and estate. Compel yourself, children, and servants to go to bed at some early hour and to rise the moment they wake of themselves, and within a fortnight Nature will unloose the bonds of sleep the moment enough repose has been secured.

Take a gentle walk before breakfast.

Where water does not disagree, value the privilege and continue it.

Anxious pursuits exhaust the nervous system; therefore, avoid them as much as possible.

Food should be well-chewed; the stomach will not deal with it in lumps.

A person should calculate the number of hours between rising in the morning and retiring to bed at night, then divide this time into four equal spaces and assign each as an hour for a meal. Thus we advocate the old-fashioned sequence of meals in preference to the modern and more artificial mode of living. The usual number of working hours averages from fifteen to sixteen a day; divide this by four or three but never below that. No opinion is more fallacious than that the stomach, jilted of its midday meal, can compensate itself from a richer and more varied repast in the evening, or that three courses at six o'clock will more than atone for a plate of roast meat and potatoes at one or two. The stomach, rendered torpid by long abstinence, will not be flattered into performing double duty by a multiplicity of rich foods as badly assorted for the purposes of digestion as out of character by their number and incongruity.

It is also a great mistake to suppose that the breakfast is required as soon as the individual is out of bed; the stomach has hardly recovered from the torpidity of the night. Those, however, who are obliged to work for two or three hours before breakfast should take with them a few mouthfuls of biscuit to give the gastric juice some solid on which to operate instead of irritating the coats of the stomach by that gnawing feeling known as the sense of hunger.

Those whose labors do not commence till after their first meal should not partake of breakfast for half an hour after leaving their beds or till the body has been actively excited by a brief exercise, some gymnastic feat, or free use of the flesh brush over the trunk.

When the breakfast has been at eight, the dinner should be at one o'clock, and the best hour for tea is six, so as to leave three clear hours before the supper. Nor will there be any fear of nightmares if the person adjourns to bed within a quarter of an hour of such a meal.

With literary men and those whose occupations perpetually tax the brain, if the day's toil can be conveniently brought to a close by five or six o'clock, it is beneficial to take a slight repast at one o'clock and delay dinner till the day's work is over.

The habit of taking provocatives before dinner, in the shape of brandy or bitters, is very objectionable and can be excused only where the stomach is cold and the appetite languid. In such cases, about half an ounce of the compound tincture of gentian or an ounce of the compound tincture of cardamoms may, however, often be taken with great benefit.

How To Keep Well

Don't go to bed with cold feet.

Don't stand over hot-air registers.

Don't eat what you do not need just to save it.

Don't try to get cool too quickly after exercising.

Don't stuff a cold lest you should next be obliged to starve a fever.

Don't sit in a damp or chilly room without a fire.

Don't try to get along without flannel underclothing in winter.

DIPHTHERIA

A gargle of sulphur and water has been used with much success in cases of diphtheria. Let the patient swallow a little of the mixture. Or, when you discover that your throat is a little sore, bind a strip of flannel around the throat, wet in camphor, and gargle salt and vinegar occasionally.

[*Note:* Only this useless treatment for diphtheria! Poor mothers, poor children. Diphtheria antitoxin was not developed until 1892, in Germany.]

COLDS AND HOARSENESS

Borax has proved a most effective remedy in certain forms of colds. In sudden hoarseness or loss of voice in public speakers or singers from colds, relief for an hour or so may be obtained by slowly dissolving and partially swallowing a lump of borax the size of a garden pea, or about three or four grains held in the mouth for ten or fifteen minutes before speaking or singing. This produces a profuse secretion of saliva or "watering" of the mouth and throat, just as wetting brings back the missing notes to a flute when it is too dry.

A flannel dipped in boiling water and sprinkled with turpentine, laid on the chest as quickly as possible, will relieve the most severe cold or hoarseness.

Another simple, pleasant remedy is furnished by beating up the white of one egg, adding to it the juice of one lemon, and sweetening with white sugar to taste. Take a teaspoonful from time to time. It has been known to effectually cure the ailment.

Or bake a lemon or sour orange twenty minutes in a moderate oven. When done, open at one end and take out the inside. Sweeten with sugar or molasses. This is an excellent remedy for hoarseness.

An old-time and good way to relieve a cold is to go to bed and stay there, drinking nothing, not even water, for twenty-four hours and eating as little as possible.

[*Note:* The exact opposite of modern medical advice to "drink plenty of liquids."]

Or go to bed, put your feet in hot mustard and water; put a bran or oatmeal poultice on the chest; take ten grains of Dover's powder and, an hour afterwards, a pint of hot gruel. In the morning rub the body all over with a coarse towel and take a dose of aperient medicine.

Violet, pennyroyal, or boneset tea is excellent to promote perspiration in case of sudden chill. Care should be taken next day not to get chilled by exposure to fresh outdoor air.

MOLASSES POSSET

The old-fashioned remedy for a cold is as effectual now as it was in old times. Put into a saucepan a pint of the best West India molasses, a teaspoonful of powdered white ginger, and a quarter of a pound of fresh butter. Set it over the fire and simmer it slowly for half an hour, stirring it frequently. Do not let it come to a boil.

Then stir in the juice of two lemons or two tablespoonfuls of vinegar; cover the pan and let it stand by the fire five minutes longer. This is good for a cold. Some of it may be taken warm at once and the remainder kept at hand for occasional use. It is the preparation absurdly called by the common people a "Stewed Quaker."

Half a pint of strained honey mixed cold with the juice of a lemon and a tablespoonful of sweet oil is another remedy for a cold; a teaspoonful or two to be taken whenever the cough is troublesome.

COUGH SYRUP

Syrup of squills, four ounces; syrup of tolu, four ounces; tincture of bloodroot, one and one-half ounces; camphorated tincture of opium, four ounces. Mix. Dose for an adult: One teaspoonful repeated every two to four hours or as often as necessary.

LEANNESS

Is generally caused by lack of power in the digestive organs to digest and assimilate the fat-producing elements of food. First restore digestion, take plenty of sleep, drink all the water the stomach will bear in the morning on rising, take moderate exercise in the open air, eat oatmeal, cracked wheat, graham mush, baked sweet apples, roasted and broiled beef. Cultivate jolly people and bathe daily.

FOR TOOTHACHE

The worst toothache or neuralgia coming from the teeth may be speedily and delightfully ended by the application of a bit of clean cotton saturated in a solution of ammonia to the defective tooth. Sometimes the late sufferer is prompted to momentary laughter by the application, but the pain will disappear.

[*Note:* When you stop laughing, see your dentist.]

WRINKLES

There is almost nothing that can be done to prevent wrinkles. The best advice is to go on a diet of milk, beer, and cake in order to grow fat and thus extend the skin to its full tightness.

AGUE

This disease is caused by decaying vegetable matter. It prevails in new countries, river bottoms, districts which overflow, or in the neighborhood of canals or millponds. It may prevail in houses with bad cellars or where the sills and floors are in a state of decay. It does not make its appearance while the land is under water, but when the water recedes and exposes the half-rotten vegetable matter to the sun. Some physicians

261

suppose this disease to be caused by a microscopic vegetable germ which enters the system, contaminating the blood.

Some persons are never free from the intermittent fever while they reside in a malarial district.

Treatment: The night air contains the malarial poison in greater abundance than that of the day; so that if persons must live in a malarial region, they can lessen the liability to contract disease by being in the house before sunset and remaining there until after sunrise in the morning. An attack may be induced in some persons by eating anything which is difficult to digest. It becomes those who are susceptible to the influence of this virus to look well to their food.

Quinine is the king in this realm of remedies.

[*Note:* Ague was malarial fever. It was a disease that plagued pioneers from the New England coast to the Midwest. Old-timers were correct in thinking it more prevalent in low, swampy areas; mosquitoes were the chief carriers. As new areas were settled and damp lowlands were planted with trees and dried up, "ague" became less troublesome. It continued to be a threat for years, however. Many Presidents and First Ladies suffered from it at one time or another. Even before mosquitoes were identified as the chief culprits, it was well-known that one of the least healthful and most ague-inviting sites in the country was the humid city of Washington and the damp, drafty old White House.]

CROUP

Croup, it is said, can be cured in one minute, and the remedy is simply alum and sugar. Take a knife or grater and shave off in small particles about a teaspoonful of alum; then mix it with twice its amount of sugar to make it palatable and administer it as quickly as possible. Almost instantaneous relief will follow. Turpentine is said to be an excellent remedy for croup. Saturate a piece of flannel and apply it to the chest and throat and take inwardly three or four drops of turpentine on a lump of sugar.

BURNS AND SCALDS

A piece of cotton wadding spread with butter or sweet oil and bound on the burn instantly will draw out the pain without leaving a scar. The object is to entirely exclude the air from the part affected. Some use common baking soda, dry or wet, often giving instant relief, withdrawing the heat and pain. Some recommend the white of an egg, applied with a feather, which is very cooling and soothing and soon allays the smarting pain.

TO STOP THE FLOW OF BLOOD

For a slight cut there is nothing better to control the hemorrhage than common unglazed brown wrapping paper, such as is used by marketmen and grocers, a piece to be bound over the wound. Or cobwebs and brown sugar, pressed on like lint. When an artery is cut, the red blood spurts out at each pulsation. Press the thumb firmly over the artery near the wound and on the side near the heart. Press hard enough to stop the bleeding and wait till a physician comes. The wounded person is often able to do this himself if he has the requisite knowledge.

GRAVEL

Into a pint of water put two ounces of bicarbonate of soda. Take two tablespoonfuls in the early forenoon and the same towards night; also drink freely of water through the day. Inflammation of the kidneys has been successfully treated with large doses of limewater. Persons troubled with kidney difficulties should abstain from sugar and things that are converted into sugar in digestion, such as starchy food and sweet vegetables.

SORE THROAT

Everybody has a cure for this trouble, but simple remedies appear to be the most effectual. Salt and water is used by many as a gargle, but a little alum and honey dissolved in sage tea is better. An application of cloths wrung out of hot water and applied to the neck, changing as often as they begin to cool, has the most potency for removing inflammation of anything we ever tried. It should be kept up for a number of hours; during the evening is usually the most convenient time for applying this remedy.

Cut slices of salt pork or fat bacon, simmer a few moments in hot vinegar, and apply to throat as hot as possible. When this is taken off, as the throat is relieved, put around a bandage of soft flannel.

Camphorated oil is an excellent rubbing lotion for sore throat, sore

263

chest, aching limbs, etc. For a gargle for sore throat, put a pinch of chlorate of potash in a glass of water. Gargle the throat with it twice a day or oftener, if necessary.

CONSTIPATION

One or two figs eaten while fasting are sufficient for some, and they are especially good for children, as there is no trouble getting them to take them. A spoonful of wheaten bran in a glass of water is a simple remedy and quite effective, taken half an hour before breakfast; fruit eaten raw; partake largely of laxative food; exercise in the open air; drink freely of cold water during the day, etc. It is impossible to give many of the numerous treatments in so short a space; suffice it to say that the general character of our diet and experience is such as to assure us that at least one-quarter of the food that we swallow is intended by Nature to be evacuated from the system; and if it is not, it is again absorbed into the system, poisoning the blood and producing much suffering and permanent disease.

RELIEF FROM ASTHMA (MUSKRAT POULTICE)

Sufferers from asthma should get a muskrat skin and wear it over their lungs with the fur side next to the body. It will bring certain relief.

Or soak blotting paper in saltpeter water, then dry, burning at night in the patient's bedroom.

RECIPE FOR FELONS

Take common rock salt, as used for salting down pork or beef, dry in an oven, then pound it fine and mix with spirits of turpentine in equal parts; put it in a rag and wrap it around the parts affected; as it gets dry put on more, and in twenty-four hours you are cured. The felon will be dead.

Or saturate a bit of grated wild turnip, the size of a bean, with spirits of turpentine and apply it on the affected part. It relieves the pain at once; in twelve hours there will be a hole to the bone and the felon destroyed; then apply healing salve and the finger is well.

Or fill a tumbler with equal parts of fine salt and ice; mix well. Sink the finger in the center, allow it to remain until it is nearly frozen and numb; then withdraw it and, when sensation is restored, renew the operation four or five times, when it will be found the disease is destroyed. This must be done before pus is formed.

REMEDY FOR LOCKJAW

If any person is threatened with or taken with lockjaw from injuries of the arms, legs, or feet, *first call the doctor*, then put the part injured in the following preparation: Put hot wood-ashes into water as warm as can be borne; if the injured part cannot be put into water, then wet thick folded cloths in the water and apply them to the part as soon as possible; at the same time bathe the backbone from the neck down with some laxative stimulant—say, cayenne pepper and water or mustard and water (good vinegar is better than water); it should be as hot as the patient can bear it.

[*Note:* In case of lockjaw, call the doctor and forget the rest of this treatment!]

BLEEDING AT THE NOSE

Roll up a piece of paper and press it under the upper lip. In obstinate cases blow a little gum arabic up the nostril through a quill, which will immediately stop the discharge; powdered alum, dissolved in water, is also good. Pressure by the finger over the small artery near the ala (wing) of the nose, on the side where the blood is flowing, is said to arrest the hemorrhage immediately. Sometimes wringing a cloth out of very hot water and laying it on the back of the neck gives relief. Napkins wrung out of cold water must be laid across the forehead and nose, the hands dipped in cold water, and a bottle of hot water applied to the feet.

SUNSTROKE

Wrap a wet cloth bandage over the head; wet another cloth, folded small, square, cover it thickly with salt and bind it on to the back of the neck; apply dry salt behind the ears. Put mustard plasters to the calves of the legs and soles of the feet. This is an effectual remedy.

Good Morning, Have You Used Pear's Soap? —(*old adv.*)

FAINTING (SYNCOPE)

Immediately place the person in a lying position with head lower than body. In this way consciousness returns immediately, while in the erect position it often ends in death.

SWAIM'S VERMIFUGE

Worm seed, two ounces; valerian, rhubarb, pink root, white agaric, senna, of each one ounce and a half. Boil in sufficient water to yield three quarts of decoction. Now add to it ten drops of the oil of tansy and forty-five drops of the oil of cloves, dissolved in a quart of rectified spirit. Dose: One tablespoonful at night.

[*Note:* Not recommended! This concoction was much in favor years ago, when it was assumed that every fidgety child had worms. The modern approach is to provide fidgety children with "creative outlets" —sailboats, riding horses, color TV sets.]

FOR SEVERE SPRAINS

The white of an egg, a tablespoonful of vinegar and a tablespoonful of spirits of turpentine. Mix in a bottle, shake thoroughly, and bathe the sprain as soon as possible after the accident. This was published in *Life Secrets*, but it is republished by request on account of its great value. It should be remembered by everyone. An invaluable remedy for a sprain or bruise is wormwood boiled in vinegar and applied hot with enough cloths wrapped around it to keep the sprain moist.

CAMPHORATED OIL

Best oil of Lucca; gum camphor. Pound some gum camphor and fill a wide-necked pint bottle one-third full; fill up with olive oil and set away until the camphor is absorbed. Excellent lotion to rub on sore chest, sore throat, aching limbs, etc.

LINIMENT FOR CHILBLAINS

Spirits of turpentine, three drachms; camphorated oil, nine drachms. Mix for a liniment. If for a young child or if the skin be tender, the camphorated oil is used without the turpentine.

THE SUN'S CHOLERA MIXTURE

More than forty years ago, when it was found that prevention for the Asiatic cholera was easier than cure, the learned doctors of both hemispheres drew up a prescription which was published (for working people) in *The New York Sun* and so took the name of "The Sun's Cholera Mixture." It is found to be the best remedy ever yet devised. It is to be commended for several reasons. It is not to be mixed with liquor and therefore will not be used as an alcoholic beverage. Its ingredients are well known among all the common people, and it will have no prejudice to combat; each of the materials is in equal proportions to the others, and it may therefore be compounded without professional skill; and as the dose is so very small, it may be carried in a tiny phial in the waistcoat pocket and be always at hand. Dose according to age and violence of attack. No one who takes it in time will ever have the cholera. Even when no cholera is anticipated, it is a valuable remedy for ordinary summer complaints and should be kept always in readiness.

[*Note:* Mrs. Gillette did not give the prescription, so anyone interested may write to *The New York Sun* of 1840, care of the Cholera Editor.]

GRANDMOTHER'S COUGH SYRUP

Take half a pound of dry hoarhound herbs, one pod of red pepper, four tablespoonfuls of ginger. Boil all in three quarts of water, then strain and add one teaspoonful of good, fresh tar and a pound of sugar. Boil slowly and stir often until it is reduced to one quart of syrup. When cool, bottle for use. Take one or two teaspoonfuls four or six times a day.

GRANDMOTHER'S UNIVERSAL LINIMENT

One pint of alcohol and as much camphor gum as can be dissolved in it; half an ounce of the oil of cedar; one-half ounce of the oil of sassafras; aqua ammonia, half an ounce; and the same amount of the tincture of morphine. Shake well together, and apply it by the fire; the liniment must not be heated or come in contact with the fire, but the rubbing is to be done by the warmth of the fire.

These recipes of Grandmother's are all old, tried medicines and are more effectual than most of those that are advertised, as they have been thoroughly tried and proved reliable.

267

GRANDMOTHER'S FAMILY SPRING BITTERS

Mandrake root, one ounce; dandelion root, one ounce; burdock root, one ounce; yellow-dock root, one ounce; prickly-ash berries, two ounces; marshmallow, one ounce; turkey rhubarb, half an ounce; gentian, one ounce; English camomile flowers, one ounce; red clover tops, two ounces.

Wash the herbs and roots; put them into an earthen vessel; pour over them two quarts of water that has been boiled and cooled; let it stand overnight and soak; in the morning, set it on the back of the stove and steep it five hours. It must not boil but be nearly ready to boil. Strain it through a cloth, and add half a pint of good gin. Keep it in a cool place. Half a wineglass taken as a dose twice a day.

This is better than all the patent blood medicines that are in the market—a superior blood purifier—and will cure almost any sore, by taking it according to directions, and washing the sore with strong tea of raspberry leaves steeped, first washing the sore with castile soap, then drying with a soft cloth.

HUNTER'S PILLS

These pills can be manufactured at home and are *truly reliable*, having been sold and used for more than fifty years in Europe. The ingredients may be procured at almost any druggist's. The articles should be all in the powder. Saffron, rue, Scot aloes, savin, cayenne pepper. Mix all into a very thick mass by adding sufficient syrup. Rub some fine starch on the surface of a platter or large dinner plate; then with your forefinger and thumb nip off a small piece of the mass the size of a pill and roll it in pill form, first dipping your fingers in the starch. Place them as fast as made on the platter, set where they will dry slowly. Put them into a dry bottle or paper box. Dose: One every night and morning as long as occasion requires. This recipe is worth *ten times* the price of this book to any female requiring the need of these regulating pills.

Hints in Regard to Health

It is plainly seen by an inquiring mind that, aside from the selection and preparation of food, there are many little things constantly arising in the experience of everyday life which, in their combined effect, are powerful agents in the formation (or prevention) of perfect health. A careful observance of these little occurrences, an inquiry into the philosophy attending them, lies within the province, and indeed should be considered among the highest duties, of every housekeeper:

One should be cautious about entering a sick room in a state of perspiration, as the moment you become cool your pores absorb. Do not approach contagious diseases with an empty stomach nor sit between the sick and the fire, because the heat attracts the vapor.

The flavor of cod-liver oil may be changed to the delightful one of fresh oyster if the patient will drink a large glass of water poured from a vessel in which nails have been allowed to rust.

A bag of hot sand relieves neuralgia.

Warm borax water will remove dandruff.

Salt should be eaten with nuts to aid digestion.

It rests you, in sewing, to change your position frequently.

A little soda water will relieve sick headache caused by indigestion.

A cupful of strong coffee will remove the odor of onions from the breath.

Well-ventilated bedrooms will prevent morning headaches and lassitude.

A cupful of hot water before meals will relieve nausea and dyspepsia.

A fever patient can be made cool and comfortable by frequent sponging off with soda water.

Consumptive night-sweats may be arrested by sponging the body nightly in salt water.

Hot, dry flannels, applied as hot as possible, for neuralgia.

For bilious colic, soda and ginger in hot water. It may be taken freely.

Tickling in the throat is best relieved by a gargling of salt and water.

Pains in the side are most promptly relieved by the application of mustard.

For cold in the head, nothing is better than powdered borax sniffed up the nostrils.

A drink of hot, strong lemonade before going to bed will often break up a cold and cure a sore throat.

Nervous spasms are usually relieved by a little salt taken into the mouth and allowed to dissolve.

Sleeplessness caused by too much blood in the head may be overcome by applying a cloth wet with cold water to the back of the neck.

Earache—Tobacco smoke, puffed into the ear, has oftentimes been effectual.

For stomach cramps, ginger ale or a teaspoonful of the tincture of ginger in a half glass of water in which a half teaspoonful of soda has been dissolved.

Sickness of the stomach is most promptly relieved by drinking a teacupful of hot soda and water. If it brings the offending matter up, all the better.

A teaspoonful of ground mustard in a cupful of warm water is a prompt and reliable emetic and should be resorted to in cases of poisoning or cramps in the stomach from overeating.

Avoid purgatives or strong physic, as they not only do no good but are positively harmful. Pills may relieve for the time, but they seldom cure.

Hot water is better than cold for bruises. It relieves pain quickly and by preventing congestion often keeps off the ugly black and blue mark. "Children cry for it," when they experience the relief it affords their bumps and bruises.

A Becoming Figure

Young girls are not as heavy in proportion to their height as grown women are. Many persons, however, have very erroneous ideas of what constitutes a becoming figure. The following table will show what are the proper proportions of height and weight in a well-developed woman:

Five feet in height	About 100 pounds
Five feet, one inch	106
Five feet, two	113
Five feet, three	119
Five feet, four	130
Five feet, five	138
Five feet, six	144
Five feet, seven	150
Five feet, eight	155
Five feet, nine	163
Five feet, ten	169
Five feet, eleven	176
Six feet	180
Six feet, one inch	186

Medicinal Food

Spinach has a direct effect upon complaints of the kidneys; the common dandelion, used as greens, is excellent for the same trouble; asparagus purifies the blood; celery acts admirably upon the nervous system, and is a cure for rheumatism and neuralgia; tomatoes act upon the liver; beets and turnips are excellent appetizers; lettuce and cucumbers are cooling in their effects upon the system; beans are a very nutritious and strengthening vegetable; while onions, garlic, leeks, chives and shallots, all of which are similar, possess medical virtues of a marked character, stimulating the circulatory system and the consequent increase of the saliva and the gastric juice promoting digestion. Red onions are an excellent diuretic, and the white ones are recommended raw as a remedy for insomnia. They are tonic, nutritious. A soup made from onions is regarded by the French as an excellent restorative in debility of the digestive organs. We might go through the entire list and find each vegetable possessing its especial mission of cure, and it will be plain to every housekeeper that a vegetable diet should be partly adopted and will prove of great advantage to the health of every member of the family.

FRUITS AS MEDICINE

The famous French doctor, Dupoury, divides fruits into five classes: 1. Acid 2. Sweet 3. Astringent 4. Oily 5. Mealy. In the first class he counts cherries, strawberries, raspberries, gooseberries, peaches, apples, lemons, oranges, and regards them as of great hygienic value.

Cherries he prohibits to those affected with neuralgia of the stomach;

Strawberries and raspberries he recommends to the bilious and gouty and denies them to those affected with diabetes;

Of the sweet fruits he particularly values plums, especially for the gouty and rheumatic;

Grapes he awards the first place and thinks them the cure par excellence for the anaemic, dyspeptic, consumptive, gouty and bilious;

Bananas are recommended for the typhoid patient;

Lemons and tomatoes are cooling;

Lemonade is the best drink in fevers;

The juice of half a lemon in one teacupful of strong black coffee without sugar often cures a sick headache;

Green figs are an excellent food and are laxative;

Prunes supply the highest nerve or brain food; dried figs contain heat, nerve, and muscle food, hence are good for both cold and warm weather;

The acid of small seeded fruits (strawberries, etc.) is cooling and purifying.

271

Cure for Alcoholism—In the morning before breakfast one orange should be eaten, one about nine o'clock, one before dinner, one before supper and one before retiring. Continue one week. The second week four oranges per day will be sufficient, the third week, three, and the fourth week the tippler won't be able to bear the smell of alcohol. Try it.

Blackberry Syrup Remedy for Diarrhea—To every quart of strained blackberry juice use one-half pound of loaf sugar, one teaspoonful of powdered cloves, one teaspoonful of cinnamon, one teaspoonful of powdered nutmeg. Mix. Boil all together in a porcelain kettle, skimming well. When cold add one-half pint of best brandy.

[*Note:* Blackberry brandy—the popular "soldier's medicine" for a common Civil War disease.]

Watercress contains much iron and this is a real blood medicine. It is a destroyer of pimples and a cleanser of the system. Watercress will neutralize chalk in the blood, which limy matter is the great cause of aging and stiffening of the fibers. Those who would feel young and look young, therefore, should eat watercress.

Black Tea is much more suitable than green for sick persons, as it does not affect the nerves. Nervous persons who sleep badly rest much better after a supper of corn or rye mush than if they take tea or coffee.

Boneset for a Cough or Cold—Pour one and one-half pints of boiling water on a ten-cent package of boneset. Let it steep near the fire for ten or fifteen minutes, then strain it. Sweeten it with two and one-half coffee cups of loaf sugar, then bottle it. It will keep longer if one-half pint of Jamaica rum be added. A child may take one teaspoonful before each meal. A grown person, one small wineglass.

Nervousness—Herb teas are very useful. Camomile for nervousness and sleeplessness. Calamus for infants. The tea must be sweetened to taste.

To Catch Flies—Put into a saucepan one pint of molasses, one-half pint of linseed oil, one pound of resin. Cook for thirty-five minutes after the mixture begins to boil, stir frequently, spread this on common brown paper, and spread another sheet of paper on the first one. Continue until the mixture is all used. If you want to use any of it, cut off a piece and draw the sheets apart so you have "fly" paper.

A new broom should be dipped into boiling water before using to soften the straw and to make it less brittle. Longer service will be the result.

Cooking Aprons—Two wide, long aprons of fine, unbleached muslin of soft sheer quality, with generous strings and feather-stitched hems, will be an acceptable gift to any woman. A nice long holder of white or brown linen for removing pies and other hot dishes from the oven might appropriately be added.

Toilet Recipes, Items

COLOGNE WATER (SUPERIOR)

Oil of lavender, two drachms; oil of rosemary, one drachm and a half; orange, lemon, and bergamot, one drachm each of the oil; also, two drachms of the essence of musk; attar of rose, ten drops; and a pint of proof spirit. Shake all together thoroughly three times a day for a week.

JOCKEY CLUB BOUQUET

Mix one pint extract of rose, one pint extract of tuberose, half a pint of extract of cassia, four ounces extract of jasmine and three ounces tincture of civet. Filter the mixture.

ROSEWATER

Preferable to the distilled for a perfume or for culinary purposes. Attar of rose, twelve drops; rub it up with half an ounce of white sugar and two drachms carbonate magnesia; then add gradually one quart of water and two ounces of proof spirit and filter through paper.

LAVENDER WATER

Oil of lavender, two ounces; orris root, half an ounce; spirit of wine, one pint. Mix and keep two or three weeks. It may then be strained through two thicknesses of blotting paper and is ready for use.

273

BAY RUM

French proof spirit, one gallon; extract bay, six ounces. Mix and color with caramel. Needs no filtering.

CREAM OF LILIES

Best white castor oil; pour in a little strong solution of sal tartar in water and shake it until it looks thick and white. Perfume with lavender.

CREAM OF ROSES

Olive oil, one pound; attar of roses, fifty drops; oil of rosemary, twenty-five drops. Mix and color it with alkanet root.

COLD CREAM

Melt one ounce oil of almonds, half-ounce spermaceti, one drachm white wax, and then add two ounces of rose water and stir it constantly until cold.

LIP SALVE

Melt one ounce white wax, one ounce sweet oil, one drachm spermaceti and throw in a piece of alkanet root to color it and, when cooling, perfume it with oil rose, and then pour it into small white jars or boxes.

FOR DANDRUFF

Take glycerine, four ounces; tincture of cantharides, five ounces; bay rum, four ounces; water, two ounces. Mix and apply once a day, and rub well down the scalp.

HAIR INVIGORATOR

Bay rum, two pints; alcohol, one pint; castor oil, one ounce; carb. ammonia, half an ounce; tincture of cantharides, one ounce. Mix them well. This compound will promote the growth of the hair and prevent it from falling out.

MACASSAR OIL FOR THE HAIR

Renowned for the past fifty years is as follows: Take a quarter of an ounce of the chippings of alkanet root, tie this in a bit of coarse muslin, and put it in a bottle containing eight ounces of sweet oil; cover it to keep out the dust; let it stand several days; add to this sixty drops of tincture of cantharides, ten drops of oil of rose; neroli and lemon, each sixty drops; let it stand one week and you will have one of the most powerful stimulants for the growth of hair ever known.

Another hair oil: To a pint of strong sage tea, a pint of bay rum, and a quarter of an ounce of the tincture of cantharides, add an ounce of castor oil and a teaspoonful of rose or other perfume. Shake well before applying to the hair, as the oil will not mix.

INSTANTANEOUS HAIR DYE

There is danger in some of the patent hair dyes, and hence the *Scientific American* offers what is known as the walnut hair dye. The simplest form is the expressed juice of the bark or shell of green walnuts. To preserve the juice a little alcohol is commonly added to it with a few bruised cloves, and the whole digested together, with occasional agitation for a week or fortnight, when the clear portion is decanted and, if necessary, filtered. Sometimes a little common salt is added with the same intention. It should be kept in a cool place. The most convenient way of application is by means of a sponge.

DYE FOR WHITE OR LIGHT EYEBROWS

Boil an ounce of walnut bark in a pint of water for an hour. Add a lump of alum the size of a filbert, and when cold, apply with a camel's-hair brush.

HAIR WASH

One pennyworth of borax, half a pint of olive oil, one pint of boiling water. Pour the boiling water over the borax and oil; let it cool; then

275

put the mixture into a bottle. Shake it before using and apply it with a flannel. Camphor and borax, dissolved in boiling water and left to cool, make a very good wash for the hair, as also does rosemary water mixed with a little borax. After using any of these washes, when the hair becomes thoroughly dry, a little pomatum or oil should be rubbed in to make it smooth and glossy—that is, if one prefers oil on the hair.

OX-MARROW POMADE FOR THE HAIR

One marrow bone, half a pint of oil, ten cents' worth of citronella. Take the marrow out of the bone, place it in warm water, let it get almost to boiling point, then let it cool and pour the water away; repeat this three times until the marrow is thoroughly "fined." Beat the marrow to a cream with a silver fork, stir the oil in, drop by drop, beating all the time; when quite cold add the citronella, pour into jars, and cover down.

"What! Corns and Bunions all gone?"
"Yes, I am happy to say, through the merits of Hanson's Magic Corn Salve I can now walk with ease."

TO INCREASE THE HAIR IN THE BROWS

Clip them and anoint with a little sweet oil. Should the hair fall out, having been full, use one of the hair invigorators.

BANDOLINE

To one quart of rose water add an ounce and a half of gum tragacanth; let it stand forty-eight hours, frequently straining it, then strain through a coarse linen cloth; let it stand two days and again strain; add to it a drachm of oil of roses. Used by ladies dressing their hair to make it lie in any position.

COMPLEXION WASH

Put in a vial one drachm of benzoin gum in powder, one drachm nutmeg oil, six drops of orange-blossom tea or apple blossoms; put in half pint of rain water and boil down to one teaspoonful and strain; add one pint of sherry wine. Bathe the face morning and night; will remove all flesh worms and freckles and give a beautiful complexion. Or put one ounce of powdered gum of benzoin in a pint of whiskey; to use, put in water in washbowl till it is milky, allowing it to dry without wiping. This is perfectly harmless. Cream cures sunburn on some complexions; lemon juice is best on others, and cold water suits still others best.

BURNET'S CELEBRATED POWDER FOR THE FACE

Five cents' worth of bay rum, five cents' worth of magnesia snowflake, five cents' worth of bergamot, five cents' worth of oil of lemon. Mix in a pint bottle and fill up with rain water. Shake well and apply on a soft sponge or cloth.

TOILET OR FACE POWDER

Take a quarter of a pound of wheat starch pounded fine; sift it through a piece of lace; add to it eight drops of oil of rose, oil of lemon, thirty drops, and oil of bergamot, fifteen drops. Rub thoroughly together. The French throw this powder into alcohol, shaking it, letting it settle, then pouring off the alcohol and drying the powder. In that case, the perfume is added lastly.

277

TO REMOVE FRECKLES

The following lotion is highly recommended: One ounce of lemon juice, a quarter of a drachm of powdered borax, and half a drachm of sugar. Mix in a bottle and allow them to stand a few days, when the liquor should be rubbed occasionally on the hands and face. Another application is: friar's balsam, one part; rose water, twenty parts.

Also a tablespoonful of freshly grated horse-radish stirred into a cupful of sour milk; let it stand for twelve hours, then strain and apply often. This bleaches the complexion also and takes off tan.

TO REMOVE MOTH PATCHES

Into a pint bottle of rum put a tablespoonful of flour of sulphur. Apply this to the patches once a day, and they will disappear in two or three weeks.

PEARL SMELLING SALTS

Powdered carbonate of ammonia, one ounce; strong solution of ammonia, half a fluid ounce; oil of rosemary, ten drops; oil of bergamot, ten drops. Mix and while moist put in a wide-mouthed bottle.

PEARL TOOTH POWDER

Prepared chalk, half a pound; powdered myrrh, two ounces; camphor, two drachms; orris root, powdered, two ounces. Moisten the camphor with alcohol and mix well together.

BAD BREATH

Bad breath from catarrh, foul stomach, or bad teeth may be temporarily relieved by diluting a little bromochloralum with eight or ten parts of water and using it as a gargle and swallowing a few drops before going out. A pint of bromochloralum costs fifty cents, but a small vial will last a long time.

RAZOR-STROP PASTE

Wet the strop with a little sweet oil and apply a little flour of emery evenly over the surface.

278

SHAVING COMPOUND

Half a pound of plain, white soap, dissolved in a small quantity of alcohol, as little as can be used; add a tablespoonful of pulverized borax. Shave the soap and put it in a small tin basin or cup; place it on the fire in a dish of boiling water; when melted, add the alcohol and remove from the fire; stir in oil of bergamot sufficient to perfume it.

BARBER'S SHAMPOO MIXTURE

Dissolve half an ounce of carbonate of ammonia and one ounce of borax in one quart of water; then add two ounces of glycerine in three quarts of New England rum and one quart of bay rum. Moisten the hair with this liquid, shampoo with the hands until a light lather is formed, then wash off with plenty of clean water.

CAMPHOR ICE

Melt together over a water bath white wax and spermaceti, each one ounce; camphor, two ounces, in sweet almond oil, one pound; then triturate until the mixture has become homogeneous, and allow one pound of rose water to flow in slowly during the operation. Excellent for chapped lips or hands.

ODORIFEROUS OR SWEET-SMELLING BAGS

Lavender flowers, one ounce; pulverized orris, two drachms; bruised rosemary leaves, half-ounce; musk, five grains; attar of rose, five drops. Mix well. Sew up in small flat muslin bags and cover them with fancy silk or satin. These are very nice to keep in your bureau drawers or trunk, as the perfume penetrates through the contents of the trunk or drawers. An acceptable present to a single gentleman.

HOW TO KEEP BRUSHES CLEAN

The best way in which to clean hairbrushes is with spirits of ammonia, as its effect is immediate. No rubbing is required, and cold water can be used just as successfully as warm. Take a tablespoonful of ammonia

279

to a quart of water, dip the hair part of the brush without wetting the ivory, and in a moment the grease is removed; then rinse in cold water, shake well, and dry in the air, but not in the sun. Soda and soap soften the bristles and invariably turn the ivory yellow.

TOILET SOAP

One pound of washing soda, one pound of lard or clear tallow, half a pound of unslaked lime, one tablespoonful of salt, three quarts of water. Put the soda and lime in a large dish and pour over the water, boiling hot; stir until dissolved; let it stand until clear, then pour off the clear liquid, add the grease and salt; boil four hours, then pour into pans to cool. If it should be inclined to curdle or separate, indicating the lime to be too strong, pour in a little more water and boil again. Perfume as you please and pour into molds or a shallow dish and, when cold, cut into bars to dry.

CURE FOR PIMPLES

It is advisable, in order to clear the complexion, to cleanse the blood. Diet should receive first attention. Strong tea used daily will give the skin the color and appearance of leather. Coffee affects the nerves more but the skin less, and a healthy nervous system is necessary to beauty. Eating between meals, late suppers, overeating at meals, eating sweet-meats, candies, etc., all these tend to disorder the blood, producing pimples and blotches.

If suds are left or wiped off the skin, the action of the air and sun will tan the surface and permanently deface the complexion; therefore, one should be sure to thoroughly rinse off all soap from the skin to avoid the tanning, which will leave a brown or yellow tinge impossible to efface.

TOILET ITEMS

Mutton tallow is considered excellent to soften the hands. An old pair of soft, large gloves thoroughly covered on the inside with the tallow and glycerine in equal parts, melted together, can be worn during the night with the most satisfactory results.

Four parts of glycerine and five parts of yolks of eggs thoroughly mixed and applied after washing the hands is also considered excellent.

For chapped hands or face, one ounce of glycerine, one ounce of alcohol mixed, then add eight ounces of rose water.

280

Another good rule is to rub well in dry oatmeal after every washing and be particular regarding the quality of soap. Cheap soap and hard water are the unknown enemies of many people and the cause of rough skin and chapped hands. Castile soap and rainwater will sometimes cure without any other assistance.

Camphor ice is also excellent and can be applied with but little inconvenience. Borax dissolved and added to the toilet water is also good.

For chapped lips, beeswax dissolved in a small quantity of sweet oil by heating carefully. Apply the salve two or three times a day and avoid wetting the lips as much as possible.

To soften the hands, one can have the hands in soapsuds with soft soap without injury to the skin if the hands are dipped in vinegar or lemon juice immediately after. The acids destroy the corrosive effects of the alkali and make the hands soft and white. Indian meal and vinegar or lemon juice used on hands where roughened by cold or labor will heal and soften them. Rub the hands in this, then wash thoroughly and rub in glycerine. Those who suffer from chapped hands will find this comforting.

To remove stains rub a slice of raw potato upon the stains, or wash the hands in lemon juice or steeped laurel leaves.

To give a fine color to the nails, the hands and fingers must be well lathered and washed with fine soap; then the nails must be rubbed with equal parts of cinnebar and emery, followed by oil of bitter almonds. To take white spots from the nails, melt equal parts of pitch and turpentine in a small cup, add to it vinegar and powdered sulphur. Rub this on the nails, and the spots will soon disappear.

Miscellaneous Household Recipes

USES OF AMMONIA

All housekeepers should keep a bottle of liquid ammonia, as it is the most powerful and useful agent for cleaning silks, stuffs, and hats—in fact, cleans everything it touches. A few drops in water will take off grease from dishes, pans, etc. A spoonful in a quart of warm water for cleaning paint makes it look like new. If a cupful of ammonia is put into the water in which clothes are soaked the night before washing, the ease with which the articles can be washed and their great whiteness and

281

clearness when dried will be very gratifying. Remembering the small sum paid for three quarts of ammonia of common strength, one can easily see that no bleaching preparation can be more cheaply obtained.

No articles in kitchen use are so likely to be neglected and abused as dishcloths and dish towels. In washing these, ammonia can be a greater comfort than anywhere else. A few drops in water will brighten the colors in dark carpets, clean hairbrushes, and use the waste water afterwards, if not too soiled, to fertilize and nourish house plants. In every way, in fact, ammonia is the housekeeper's friend.

Ammonia is not only useful for cleaning but as a household medicine. Half a teaspoonful in half a tumbler of water is far better for faintness than alcoholic stimulants. In the Temperance Hospital in London, it is used with the best results. It was used freely by Lieutenant Greely's Arctic party for keeping up circulation. It is a relief in nervousness, headache, and heart disturbances.

TO DESTROY INSECTS AND VERMIN

Mix equal quantities of pulverized borax, camphor gum, and saltpeter together, making a powder. If the housekeeper will begin at the top of her house with a powder bellows and a large quantity of this fresh powder and puff it thoroughly into every crack and crevice, whether or not there are Croton bugs in them, to the very bottom of her house, special attention being paid to old furniture, closets, and wherever Croton water is introduced, she will be freed from these and other torments. The operation may require a repetition, but the end is success.

Dissolve two pounds of alum in three or four quarts of water. Let it remain overnight till alum is dissolved. Apply with brush, boiling hot, to every joint and crevice where Croton bugs, ants, cockroaches, or bedbugs intrude.

To keep woolens and furs from moths: Tie up articles in strong brown paper with several lumps of gum camphor between the folds. Place in close box or trunk. Wherever a knitting needle can pass, the parent moth can enter.

Or place pieces of camphor, cedar wood, Russia leather, tobacco leaves, whole cloves, or anything strongly aromatic in drawers.

Hair on the Face, Neck, Arms or Any Part of the Person Quickly Dissolved and Removed with the New Solution, MODENE! *Does Away with Shaving Forever. Discovered by Accident.* —(old adv.)

MOTHS IN CARPETS

If you fear that they are at work at the edge of carpets, it will sometimes suffice to lay a wet towel and press a hot flatiron over it; but the best way is to take the carpet up and clean it, look in the floor cracks, and if you discover signs of moths, wash the floor with benzine and scatter red pepper on it before putting the carpet lining down.

A good way to clean old carpets until you would think them new: Put half a tumbler of spirits of turpentine in a basin of water and dip your broom in it and sweep over the carpet once or twice; or rub carpet over with meal. Just dampen it a very little and rub with it and when perfectly dry, sweep over with meal. After a carpet is thoroughly swept, rub it with a cloth dipped in water and ammonia.

CLEANING OILCLOTHS

A dingy oilcloth may be brightened by washing it with clear water with a little borax dissolved in it; wipe it with a flannel cloth that you have dipped into milk and then wrung as dry as possible.

TO STARCH, FOLD, AND IRON SHIRTS

To three tablespoonfuls of dry, fine starch allow a quart of water. First wet the starch smooth in a little cold water in a tin pan. Put into it a little pinch of salt and a piece of enamel or shirt polish, the size of a bean, or a piece of clean tallow or a piece of butter the size of a cranberry. Pour over this a quart of boiling water, stirring rapidly, placing it over the fire. Cook until clear, then remove it from the fire and set the pan in another of warm water to keep the starch warm.

Turn the shirt wrong side out and dip the bosom in the hot starch as warm as the hands can bear the heat. Rub the starch evenly through the linen, saturating it thoroughly, and wring hard to make dry as possible. Starch the collar and wristbands the same way, then hang them out to dry. Three hours before ironing them, wet the bosoms and cuffs in cold water, wring out, shake and fold, roll up tightly, wrap in a towel, and let remain two or three hours.

The back of the shirt should be ironed first by doubling it lengthwise through the center; the wristbands may be ironed next and both sides of the sleeves, then the collarband. Now place a bosom board under the bosom and with a fresh clean napkin dampened a little, rub the bosom

283

from the top towards the bottom, arranging and smoothing each plait neatly; then, with a smooth, moderately hot flatiron, begin ironing from the top downward, pressing hard until the bosom becomes smooth, dry, and glossy. Remove the bosom board and iron the front, fold both sides of the shirt towards the center of the back, fold together below the bosom, and hang on the bars to air.

[*Note:* After ironing this shirt, you may want to hang on the bars a little while yourself.]

TO CLEAN BLACK LACE

A teaspoonful of gum arabic, dissolved in one teacupful of boiling water; when cool, add half a teaspoonful of black ink, dip the lace and spread smoothly between the folds of a newspaper, and press dry with book or the like. Lace shawls can be dressed over in this way: Pin a sheet to the carpet and stretch the shawl upon that, or black lace can be cleaned the same as ribbon and silk:

Take an old kid glove (black preferable) no matter how old and boil it in a pint of water for a short time; then let it cool until the leather can be taken in the hand without burning; use the glove to sponge off the ribbon. After cleaning, lay a piece of paper over the ribbon and iron. The ribbon will look like new.

Or throw black laces boldly into alcohol, churn them up and down until they foam, squeeze them out, "spat" them, pull out the edges, lay them between brown paper, leave under a heavy weight until dry; do not iron.

TO WASH WHITE LACE

Cover a bottle with linen stitched smoothly to fit the shape. Wind the lace about it, basting both edges to the linen. Wash on the bottle, soaping and rinsing, then boil in soft water. Dry in the sun. Clip the basting threads and do not iron. If carefully done, it will look like new lace.

TO CLEAN SILKS OR RIBBONS

Half a pint of gin, half a pound of honey, half a pound of soft soap, one eighth of a pint of water. Mix the above ingredients together, then lay each breadth of silk upon a clean kitchen table and scrub it well on the soiled side with the mixture. Have ready three vessels of cold water. Take each piece of silk at two corners and dip it up and down in each vessel, but do not wring it, and take care that each breadth has one vessel of quite clean water for the last dip. Hang it up dripping for a minute or two, then dab in a cloth and iron it quickly with a very hot iron.

Where the lace or silk is very much soiled, it is best to pass them through a warm liquor of bullock's gall and water. Rinse in cold water, then take a small piece of glue, pour boiling water on it, and pass the veil through it; clap it and frame to dry. Instead of framing, it may be fastened with drawing pins closely fixed upon a very clean paste or drawing board.

TO CLEAN BLACK SILK DRESSES

One of the things "not generally known," at least in this country, is the Parisian method of cleaning black silk; the *modus operandi* is very simple and the result infinitely superior to that achieved in any other manner. Brush and wipe silk, then lay flat on board and sponge well with hot coffee thoroughly freed from sediment by being strained through muslin. Sponge on side intended to show; allow to become partially dry and iron on wrong side. The coffee restores the brilliancy of silk without imparting to it either the shiny appearance or crackly stiffness obtained by beer. The silk really appears thickened by the process, and this good effect is permanent. Our readers who will experimentalize on an apron or cravat will never again try any other method.

TO WASH FEATHERS

Wash in warm soapsuds and rinse in water a very little blued; if the feather is white, let the wind dry it. When the curl has come out by washing or getting the feather damp, place a hot flatiron so that you can hold the feather just about it while curling. Take a bone or silver knife and draw the fibers of the feather between the thumb and the dull edge of the knife, taking not more than three fibers at a time, beginning at the point of the feather and curling one half the other way. After a little practice one can make them look as well as new feathers.

A FILTHY HOME *is rarely found where the Hartman Flexible Wire Mat is to be seen at the outer door. Its cleanliness is an inspiration.* —(*old adv.*)

HOW TO FRESHEN UP FURS

Furs when taken out in the fall are often found to have a mussed, crushed-out appearance. They can be made to look like new. Wet the fur with a hairbrush, brushing up the wrong way of the fur. Leave it to dry in the air for about half an hour, then give it a good beating on the right side with a rattan and comb it with a coarse comb.

NOVEL DRESS MENDING

A novel way of mending a woolen or silk dress: The frayed portions around the tear should be carefully smoothed and a piece of the material, moistened with a very thin mucilage, placed under the hole. A heavy weight should be put upon it until it is dry, when it is only possible to discover the mended place by careful observation.

[*Note:* The forerunner of "iron-on" patches and fabric glue!]

TO RAISE THE PILE ON VELVET

Put on a table two pieces of wood; place between them, bottom side up, three very hot flatirons, and over them lay a wet cloth. Hold the velvet over the cloth with the wrong side down; when steamed, brush the pile with a light wisp, and the velvet will look as good as new.

When it is feared that soap may change the color of an article as, for instance, scarlet hosiery, if the garment be not badly soiled it may be cleansed by washing without soap in water in which pared potatoes have been boiled. This method will also prevent color from running in washing prints.

To keep colors from running in washing black prints, put a teaspoonful of black pepper in the first water.

Salt or beef's gall in the water helps to set black.

Dark calicoes should be stiffened with gum arabic—five cents' worth is enough for a dress.

Lard will remove wagon grease.

CEMENT FOR CHINA AND GLASS

To half a pint of milk put an equal quantity of vinegar in order to curdle it; then separate the curd from the whey and mix the whey

286

with the whites of four or five eggs, beating the whole well together. When well mixed, add a little quicklime through a sieve until it has acquired the consistency of a thick paste. With this cement broken vessels may be mended.

LEAKS IN WASTE PIPES

Shut yourself into a room from which the pipe starts. Put two or three ounces of oil of peppermint into a pail of boiling hot water and pour down the pipe. Another person who has not yet inhaled the strong odor should follow the course of the pipe through the house. The peppermint will be pretty sure to discover a break that even an expert plumber might overlook.

TO CLEAN KID GLOVES

Boil a handful of flaxseed, add a little dissolved toilet soap; when mixture cools, put the glove on the hand and rub with a piece of white flannel wet with the mixture.

Xmas Pleasures
The mistletoe hung on the chandelier
And he kissed her there with never a fear,
For the soup was delicious, the turkey fine,
The pudding was rich, the sauce divine,
And then came the fruits and confections so sweet,
But none of them better than Cream of Wheat!
So the lovers were left to their billing and cooing
And all the sweet nothings which constitute wooing.

Cream of Wheat meets every requirement of the growing body and supplants the waste of age. It is Brain and Muscle Food, as it is chiefly Gluten and Phosphates. Your grocer will give you a really beautiful picture of northwestern scenery whenever you buy two packages of Cream of Wheat. —(old adv.)

THE ONEITA—*Elastic Ribbed Union Suits, perfectly elastic, fitting like a glove.* NO BUTTONS DOWN THE FRONT. *Made especially for Women and Misses. Convenient to put on, being entered at top and drawn on like trousers.* —*(old adv.)*

STARCH POLISH

Take one ounce of spermaceti and one ounce of white wax; melt and run it into a thin cake on a plate. A piece the size of a quarter dollar added to a quart of prepared starch gives a beautiful luster to the clothes and prevents the iron from sticking.

TO CLEAN SILVER PLATE

Wash in soapsuds, rinse, and dry; mix hartshorn powder into a thick paste with cold water; spread this over silver. When dry, brush off and polish with chamois skin.

TO WASH COLORED GARMENTS

For calicoes that fade, put a teaspoonful of sugar of lead into a pailful of water and soak fifteen minutes before washing.

THE MARKING SYSTEM

Mark all your own personal wardrobe. A bottle of indelible ink is cheap, a clean pen still cheaper, and a bright, sunny day or a hot flatiron will complete the business. Then there are the paper patterns, of which every mother has a store. On the outside of each, the name of the pattern should be plainly written. There are the rolls of pieces which may contain a good deal not apparent from the outside. All these hidden mysteries should be indicated.

MANAGEMENT OF STOVES

If the fire in a stove has plenty of fresh coals on top not yet burned through, it will need only a little shaking to start it up, but if the fire looks dying and the coals look white, don't shake it. When it has drawn till it is red again, if there is much ash and little fire, put coals on very carefully. A mere handful of fire can be coaxed back to life by adding another handful or so of new coals on the red spot and giving plenty of draught, but don't shake a dying fire or you lose it. This management is often necessary after a warm spell, when the stove has been kept dormant for days, though I hope you will not be so unfortunate as to have a fire to coax up on a cold winter morning. They should be arranged overnight so that all that is required is to open the draughts in order to have a cheery glow in a few minutes.

TO REMOVE STAINS AND SPOTS

A tablespoonful of white currant juice, if any can be had, is even better than lemon. This preparation may be used on delicate articles. Mark it "poison" and put it where it will not be meddled with.

POSTAGE STAMP MUCILAGE

Take of gum dextrine, two parts; acetic acid, one part; water, five parts; dissolve in a water bath and add alcohol, one part.

FAMILY GLUE

Crack the glue and put it in a bottle; add common whisky. Shake up, cork tight, and in three or four days it can be used. Keep tight so whisky will not evaporate. Warm up in cold weather. Use tin stopper fitting as closely as possible.

FURNITURE CREAM

Shred finely two ounces of beeswax and half an ounce of white wax into half a pint of turpentine; set in a warm place until dissolved, then pour over the mixture the following, boiled together until melted: half a pint of water, an ounce of castile soap, and a piece of resin the size of a small nutmeg. Mix thoroughly and keep in a wide-necked stone bottle for use. This cleans well and leaves a good polish and may be made at a fourth of the price it is sold at.

POLISH FOR LADIES' KID SHOES

A fine liquid polish for ladies' kid shoes, satchels, etc., that is easy of application, recommended as containing no ingredients in any manner injurious to leather, is found by digesting in a close vessel at gentle heat and straining a solution made as follows: lampblack, one drachm;

oil turpentine, four drachms; alcohol (trimethyl), twelve ounces; shellac, one and one-half ounces; white turpentine, five drachms; sandarac, two drachms.

PASTE FOR SCRAPBOOKS, ETC.

Dissolve a teaspoonful of alum in a quart of water. When cold, stir in flour to give it the consistency of thick cream. Beat up all the lumps. Stir in as much powdered resin as will lie on a dime, and throw in half a dozen cloves to give it a pleasant odor. Have on the fire a teacupful of boiling water; pour flour mixture into it, stirring. In a few minutes it will be the consistency of molasses. Cool and stir in a small teaspoonful of oil of cloves and sassafras. When needed, soften a portion with warm water. This is a fine paste to use to stiffen embroidery. Will keep.

TO KEEP CIDER

A gentleman of Denver writes he has a sure preservative. Put eight gallons of cider into a clean barrel, take one ounce of powdered charcoal and one ounce of powdered sulphur, mix and put it into some iron vessel that will go down through the bunghole of the barrel. Now put a piece of red-hot iron into the charcoal and sulphur and while it is burning, lower it through the bunghole to within one foot of the cider, and suspend it there by a piece of wire. Bring it up, and in twelve hours you can cure another batch. Put the cider in a tight barrel and keep in a cool cellar, and it will keep for years.

A Holland recipe: To one quart of new milk fresh from the cow (not strained) add one-half pound of ground black mustard seed and six eggs. Beat the whole well together and pour into a barrel of cider. It will keep cider sweet for one year or more.

WASHING FLUID

This is the article that is used in the Chinese laundries for whitening their linen and is called "Javelle Water." One gallon of water and four pounds of ordinary washing soda and a quarter of a pound of soda. Heat the water to boiling hot, put in the soda, boil about five minutes, then pour it over two pounds of unslaked lime; let it bubble and foam until it settles, turn it off, and bottle for use. A tablespoonful put into a suds of three gallons in the boiler when boiling the clothes makes them very white and clear. Clothes should not be left long in it. Rinse them well afterwards.

HARD SOAP (WASHING)

Six pounds of washing soda and three of unslaked lime. Pour on four gallons of boiling water, let it stand until perfectly clear, then drain off and put in six pounds of clean fat. Boil it until it begins to harden, about two hours, stirring most of the time. Thin it with two gallons of cold water. Add it when there is danger of boiling over. Try the thickness by cooling a little on a plate. Put in a handful of salt just before taking from the fire. Wet a tub to prevent sticking, turn in the soap, and let it stand until solid. Cut into bars, put on a board, and let it dry. This makes about forty pounds of soap. It can be flavored just as you turn it out.

OLD-STYLE FAMILY SOFT SOAP

To set the leach, bore several holes in the bottom of a barrel, or use one without a bottom. Prepare a board larger than the barrel, then set the barrel on it and cut a groove around just outside the barrel, making one groove from this to the edge of the board to carry off the lye as it runs off, with a groove around it running into one in the center of the board. Place all two feet from the ground and tip it so that the lye may run easily from the board into the vessel below prepared to receive it. Put half bricks or stones around the edge of the inside of the barrel; place on them one end of some sticks about two inches wide, inclining to the center; on those place some straw to the depth of two inches, and over it scatter two pounds of slaked lime.

Put in ashes, about half a bushel at a time; pack it well by pounding down, and continue doing so until the barrel is full, leaving a funnel-shaped hollow in the center large enough to hold several quarts of water. Use rain water boiling hot. Let the water disappear before adding more. If the ashes are packed very tightly it may require two or three days before the lye will begin to run, but it will be the stronger for it and much better.

Put in a kettle the grease consisting of all kinds of fat that has accumulated in the kitchen, such as scraps and bones from the soup kettles, rinds from meat, etc. Fill the kettle half full. If there is too much grease it can be skimmed off after the soap is cold for another kettle of soap. This is the only true test when enough grease is used, as the lye will consume all that is needed and no more. Make a fire under one side of it. The kettle should be in an outhouse or out-of-doors.

Let it heat very hot so as to fry; stir occasionally to prevent burning. Now put in the lye a gallon at a time, watching it closely as it boils, as it sometimes runs over at the beginning. Add lye until the kettle is full enough but not too full to boil well. Soap should boil from the side and not the middle, as this would be more likely to cause it to boil over. To test the soap, to one spoonful add one of rain water. If it stirs up very thick, the soap is good and will keep. If it becomes thinner, it is not good. This is the result of one of three causes: either it is too weak or there is a deposit of dirt or it is too strong. Continue to boil for a few hours, when it should flow from the stick like thick molasses.

TO SOFTEN WATER

Put a gallon of lye into a barrelful of water, or two or three shovelsful of wood ashes, and let stand overnight; it will be clear and soft.

MILK PAINT

Mix water lime with skim milk to proper consistency to apply with brush; will adhere well to wood, brick, mortar, or stone where oil has not been used. Any color desirable may be had by using colors dissolved in whisky.

TO CLEAN WOODWORK

Fuller's earth will be found cheap and useful. Where extreme nicety is required, use a mixture of one pound of soft soap, two ounces of pearl ash, one pint of lard, and one pint of table beer; simmer in pipkin till well mixed. This will clean woodwork without removing the paint.

CLEAN GILT FRAMES

White of an egg gently rubbed on with a camel-hair pencil.

What Every Housekeeper Should Know

Agreeable Disinfectant: Sprinkle fresh ground coffee on a shovel of hot coals or burn sugar on hot coals. Vinegar boiled with myrrh, sprinkled on the floor and furniture of a sickroom, is an excellent deodorizer. Superior to pastiles and very much cheaper.

To Blacken Hearths: Mix black lead and whites of eggs well beaten together. With painter's brush wet hearth, then rub bright.

To Polish Stoves: Rub with newspaper instead of a brush.

To Preserve Brooms: Dip for a minute in a kettle of boiling suds once a week, and they will last much longer, making them tough and pliable. A carpet wears much longer swept with a broom cared for in this manner.

To Remove Old Putty from Windows: Pass red-hot poker over it.

To Keep Milk Sweet: Put into a panful a spoonful of grated horse-radish, and it will keep sweet for days.

Poison Water: Water boiled in galvanized iron becomes poisonous, and cold water passed through zinc-lined iron pipes should never be used for cooking or drinking.

To Ventilate a Room: Place a pitcher of cold water on a table in your room, and it will absorb all the gases with which the room is filled from the respiration of those eating or sleeping in the apartment. Very few realize how important such purification is for the health of the family or, indeed, understand or realize that there can be any impurity in the rooms; yet in a few hours a pitcher or pail of cold water—the colder the more effective—will make the air of a room pure; but the water will be entirely unfit for use.

Hold a hot stove lid over white spots on varnished furniture, and they will disappear.

Troublesome Ants: A heavy chalk mark laid a finger's distance from your sugar box and all around (there must be no space not covered) will surely prevent ants from troubling.

To Remove Discoloration From Bruises: Apply raw beefsteak.

Slicing Pineapples: The knife used for peeling a pineapple should not be used for slicing it, as the rind contains an acid that is apt to cause a swollen mouth and sore lips. The Cubans use salt as an antidote for the ill effects of the peel.

To Destroy Ants: Ants in house and garden may be destroyed by taking flour of brimstone, half a pound, and potash, four ounces; set them in an iron or earthen pan over the fire until dissolved and united. Afterwards beat them to a powder and infuse a little of this powder in water, and wherever you sprinkle it, the ants will fly the place.

Cure for Hiccoughs: Sit erect and inflate the lungs fully. Then, retaining the breath, bend forward slowly until the chest meets the knees. After slowly rising again to the erect position, slowly exhale the breath. Repeat this process a second time, and the nerves will be found to have received an access of energy that will enable them to perform their natural functions.

Mosquitoes and Rats: Leave a bottle of oil of pennyroyal uncorked in a room at night and not a mosquito, nor any other bloodsucker, will be found there in the morning.

Mix potash with powdered meal and throw it into the ratholes of a cellar, and the rats will depart. If a rat or mouse gets into your pantry, stuff into the rathole or mousehole a rag saturated with a solution of cayenne pepper, and no rat or mouse will touch the rag for the purpose of opening communication with a depot of supplies.

Salt will curdle new milk.

To prevent rust on flatirons and keep them smooth and clean as glass, rub first with beeswax in a rag, then with a cloth sprinkled with salt.

See if your knives do not polish better if you mix a small quantity of baking soda with your brick dust.

To soften boots and shoes, rub with kerosene; it also makes tin teakettles bright as new.

A white satin wedding dress should be pinned up in blue paper with brown paper outside sewn together at the edges.

To Preserve Bouquets: Put a little saltpeter in the water, and the flowers will live for a fortnight.

To Destroy Cockroaches: Hellebore sprinkled on the floor at night; they will eat it and are poisoned.

Silver Tea and Coffeepots: When putting away, lay a little stick across the top under the cover. This will allow fresh air to get in and prevent the mustiness of the contents, familiar to hotel and boardinghouse sufferers.

Creaking of Bedsteads: If a bedstead creaks at each movement of the sleeper, remove the slats and wrap the ends of each in some old newspapers.

To Prevent Lampwicks from Smoking: Soak them in vinegar and dry them thoroughly.

Rub nickel stove trimmings with kerosene and whiting.

Death to Bedbugs: Varnish is death to the most persistent bug. It is cheap—ten cents' worth will do for one bedstead—is easily used, safe, and improves the looks of the furniture.

Milk which stands too long makes bitter butter.

To Toughen Lamp Chimneys: Immerse article in pot of cold water to which common salt has been added. Boil well, then cool slowly. Glass treated in this way will resist any sudden change of temperature.

To Clean Stovepipes: Put piece of zinc on the live coals.

Hartshorn will allay the pain of stings of poisonous insects; oil of sassafras is even better.

To Clean Glass Bottles: Crush eggshells into small bits or a few carpet tacks or a small quantity of gunshot; put into bottle; fill one-half full of strong soapsuds; shake; rinse. Will look like new.

Cutting Off Glass Bottles To Make Cups or Jars: A simple, practical way is to take a red-hot poker with a pointed end. Make a mark with a file to begin the cut, then apply the hot iron and a crack will start which will follow the iron wherever it is carried. This is, on the whole, simple and better than the use of strings wet with turpentine, etc.

Never use water which has stood in a lead pipe overnight. Not less than a wooden bucketful should be allowed to run.

To Prevent the Odor of Boiling Cabbage: Throw red pepper pods or a few bits of charcoal into the pan.

Never keep vinegar or yeast in stone crocks or jugs; their acid attacks the glazing, which is said to be poisonous.

Never allow opened fruit, fish, or vegetables to stand in the tin can. Never stir anything in tin, or, if done, use a wooden spoon. Take great caution not to scrape off flecks of bright metal.

If the oven is too hot when baking, place a small dish of cold water in it.

Mend a crack in the stove by mixing ashes and salt with water.

Wings of turkeys, geese, and chickens are good to wash and clean windows, as they leave no dust nor lint.

To remove tea stains from cups, scour with ashes.

If nutmegs are good, when pricked with a pin, oil will ooze out.

To prevent mustard plasters from blistering, mix with the white of an egg.

Fresh meat beginning to sour will sweeten if placed out-of-doors in the cool air overnight.

Wash the hair in cold sage tea.

Bent whalebones can be restored and used again by simply soaking in water a few hours, then drying them.

If you are troubled with moths in your feather beds, boil the feathers in water for a short time; then put them in sacks and dry them, working them with the hands all the time.

To test oleomargarine, place small bit between two pieces of thin common window glass; press together until only a film remains. When held up to the light, white, opaque spots are always to be seen. These are crystals of fat. Pure butter does not show such specks. This is an excellent means of cultivating the eye and qualifying one to determine the imitation from the genuine.

Linament for Rheumatism—Take one pint good cider vinegar, add a heaping teaspoon each of salt and pepper, boil down to half pint and use.

To Stop Hiccoughs—One tablespoonful quince juice.

To Keep Flies from Horses—Take two or three handfuls of green walnut leaves; pour over them two or three quarts of soft cold water; let stand one night; pour in a kettle and boil fifteen minutes. When cold, wet a sponge and, before the horse goes out of the stable, let those parts which are most irritated be washed over with the liquid.

Sure Cure for Ague—Five cents' worth frankincense, crushed, and one grated nutmeg put in thin muslin bag. To be worn over the pit of the stomach.

Recipe for Quarreling—Take a root of sassafras and steep in a pint of water and put in a bottle. When your husband comes in to quarrel, fill your mouth with it and hold until he goes away. A sure cure.

HOW TO PRESERVE A HUSBAND

Be careful in your selection; do not choose too young and take only such as have been reared in a good atmosphere. Some women insist on keeping them in a pickle, while others keep them in hot water. This only makes them sour, hard, and sometimes bitter. Even poor varieties may be made sweet, tender, and good by garnishing them with patience, well-sweetened with smiles and flavored with kisses to taste. Then wrap them in a mantel of charity, keep warm with a steady fire of domestic devotion, and serve with peaches and cream. When thus prepared they will keep for years.

MAGNETIC BELT *for either lady or gent. Most Powerful Curative Agent ever made for Lame Back, Weakness of Spine and Kidneys and pains arising from derangement of the abdominal organs. Made of* GENUINE MAGNETS—*the genius of man has not produced its equal since the days of Paracelsus, the world-renowned physician who cured all diseases with magnetism.* —(old adv.)

HOW TO ACCUMULATE A FORTUNE

The following steps show how easy it is, provided certain steps are taken. The table shows what would be the result at the end of fifty years by saving a certain amount each day and putting it at interest at the rate of six per cent:

Daily Savings	The Result
One cent	$ 950
Ten cents	9,504
Twenty cents	19,006
Thirty cents	28,512
Forty cents	38,015
Fifty cents	47,520
Sixty cents	57,024
Seventy cents	66,528
Eighty cents	76,032
Ninety cents	85,537
One dollar	95,041
Five dollars	475,208

Nearly every person wastes enough in twenty or thirty years which, if saved and carefully invested, would make a family quite independent; but the principle of small savings has been lost sight of in the general desire to become wealthy.

[*Note:* Permanent federal income tax did not come onto the American scene until 1913!]

DYEING AND COLORING

Everything should be clean. The goods should be scoured in soap and the soap rinsed out. They are often steeped in soap lye overnight. Dip them into water just before putting them into dye to prevent spotting. Soft water should be used, sufficient to cover goods well. Air dyed goods, rinse them, hang up to dry. Do not wring silk or merino dresses.

COTTON GOODS

Black: For five pounds of goods, boil them in a decoction of three pounds of sumach one-half hour and steep twelve hours; dip in lime water one-

297

half hour; take out and let them drip one hour; run them through the lime water again fifteen minutes. Make a new dye with two and one-half pounds logwood (boiled one hour), and dip again three hours. Add bichromate potash, two ounces, to the logwood dye and dip one hour. Wash in clear, cold water and dry in the shade. Only process for permanent black.

Sky Blue: For three pounds of goods, blue vitriol, four ounces; boil a few minutes, then dip the goods three hours; then pass them through a strong limewater. A beautiful Snuff Brown can be obtained by next putting the goods through a solution of prussiate of potash.

Green: Dip the goods in homemade blue, then make a dye with fustic, three pounds; logwood, three ounces, to each pound of goods. When cooled so as to bear the hand, put in the goods, move briskly a few minutes, and let lie one hour. Take out and drain. Add to dye for each pound of cotton, blue vitriol, one-half ounce, and dip another hour. Wring and dry in shade. By adding or diminishing the logwood and fustic any shade may be had.

Orange: For five pounds of goods, sugar of lead, four ounces. Boil. When cool put in the goods, dip two hours, wring. Make a new dye with bichromate potash, eight ounces; madder, two ounces. Dip until it suits. If color is too red, take a small sample and dip into limewater and choose between them.

Yellow: Seven ounces of sugar of lead to five pounds of goods. Dip two hours. Make a new dye with bichromate of potash, four ounces. Dip until the color suits; wring out and dry. If not yellow enough, repeat.

Red: Muriate of tin, two-thirds of a teacupful; add water to cover the goods; raise to boiling point. Leave goods in one hour. Stir often. Take out, empty the kettle, put in clean water with nic-wood, one pound. Steep one-half hour at hand heat, then put in goods and increase the heat one hour—not boiling. Air the goods and dip them one hour as before. Wash without soap.

Nice Crimson for Wools: Alum, three ounces. Dip at hand heat one hour. Take out and drain while making new dye by boiling ten minutes cochineal, three ounces; bruised nutgalls, two ounces; cream-tartar, one-fourth ounce, in one pail of water. When cool, begin to dip, raising heat to boil. Dip one hour. Wash and dry.

Sky Blue on Silk or Cotton: Very beautiful. Give goods as much color from a solution of blue vitriol, two ounces, to water, one gallon, as it will take up in dipping fifteen minutes, then run it through limewater. This will make a beautiful and durable sky blue.

Madder Red for Wools: Alum, five ounces; red or cream-tartar, one ounce. Put in goods and bring kettle to a boil, one-half hour, then air them and boil one-half hour longer. Empty the kettle and fill with clean water. Put in bran, one peck. Make it milk-warm, and let it stand until the bran rises; then skim off the bran and put in one-half pound madder. Put in the goods, and heat slowly until it boils and is done. Wash in strong suds.

Purple Wool: For each pound of goods, two ounces of cudbear. Rinse the goods well in soapsuds, then dissolve cudbear in hot suds—not quite boiling—and soak the goods until of required color. The color is brightened by rinsing in alum water.

Dove and Slate Colors of All Shades: Boil in an iron vessel a teacupful of black tea with a teaspoonful of copperas and sufficient water. Dilute till you get the shade wanted.

Any Shade: Boil goods in a mordant of alum, two parts; copperas, three parts. Then rinse them through a bath of madder. The tint depends on the proportions of copperas and alum. The more copperas, the darker the dye. Mixtures of red and yellows with blues and blacks, or simple dyes, will make any shade.

Flowers

HOW TO KEEP THEM FRESH

Every lover of flowers must deplore their extreme frailty. It is a sad thing to see how soon the splendid bloom, the pretty blossoms plucked with pride in our own beds, and the sweet nosegay sent to us by a friend all wither with hopeless persistency. There is no known means to keep a flower from fading, but carelessness will often hasten its decay and spend its beauty before its time:

1. If you wish to preserve cut flowers longer, do not rend them from the parent stalk with your fingers. Cut flowers with sharp shears or knife.

2. Keep the flowers loosely arranged. They need air quite as much as moisture. They will wilt much more quickly if tied in bunches than if they are loosely grouped in some commodious vessel.

3. Keep them in a cool room where the air is pure. Smoke is apt to injure them, especially stale tobacco smoke.

DON'T WEAR FALSE BANGS *unless they are made of natural curly hair. We have them from $2.00 up. Keep in shape simply by combing. S. C. Beck, Philadelphia, Pa.* —(old adv.)

TO RESTORE AND PRESERVE FLOWERS

Immerse them halfway up their stems in very hot water, and allow them to remain in it until it cools or they have recovered. The scalded portion of the stem must then be cut off and the flowers placed in clear, cold water. However, on some of the more fugacious kinds this proves useless.

Flowers may be preserved and their tints deepened by adding to the water a little solution of carbonate of ammonium and a few drops of phosphate of sodium. The effect of this, in giving the flowers a deeper color and stronger appearance, is quite wonderful, and by cutting off every other day about half an inch of the stems of the flowers with a sharp knife, they may be kept as long as their natural life would last in the fields or woods.

HOW TO MAKE THEM GROW

1. Keep them clean—out of the dust if possible—with plenty of pure air, water, and sunshine. Do not have any regular times for watering them. Judge by the surface soil whether they are thirsty.

2. Water thoroughly to feed the roots well. Use rainwater if you can get it, tepid in temperature. A plant may be chilled by a cold bath as well as a person. Stale water is as unwholesome for plants as it is for people. Too much water is as bad as none.

3. The soil in the pot should be light and porous; the bottom of the pot should be filled with broken bits of crockery or any substance that will admit of free percolation.

4. Evening is the best time for watering. Evaporation goes on more slowly at night time.

5. A few drops of ammonia in a quart of water is occasionally good for plants, but a frequent recourse to stimulants is inadvisable. Manures of this sort are apt to favor the growth of foliage and stalk while they retard the development of flowers.

6. Common glue is a good fertilizer; one ounce to one gallon of water. Also soot from a stove or chimney where wood is burned; mix with hot water and allow to cool before use.

7. Let plants have *morning* sunshine if possible. Give plants a shower bath once a week to cleanse leaves of dust, which often clogs up their respiratory organs.

MOXIE NERVE FOOD—*the greatest remedy for nervousness, exhaustion, dissipation and all its results.—(old adv.)*

300

The House of 2,000 A. D.?

The electronic home of tomorrow with "automatic bacon and eggs" was predicted in a speech here. . . . A household electronic center will, when fed instructions on magnetic tape:

Wake you up in the morning
Start the coffeemaker
Cook the bacon and eggs
Open the garage door and warm up the car
Do the laundry
Regulate the heat
Wash the dishes
Clean the house
Pay the milkman
Balance your checkbook
Complete your income tax forms

— *The Milwaukee Journal*
January 20, 1963

The Presidents' Wives and Official Hostesses of The White House 1789–1964

BRIEF BIOGRAPHIES

FAVORITE RECIPES

SELECTED MENUS

"*The government of a family bears a Lilliputian resemblance to the government of a nation.*" — *The Virginia Housewife, 1824*

Martha Dandridge Custis Washington

OF VIRGINIA

First Lady 1789–1797

"I—who had much rather be at home—occupy a place with which many younger and gayer women would be extremely pleased."

WHEN MRS. GEORGE WASHINGTON went up to New York to become the first First Lady of the United States, she took along her "receipt book." It contained instructions for great cakes, fools, trifles, syllabubs, blanc manges, piggs, fowles, apricocks, hartychoakes, beef pyes, and chickin frykasies. At fifty-eight, Martha Washington was resigned to the extensive entertaining her elegant new position would impose.

The War over, she had hoped to retire with the General to a quiet plantation life. But she was accustomed to sacrificing her wishes to those of her "old man"—as she called him—and their country. So, on to the Presidential Mansion, to receptions and levees and "at-homes."

Plump, matronly, simply dressed, yet possessing an air of queenly aloofness, Mrs. Washington was well suited to the role. As a girl, she had been presented at the Governor's Mansion in Williamsburg; as a woman, she had been twice-married, once widowed. She was a mother and a grandmother, the chatelaine of an enormous estate, an army wife and a General's lady, and she was used to managing and entertaining. A houseful of guests was the rule at Mount Vernon. Her knowledge of the social graces found her better prepared than her guests for the official whirl that began New Year's Day, 1790, at the red brick house on Cherry Street in New York City.

Curtseying to the guests, Martha Washington would invite them to partake of the plum cake and tea being offered by "Black Sam," dignified in black silk knee breeches and white ruffled shirt. The ladies

305

curtseyed in return, anxiously calculating their dips to match hers—no more, no less—while they mentally debated whether to call her Lady Washington or Your Elective Majesty. (They were still under the spell of British court manners.) At last the decorous but rather dull evening would be brought to an end when Her Majesty would rise and say: "The General always retires at nine."

Martha seldom rested from her duties. Between entertainments she could be seen going about New York in her cream and gold chariot, "returning calls"—a custom that was to plague First Ladies in years to come. But near the end of her husband's second term Martha was sixty-six and the burdens of public life were weighing heavily on her. Sometimes, when it seemed she had no privacy at all, the staunch army wife could give way to self-pity: "I am more like a State prisoner than anything else. . . ."

Still, the Washingtons' popularity did not wane. The guests came in droves. Food bills for the Presidential table mounted to one hundred and sixty-five dollars weekly and were paid by the First Family. Expense accounts had not yet been invented.

Favorite Recipes of Martha Washington

MRS. WASHINGTON'S RICH, BLACK GREAT-CAKE

Take twenty eggs and divide the whites from the yolks and beat the whites to a froth, then work two pounds of butter to a cream and put the whites of eggs to it, a spoonful at a time until well worked; then put two pounds of sugar finely powdered in it in the same manner, then add the yolks of the eggs well beaten and two and a half pounds of flour and five pounds of fruit. Add to this one-quarter ounce of mace, a nutmeg, a half pint of wine and some French brandy. Five and a half hours will bake it.

After one hundred years Mrs. Washington's Great Cake had become a "small" cake, calling for only ten to twelve eggs. (Actually the name

Martha Washington, the Nation's first First Lady, holds a reception

306

"Great Cake" meant fruit cake and did not refer to the size.) Here is her recipe as modified for the *New World's Fair Cookbook* of 1891:

WASHINGTON CAKE

One pound of butter, one pound of sugar, one and a quarter pounds of flour, ten eggs, one gill of cream, one wineglassful of wine, one pound of raisins (seeded and chopped), one pound of currants (washed, dried, and picked), one teaspoon of cinnamon and cloves mixed, grating of one nutmeg. Beat the butter and sugar light, to which add the cream with a quarter of the flour. Whisk the eggs until thick and stir in by degrees. After mixing well, add remainder of flour, spice, and wine alternately. Beat all well together, then stir in the fruit. Butter and paper your pan. Put in the batter, spread it over smooth and bake in a moderate oven.

PRESIDENT AND MARTHA WASHINGTON AND HER
CHILDREN AT MOUNT VERNON

Martha Washington as
a young woman

A Receipt for All Young Ladies That Are Going To Be Married

TO MAKE A SACK POSSET—1743

From famed Barbados on the western Main
Fetch Sugar half a pound; fetch Sack from Spain
A pint, and from the Eastern Indian Coast
Nutmeg, the Glory of our Northern Toast.
O'er flaming coals together let them heat
Till the all-conquering Sack dissolved the Sweet.
O'er such another fire set Eggs twice ten,
New-born from foot of Cock and Rump of hen,
Stir them with steady Hand and Conscience pricking
To see the untimely Fate of twenty Chicken.
From shining shelf take down your brazen skillet,
A quart of milk from gentle Cow will fill it,
When boil'd and cool'd put Milk and Sack to Egg,
Unite them firmly like the triffle League;
Then covered close, together let them dwell
Till Miss twice sings—you must not Kiss and Tell.
Each Lad and Lass snatch up their murdering Spoon
And fall on fiercely like a Starved Dragoon.

[*Note: Sack* is a dry, white wine; *posset,* a drink of hot milk curdled with
wine, thought to be good for "a cold in the head."]

OLIJKOECKS OR OLY-KOCKS OR OLIE CAKES
[*Oil Cakes*]

[*Note:* This is a Colonial recipe that dates from about 1730.]

About twelve o'clock set a little yeast to rise to be ready at five P.M. Mix with the following ingredients: three and three-fourths pounds of flour, one pound of sugar, one-half pound of butter and lard mixed, one and a half pints of milk, six eggs, one pint of raised yeast. Warm the butter, sugar, and milk together, grate a nutmeg into the flour, add the eggs last. Put in a warm place to rise. If quite light at bedtime, work down. At nine o'clock the next morning make into small balls with the hands and place in the center of each a bit of raisin, citron, and apple, chopped fine. Lay on a well-floured pieboard and let rise. They are frequently ready to boil at two P.M. Put into boiling lard [or oil] and boil five minutes. Roll in powdered sugar.

Modern olykoeks (still another version of spelling) may be made from sweet-roll dough:

SWEET-ROLL DOUGH FOR OIL CAKES ☆

1 cup milk, scalded	½ to 1 cake compressed yeast
1 teaspoon salt	1 egg, well beaten
¼ cup sugar	3½ to 4 cups sifted flour
⅙ cup shortening	

Place milk, salt, sugar, and shortening in mixing bowl and cool. When they are lukewarm, add crumbled yeast, egg, and half of flour and beat thoroughly. Gradually stir in remaining flour. Turn out on floured board and knead until smooth and elastic, adding flour as necessary to keep from sticking. Place dough in greased bowl and brush with melted shortening. Cover and let rise in warm place until doubled in bulk, about two to four hours. Knead, cut off small pieces, roll into balls, enclosing brandied raisins, plain raisins, citron, etc. Let rise until very light, one to two hours. Fry in deep fat (360°) three minutes, drain and roll in powdered sugar.

You have heard of birthday cakes and wedding cakes, but do you know about Doed Koecks? This recipe dates from about 1680:

DOED KOECKS

Two pounds of flour, one pound of sugar, one-half pound of butter, one and a half teacups of milk, one-half teaspoon of pearl ash, one ounce of carraway. Cut thick and stamp with the name and date of death.

[*Note:* Dead Cakes were given to each person attending a funeral and were kept for years as souvenirs.]

Abigail Smith Adams

OF MASSACHUSETTS

First Lady 1797–1801

*"I had much rather live in the
house at Philadelphia."*

ABIGAIL ADAMS was the first mistress of the White House. A most inconvenient house it was, too. Half-finished, damp, drafty, with only six habitable rooms, it was located in a swampy village called "Washington"—population: three thousand. Not the least of its inconveniences was the lack of a yard to hang the laundry. Abigail, a resourceful New Englander, knew how to "make do"; she turned the great East Room into a drying room.

Heroic was the word for Abigail; her own husband, John Adams, had called her that. From a minister's delicate child who had to be tutored at home, she had grown into a thrifty Yankee wife with a sturdy backbone. During the war years, when John was frequently away—in the Congress at Philadelphia and in Europe—she raised their children and put their farm on a paying basis so that they would have something to live on when her great (but poor) statesman came home. At one time he was gone for four years. So slow was the mail that once, six months

311

passed without a letter. When it finally came, it told Abigail everything except what she wanted to hear—that John missed her. She was disappointed and lonely and said so and was scolded by mail for expecting such "intimacies" on paper. But John and Abigail were kindred spirits and were in love all their long married life.

When the Revolutionary War was over, Abigail and the children made the rough voyage to England, where she was presented at court. But there was still much hostility toward the former "colonies," and her position as ambassador's wife required much tact and dignity. Abigail possessed both.

She saw her husband become Vice-President and, when she was fifty-three, President of the United States. Over the muddy cowpaths of Washington she traveled, making calls, sometimes fifteen a day. Together she and her dear friend, Martha Washington, worked out an official social schedule. On New Year's Day, 1801, the President's Palace was formally opened to the public. Handsome in brocade and velvet, Mrs. Presidentess remained seated, the President standing at her side, to receive their guests, who then partook of cakes and tarts, curds and creams, trifles, syllabub, and Floating Island.

At the end of her husband's term of office, Abigail turned her eyes again toward Massachusetts, saying, "I can return to my little cottage and be happier." Behind her she left the influence of a First Lady who had championed causes far in advance of her era—the vote for women, the abolition of slavery, and extended education of the young. Her brusque, distant husband had been a better President because of her, and her son, although she did not live to see it, was also to be President.

Favorite Recipes of Abigail Adams

FLOATING ISLAND 1

One quart of milk, scalded; five egg yolks and one white beaten together with five tablespoonfuls of sugar and one-eighth teaspoon salt. Stir a little of the scalded milk into the yolks to prevent curdling, then stir all the milk in. Cook till thickened, remove from fire, cool, flavor with vanilla if wished. Pour into glass bowl and let custard become very cold. Now whip whites of eggs to a stiff froth, adding three tablespoonfuls of sugar. Pour this froth upon a shallow dish of boiling water; the steam passing through it cooks it. When sufficiently cooked, take a tablespoon and drop spoonfuls over the top of the custard far enough apart so the "little white islands" will not touch each other.

Mrs. John Adams served Floating Island at her White House reception in 1801. *The White House Cookbook* of 1887 featured it. My grandmother made it exactly as above in the 1930s, and it was our favorite childhood dessert. Now I hope your children enjoy this wonderful old classic as much as mine do.

FLOATING ISLAND 2 ☆

A modern recipe for Floating Island, which makes only half the above amount:

2 cups scalded milk	½ teaspoon vanilla or sherry
3 eggs or 6 egg yolks	to taste, added when
¼ cup sugar	mixture cools
⅛ teaspoon salt	

Cook in double boiler over hot water until mixture coats the spoon— about seven minutes. Do not overcook or custard may curdle. Beat three egg whites with sugar for "islands" and steam-cook as in preceding recipe. Cool and serve.

RASPBERRY FOOL

Put your fruit into an oven for quarter of an hour. When tender, pulp it through a sieve, sugar it, add the crumbs of sufficient sponge cake to thicken it. Put into a glass mould or into custard cups and lay some thick cream on top. If for immediate use, the cream may be beaten up with the fruit. Other light berries and fruit may be treated in the same way.

With boiled custard or heavy cream, whipped or unwhipped, "fools" were popular desserts from Martha Washington's day clear through the nineteenth century to the times of Carrie Harrison.

RASPBERRY SHRUB

One quart raspberry juice, half a pound of loaf sugar, dissolved; a pint of rum or part rum and brandy. Mix and bottle.

MEAD, METHELIN, OR HONEY WINE

To some new honey strained add spring water; put a whole egg in it, boil this liquor till the egg swims above the liquor, strain, pour it in a cask. To every fifteen gallons add two ounces of white Jamaica ginger, bruised, one ounce cloves and mace, one and a half ounces of cinnamon, all bruised together and tied up in a muslin bag; accelerate the fermentation with yeast. When worked sufficiently, bung up; in six weeks draw off into bottles.

Another Mead: Boil the combs, from which the honey has been drained, with sufficient water to make a tolerably sweet liquor; ferment this with yeast and proceed as per preceding formula.

Sack Mead: Add a handful of hops and sufficient brandy to the comb liquor.

ROSE PETAL TEA

Gather wild roses in bud, unfold leaves, let them dry in sunny window, then store in tin or jar. To use, pour boiling water over dried leaves.

BUILDING THE FIRST WHITE HOUSE, CA. 1798

BISHOP [*for Winter Nights*] ☆

Stick cloves thick in two oranges, roast oranges in oven, quarter them. In saucepan with roast oranges put twelve lumps of sugar rubbed with lemon half, juice of one lemon, and three bottles of port wine. Simmer gently a few minutes, sprinkle with nutmeg and serve in a mug.

ARCHBISHOP ☆ AND POPE ☆

The first is Bishop made with claret; The second, Bishop made with Burgundy.

The following recipes are good to serve with Bishop for a late party snack.

SWISS PIES ☆

6 slices bacon, cut in ¼-inch strips	½ teaspoon salt
	Dash of pepper
1 cup chopped onion	2¾ cups Swiss cheese
2 beaten eggs	cut in ¼-inch cubes
¾ cup sour cream	6 unbaked tart shells

Fry bacon till crisp. Drain on paper towels and add onion to fat and cook till tender but not brown; drain off fat. Combine eggs, sour cream, salt, pepper, cheese, and bacon. Pour into tart shells and bake at 375° till knife inserted in center comes out clean—about twenty-five minutes. Filling may be cooked first, then put into pre-baked pastry shells and slipped into oven to warm.

HOT CRAB SALAD ☆

2 tablespoons butter	1 can crabmeat
2 tablespoons flour	½ can pimientos
1 cup milk	½-1 pound blanched almonds

Make stiff cream sauce with butter, flour, and milk. Remove from heat and add crab, pimiento, and nuts. Serve in small lettuce cups or in pre-baked pastry shells or cream puffs.

Martha Wayles Skelton Jefferson

OF VIRGINIA

HISTORY RUMORS THAT Martha Jefferson, though she had been married twice, extracted a promise from her lawyer-husband that he would never remarry. Martha, a Virginia aristocrat, died at age thirty-four, eighteen years before Jefferson became President. All his life, until his death at eighty-three, he kept a lock of her auburn hair in a secret drawer in his cabinet. No known portrait of her exists.

Though accomplished in law, statesmanship, astronomy, agriculture, architecture, botany, music, and mathematics—to name only a few of his fields of interest—Jefferson, like his fellow genius Benjamin Franklin, did not consider details of household management beneath his notice. A widely traveled man of the world, he was an epicure who delighted in importing unheard-of delicacies for his table: waffles from Holland, macaroni from Italy, almonds, anchovies, and "Baked Alaska" from France, vanilla flavoring, Parmesan cheese, figs, raisins, mustard. Many of his unique inventions were designed to simplify or enhance entertaining. He used a round table for dining because it made all seats equal in importance and a dumbwaiter because it eliminated eavesdropping servants.

Etienne Lemaire, the famous French steward, headed the staff, which was the best-paid in Washington. Jefferson set the most lavish table in the city, spending almost eleven thousand dollars on imported wines during his tenure. Every expenditure was supervised and itemized, as had always been done at Jefferson's home, Monticello. His income could

THE WHITE HOUSE DURING JEFFERSON'S ADMINISTRATIONS

316

not support his lavish hospitality, however, and like many a future President, when he left the White House he was in debt.

Washington society ladies were both charmed and disturbed by the dramatic democrat who walked from his boardinghouse to the Capitol for his inauguration, who initiated handshaking to replace bowing, and who refused to celebrate his own birthday with the usual President's Ball, saying that Independence Day was the only birthday he cared to commemorate. He held only two receptions each year—on July 4 and New Year's Day—and they were open to one and all.

President Jefferson kept his promise to Martha. He did not remarry but relied on Dolley Madison and his daughters, Martha and Maria, to act as his hostesses.

The Virginia Housewife and Her Father, Thomas Jefferson

Long counted among the treasures of the White House is a small, yellowed book, both printed and closely written in fine script, called "The Virginia Housewife." It is Martha Jefferson Randolph's cookbook. Published and presented to her by her sister-in-law, it attracted the interest of the versatile Jefferson, who lent his genius as readily to domestic arrangements as to state affairs and the arts and sciences. He could not resist "improving" the cookbook; the same steady hand that had penned the Declaration of Independence jotted down, on a few blank pages, his own favorite recipes.

Years later, in 1904, the book came home to the White House as a surprise gift to the First Lady, Mrs. Theodore Roosevelt, from George A. Satterlee, of the Soldiers' Home, Los Angeles County, California, in whose family it had been handed down for generations. The title page reads as follows:

THE VIRGINIA HOUSEWIFE

"METHOD IS THE SOUL OF MANAGEMENT"

WASHINGTON

PRINTED BY DAVIS AND FORCE

(FRANKLIN'S HEAD)

PENNSYLVANIA AVENUE

1824

FOR MRS. RANDOLPH, MONTICELLO

FROM HER AFFECTIONATE FRIEND AND SISTER

317

PREFACE

"The difficulties I encountered when I first entered on the duties of a housekeeping life, from the want of books sufficiently clear and concise to impart knowledge to a Tyro, compelled me to study the subject and by actual experiment to reduce everything in the culinary line to proper weights and measurements. This method I found not only to diminish the necessary attention and labor but to be also economical; for when the ingredients employed were given in just proportions, the article made was always equally good.

"The government of a family bears a Lilliputian resemblance to the government of a nation. The contents of the treasury must be known and great care taken to keep the expenditures from being equal to the receipts. . . .

"Let everything be done at the proper time, keep everything in its proper place and put everything to its proper use.

"Early rising is also essential to the good government of a family. A late breakfast deranges the whole business of the day and throws a portion of it on the next which opens the door for confusion to enter.

"Should [the following recipes] prove serviceable to the young, inexperienced housekeeper, it will add greatly to that gratification which an extended circulation of the work will be likely to confer."

M. RANDOLPH
WASHINGTON
January, 1824

Thomas Jefferson's Recipes
[*inserted in his daughter's cookbook in his own handwriting*]

OBSERVATIONS ON SOUP

Always observe to lay your meat in the bottom of the pan with a lump of fresh butter. Cut the herbs and roots small and lay them over the meat. Cover it close and put it over a slow fire. This will draw forth the flavors of the herbs and in a much greater degree than to put on the water at first. When the gravy produced from the meat is beginning to dry put in the water, and when the soup is done take it off. Let it cool and skim off the fat clear. Heat it again and dish it up. When you make white soups never put in the cream until you take it off of the fire.

318

CABBAGE PUDDING

Shred one-half pound of lean beef and a pound of suet very fine, the yolks of three eggs, one spoonful grated bread, some sweet herbs, pepper, salt, and onion. It will fill a cabbage which must be parboiled and opened at the top. Scoop it out till you think it will receive the meat. Fill it, close it up, tie it hard and close in a cloth. When it has boiled a little, tie it closer. It must boil two and a half hours.

DRIED BEANS

Boil them till done but not mashed. Take a bit of butter the size of a walnut, half an onion chopped fine. Do them together in a frying pan till the onion is done. Dash in a little flour and soup enough to make a gravy. Put in your beans, let them boil and season with pepper and salt.

TO DRESS POTATOES [*Mashed Potatoes*]

Wash your potatoes well and peel them. Let them lay fifteen minutes in cold water. Take them out and throw them into as much boiling water and salt as will boil them tender, soft. When done take them out of the water and mash them with a spoon, add cream and butter equal quantities, enough to make them liquid (one-quarter pound of butter to two quarts of potatoes) with a little nutmeg. Stir them until perfectly light and white. If too stiff they may be liquefied with good milk.

CHINESE MODE OF BOILING RICE

Wash it well in cold water. Drain it in a sieve and throw it into boiling water. When pulpy, take it with a ladle, put it in a clean vessel. Let it remain (near the fire) till it becomes white and dry. In this form it is used for bread.

BEEF À LA DARIBE LEMAIRE

Take a round of beef, lard it well and put it in a dutch oven. Take the meat from a shin of beef, cut it in pieces with small slices of any other fresh meat and a little bacon. Season them with salt, pepper, thyme, carrots, and a little onion. Put it round and over the beef, cover the whole with water, let it stew very slowly until perfectly done. Take out

319

the round and set it by to cool. The jelly is now to be made. Begin by taking out all the meat and leave in the oven all the juices or broth, which must be strained through a sieve and the grease skimmed from the top. Put it back on the fire with a few grains of pepper and let it simmer slowly. Beat up four eggs in a cup of water and mix them in, stirring all together for about five minutes. Then let it remain a little while longer until the side next the fire begins to look clear. You may try whether it is sufficiently clear by taking a little in a silver spoon. Take the oven off and, setting it near the fire, put a few coals on the top and let it stand for about a quarter of an hour. Your jelly is now ready for straining and after it cools garnishes the beef. This dish should be prepared a day before it is wanted. The oven should not be too large.

[*Note:* Apparently, this was one of M. Lemaire's specialties.]

Martha Jefferson Randolph, the President's daughter

The following recipes are taken from Mrs. Randolph's cookbook used at Monticello:

HUNTER'S BEEF

Select a fine fat round weighing about twenty-five pounds. Take three ounces of saltpeter, three of brown sugar, one ounce of cloves, a half-ounce of allspice, a large nutmeg, and a quart of salt. Put them all together very fine. Take the bone out. Rub it well with this mixture on both sides. Put some of the mixture in the bottom of a tub just large enough to hold the beef. Lay the beef in and strew the remainder of the mixture on the top. Rub the beef well every day for two weeks and spread the mixture over it; at the end of this time wash the beef, bind it with tape to keep it round and compact, filling the hole where the bone was with a piece of fat. Lay it in a pan of convenient size, strew a little suet over the top and pour in a pint of water. Cover the pan with a coarse crust and a thick paper over that. It will take five hours baking; when cold, take off the tape. It is a delicious relish at twelve o'clock or for supper eaten with vinegar, mustard, oil, or salad. Skim the grease from the gravy and bottle it; it makes an excellent seasoning for any made dish.

GOOSEBERRY FOOL

Pick the stems and blossoms from two quarts of green gooseberries. Put them in a stewpan with their weight in loaf sugar and a very little water; when sufficiently stewed, pass the pulp through a sieve, and when cold, add rich boiled custard till it is like thick cream. Put it in a glass bowl and lay the brothed cream on the top.

VINEGAR OF THE FOUR THIEVES

Take lavender, rosemary, sage, wormwood, rue, and mint—of each a large handful. Put them in a pot of earthenware, pour on them four quarts of very strong vinegar. Cover pot closely and put a board on the top; keep it in the hottest sun two weeks. Then strain and bottle, putting in each bottle a clove of garlic. When it has settled in the bottle and become clear, pour it off gently; do this until you get it all free from sediment. The proper time to make it is when the herbs are in full vigor in June. This vinegar is very refreshing in crowded rooms, in the apartments of the sick, and is peculiarly grateful when sprinkled about the house in damp weather.

Dolley Payne Todd Madison

OF NORTH CAROLINA

First Lady 1809–1817

"I derived pleasure from my indulgence."

DOLLEY MADISON seemed born to be First Lady, yet she would have handled any job as well. She loved people and parties and projects. Dolley was in the habit of saying "Yes" to life.

She was a vivacious young Quaker widow from Philadelphia when she met quiet Jamie Madison, a prominent lawyer and close friend of Thomas Jefferson and a man whose temperament complemented her own. She and Jamie were married, whereupon Dolley was promptly "read out of" the Pine Street Meeting. The gray Quakers had never approved of her; surely anyone so pretty and happy could not be *good*, they reasoned. Dolley accepted the rebuke with her usual optimism. Now she was free to wear the bright colors and beautiful clothes she had always loved.

Her flair for entertaining brightened official Washington even before Madison became president. President Jefferson, a widower, when besieged by cabinet ladies to give a "dove party," would speed a note to the wife of his Secretary of State: "Thomas Jefferson begs Mrs. Madison to take care of female friends expected."

When the Jefferson daughters came up from Monticello, not wanting to appear countrified, they called on Dolley to help them choose proper clothes. With her French gowns and feathered and jeweled turbans, which were her trademark, she was already a pace-setter in fashion as well as in entertaining.

As First Lady at forty-one, she redecorated the White House with gold satin and damask (sunny yellow was her favorite color) and inaugurated a staggering social schedule that has never been excelled.

With the help of her steward, French John, she set a fine table. Waterfowl, deer, game birds, and oysters were plentiful in the vicinity. Ham, fish, and game appeared four times a day, accompanied by potatoes, beets, puddings, and pies and, later, by such "fancy" vegetables as celery, spinach, salsify, and cauliflower. Dolley had a household staff of thirty, which she often supplemented with extra slaves from neighboring plantations at thirty-five cents each for the evening, providing one waiter for each guest.

Her success secrets were congenial guests, abundant food, superb service, and a generous smattering of friendly small talk, at which she, herself, was adept. Many a dreary conference was pleasantly interrupted by the arrival of her famous seed cake and bouillon, both of which were widely imitated by envious hostesses. ("She dips snuff, you know, and I think she *paints!*")

Did Dolley's apparently frivolous nature indicate a lack of character and courage?

In 1814, when the British were advancing on and burning the Capitol City, she was among the last to leave. Finally, at the frantic urging of servants, she came down from the roof of the White House, her spyglass in hand, gathered together valuable state papers, ordered the Stuart portrait of Washington taken from the wall, wrote a letter to her sister, and, dressed as a farmer's wife, left the city in a wagon and spent the night in an army tent.

She led the women of Washington in equipping the Lewis and Clark expeditions, raised money for the Washington Monument, nursed the wounded after the explosion of the *USS Princeton* on the Potomac (she was a not-so-young passenger on that ill-fated trip). She took tender loving care of Madison and his elderly mother until their deaths. Her mother-in-law adored her.

When President Van Buren, a widower, entered the White House, promising a rather dull social season, Dolley ingeniously provided him with just the right hostess. She brought an attractive relative, Angelica Singleton, from the South, introduced her to Van Buren's oldest son, and danced at their wedding. For years it was the custom in Washington, on New Year's Day, to call first on the President and his wife, then on Mrs. Madison, who lived in the shadow of the White House.

Plagued in her later years with an eye affliction and a ne'er-do-well son, whose extravagances forced her to pawn her silverware, she was poor in resources but not in spirit. She still loved to waltz, play cards,

A LEVEE AT THE WHITE HOUSE WHEN DOLLEY
MADISON WAS FIRST LADY

and dip snuff and enjoyed a rousing game of whist with John Quincy Adams and Lord Ashburton when they were all crowding eighty.

Living alone now with her only valuables—her husband's papers (which she rescued from fire a second time when she was eighty)—Dolley was forced to depend on the charity of former servants. She had one rusty, black "good dress." But life had two surprises in store:

Congress voted her a lifetime seat on the floor of the House of Representatives—an unprecedented honor—and bought the Madison papers for $25,000. She celebrated by giving a boat party on the Potomac for her many friends and by ordering a gown of white satin with matching turban. She wore this dazzling costume to President Polk's reception. Promenading the crowded rooms at midnight on the arm of the President, she still looked, they said, "every inch a Queen." She was eighty-one. It was her last big party.

The Quakers had been wrong about Dolley. She was not too happy to be good. All her life she was too goodhearted to turn her back on happiness. She died, but her spirit did not. Washington hostesses have been trying to recapture it ever since.

Famous Recipes of a Famous Doll

When Dolley Madison turned over her housekeeping keys to her successor, Elizabeth Monroe, in 1817, she left behind two recipes that were to be used by First Ladies well into the twentieth century. Dolley's Layer Cake (see page 327) graced many a White House tea, and her Bouillon warmed countless official stomachs on blustery March Fourths at the buffet luncheons that followed oath-taking ceremonies at the Capitol.

DOLLEY'S BOUILLON

4 pounds juicy beef	1 small pod red pepper
1 knuckle of veal	2 small white onions
2 small turnips	Salt
2 small carrots	6 quarts water
1 soup bunch	

Simmer six hours, strain through fine sieve, let stand overnight and congeal. Skim off all grease, put into kettle to heat and just before serving add sherry to taste.

DOLLEY'S FRUIT CAKE

1 pound butter
1 pound brown sugar
1 gill molasses
2 teaspoons cream of tartar
12 eggs separated
1 teaspoon allspice
2 teaspoons cinnamon
2 teaspoons grated nutmeg

1 pound flour
1 teaspoon soda
2 pounds raisins, seeded
2 pounds currants
1 pound citron
1 pound blanched almonds,
    chopped fine

Cream butter, sugar, molasses, and tartar. Add well-beaten egg yolks. Sift spices, flour, soda; add alternately with beaten egg whites. Add floured fruit and nuts. Bake in pans lined with greased paper in slow oven (250°) for five hours.

Dolley was renowned for her Seed Cake as well as for her Bouillon and her Layer Cake. The following up-to-date recipe for a Seed Cake may lack authenticity, but it makes up for it in speed, efficiency, and sure-fire results!

DOLLEY MADISON'S BRANDIED SEED CAKE, MODERN STYLE ☆

1 package (1 pound, 1 ounce)
    white or yellow cake mix
⅛ teaspoon nutmeg
½ cup milk

2 eggs
1 tablespoon caraway seeds
¼ cup brandy

Preheat oven to 325°. Mix cake with nutmeg, add milk, stir until mix is moistened. Beat one minute at medium speed with electric mixer or 150 strokes by hand. Add eggs, stir and beat one minute. Add seeds and brandy and beat one minute. Bake in ungreased nine-inch loaf pan about one and a quarter hours or until golden brown and crust springs back when lightly touched with finger. Let cool in pan on rack thirty minutes. Loosen with spatula, remove cake and place it on rack for complete cooling.

If you *must* have an authentic old Seed Cake, here is one from *Mrs. Winslow's Domestic Receipt Book for 1865:*

SEED CAKE, 1865 STYLE

Four cups of flour, one and a half cups of cream or milk, half a cup of butter, three eggs, half a teacupful of caraway seeds, a teaspoonful of saleratus [the great-grandmother of our modern baking soda], the same of rose water. Make mixture into a stiff paste and cut it with a tumbler or biscuit-cutter; bake about twenty minutes.

Incidentally, Mrs. Winslow was widely known not for her Seed Cake but for another original concoction:

> MOTHERS! MOTHERS! MOTHERS!
> *Don't fail to procure*
> MRS. WINSLOW'S SOOTHING SYRUP
> *For Children Teething*
>
> *An old nurse for children, Mrs. Winslow is becoming world renowned as a benefactor of her race. Children certainly do rise up and bless her. Indispensable Nursery Article! A Perfect Charm! Try it, Mothers!* TRY IT NOW. —*(old adv.)*

DOLLEY'S LAYER CAKE

1 small cup butter	1 cup milk
2½ cups sugar	2½ teaspoons vanilla
3 cups flour (cake flour)	White of 8 eggs beaten
¾ cups cornstarch	stiff with ⅛ teaspoon
½ teaspoon salt	salt

Beat butter till soft, add sifted sugar gradually, beat till creamy. Sift flour, cornstarch, and salt and add to butter mixture alternately with milk, using thirds each time. Beat batter till smooth after each addition. Beat in vanilla. Whip egg whites with salt, fold lightly into batter. Bake in three greased eight-inch layer pans at 375° for twenty-five minutes or in a greased nine-by-thirteen pan at 350° for forty minutes. After cool, spread the following between the layers and over the top:

CARAMEL FILLING

3 cups brown sugar   Butter the size of an egg
1 cup sweet cream   1 teaspoonful vanilla

Cook sugar, cream, butter in double boiler twenty minutes, add more sugar if desired. Just before removing from fire, add vanilla to the mixture.

LADY BALTIMORE CAKE

Dolley's Layer Cake is similar to Lady Baltimore Cake. A modern Lady Baltimore would call for:

2 cups sugar instead of 2½   No cornstarch
3½ cups flour instead of 3   Only 1 teaspoon vanilla
3½ teaspoons baking powder   extract

Prepare as for preceding recipe.

DOLLEY MADISON SAVES THE
STUART PORTRAIT OF WASHINGTON

328

Elizabeth Kortright Monroe

OF NEW YORK

First Lady
1817–1825

MRS. JAMES MONROE drew a difficult assignment as First Lady. She had to follow popular Dolley Madison. She soon made it clear, however, that she intended to "follow" no one:

She would *not* continue the tiresome custom of making and returning calls;

Her older daughter, Eliza (whom John Quincy Adams had called "an obstinate little firebrand"), would *not* call on diplomats' wives until they had first called on her;

The wedding of her daughter, Maria—the first President's daughter married in the White House—would *not* be a big social affair; only relatives and close friends would be invited.

At once a furor of ill-feeling that rocked the Cabinet arose among Washington ladies. Elizabeth Monroe had been called "the belle of New York" and a "serene aristocrat." Now she was called a snob—a British snob (the new President had been a diplomat abroad). For almost his entire first term Monroe and his wife were boycotted socially, their receptions sparsely attended. Mrs. Monroe was as stubborn as she was stately, however, and eventually the ladies made peace with her. Washington society could not hold out forever against the White House.

Influenced by their experiences abroad, the Monroes lived graciously

329

and entertained in formal, European style, serving French cuisine at beautifully appointed tables. Washington residents grumbled about the stiffly dignified affairs, but British and French visitors were impressed. They began to look upon Americans—perhaps for the first time—as something other than gawky colonials.

Tuesday-night receptions were popular. Mrs. Monroe, handsome in black velvet and pearls, her hair piled high in puffs and enhanced with ostrich plumes, received guests, while Negro servants in livery served wine, tea, coffee, and little cakes from silver trays near the fireplace.

Congress may have gasped at the bills for furnishings the Monroes imported from France, but these objects always have been among the most valuable possessions in the White House. Many a First Lady has admired them and their original owner, haughty Elizabeth Monroe, who banished the burdensome custom of "calling."

SHREWSBURY CAKES (A RICH SHORTBREAD)
[a 400-year-old recipe brought to the Colonies from England]

Take quarter of a pound of butter well worked, mix it with one pound brown sugar, one egg well beaten, as much flour as will make it stiff. Roll, then cut with a tin mold and bake the cakes in a slow oven.

THE THIRTEEN-FOOT-LONG MIRRORED BRONZE DORÉ
CENTERPIECE PURCHASED BY MONROE
AND STILL USED IN THE STATE DINING ROOM

330

MAIDS OF HONOR 1 ☆

[*Note:* This is said to have been named after Queen Elizabeth's ladies-in-waiting. It is another old English recipe.]

1¼ cups milk	2 tablespoons sugar
8 teaspoons bread crumbs	1 grated lemon rind
⅛ teaspoon salt	3 eggs
½ cup butter	⅔ cup blanched almonds, ground

Scald milk, add crumbs and salt. Let stand ten minutes. Add butter, sugar, and lemon rind. Add beaten eggs. Stir in almonds. Mix well. Line tart tins with puff paste or short pastry and fill two-thirds with mixture. Bake till golden brown in 300° oven.

MAIDS OF HONOR 2

Take one cupful of sour milk, one of sweet milk, a tablespoonful of melted butter, yolks of four eggs, juice and rind of one lemon, and a small cupful of white pounded sugar. Put both kinds of milk together in a vessel which is set inside another and let the mixture become sufficiently heated to set the curd; then strain off the milk, rub the curd through a strainer, add butter to the curd, the sugar, well-beaten yolks, and lemon. Line little pans with richest of puff-paste and fill with the mixture; bake until firm in the center, from ten to fifteen minutes.

TIPSY PUDDING OR TIPSY CHARLOTTE

Take a stale sponge cake, cut the bottom and sides of it to make it stand even in a glass fruit dish; make a few deep gashes through it, pour over it a pint of good wine and let it stand and soak into the cake. Blanch, peel and slice lengthwise half a pound of sweet almonds and stick them all over top of cake. Have ready a pint of good boiled custard and pour over the whole. To be dished with a spoon.

SPONGE CAKE

Ten eggs, the weight of them in sugar, the weight of five of them in flour, the juice and rind of one lemon. Beat eggs separately, then mix, adding sugar and flour, lastly the lemon.

331

JUMBLES

One pound of flour, one-half pound butter, three-fourths pound brown sugar, two eggs, half a nutmeg grated, two tablespoonfuls rose water. Roll out long with hands till width of finger, then join in rings. Bake moderately.

SYLLABUB

One quart of rich milk or cream, a cupful of wine, half a cupful of sugar. Put the sugar and wine into a bowl and the milk lukewarm in a separate vessel. When the sugar is dissolved in the wine, pour the milk in, holding it high; pour mixture back and forth until it is frothy. Grate nutmeg over.

[*Note:* In Martha Washington's day a popular drink was Syllabub Made Under the Cow. No explanation necessary!]

Louisa Catherine Johnson Adams

OF LONDON, ENGLAND

First Lady 1825–1829

LOUISA ADAMS, America's only foreign-born First Lady, was a frail, charming girl who won the admiration even of her gruff father-in-law, former President John Adams. He at first had opposed her marriage to his son but finally decided that John Quincy's choice of a wife was "the wisest choice of his career."

Louisa became the mother of four children. As the wife of a diplomat, senator, and Secretary of State, she had visited most of Europe's courts before coming to Washington and was an experienced hostess. She could play the harp and spinet, sing, sketch, write verse, and read French and Greek. She was pretty and always dressed in the latest fashion with glamorous coiffures. Her drawing rooms became more and more popular, with the doors open to all (at one a general's pocket was picked of eight hundred dollars). If her elaborate dinner parties had not quite the sparkle of Dolley Madison's, neither had they the chilly dignity of Elizabeth Monroe's.

In a popular verse of the time:

> Belles and matrons, maids and madams,
> All are gone to Mrs. Adams'.

Louisa was somewhat too retiring and studious to capture the public fancy, however. Americans have always preferred their First Ladies to be either highly glamorous or down-to-earth domestic types. Louisa Adams was somewhere in between.

GOOD PLUM CAKE

An equal weight of butter and flour, quarter of a pound of cut peels and citrons, double the weight of butter in currants, the grating of three lemons, and half a nutmeg, half an ounce of pudding spice, one glass of brandy, and the same quantity of eggs as the weight in butter. Beat your butter as for pound cake, put in a few chopped sweet almonds, then paper and butter a hoop, bottom and sides, and put in your mixtures and bake in a slow oven. Take off the hoop when done, but not the paper.

BIRD'S NEST PUDDING

Mix two large tablespoonfuls of flour with a pint of milk, a little salt, and two well-beaten eggs. Have ready six tart apples peeled, cored, and filled with sugar, strips of citron, and spice to taste; set the apples in a buttered earthen pudding dish; pour over them the batter and bake three-quarters of an hour. Eat with sweet sauce flavored with lemon.

333

COLD CUSTARD

Take one-fourth of a calf's rennet, wash it well, cut it in pieces and put it into a decanter with one pint of Lisbon wine. In a day or two it will be fit for use. To one pint of milk add one teaspoonful of the wine; sweeten the milk and flavor it with vanilla, rose water, or lemon; warm it a little and add the wine, stirring it slightly; pour it immediately into cups or glasses, and in a few minutes it will become a custard. It makes a firmer curd to put in the wine, omitting the sugar. It may be eaten with sugar and cream.

Rachel Donelson Robards Jackson

OF VIRGINIA

"For Mr. Jackson's sake I am glad; for my own part I never wanted it."

RACHEL JACKSON missed the White House by only three months. She died shortly before her husband's inauguration, "done to death by slanderous tongues," said the heartbroken President.

Though dead, Rachel greatly influenced the administration. His fierce loyalty to her, magnified by grief and anger, caused Jackson to champion other "martyrs" whom he mistakenly identified with her. Sometimes these protégées were ill-chosen and caused upsets in the Cabinet.

334

Old Hickory was the first President not descended from aristocracy. He was a soldier and frontiersman who settled arguments with battles and bullets. Until his death he carried a bullet in his chest—the result of a duel over Rachel's honor. (The other man was killed.)

Gossip and scandal had plagued the Jacksons from the day of their marriage. The question was this: Were they really married or living in sin? Rachel had been wed previously to a man named Robards. They proved incompatible and soon separated, and Robards filed for a divorce. Divorce, in those days, was almost unknown; lawyers knew as little about the necessary procedures as their clients. But assuming she was legally free, Rachel and Andrew married. Troublemakers, possibly led by her first husband, instigated a search for the divorce records. They could not be found. From that day until her death, Rachel knew no peace. By the time Jackson ran for President, the tale was forty years old, but wagging tongues of political enemies and self-righteous house-wives kept it alive.

While shopping for her inaugural gown, Rachel, then sixty-one, over-heard two women viciously discussing her and questioning her fitness to be First Lady of the land. It was said that this episode brought on the heart attack from which she died soon after. She was buried in her white satin inaugural dress, and on her tombstone Jackson had these words engraved: "A being so gentle and so virtuous that slander might wound but could not dishonor." It was true that Rachel's good character and good works were well-known among her acquaintances in Tennessee. With no children of her own, she had helped clothe, house, and educate many young relatives.

"Nothing but her care and industry saved me from ruin," Jackson once said.

The lonely President moved into the White House, and one of his first acts was to place an ivory miniature of Rachel and a Bible on his bedside table, where they remained throughout his stay. Emily Donelson, his wife's attractive, auburn-haired niece from Tennessee, became Uncle Andy's hostess. The four Donelson children were born at the White House and enjoyed the distinction of being worried over, sung to, and rocked to sleep by the tough old President.

Eight flamboyant years followed, during which the public made free with the mansion. Two of Jackson's parties vied for honors as the most destructive affair ever held at the White House. His first inaugural reception was attended by twenty thousand people, fainting and fighting for a glimpse of the President. Damage to rugs, furniture, and glassware was estimated in the thousands. Eight years later, shortly before leaving office, Jackson was presented by an admirer with a fourteen-hundred-

335

pound cheese. After it was thoroughly aged and ripened, he invited the public, and it came to eat cheese, step in cheese, and smear cheese all over the carpets, draperies, and walls. The fragrance lingered for months.

No Spartan at the dinner table, the President employed a French chef and imported servants from The Hermitage, his Tennessee home, to keep the horseshoe-shaped table in the state dining room heaped with elaborate French dishes and such American delights as "monster salmon in meat jelly." Never hesitating to ask Congress for additional appropriations, he spent $10,000 to turn the East Room into a show-place and another $45,000 to provide the house with the finest china, silver, and furniture. The public began to call him "King Andrew."

Though Rachel Jackson never lived in the White House, she is not forgotten there. On the south grounds still bloom the magnolia trees that her grieving husband, Old Hickory, planted in her memory.

Favorite Recipes of General Andrew Jackson
[*as prepared by Rachel Jackson*]

LEG OF LAMB WITH ROSEMARY ☆

5-pound leg of lamb	2 cloves of garlic
2 strips bacon	1½ teaspoons rosemary
2 lamb kidneys (these can be	2 teaspoons salt
omitted, but they enhance	¼ teaspoon pepper
the flavor)	

Start your oven at 325° or slow. Wrap bacon strips around lamb kidneys and skewer to the underside concavity of the leg. Put lamb, fell side up, in a shallow roasting pan and rub surface with a mixture of crushed garlic, rosemary, salt and pepper. Bake two to two and a half hours (twenty minutes per pound for best tasting) and serve on a hot platter. Serves six with enough left over for sandwiches.

The crush outside the White House at Andrew Jackson's
inauguration

GENERAL JACKSON'S FAVORITE TRIFLE ☆

2 cups milk
⅓ cup sugar
Dash of salt
1½ tablespoons cornstarch
2 eggs
½ teaspoon almond extract

½ pound macaroons
½ cup sherry
1 cup orange marmalade
½ pint heavy cream
2 teaspoons sugar
1 teaspoon sherry

Heat milk until a film shines on top. Mix sugar, salt, cornstarch, and eggs together in a bowl until smooth. Now add the hot milk dribbled a little at a time, stirring the mixture vigorously as you pour. Transfer to top of double boiler and cook over hot water until thick as mayonnaise, stirring constantly. Remove from heat, flavor with almond extract and cool. Lay macaroons on the bottom of a serving dish [a glass bowl is traditional] and pour in a half cup of sherry. Let the wine soak into the macaroons. Now spoon the cool custard on the top and cover with marmalade. Beat heavy cream, sugar, and one teaspoon sherry together until mixture holds a shape. Pile on top of marmalade and chill. Serve very cold to eight to ten guests.

ANDREW JACKSON'S FAMOUS CHEESE LEVEE

Emily Donelson, Rachel
Jackson's niece

SHRIMP PIE ☆

1 cup pastry
1½ pounds fresh shrimp
1 teaspoon mace
3 whole cloves

3 anchovies
3 tablespoons butter
½ cup white wine

Make up pastry and chill. Toss shrimp into boiling salted water, cover, reduce heat and cook slowly for about five minutes. Drain and if necessary remove shells. Start your oven at 425° or hot. Put shrimp in a buttered nine-inch pie pan and season with mace and cloves. Lay anchovies on top of shrimp, dot with butter and pour in wine. Cover with pastry, seal edges securely. Bake fifteen to twenty minutes or until pastry is golden. Serves four generously.

[*Note:* Unlike our modern recipes for shrimp pie, there is no binding nor thickening agent used in this filling. Be sure to spoon the good shrimp-flavored wine liquid over the servings.]

VIRGINIA SYLLABUB ☆

Pour one cup of sherry or Madeira wine in a punch bowl and stir in the same amount of sugar until dissolved. Beat one quart of heavy cream until it holds a shape, then stir in juice and grated rind of one lemon. Mix the lemon-flavored cream into the wine gently. Serve in glasses or a punch bowl.

After President Jackson's hectic White House inaugural reception, where jostling crowds stood on satin chairs with muddy boots and otherwise "made merry," he and Vice-President Calhoun slipped away to dine quietly on sirloin steak from a prize ox sent them by an admiring butcher in New York City.

Hannah Hoes Van Buren

OF NEW YORK

IN THE SHADOWS behind Martin Van Buren stands his almost-unknown wife, Hannah, who died at age thirty-six, nineteen years before he became President, leaving him to bring up their four sons alone. Van Buren never remarried.

Single Presidents never have promised the gay social seasons that the Capitol City craves, and Washington ladies sighed over the lack of a charming hostess for the executive mansion. Matchmaking efforts seemed lost on the President himself, but happily his oldest son, Abraham, proved susceptible to the charms of beautiful Angelica Singleton, a relative of Dolley Madison.

Angelica Van Buren fitted the role of hostess perfectly. She was well-

340

educated, graceful, vivacious, and queenly in her tiny-waisted, hooped-skirted costumes. Probably these graces did not save her from sharing the criticism that the President received for his extravagances.

An epicure and bon vivant, Van Buren had cultivated tastes, exquisite manners, and a polished, elegant style of living that was too dandified to suit democratic Americans. He imported a chef from London. He gave small, beautifully appointed and snobbish dinners. His public receptions were infrequent, stiff, and formal, with no refreshments served and with a police guard employed to screen out the "mobocracy" that President Jackson had made welcome.

In the miserable winter of 1839 fashionable guests, who had struggled through Washington's poorly lighted, frozen, rutted streets to get to the White House, said it was hardly worth the effort. Such a sameness of food and entertainment! The public was even more dissatisfied. The first great American depression had begun, and the people were in no mood for a high-living, free-spending President. They could hardly wait to vote gold-plated flatware, emerald green finger bowls, and royal-blue velvet gowns out of office.

Angelica Single-ton Van Buren, the President's daughter-in-law

Anna Symmes Harrison

OF

NEW JERSEY

First Lady
March–April, 1841

*"I wish they would
leave him happy and
contented in retirement."*

MRS. WILLIAM HENRY HARRISON was the wife of one President and the grandmother of another (Benjamin Harrison) and, though she served the shortest term of any First Lady—one month—she lived longer than any other President's wife. She was born during the first year of the Revolutionary War and died, at the age of eighty-nine, during the Civil War.

Mrs. Harrison was ill and not able to attend her husband's inauguration. By the time she was able to travel to Washington, the sixty-eight-year-old President, who had caught cold at his inauguration, had died of pneumonia. He was Chief Executive exactly four weeks. For the first time a President lay in state in the East Room. It was the era of splendid funerals, and the sad ceremony was conducted with great pomp.

Anna Symmes, the young daughter of an Ohio Supreme Court justice, and William Henry Harrison had eloped when he was an army officer and Indian fighter. General Anthony Wayne called her "the fairest bride in the Northwest Territory." Harrison became the first territorial governor of Indiana and was nicknamed "Old Tippecanoe" after his defeat of the Indians at the Battle of Tippecanoe. Later he served in both Houses of Congress and was American minister to

The inauguration of President William Henry Harrison

342

Colombia. Anna, in those famous and recurring words, "stayed home and raised the children and ran the farm."

For the fleeting month that Harrison was President, his daughter-in-law served as White House hostess.

There is little doubt that Mrs. Harrison would have been a popular and successful First Lady. As wife of the territorial governor, she had made their home, *Grouseland*, in Vincennes, Indiana, the center of hospitality and social life on the frontier. It was called "The White House of the West."

Pioneer "Apple" Pie

Ma, why can't we have us an apple pie?
'Cause we're plumb out of apples, that's why.
Then let's have us a vinegar pie!

Westering pioneer families couldn't take their orchards with them, so they did the next best thing. They took as many barrels of dried apples as the wagons would hold to tide them over till spring. When they got to the bottom of the last barrel, there was nothing to do but make Vinegar Pie to recall that good, apple flavor.

VINEGAR PIE 1 ☆

Beat three egg yolks till thick, add one cup of brown sugar, level, not pressed down, and one-quarter cup of white sugar, three tablespoons of cornstarch, a quarter teaspoon of salt, and a quarter cup of vinegar. Add two cups of boiling water, stirring all the time. Cook in double boiler till thick and smooth. Add one tablespoon butter just before removing from stove. Meanwhile, bake one crust at 400° three minutes. Fill crust, put back in oven at 325° and bake till light brown. Make meringue: three egg whites beaten with three tablespoons sugar [one tablespoon at a time] and flavored with lemon extract. Cover pie with meringue and bake till both crust and meringue are brown.

VINEGAR PIE 2 [1879]

One cup of sugar, one-half cup of cider vinegar, two tablespoons of flour, one teaspoon of butter, one teaspoon of cinnamon, two cups of water. Boil together. Bake as you would custard pie.

344

OLD-FASHIONED SUGAR CREAM PIE ☆

1 cup sugar
4 tablespoons flour
¼ teaspoon salt

1 pint heavy cream
1 teaspoon vanilla

Mix dry ingredients, blend in cream and vanilla. Bake in unbaked pie shell thirty-five minutes at 450° or an hour or more at 350°.

OLD-FASHIONED CREAM PIE ☆

1½ cups sugar
⅓ cup flour
½ teaspoon salt

2½ cups light coffee cream
2 teaspoons vanilla
1 tablespoon melted butter

Mix sugar, flour, and salt thoroughly. Add cream, vanilla, and butter. Beat thoroughly! Fill unbaked pie shell and bake in 450° oven ten minutes, then reduce heat to 325° and bake forty-five minutes longer or until knife comes out clean.

Letitia Christian Tyler

OF VIRGINIA

First Lady 1841–1842

LETITIA TYLER, a well-born woman of Virginia, was the nation's First Lady for one and a half years. She had suffered a paralytic stroke before Tyler became President and thereafter, until her death at age fifty-two, was an invalid. She had appeared in public at the White House only once—at the wedding of her daughter.

345

Julia Gardiner Tyler

OF NEW YORK

First Lady 1844–1845

"Fifty members of Congress paid their respects to me and all at one time!"

JULIA GARDINER, the Rose of Long Island, was twenty-four years old when she married the fifty-four-year-old widower president, John Tyler. Gay, sophisticated, with large gray eyes, raven hair, and a clear olive

346

complexion, Julia had left a trail of broken hearts from New York to Paris.

The May-December romance with Tyler bloomed in the shadow of tragedy. President Tyler, Julia, and her father, a senator, were among the passengers on the *USS Princeton* when it exploded on the Potomac River. Senator Gardiner was killed. Julia fainted and, some say, the President carried her ashore. At any rate, he consoled her so effectively that, after four months, they were secretly married in New York. It was the first marriage of a President while in office and occasioned much excitement in Washington and in Virginia, where Tyler's seven children, most of whom were near Julia's age, kept a shocked silence.

At once the Capitol became lively and more interesting; so did the previously staid President, who now composed serenades to his bride. She loved clothes, jewels, and compliments, and he enjoyed indulging her. It was a pact of mutual admiration. Julia's infatuation with her fatherly bridegroom amounted to hero-worship. She found his speeches "inspired and truly elegant." After he had signed the Texas Annexation Bill, she wore the gold pen with which he had signed it on a chain around her neck. It was she who ordered the Marine Band to play "Hail to the Chief" when the President entered an official gathering—a custom that persists to this day.

White House entertainments began to resemble European court life. Dressed in a long-trained purple gown with feathered headdress and seated on a raised platform that suggested a throne, Julia received each announced guest in regal splendor. Mrs. Presidentess—as she loved to be called—rode around Washington in a handsome coach-and-four, putting on a show that called forth a variety of comments—some awed, some amused, many enraged. Julia's mother wisely counseled her to "avoid display," but the starry-eyed young First Lady found it hard to do so. She gave Washington the biggest social whirl since Dolley Madison.

President Tyler was the father of fourteen children by his two wives, the last child born when he was seventy.

FIRST FAMILIES OF VIRGINIA CAKE

A half pound of flour, six ounces sugar, four ounces butter, two eggs, one wineglassful new milk, one small teaspoonful ammonia. Beat butter, add eggs and sugar, then flour. Dissolve ammonia in the milk and add with currants and candied peel to taste. Bake in loaf or cakes.

347

SEED CAKES

Two pounds of flour, one pound of sugar, fourteen ounces of butter, one tablespoonful of caraway seed, half a pint of milk, two tablespoonfuls of saleratus. Rub butter, sugar, and flour together, then add all the other ingredients. Knead all well together into a smooth dough. Roll out quite thin, cut with round cutter, place on tins and bake in moderate oven. The quantity of milk in this, as in all other hard cakes, appears small, but after kneading a little while, it will be found quite sufficient; to add more would spoil the cakes.

Recipes of the Old South

SWEET POTATO PUDDING ☆

2 sweet potatoes, peeled and grated	1 cup brown sugar
	4 tablespoons butter
1¾ cups cold water	½ teaspoon ginger

Mix all and bake in moderate oven (350°) one and a half to two hours.

IRISH POTATO PUDDING

To two pounds of potatoes, boiled and mashed, add one pound of butter while potatoes are hot. Take one pound of white sugar and beat into it eight eggs. When potatoes cool, add sugar and eggs, then add a half pint of sweet cream. Flavor with a half tumbler of brandy and nutmeg to taste. Bake in an under crust.

VUHGINIA MINT JULEP, SUH!

Gather mint when dew is on it; sprinkle with pulverized sugar and a few drops of brandy and water. Bruise it with beechwood pestle gently till mint oil comes. Put bruised mint in a glass and pour over it a cup of boiling water. Let set for fifteen minutes, then strain mint and pour juice in silver tankard filled with crushed ice. Let set a few minutes and pour into French brandy that has been kept at about 40°.

SALLY LUNN ☆

3 tablespoons butter
½ cup sugar
2 eggs
1 cup sweet milk

3 teaspoons baking powder
2 cups flour
1 teaspoon salt

Cream butter, add sugar, beating till fluffy, then add beaten eggs and milk alternately with sifted dry ingredients. Beat thoroughly. Pour into two well-greased and floured pans (8x8x2) and bake at 425° for twenty to twenty-five minutes. Serve hot with butter.

Sarah Childress Polk

OF TENNESSEE

First Lady 1845–1849

*"I have always belonged
to the whole country."*
(*Said during the Civil War.*)

THE PURITANICAL PUBLIC that had disapproved of Julia Tyler's frivolities had a pleasant surprise when Sarah Polk came into the White House. Sarah, age forty-two, a devout Presbyterian with a strict upbringing, frowned on fun—specifically dancing, card-playing and wine-drinking— as "time unprofitably spent." At the Inaugural Ball waltzing ceased when the President and his wife arrived and was resumed only after they left. Receptions were held twice each week, but guests did not linger long; no refreshments were served. It would have been a dreary

349

four years for Washington party-lovers had it not been for Dolley Madison, who lived close by at Lafayette Place and who, at eighty, still gave the best parties in town.

Sarah also proved a faithful guardian of the White House purse strings, to the disappointment of local tradesmen, who had hoped to redecorate the mansion. She ordered only the most necessary repairs and those at a modest cost.

Grave, formal, and dignified, Sarah was a perfect companion for the hard-working Polk. She was the first First Lady to serve as confidential secretary to her husband. As he worked late at his desk, she read and marked newspaper articles for his attention. They took fewer vacations than any First Family before or since. With no children, Sarah had always devoted all her time to her husband and his career and his character. It was one of the great satisfactions of her life when she persuaded James to be baptized.

Though the Polk receptions were dull and pinch-penny, Sarah herself was neither dull nor dowdy. She was charming and clever in conversation and handsome in appearance, with dark, Spanish good

Christmas Dinner at the Polks in Tennessee

OYSTER SOUP

| CELERY | TURKEY | HOMEMADE WAFERS |

HAM   SPICED ROUND

SALSIFY   CARAMEL SWEET POTATOES

PICKLES   RICE   CRANBERRY SAUCE

BLAZING PLUM PUDDING

WINE JELLY   CHARLOTTE RUSSE

GRAPEFRUIT SALAD   FRUIT CAKE

NUTS   RAISINS

WINE   COFFEE

looks. A member of a family of merchants, she always dressed in high fashion and fine taste, favoring rich satins and velvets.

Religious groups and the public in general heartily approved of the Polk austerity program. When Sarah left the White House, she left behind the reputation of a good woman who:

Once asked a band to stop playing for her entertainment because it was Sunday;

Refused all costly gifts;

Never attended the theater;

Always went to church but never received on the Sabbath.

In 1848 when candles and oil lamps in the White House were replaced by gaslights, Sarah Polk insisted on keeping one candle chandelier in the reception hall. Shortly after, the new-fangled gaslights faltered, and only the one chandelier was left burning bravely. It was sure proof, people said approvingly, of Mrs. Polk's good sense.

CHARLOTTE POLONAISE

[This recipe has been handed down from generation to generation in the Polk family of North Carolina.]

1½ pint milk	½ cup citron, chopped
6 egg yolks	½ cup powdered sugar
2 squares chocolate, grated	(generous)
½ cup granulated sugar	Large sponge cake
½ cup macaroons, crumbled	Icing or whipped cream
1 teaspoon almond flavoring	1 pint wine (if desired)
1 cup almonds, ground	

With sweet milk and yolks of eggs, make a rich custard. Let it boil, stirring, for ten minutes. Divide the custard in two equal parts by putting it into separate saucepans. Into one part put the pulverized chocolate, granulated sugar, and macaroons. Into the other half of custard put almond flavoring, pounded almonds, citron, and powdered sugar; after this has come to a boil, stir well and set aside to cool. Cut a large sponge cake in slices half an inch thick; spread one slice thickly with the chocolate mixture and one slice with almond mixture. Do this alternately until all ingredients are used. Put slices together. Cover with icing or garnish with whipped cream. This is improved by first pouring over it a pint of wine before icing. Serves twenty-five to thirty.

351

A Favorite Recipe of Church Ladies
Since Nobody-Knows-When

SCRIPTURE CAKE

3½ cups I Kings 4:22
  ½ cup Judges 5:25 (last clause)
  2 cups Jeremiah 6:20
  2 cups I Samuel 30:12
  2 cups Nahum 3:12
  2 cups Numbers 17:8
  ½ cup Judges 4:19 (last clause)

2 tablespoons I Samuel 14:25
2 teaspoons Amos 4:5
  Season to taste with
    II Chronicles 9:9; a pinch
    of Leviticus 2:13
Six of Jeremiah 17:11

Follow Solomon's advice for making a good boy, and you will have a good cake—Proverbs 23:14.

Margaret Mackall Smith Taylor

OF MARYLAND

First Lady 1849–1850

"It is all a plot to deprive me of his society."

"SHE PRAYED EVERY NIGHT my opponent would become President," laughed Zachary Taylor after his election. Doubtless his wife, Peggy, was worn out from years of following him from army post to army

post, from the Great Lakes to Baton Rouge. She had met Old-Rough-
and-Ready on the Kentucky frontier, married him in a log cabin
and borne him six children, two of whom died of swamp fever in one
month. Leaving their older children behind with relatives, she had
shared her husband's rough life and had nursed countless sick and
wounded soldiers in the Indian Wars.

"She was as much of a soldier as I was," said Taylor.

Now sixty-one and in ill health, Peggy was ready to settle down
quietly. Instead, as First Lady, she was elevated to a position that
involved social procedures about which she knew little and cared
nothing. With all the determination of an old soldier she retired to her
private apartment and turned over the duties of White House hostess
to her youngest daughter.

The executive mansion never had a sweeter, gentler mistress than
blonde, blue-eyed Betty Taylor Bliss. It was a year of informal hospitality and friendliness, brightened by the winning of the Mexican War.
There was a folksy air about; people liked to see Old Whitey, Taylor's
campaign horse, cropping grass on the White House lawn.

Betty Bliss entertained often and well at state dinners, morning
receptions, and tea parties at which she served homemade cakes
and tarts.

Meanwhile, Mrs. Taylor rocked in her cozy quarters upstairs,
sipping tea, chatting with family and old friends and—said some
people who had never even met her—smoking her corncob pipe.
President Taylor died after only one year in office. His wife never
afterward referred to their stay in the White House except in relation
to this sad event.

SWEET POTATO JOHNNY CAKE

[*Note:* Johnny Cake was originally "journey cake"—a corn bread that
was easily carried on trips by the early pioneers. It was also baked on
a hot, greased skillet.]

Take one pint of best cornmeal and salt it to taste (half a teaspoonful
is the ordinary seasoning). Rub into the meal a large tablespoonful of
lard. Next, add to it one pint of smoothly mashed sweet potatoes. If the
potatoes are not very sweet, add a tablespoonful of sugar. Mix thoroughly to a rather soft dough but not too soft to handle. Have the
middle stave of a barrel head (oak wood) washed clean. Rinse it, leaving
it wet, and on this evenly spread the dough not quite out to the edges of
the board. Dip a knife blade in cold water and smooth it over the surface

353

of the Johnny Cake; stick the cake with a fork as you would biscuit. Set it before the fire with a brick or flatiron to support it. Let it brown nicely, then loosen it from the board by means of a coarse thread passed between the Johnny Cake and the board, close to the latter. Turn the board over and lay the browned side of the Johnny Cake down on it, again setting it before the fire to brown the other side. When that is done, cut it in three-inch wide pieces; there will be about five of them. Send them to the table hot from the board, butter well and eat immediately.

This is a delicious bread for a winter supper or breakfast. But it must be cooked by the reflection of the fire to have the genuine Johnny Cake taste. In the stove? No! Before the fire!

LAYOVER FOR MEDDLERS ☆

Beat the yolks of four eggs, add one and a half cups of powdered sugar, two scant tablespoons cornstarch, and a good pinch of salt. Put a quart of milk in a double boiler, then add egg mixture and cook till it thickens (do not overcook) and flavor with vanilla if desired. Cool and cover with meringue made by beating two tablespoons of sugar with each egg white. Put into 300° oven for fifteen to twenty minutes. Use half the recipe for a small family.

"Scarlett was going to Atlanta to borrow money or to mortgage Tara if necessary. . . . And when they asked who was going to lend the money she said: 'Layovers catch meddlers,' so archly they all laughed and teased her about her millionaire friend."—*Gone With the Wind*, by *Margaret Mitchell*

Of all the old recipes in the new *White House Cookbook* none is more intriguing than Layover for Meddlers. What does the phrase mean? Stephens Mitchell, brother of the late Margaret Mitchell, and others have suggested that it is one of those teasing replies that adults give to children's persistent questions. As for the recipe:

One day, almost a century ago, a little boy came into the kitchen and asked his mother—a Virginian—what she was cooking. She answered, "Layover for Meddlers." That little boy is now one hundred years old, and the recipe is still a family favorite. An interesting title! But the expression is much older than the recipe; it goes back to the seventeenth century. Some people say it means, "Meddlers get leftovers." There will be no leftovers from this dish, however; it is delicious.

354

OF NEW YORK
First Lady 1850–1853

MILLARD FILLMORE often was called a "wife-made man." Abigail was two years older than he and had been his first and only teacher. The auburn-haired daughter of a Baptist minister, she was in charge of a village school when she met Fillmore, a poor boy who had gone to work at twelve as a clothier's apprentice. In his teens he enrolled in her school—the first he had ever attended—and she taught him to read and write. After they were married she continued to teach while he studied law. In the evenings she tutored him. After he went to Congress, she spent her spare time learning French and music.

At fifty-two, Abigail was equal to the intellectual but not the physical demands of the White House. Though frail, she did not want to be considered a recluse; she took an active part in official life, sometimes spending several hours in bed before a large party. Her most important accomplishment as First Lady was the establishment of the first library in the White House. Congress appropriated five thousand dollars for the purpose. She also had a piano installed.

Musical evenings were popular during her term. She and her daughter, Mary Abigail, played and sang duets, attended public lectures, art exhibits, and literary meetings. Despite her intellectual interests. Abigail was a homebody who saw to it that the President's house was closed to

355

visitors on Sunday so that the family might all go to church and rest.

Exciting innovations during this time were a bathtub and water pipes and a hotel-size cookstove that replaced the open fireplaces with their pots and pans on hooks and cranes. The new stove was so complicated, however, that President Fillmore had to be summoned to the kitchen to demonstrate its operation to the chef.

A fashion note introduced by the First Lady and widely copied was the wearing of a lacc handkerchief suspended elegantly by a thin golden chain from a ring.

The Fillmores were a devoted couple who wrote each other daily when apart. Less than a month after the end of her husband's term, Abigail died. She had caught cold at the inauguration ceremony for his successor, Franklin Pierce.

Jane Appleton Pierce

OF NEW HAMPSHIRE
First Lady 1853–1857

"Oh, how I wish he was out of political life! How much better it would be for him on every account!"

"THE VERY PICTURE of melancholy," they called her, poor Jane Pierce, the saddest of all the First Ladies.

No President's wife entertained with less enthusiasm; none gave of herself more reluctantly. The woeful face and slight figure, always

Arriving for a White House levee, 1856

356

garbed in black, banished all joy in others. Yet there was little criticism of her by the women of mid-nineteenth-century America; they understood only too well death in the nursery. Jane Pierce had had three sons and lost them all, one in infancy, one at the age of four, and the last at twelve in a railroad accident in which his parents were only slightly injured. The tragedy occurred less than two months before Pierce's inauguration, which the First Lady did not attend. The Inaugural Ball was canceled.

Long before these sad events, however, Jane Pierce had tried to stifle her husband's career. She had always begged him to give up politics and succeeded in persuading him to refuse the nomination for governor of New Hampshire. When he finally went to Congress, she did not go to Washington with him, and when a messenger brought the news of his nomination for President, she fainted. She was then forty-seven years old.

Her father, the president of Bowdoin College and a man fervidly occupied with religion, died at a young age. Jane was then a shy, impressionable child and, later, a fragile young woman with delicate features, ivory skin, black hair, and large dark eyes. She and Pierce were engaged for six years before they married; her family considered him "too worldly." He was said to be overly fond of liquor, though later he supported the temperance movement. Friends and associates in the Mexican War described the future President as handsome, gallant, and genial.

Although overwhelmed by Washington social life, Jane tried to do her part—especially near the end of her husband's term. She usually presided at the weekly state dinners, gave Friday-evening receptions and made an appearance at the New Year's Day reception of 1855, but her heart was in none of it. Her aunt often acted as official hostess in her place, and much important entertaining was done by the young and beautiful Mrs. Jefferson Davis, wife of the Secretary of War.

The only activities Jane allowed herself to enjoy were those she perhaps felt would not bring harsh Divine judgment upon her—religious and charitable work. One Christmas Day she entertained the entire Sunday School of the New York Avenue Presbyterian Church at the White House.

Meanwhile, Franklin Pierce went through the motions of being President, spent an appropriated twenty-five thousand dollars on the painting of the mansion inside and out, a new one-ton carpet for the East Room, a furnace, and a hot-water heating system. For relaxation he attended plays and concerts and other "worldly" events alone. He is called "The Forgotten President."

OF PENNSYLVANIA

White House Hostess for
President James Buchanan
1857–1861

"SHE HAS ENTICED back the merry laugh!" said a journalist about
Harriet Lane. The orphan niece of President Buchanan was to be
far more successful as acting First Lady than her uncle was as Chief
Executive.

The country was bored with delicate First Ladies who hid away on
the second floor. It warmly welcomed twenty-four-year-old Harriet,
who was as healthy and energetic as she was poised and worldly. Soon
the tall, willowy blonde with the violet eyes was America's pace-setter
in fashion. Home seamstresses everywhere furiously pedaled their
sewing machines as they hurried to copy her lace berthas, low necklines,
and full, stiff skirts. Down at the corner saloon the boys added a new
song to their repertory, one that had been especially written for and
dedicated to Harriet: "Listen to the Mockingbird."

Romanticists whispered that Bachelor Buchanan had lost his one
true love early in life and had vowed never to marry. True or not, it
was obvious that for years he had been grooming Harriet to take her
place by his side in political life. As carefully trained as a princess,
she had spent her formative years in the best boarding schools and
convents, and when Uncle Jim had become ambassador to the Court
of St. James's, she had gone along and become a favorite of Queen
Victoria.

Buchanan was distinguished in appearance and an excellent host,
and the handsome pair quickly dispelled the "Pierce gloom" that had
hung over the White House. Experienced in diplomacy, they managed

359

in this difficult pre-Civil War period to keep peace—socially, at least—between the "Dixies" and the "Yankee Doodles." The Royal Family's warm regard for the President and Harriet was credited with keeping England from entering the war on the side of the Confederacy.

As many titled visitors, including the Prince of Wales and members of the Japanese embassy, came to pay their respects, the White House took on the air of a European court. Entertaining reached a new high, and the Presidential salary of twenty-five thousand dollars no longer was adequate. Buchanan liked elaborate parties and paid for many of them from his own pocket, while Harriet—no scatterbrain, but a good manager—kept her eye on the bills. A lover of flowers and exotic plants, she spent much time in the newly built White House conservatory, which was open to the public on reception days. A proposal that a private residence be built for the President, with the White House to be used for offices and reception rooms, was much discussed but never acted upon.

Harriet was married during her uncle's term of office. One of her last gracious acts, before her uncle left the White House, was to see that a dinner was prepared and waiting for the incoming tenants—President and Mrs. Abraham Lincoln. Mr. Buchanan also left some things for Mr. Lincoln—a nation divided over the slavery question and unresolved problems regarding the course of the Union.

Said Old Buck to Honest Abe: "If you, my good man, are as happy

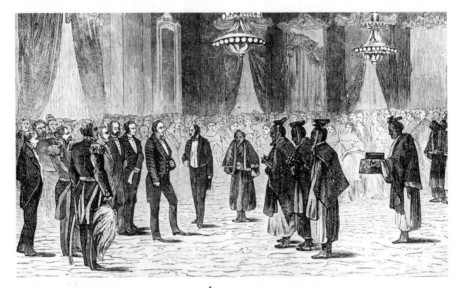

PRESIDENT BUCHANAN'S RECEPTION OF THE GRAND
EMBASSY FROM JAPAN

upon entering this house as I am on leaving it, then you are the happiest man in the country."

The happiest woman in the country at that moment was Mary Lincoln.

The Buchanan Inaugural Ball—March 4, 1857

In a new fifteen-thousand-dollar building especially erected for the Inaugural Ball guests danced beneath a white ceiling studded with gold stars. From long tables set up against the red, white, and blue walls they were served:

> 400 gallons of oysters
> 60 saddles of mutton
> 4 saddles of venison
> 125 beef tongues
> 75 hams
> 500 quarts of chicken salad
> 500 quarts of jellies
> 1,200 quarts of ice cream
> A four-foot cake
> $3,000 worth of wine

President Buchanan's Pennsylvania-Dutch tastes are reflected in the following recipes for his favorite foods:

BAKED SAUERKRAUT—PENNSYLVANIA DUTCH STYLE ☆

Boil a piece of pork until tender, then remove from the water, rub with salt and pepper, dredge with flour and place in pan on top of the stove. Sear quickly in a little fat. Put in roasting pan and sprinkle lightly with brown sugar, cover with sauerkraut and bake about ½ hour or until kraut is well cooked. Remove pork to large platter. Circle it with kraut, then with mashed potatoes. Entire platter may be returned to oven to brown potatoes slightly.

SAUERKRAUT

Make early in the light of the moon. Use just one pint of salt to a thirty-two-gallon barrel of kraut, and you will not fail to have it first-class.

PORK AND SAUERKRAUT WITH SOUR CREAM ☆

1½ pounds pork shoulder,
  cut into cubes
2 cups sliced onions
1 tablespoon paprika

1 to 1½ cups warm water
1 can sauerkraut [#2½ size]
Salt
1 cup sour cream

Brown cubed pork. Sauté onions and add to pork. Add paprika and water. Simmer until pork is done [about one and a half hours]. Then add the drained sauerkraut to the cooked meat and about two teaspoons salt. If this mixture should be too watery, sprinkle a small amount of flour on top and mix. Just before serving add sour cream and mix thoroughly. Serve over noodles or baked potato.

Three Versions of an Old Standby

PORK CAKE 1 [*1905*]

Two cupfuls of sugar, one cupful of molasses, one cupful of sour milk, one pound of pork minced fine, one pound of raisins, four eggs, one nutmeg, one teaspoonful of soda, one tablespoonful of cinnamon, four cupfuls of flour. Will keep three months.

PORK CAKE 2

One pound pork chopped fine, one pound dark sugar, one pound raisins, one pound currants, one pint baking molasses, one tablespoon each of cloves, cinnamon, allspice, and pepper, one nutmeg, butter the size of an egg, two eggs, one tablespoon soda dissolved in one pint of hot water. Stir stiff with flour and bake in loaf pans.

PORK CAKE 3 [*Mid-Twentieth Century*] ☆

Pour one pint of boiling water on thirteen ounces of ground fresh fat pork and cook for eight minutes. Let pork cool, add pinch of salt, then add pork to two cups of dark brown sugar, three eggs, one-half teaspoon each of allspice, cinnamon, and nutmeg, one cup each of nuts, raisins, and figs or dates, three cups of flour and two scant teaspoons of soda dissolved in a little hot water. Bake slowly in a moderate oven.

Mary Todd Lincoln

OF KENTUCKY

First Lady 1861–1865

"We are pleased with our advancement."

MARY LINCOLN wanted to be the best First Lady in the history of the country. She had the background for it. As the daughter of the president of the Bank of Kentucky, she had been well educated and "finished" in fashionable schools. She was somewhat spoiled and willful, but a great many daughters of indulgent fathers are that.

When, at twenty-one, she came up to Springfield, Illinois, to visit her sister, who had married the governor's son, Mary was a short, pleasingly rounded, and pretty girl with a dimpled face, a quick wit, and a sharp tongue. Abraham Lincoln was charmed by her. Probably she was the most interesting girl the easy-going, slow-moving lawyer had ever met. Certainly, she was the most attractive and accomplished who had ever shown romantic interest in him; he was not a ladies' man. After becoming engaged, breaking off, meeting again, they were married.

Considering the luxury of her upbringing, Mary did well as the young wife of a dreamy, impractical genius. True, she was always on her high horse about something, but then Abe was not an ideal husband. He was often away, riding the law circuit. At home he was somber, silent, and abstracted much of the time and indifferent to such amenities as tidy dress and proper meals. Deep in books or thoughts, he did not seem to care when nor what nor whether he ate. (Probably he was the smallest eater of all the Presidents, being well satisfied with an apple or crackers and cheese in his office.) He hated to pester clients for money

ABRAHAM LINCOLN AND HIS FAMILY

they owed him. Mary always had to be the manager. She was devoted—almost desperately—to her four sons and to her husband, whose abilities she recognized. Abraham Lincoln was eminently capable of handling the Presidency; his wife knew that long before anyone else.

And so, having coveted the position of First Lady, she entered Washington at age forty-two, prepared to enjoy her husband's triumph. No time was lost launching her career, no expense spared in her wardrobe—white satin and Chantilly lace with pearls for the Inaugural Ball, magenta silk with a lace cape for the first reception. Official Washington and social-minded Easterners began to sit up and take notice, precisely as the midwestern lawyer's wife had intended.

Early comments were favorable. Newspapers praised her entertaining as "most recherché and elegant." They called attention to her "exquisite taste and practical good sense," which, they said, equaled her "graceful courtesy and charming manners."

Then the Civil War began, casting a pall over the country. Extravagant entertaining and fashionable display ceased—but not at the White House. On February 5, 1862, Mrs. Lincoln, elegant in purple velvet *en train* (and with a sick child upstairs about whom she was terribly worried) gave her most elaborate soirée. She had imported a New York caterer for the occasion. The menu:

CHAMPAGNE PUNCH

STEWED AND SCALLOPED OYSTERS

BONED, TRUFFLE-STUFFED TURKEY

PÂTÉ DE FOIS GRAS

ASPIC OF TONGUE

CANVASBACK DUCK

PARTRIDGE

FILLET OF BEEF

HAM   VENISON

PHEASANT TERRAPIN

CHICKEN SALAD

SANDWICHES AND JELLIES

CAKES   ICES

It was, reporters said, "one of the finest displays of gastronomic art ever seen," but the meal did not go down well with the public.

"Are the President and Mrs. Lincoln aware there is a Civil War?" someone asked bitterly.

The President was aware. Mrs. Lincoln, however, had become so embroiled in personal wars with her budget, with her nerves, with the critical public, who had begun to question even her loyalty (she was a Southerner with relatives in the Confederate forces), that she had little energy left for the larger issue. Fifteen days after the soirée her son, Willie, died. He was the second son she had lost, but she did not receive the sympathy that had been extended to Jane Pierce. Many women were losing sons on battlefields. "At least she could be with her boy," some said callously. Her mail became vicious.

So often now was she the target of criticism that she became defensive and suspicious, seeing enemies everywhere. She never had the knack of "taking it easy" or "shrugging things off," nor had she any saving philosophy. She couldn't bend; she could only break. Little by little, the intensity and the temper and the tantrums she had never learned to control began to control her. Thus, from the high-spirited girl who had attracted Lincoln, there emerged the self-centered, irresponsible woman who was subject to violent headaches and uncontrollable outbursts. His re-election became an anguished question for her; she was deeply in debt. Wildly she swung from one extreme to the other, trying to offset large expenditures with petty household economies. If he was re-elected, she could continue to conceal her extravagances from him. Victory assured, she relaxed and celebrated with a new white silk and lace inaugural costume costing two thousand dollars.

"Through the whole War," one correspondent observed, "Mrs. Lincoln shopped."

Such peculiar shopping it became. Three hundred pairs of gloves in four months. The public stopped referring to "Her Satanic Majesty" and began, more understandingly, to call her "a sad case." Then came the assassination, and the only person who had made allowances for her was gone. ("If you only knew how much good these little outbursts do Molly—" President Lincoln had said protectively.)

There have been thousands of American women, well born, well educated, talented, and ambitious who would not have been suited by

New Year's Day reception at the White House during Lincoln's first administration

temperament to the demanding job of First Lady. Mary Lincoln was one of them. If she were writing an appraisal of her life, it might read: "I tried very hard, but I failed. I don't know exactly why."

Mr. Lincoln's Sweet Tooth

Though his law partner, Billy Herndon, had said, "Abe can sit and think longer without food than any man I ever met," other acquaint-ances remembered his fondness for desserts. A Washington, D. C., baker declared that the tall President was one of his best pecan-pie customers. Then there was the delicious vanilla-almond cake served to him at the home of General Dodge in Council Bluffs, Iowa, during the War—Mr. Lincoln remembered that cake with pleasure. Here are modern adaptations of his favorites:

LINCOLN VANILLA-PECAN PIE ☆

3 eggs, beaten
½ cup dark brown sugar
1 cup light corn syrup
3 tablespoons butter
1½ teaspoons vanilla
⅛ teaspoon salt

1 cup chopped pecans
1 tablespoon flour
1 nine-inch unbaked pie shell
Whipped cream for garnish
Pecan halves for garnish

Preheat oven to 375°. Combine eggs and brown sugar. Blend in corn syrup. Melt butter and add along with vanilla and salt. Blend chopped pecans with flour and stir into the mixture. Pour into a nine-inch pastry-lined pie plate. Bake in 375° oven forty minutes or until firm. Garnish with whipped cream and pecan halves if desired. Makes eight servings.

VANILLA-ALMOND CAKE ☆

3 cups sifted all-purpose flour
3 teaspoons double-acting
   baking powder
½ teaspoon salt
¾ cup soft butter
   or margarine

1¾ cups sugar
2 teaspoons vanilla extract
½ teaspoon almond extract
6 egg whites, unbeaten
1 cup milk
⅓ cup hot water

Sift first three ingredients together and set aside. Stir butter till fluffy and gradually blend in sugar. Stir in vanilla and almond extracts. Beat in egg whites, one at a time. Add sifted flour mixture alternately with milk. Blend in hot water. Turn into three well-greased and lightly floured nine-inch layer-cake pans. Bake in pre-heated moderate oven (375°) twenty-five minutes or till done. Cool ten minutes in pans. Turn out on wire rack. When cool, spread frosting between layers and over top and sides.

JIFFY CHOCOLATE FROSTING ☆

¼ pound marshmallows
2 squares unsweetened chocolate
2 tablespoons light corn syrup
¼ cup butter
¼ cup milk

4 cups sifted
   confectioner's sugar
2 teaspoons vanilla extract
⅛ teaspoon salt

Combine first four ingredients in top part of double boiler. Cook over hot water till marshmallows and chocolate are melted. Blend milk and sugar together, add chocolate mixture, vanilla extract, and salt. Mix till smooth.

Eliza McCardle Johnson

OF TENNESSEE

First Lady 1865–1869

*"My dears,
I am an invalid."*

ELIZA JOHNSON had much in common with two earlier First Ladies, with Abigail Fillmore, who taught her husband to read, and with Margaret Taylor, who kept to her apartment. Eliza appeared in public only once —at a party given by her grandchildren.

369

Martha Patterson,
Andrew Johnson's
daughter

At sixteen she had married Andrew Johnson, a poor widow's son. After teaching him to read, write, and cipher, she helped him rise from country tailor to alderman, mayor, state legislator, governor of Tennessee, congressman, senator, and vice-president. When he became President, Eliza was fifty-five and an invalid, having had tuberculosis for twenty years. Martha Johnson Patterson took over her mother's duties.

"We are plain people from the mountains of Tennessee; I trust too much will not be expected of us," said Martha.

If Washington was prepared to look down its official nose, it was delightfully surprised by the quiet elegance and gentle manners the Johnsons brought to the White House. Martha, no barefoot mountain girl, had been educated in private academies when her father was senator. She had spent holidays with the Polks in the executive mansion, had known Dolley Madison and other distinguished old residents. Moreover, she was a paragon housekeeper. Housewives across the nation sympathized as she undertook to refurbish the neglected mansion. They threw up their hands in horror when she discovered vermin in the

East Room. During the Civil War the White House had been used by quartered soldiers and abused by the souvenir-seeking public, who had even cut pieces from the draperies. Like any good housekeeper, Martha could not think of entertaining until she had "cleaned house." With a modest appropriation of thirty-thousand dollars, which she stretched skillfully, it was put in shape for the New Year's Day reception of 1867. Callers were impressed with the transformation and with Martha and her sister, who received, similarly dressed in modest high-necked black silk gowns with tight basque waists.

Once the White House was clean, Martha intended to keep it that way. On rainy days—no matter who called—the new velvet carpets were prudently covered with muslin. Unfortunately, some of the re-decorating had to be done over. In 1867 a twenty-thousand-dollar fire did much damage and destroyed a third of the plants in the conservatory.

Frail Eliza Johnson, the seldom-seen First Lady, did her part in maintaining good public relations by promoting harmony within the three-generation family circle. Her quiet room upstairs, where she knitted and read, became a pleasant retreat for them. The nation was fond of Grandma, who had raised a daughter with enough gumption to clean house and milk her Jerseys in the morning and give a party for Queen Emma of the Sandwich Islands at night.

Grandma Was Acting First Lady

In 1892 a three-year-old girl lost her mother and went to live with her grandmother, Martha Johnson Patterson, former acting First Lady. Today Martha Willingham, of Richmond, Virginia, reminisces about life with Grandmother Patterson in the Johnson home, Greeneville, Tennessee. Grandmother had a favorite recipe.

"It was mixed by her cook in the basement kitchen," Mrs. Willingham remembers. "But in cold weather it was brought up to Grandmother's bedroom on the first floor, in a stone jar, covered with a white cloth and set on the hearth to one side of the open fire for the night. As Grandmother was far from well, the fire was kept burning all night, but in spite of her infirmities she would get out of bed several times during the night to turn the jar so it would rise evenly. She often remarked that it was a favorite of her father [President Andrew Johnson] and that she had taught the cooks in the White House to make it as he liked it."

Here is the recipe on which Martha Patterson lavished such care:

371

MARTHA JOHNSON PATTERSON'S BUCKWHEAT CAKES

In the evening mix:

1 quart buckwheat flour
4 tablespoons of yeast
1 teaspoon salt
1 handful Indian meal

2 tablespoons molasses
  (not syrup)
Warm water, enough to make
  a thin batter

Beat very well and set to rise in a warm place. If the batter is the least bit sour in the morning, stir in a very little soda, dissolved in hot water.

Mix in an earthen crock and leave some in the bottom each morning—a cupful or so—to serve as a sponge for the next night instead of getting fresh yeast. In cold weather this plan can be successfully pursued for a week or ten days without setting a new supply. Of course, you must add the usual quantity of flour, etc., every night and beat well. Do not make your cakes too small. Buckwheats should be of generous size.

Julia Dent Grant

OF MISSOURI

First Lady
1869–1877

"Those eight years were the happiest period of my life."

THE CLOSELY KNIT Grant family brought solidity and glamour to the White House. The old mansion looked more homey than it ever had

372

before; yet there was always something exciting going on, to be read about in the newspapers.

Julia Grant, the daughter of a St. Louis judge, had known bitter years as the wife of a man who was several times a business failure before he became a war hero. At forty-three she knew good fortune when she saw it. Calling the White House "a garden spot of orchids," she prepared to enjoy her new role, and she did. She was by nature a warm and sincere person, and her training as an army wife had taught her to be adaptable. Though the family observed army regularity—breakfast at eight-thirty, dinner at five, and every member present and punctual— six extra places were always set for last-minute guests, who, Julia said, "are sure to come." Her skill and tact in handling people were demonstrated within the family. Her father and the General's—the first a Southern rebel, the other a Yankee—lived with the Grants and daily refought Antietam and Bull Run at the dinner table.

The First Family was popular with the public. After the gloomy war years, the country welcomed the glitter of gay, good times in the Capitol. Entertaining had never been so lavish. Elaborate dinners often ran to as many as twenty-nine courses and lasted two to three hours. Julia entertained at receptions and levees and graciously invited other prominent women to help her receive. Both she and the President airily did away with customs they deemed outmoded, accepting dinner invitations, making and returning calls when and where they pleased. It was the era of bustles and long trains, low-cut necklines and lace shawls. The ladies frankly "painted" with pearl powder, rouge, and enamel.

Society editors were ecstatic when it was announced that Daughter Nellie's European tour had resulted in a shipboard romance. Her wedding, May 21, 1874, to Englishman Algernon Sartoris, was the first in the White House for thirty years. The couple was deluged with gifts from their admiring public. Walt Whitman wrote a poem for the occasion. (There were to be other news-making marriages in the Grant family in years to come. Fred, the President's son, married the sister of Mrs. Potter Palmer, Chicago society queen, and Fred's daughter wed the Russian nobleman, Count Cantacuzene. After the Russian Revolution the princess and her husband opened a restaurant in London.)

The Grants decorated the White House in the gaudy, overornamented style then popular. Graperies, greenhouses, and stables were built and the grounds lighted. There was evidence—decay, cracking, and settling—that the old house needed more than redecorating, however. It was years before some of these repairs were made.

Julia saw to it that, on most occasions, the President got what he wanted to eat: for breakfast, Spanish mackerel or steak and bacon with fried apples; for dinner, rare roast beef, boiled hominy, wheaten bread, and rice pudding.

She also respected his wishes concerning her eyes. They were slightly crossed, and she had heard of a successful new operation that would "fix" them. He would not stand for it. He fell in love with those eyes, he said, and he wanted them left the way they were.

JULIA GRANT'S VEAL OLIVES

Slice as large as you can pieces from leg of veal. Make stuffing of grated bread crumbs, butter, minced onion, salt and pepper, and spread over slices of veal. Beat an egg and put over the stuffing; roll each slice up tightly and tie with thread. Stick a few cloves in them. Grate bread thickly over them after they are put in skillet with butter and chopped onions. When done, lay them on dish. Make gravy and pour over. Take threads off and garnish with eggs boiled hard and serve. To be cut in slices.

[*Note:* Mrs. Grant contributed this recipe to a church cookbook in 1892. Mrs. Sadie Allen, custodian at the Grant Home, Galena, Illinois, says she has tried it and it is very good. Following is a similar recipe from the same period which is a bit more explicit.]

VEAL BIRDS ☆

Buy veal steak about one-half an inch thick; one steak usually makes three birds. Cut steak to best advantage. Make a dressing of bread crumbs, season with salt, pepper, sage, butter, and a little onion. Spread some dressing on each strip of veal and roll as tightly as possible and fasten together with a toothpick. Roll the birds in flour and fry like chicken until they are a nice brown, about one hour, turning often. Then nearly cover them with boiling water and let simmer slowly one hour longer. Serve with sauce left in the pan.

PRESIDENT GRANT'S SPANISH MACKEREL

Split the fish down the back, take out the backbone, wash fish in cold water, dry it, sprinkle lightly with salt and lay it on a buttered gridiron over a clear fire with the flesh side downward until it begins to brown; turn to other side. Have ready a mixture of two tablespoonfuls of butter melted, a tablespoonful of lemon juice, a teaspoonful of salt, some pepper. Dish up the fish hot on a hot dish, turn the mixture over it.

374

Nellie Grant's Wedding Breakfast, May 21, 1874

STATE DINING ROOM

(Menu Printed on White Satin)

SOFT CRABS ON TOAST

CHICKEN CROQUETTES WITH FRESH PEAS

ASPIC OF BEEF TONGUE

BROILED SPRING CHICKEN

STRAWBERRIES WITH CREAM

WEDDING CAKE ICED WITH DOVES, ROSES, AND WEDDING BELLS

ICE CREAMS AND ICES

FANCY CAKES

PUNCH   COFFEE   CHOCOLATE

NELLIE GRANT SARTORIS AND HER BRIDEGROOM IN THE
PULLMAN PALACE CAR AFTER THEIR WEDDING

General Grant's Birthday Dinner at the White House

CLAMS

HAUTE SAUTERNE

Potages
CONSOMMÉ IMPERATRICE BISQUE DE CRABES

AMONTILLADO

Varies Hors d'Oeuvre Varies
BOUCHÉES À LA REGENCE

Poisson
TRUITES DE RIVIÈRE HOLLANDAISE VERT PRÉ

POMMES DE TERRE A LA PARISIENNE

JOHANNISBERGER

COUCOMBRES

Relevé
FILET DE BOEUF À LA BERNARDI

ERNEST JEROY

Entrées
AILES DE POULETS À LA PERIGORD   PETITS POIS AU BEURRE

CAISSES DE RIS DE VEAU À L'ITALIENNE

HARICOTS VERTS   ASPERGES, SAUCE CRÈME

SORBET FANTAISIE

RÔTI

SQUABS   SALADE DE LAITUE

NUITS

Entremets Sucres
CROUTE AUX MILLE FRUITS   CORNETS À LA CHANTILLY

GELÉE À LA PRUNELLE

Pièces Montées
GLACÉ VARIÉTÉES

FRUITS   PETITS FOURS   CAFÉ

376

When the old soldier with the big, black cigar was handed this menu, what was his reaction?

CLAMS

SAUTERNE

CRAB SOUP

AMONTILLADO

ASSORTED APPETIZERS

RIVER TROUT WITH HOLLANDAISE SAUCE

POTATOES

CUCUMBERS

JOHANNISBERGER

FILET OF BEEF

ERNEST JEROY

CHICKEN   PEAS IN BUTTER

VEAL SWEETBREADS

GREEN BEANS   ASPARAGUS

SHERBET

SQUAB   LETTUCE SALAD

ASSORTED FRUITS IN COMPOTE

PLUM JELLY

ASSORTED ICE CREAMS

FRUITS   LITTLE CAKES   COFFEE

Did he throw down the menu and growl, "Bring me some pickled oysters, a big steak, apple pie and coffee"?

377

Favorite Recipes of Princess Cantacuzene
[*Granddaughter of President Grant*]

CHICKEN À LA RUSSE ☆

Take two to four spring chickens well trussed and cleaned. Rub them over with flour and salt and fill them with the following stuffing: twenty-four tea rusks, well crushed; two or three tablespoonfuls of butter, one or two yolks and six tablespoonfuls of parsley. All these ingredients well mixed together. Then roast the stuffed chickens in a half pound of butter. When ready, serve them with melted butter in which a good quantity of tea rusk crumbs have been mixed. This butter is poured over as a sauce. Serves six persons.

BORSCHT FROM LITTLE RUSSIA ☆

Take three pounds of meat and put it in a saucepan with nine tumblers of cold water. Add to it two onions, two carrots, two parsnips (all whole) and two raw beets cut into long narrow strips. Salt as for consommé. Put the saucepan on the fire (not too large a fire) and bring it to boiling point. Remove it from the fire for five minutes, then put it again on the fire and let it boil well a second time. Then remove the parsnips from the soup and add half of one white cabbage chopped very fine and three sliced tomatoes and let the soup boil again. Then add six peeled, raw potatoes and a half tumbler of puree of tomato; stir well and boil for the last time. Take out the meat and cut it into large cubes, then replace it into the soup. When serving, have a cube of the meat put into each soup plate with the soup and serve sour cream with it, two teaspoonfuls per plate. A good addition is laurel leaves and black pepper.

BOEUF À LA KROGANOFF ☆

Two pounds of filet of steak or rump steak cut into thin, longish strips. Put in frying pan with salt and pepper, one onion chopped fine, and

One of the last photographs taken of President Grant

one tablespoonful of butter. Fry meat until it is a good brown color. Make following sauce: melt one tablespoonful of butter, add one tablespoonful flour, and mix thoroughly over low fire, then add two tumblers of hot stock, stirring till sauce is brown. Then add one teaspoonful of ready-made mustard, a little Worcestershire sauce, two tablespoonfuls of sour cream, and one tablespoonful of puree of tomato. When sauce is ready, put the meat into it and let it stand, covered with a lid, for half an hour in the oven. Then it is ready to serve six persons.

[*A further historical note:* President Grant's second inaugural ball was held in zero weather in an unheated building. The guests, who had paid twenty dollars for their tickets, were so cold that they danced with their hats and coats on, forsook the champagne, ice cream and punch for coffee and hot chocolate, and went home early!]

Lucy Webb Hayes

OF OHIO

First Lady 1877–1881

"No matter what they build, they will never build any more rooms like these!"

THE MOST POPULAR, best-loved First Lady ever! That was Lucy Hayes, age forty-six, daughter of an Ohio physician, the first First Lady to be graduated from a chartered college (and with highest honors).

Mrs. Rutherford B. Hayes was more than a public figure; she was almost an idol. So much good was said of her in her own day, she must have deserved it.

380

Calm, serene, cheerful, active, healthy, well-balanced—every complimentary adjective was used to describe her. "Her beauty and simplicity have taken blasé Washington by storm," said the newspapers. Three famous poets—Longfellow, Whittier, and Holmes—dedicated poems to her.

Lucy Hayes was a prime example of the New Woman in America. Though domestic and devoted to her husband and children, she had wide interests beyond her home—woman suffrage, Civil Service reform, Indian welfare, and rehabilitation of the South. She was no militant female, however, but the essence of feminine charm. When ratted coiffures were the fashion, her hair was plainly waved back to a bun and held by tortoise combs. Bustled, bejeweled lady callers at the White House were surprised to be greeted by a tastefully but modestly dressed First Lady who displayed neither bustle nor beads. Readily available to her public, she was "at home" every night to any who cared to call.

The only anti-Lucy faction was the wine-lovers. She got most of the credit or blame when liquor was banned from the White House, though President Hayes was as opposed to drinking as she was.

The grumblers dubbed her "Lemonade Lucy," which amused her, but soon they, too, were won over by her charm and meekly drank tea at official functions without complaining. Her temperance stand made her the heroine of the Women's Christian Temperance Union, which presented her portrait to the White House along with a silken banner inscribed with the Biblical quotation: "She hath done what she could."

As for the public, it smiled approvingly on the liquor ban as on everything else the Hayeses did—their morning prayers after breakfast, their Sunday morning strolls to the nearby Methodist Church, their Sunday evening hymn sessions, which were attended by many Cabinet members and Congressmen.

For all her good works, Lucy Hayes was said to be not "stuffy" but an enjoyable person with a keen sense of humor and a bright, animated face. The President's House was charming, she said, making no criticism of its shortcomings as had her predecessors. She found the position of First Lady enjoyable. When Congress appropriated a sum for her domestic needs—redecorating, and so on—she used most of it to purchase a state dinner service of nearly a thousand pieces which showed the flora and fauna of the United States. It is among the most treasured possessions in the White House today.

The Hayeses' silver wedding anniversary was celebrated December 30, 1877, with a re-enactment of the ceremony by all the principals. Lucy wore her white silk and brocade wedding gown. Immediately afterward, the two youngest Hayes children were baptized. (There had been eight children, three of whom had died in childhood.) The next night, New Year's Eve, a public reception was held. Even more exciting to the public was the revived custom of egg-rolling on Easter Monday. Dolley Madison had initiated this event on the Capitol grounds years before. When Lucy learned that the custom had been dropped because of damage to the grounds, she opened the White House gates to the children of Washington.

Lucy Hayes was the first First Lady to accompany her husband on all his political trips, the first to go to the Pacific Coast, the first to use two

RECEPTION OF GUESTS AT THE HAYESES' SILVER ANNI-
VERSARY CELEBRATION

new inventions in the White House—the telephone and the telegraph. She was the first First Lady to please most of the people most of the time. She was, in short, in tune with her times. In the Victorian era she was the kind of woman a Victorian woman was supposed to be.

Favorite Recipes of Lucy Hayes

It is usually easy to pick out a housewife's favorite recipes. Certain pages of her cookbooks are well-thumbed and dog-eared, and the margins are spotted with vestiges of long-ago puddings and pie fillings, gravies and white sauces. So it is with Lucy Hayes's cookbooks. After almost ninety years tell-tale smudges point to these favorites:

FRENCH PICKLES

[handwritten by President Hayes in a family cookbook and dated 9 Oct. 1873]

1 peck green tomatoes   6 large onions, sliced

Throw one teacup full of salt on them, let stand till morning, drain thoroughly, then boil in two quarts water and one quart vinegar fifteen or twenty minutes. Strain in a colander. Take four quarts vinegar, two pounds brown sugar, a half pound white mustard seed, two table-spoons full-grown allspice, two tablespoons each of cloves, cinnamon, ginger, and ground mustard, thrown together, and boil fifteen minutes till tender. Excellent.

CORN BREAD

[handwritten by Mrs. Hayes in her cookbook]

2 pints corn meal   1 pint jar milk with
   mixed with a little pinch   1 teaspoonful soda
   of salt   1 egg, well beaten

Add a little more milk if needed. Have the pan well buttered and very hot.

383

OFFICIAL RECEPTION OF THE FIRST CHINESE MINISTER TO
THE UNITED STATES

CORN SOUP 1

Take one can of corn. Season with a little butter, salt and pepper; add a little water if it lacks juice, not otherwise. Then, when perfectly soft, press it through a colander with potato masher, then add one quart rich milk. Let it come to a boil.

CORN SOUP 2

This is a very good soup made with either fresh or canned corn. When it is fresh, cut the corn from the cob and scrape off well all that sweetest part of the corn which remains on the cob. To a pint of corn add a quart of hot water. Boil it for an hour or longer, then press it through a colander. Put into the saucepan butter the size of a small egg and, when it bubbles, sprinkle in a heaping tablespoonful of sifted flour, which cook a minute, stirring it well. Now add half the corn pulp and, when smoothly mixed, stir in the remainder of the corn; add cayenne pepper, salt, a scant pint of boiling milk, and a cupful of cream. This soup is very nice with no more addition, as it will have the pure taste of the corn. Yet many add the yolks of two eggs just before serving, mixed with a little milk or cream and not allowed to boil. Others add a table-spoonful of tomato catsup.

President Hayes was an oyster-lover, as were many other American Presidents. Mrs. Hayes catered to his taste with the following three recipes:

SCALLOPED OYSTERS IN SHELLS

They may be served cooked in their shells or in silver scallop shells, when they present a better appearance than when cooked and served all in one dish.

If cooked in an oyster or clam shell, one large or two or three little oysters are placed in it with a few drops of the oyster liquor. It is sprinkled with pepper and salt and cracker or bread crumbs. Little pieces of butter are placed over the top. When all are ready, they are put into the oven. When they are plump and hot, they are done. Brown the tops with a salamander or with a red-hot kitchen shovel.

If they are cooked in the silver scallop shells, which are larger, several oysters are served in the one shell. One or two are put in, peppered, salted, strewn with cracker crumbs, and small pieces of butter; then more layers are added until the shell is full or until enough are used for one person. Moisten them with the oyster juice and strew little pieces of butter over the top. They are merely kept in the oven until they are thoroughly hot, then browned with a salamander. Serve one shell for each person at table, placed on a small plate. The oysters may be bearded or not.

SCALLOPED OYSTERS

Three dozen oysters, a large teacupful of bread or cracker crumbs, two ounces of fresh butter, pepper and salt, half a teacupful of oyster juice. Make layers of these ingredients, as described in the last recipe, in the top of a chafing dish or in any kind of pudding or gratin dish. Bake in a quick oven about fifteen minutes; brown with a salamander.

[*Note:* Perhaps you are wondering about the "salamander" and why it was running loose in nineteenth-century kitchens. Apparently it was a much-used culinary article, something like a poker, which was heated and used to brown the top of pastry.]

385

OYSTER STEW

Put a quart of oysters on the fire in their own liquor. The moment they begin to boil, skim them out and add to the liquor a half-pint of hot cream, salt, and cayenne pepper to taste. Skim it well, take off the fire, add to the oysters an ounce and a half of butter broken into small pieces. Serve immediately.

STEWED TOMATOES

Take the liquid in which chicken is boiled; strain through the colander. Then take half-can of tomatoes and boil together, adding as much sugar as you would put in the tomatoes. Strain through a sieve and serve.

CORNED BEEF

A good piece of beef well corned, then well boiled, is a most excellent dish. Put it into a pot with enough cold water to just cover it. When it comes to a boil, set it on the back of the range so that it will boil moderately. Too-fast boiling renders the meat tough, yet the water should never be allowed to cease boiling until the meat is done. Skim often. Let it boil at least four or five hours, according to its size. It must be thoroughly done. In England, where this dish is an especial favorite, carrots are always boiled and served with the beef. The carrot flavor improves the meat, and the meat improves the carrot. Do not put the

The Hayes residence in Fremont, Ohio

carrots into the pot however until there is only time for them to become thoroughly cooked before serving. Serve the carrots around the beef. In America, cabbage is often boiled with corned beef. This is very nice also. If cabbage is used, add at the same time one or two little red peppers. When about to serve, press out all the water from the cabbage, adding little pieces of butter. Serve the meat placed in the center of the cabbage. Little pickles are a pretty garnish for corned beef with or without the vegetables.

VEAL CUTLETS, SAUTÉED AND FRIED

These are cutlets cut from the round, although any veal cutlets may be cooked in the same way. Cut them into equal-sized pieces, beat them a little with a knife to get them into shape, season, egg and bread-crumb them. Now fry in a sauté pan or rather sauté some thin slices of ham in a little hot lard and, when done, put them on a hot dish. Fry the cutlets slowly in fat and, when done, pour out some of the fat if there is more than a teaspoonful. Add a little flour, then a little hot water and, when cooked a few minutes, season well with lemon juice, adding pepper and salt to taste, then strain. Serve the cutlets in the center of a dish with the gravy poured over and place alternate slices of the ham and lemon in a circle around them. They are also very good sautéed in a little lard and served with a cream gravy poured over them, or they are nice egged (with a little chopped parsley and onion mixed with the egg), bread-crumbed, and fried in hot lard.

FISH À LA CREME

Boil a fish weighing four pounds in salted water. When done, remove the skin and flake it, leaving out the bones. Boil one quart of rich milk. Mix butter the size of a small egg with three tablespoonfuls of flour and stir it smoothly in the milk, adding also two or three sprigs of parsley and half an onion chopped fine, a little cayenne pepper, and salt. Stir the mixture over the fire until it has thickened. Butter a gratin dish. Put in first a layer of fish, then of dressing, and continue in alternation until all the fish is used with dressing on top. Sprinkle sifted breadcrumbs over the top. Bake half an hour. Garnish with parsley and slices of hard-boiled egg.

[*Note:* "Dressing" undoubtedly refers to the white sauce.]

387

WHITE CAKE (MISS ELIZA BROWN'S)

There is not to be found a better receipt for white cake than the following. The cake is mixed contrary to the usual rules of making cake, but it is the best mode of making it fine-grained and delicate.

Ingredients: whites of six eggs, scant three-fourths cupful of butter, one and a quarter cupfuls of pulverized [confectioner's] sugar, two cupfuls cake flour, juice of a half lemon, a quarter teaspoonful of soda with a half teaspoonful cream of tartar or one teaspoonful baking powder.

Mix soda well with flour and pass it through sieve several times to distribute it equally. Beat the butter to a light cream and add the flour to it, stirring it in gradually with the ends of the fingers until it is a smooth paste. Beat the whites of eggs to a stiff froth and mix in the sugar. Now stir the eggs and sugar gradually into the flour and butter, adding also the lemon juice, and mix it smoothly with the egg whisk. As soon as it is perfectly smooth, put it into the oven, the heat of which should be rather moderate at first. [Suggestion: Bake in two greased eight-inch layer pans at 350° for about twenty-five minutes.] When done and still hot, spread over it a frosting made with the white of one egg, pulverized sugar, and a flavoring of lemon.

LUCY HAYES FOUND THE WHITE HOUSE CHARMING. PRESIDENT ARTHUR REDECORATED IT SOON AFTER WITH, AMONG OTHER THINGS, THIS TIFFANY SCREEN IN THE VESTIBULE

Lucretia Rudolph Garfield

OF OHIO

First Lady March 4, 1881–
September 19, 1881

*"It is a terrible responsibility
to come to him and me."*

LUCRETIA GARFIELD could have been expected to take her responsibilities seriously. She was the first true intellectual among the First Ladies; an "egghead," she would be called today. Her father was a farmer and one of the founders of Hiram College, where she and James Garfield were classmates who shared a love of literature, languages, science, and the fine arts. Both were studying to be teachers; later Garfield taught Greek and Latin and was president of the college.

As the wife of a struggling young teacher, Lucretia learned self-discipline. In a letter to her husband she once told how she dignified bread-making and other tedious household chores by giving her best efforts to them and elevating her thoughts.

Though somewhat overwhelmed by Garfield's nomination for the Presidency, she worked herself to exhaustion, helping with his campaign. In Washington they moved in small, select literary circles. Like Lucy Hayes, Lucretia was the New Woman type, though she was not active in temperance or woman-suffrage movements. Rather, she spent most of her spare time in the Library of Congress, looking into the history of the White House and its contents. She was the first First Lady to plan the refurnishing of the mansion with authentic pieces.

The Garfield dinner table was a classroom in miniature with the

389

President and his wife guiding their five children's conversation into intellectual channels. An important member of the family circle was the President's elderly mother, who always had the place of honor at his right. No matter how important the dinner guests, she was served first. On Inauguration Day, after taking the oath of office, Garfield turned and kissed his wife and mother—the first such public demonstration by a President.

The Garfield Inaugural Ball, March 4, 1881
HALL OF THE SMITHSONIAN INSTITUTION

Mrs. Garfield wore a light heliotrope satin gown trimmed with point lace and, in lieu of jewelry, a cluster of pansies at her neckline. The United States Marine Band played, led by John Philip Sousa, and guests marveled at an "electric light," which was featured at the entrance to the Hall. They were served:

100 GALLONS OF PICKLED OYSTERS

200 GALLONS OF CHICKEN SALAD

1,500 POUNDS OF ROAST TURKEY

50 ROAST HAMS

ROAST BEEF

BEEF TONGUES

200 GALLONS OF ICE CREAM AND WATER ICES

15,000 ASSORTED CAKES

50 GALLONS OF JELLY   3,000 ROLLS

350 LOAVES OF BREAD

FRUITS AND RELISHES

TEA   LEMONADE

250 GALLONS COFFEE

The White House family during the administration
of President Garfield

Less than four months after the Inauguration, tragedy struck the Garfields as it had the Lincolns. En route to the reunion of his college class, the President was shot by a political fanatic. For two months his wife, frail and fatigued after an attack of malaria, helped care for him, often going to the White House kitchens to prepare his food. When he died, a fund of $350,000 was raised by popular subscription to aid her and the children.

Grave, studious Lucretia Garfield then forty-nine, carried on, raising her family alone. " 'Crete grows up to every new emergency,' " her husband had once said of her. She lived to be eighty-six and to see her four sons become a lawyer, an architect, president of Williams College, and Secretary of the Interior.

Ellen Lewis
Herndon Arthur

OF VIRGINIA

ELLEN ARTHUR, who was well known in New York for her musical talents and her philanthropic work, died at age forty-two, a year and a half before her husband became President. She had caught cold singing at a charity concert. Arthur never remarried. Like Andrew Jackson, he kept his wife's picture, fresh flowers beside it, on his bedside table at the White House.

Dignified Mary McElroy, the President's sister, served as his hostess but had no monopoly on the job. Often he invited as many as forty prominent Washington women to receive with her, including those

392

Mary McElroy, President Arthur's sister

two popular matrons, Julia Tyler and Harriet Lane Johnston. This reduced charges of favoritism until the ladies began to hold second-floor teas for "selected" guests following public receptions. President Arthur was used to criticism, however. A fastidious, methodical man with a penchant for luxurious living, he was called "The Dude" by his foes, "the perfect host" by his friends. Feeling entitled to live in a manner "befitting my position," he was glad to foot the bills personally for brilliant parties.

The White House was a badly kept barracks, he said, and refused to move in until it had been completely redecorated by his friend, Louis Tiffany, in the dreadfully exotic, smothering style then so much in vogue. Satins and velvets, ferns and flowers, and colored glass prevailed with a thorough spraying of gilt paint over all.

With a wave of the hand, President Arthur disposed of twenty-four wagonloads of "clap-trap" from White House attics, basements, and storerooms. Everything from Grant geography globes to Hayes highchairs were sold at public auction, raising six thousand dollars and the eyebrows of later White House historians.

President Arthur ate small breakfasts and meatless lunches and, like President George Washington, enjoyed mutton chops with a glass of ale or rare roast beef with claret for his dinner.

393

Frances Folsom Cleveland

OF NEW YORK

First Lady 1886–1889
and 1893–1897

"I want to find everything just as it is now when we come back . . . for we are coming back four years from today."

THE YOUNGEST OF ALL the First Ladies, Frances Cleveland was the first and only one to return as mistress of the White House after retirement to private life.

Beautiful, brown-eyed Frances was fresh from college and not quite twenty-two when she married her portly forty-nine-year-old guardian, President Grover Cleveland. It was the first marriage of a President to take place at the White House, and for weeks after the announcement of the engagement an aura of wedding bells and orange blossoms hovered over the nation.

Frances could not remember a time when she hadn't known "Uncle Cleve," her father's law partner. He had dandled her on his knee, bought her dolls, helped choose her first baby carriage, and nicknamed her "Frank." When she was twelve, her father was killed in an accident, and Cleveland became the devoted guardian who supervised her education, sent her flowers on special occasions, and arranged her trip abroad after graduation from Wells College. During the years he was governor of New York, Frances and her mother were frequent guests in the governor's box at official affairs in Albany.

The simple, evening wedding took place June 2, 1886, in the Blue Room, which was banked with roses and pansies. Scarlet begonias were

394

massed in the fireplaces to simulate dancing flames. The bride wore corded ivory satin with a fifteen-foot train. At the close of the ceremony the twenty-one-gun Presidential salute sounded from the Navy Yard, and the church bells of Washington began to ring.

The love-sick public did not recover immediately. Bands played the Wedding March and romantic songs round the clock. Honeymooning at a Maryland lodge, the Clevelands were hounded by the peeking, probing public and by newsmen who camped nearby with spyglasses. The President, his plans for privacy thwarted, raged at the "colossal impertinence" of "the ghouls of the press." It was a long time before his brusqueness toward reporters changed to geniality; this happy change they credited to his bride's gentling influence.

Gracious and cordial, the new First Lady presided with a dignity and poise beyond her years. Everyone wanted to meet her, and so cooperative was she that people took outrageous advantage of her. Three receptions were held each week; one afternoon she shook hands with nine thousand guests, stopping occasionally to rest and have her arm massaged. For the first time Saturday afternoon receptions were held so that employed women might have an opportunity to meet her.

America had a new idol. Her picture could be found in almost every home, and it was said that seven out of ten women wore their hair as she did—in a low knot at the nape of the neck—although they could not copy her dimples. It was in 1887 that the first edition of *The White House Cookbook* appeared. It featured her portrait and was an immediate best-seller.

At the end of the term, the White House staff cried as they bade Mrs. Cleveland goodby. She smiled and promised that she and the President would be coming back in four years. Her prediction came true.

Rose Elizabeth Cleveland, the President's sister and White House hostess until his marriage

When she returned in 1893, as the mother of a small child, the gracious First Lady found herself harassed by excessive public attention. It was impossible for a nurse to take the child for a walk. One day a zealous crowd snatched the baby from the nurse and passed it around for inspection and fondling. The gates of the White House were then closed to the public, and rumors were circulated that "perhaps the child is retarded." It was also whispered that Cleveland was cruel to his young wife and had once driven her out of the house. This last story the First Lady personally refuted, stating that she wished all women might have husbands as "kind, attentive, considerate, and affectionate." But the fans had gone too far. The First Family spent more and more time away from the White House.

Mrs. Cleveland often visited at the executive mansion in later years and was always a welcome guest. The household staff vied for opportunities to wait on her. She lived to be eighty-three and was the first First Lady to remarry after her husband's death.

"Grover Cleveland was the second most popular person in the country," old-timers liked to reminisce. "She, of course, was first."

The Cleveland Wedding Lunch

June 4, 1886

CONSOMMÉ EN TASSE

SOFT SHELL CRABS

COQUILLES DE RIS DE VEAU   CHATEAU IQUEM

SNIPES ON TOAST

LETTUCE AND TOMATO SALADE

FANCY ICE CREAM   MOET & CHANDON

CAKES

TEA   COFFEE

FRUITS   MOTTOES

President Cleveland's marriage to Frances Folsom
in the White House

The Cleveland Wedding Supper

TERRAPIN

BREAST OF SPRING CHICKEN

COLD MEATS

SALADS

FISH

PÂTÉ DE FOIE GRAS

ICE CREAM MOLDS   BONBONS   FRUITS

This informal supper, which was served in the family dining room, featured as a centerpiece a three-masted ship made of pinks, roses, and pansies. The four-tiered wedding cake initialed "CF" rested in a double circle of roses. When champagne toasts were drunk, the young bride drank hers in mineral water. It was ever her custom, when wine was served at the White House, to turn down her glass.

Carolyn Scott Harrison

OF OHIO

First Lady 1889–1892

"While I am here I hope to get the Presidential Building put into good condition."

CAPABLE, SELF-CONFIDENT Carolyn Harrison, age fifty-seven, sailed into the White House, her head full of plans for improving the old place.

She personally drew up several elaborate designs for additions. Congress wisely rejected them. For three years she agitated for a new White House, but she never got more than an overhauling of the old.

The daughter of a Presbyterian minister who was also president of Oxford Female Seminary, Carolyn was a busy, authoritative woman who insisted on neatness, efficiency, and thrift. It was said that no dusty corner ever escaped her eye. Under her supervision, the White House underwent its most thorough housecleaning and renovation from attics to basements. Rats were methodically exterminated, rotting floorboards replaced, kitchens modernized, and bathrooms added.

"Very few people understand the lack of accommodations for the President and his family," she complained publicly.

No doubt they were crowded. The Harrison family included herself, the President, their son and wife, their daughter and husband, Mrs. Harrison's elderly father, her niece, and several grandchildren, including the famous "Baby McKee." (Baby McKee was much in the public eye as he toddled all over the White House, getting into scrapes. Once, during an official meeting in Grandpa's office, Baby was found stirring the contents of a spittoon with an important state paper.)

As the wife of a Senator, Carrie Harrison had been well known in Washington before she became First Lady. An attractive, stately woman with softly waved gray hair, a serene face, and large, expressive eyes, she was considered a good deal more charming than her standoffish husband. Only a few things could disturb her mature poise and drive her to tears; among these were the newspaper attacks on the President. She was forever exerting herself to make friends for him.

From one hobby to another she bustled, starting crazes all over the country for needlework, orchid culture, and, especially, china-painting. A teacher was imported from Indianapolis along with a kiln, and china-painting classes, as well as French classes, were held at the White House. Many a church bazaar featured articles that bore the First Lady's "signature"—a four-leafed clover.

At her request, the President ordered an inventory of White House furnishings so that pieces of historic value might be preserved. Until this time stewards often had decided which articles were to be kept and which thrown away or sold. She began the collection of china of past Presidents that has become a valuable permanent exhibit at the White House.

There was nothing fancy, pretentious, nor "foreign" about the Harrison regime. Mrs. Harrison—the first president-general of the Daughters of the American Revolution—dressed in quiet taste in American-made clothes and did her own shopping. The President liked

399

good food but no flourishes and would not allow livery on the servants; they wore kerchiefs and aprons. Hugo Ziemann, co-author of the original *White House Cookbook*, served as steward, as he had for the Clevelands.

The older Harrisons brought back family prayers to the executive mansion; the younger brought back frequent dancing. The whole family was enchanted but somewhat frightened when electricity came to the White House. Occasionally, after a four-generation conference, one of them might dare to touch a switch. It was agreed, however, that it was much safer to let the engineer turn the lights on in the evening before he left and turn them off in the morning when he came to work.

A few months before the end of the term, Mrs. Harrison died. Three years later the President married her widowed niece, who long had been a member of the family circle.

President Harrison was especially fond of chocolate or devil's food cake. The recipe given below is one modern version of this favorite dessert of his.

DEVIL'S FOOD CAKE ☆

2 cups light brown sugar	1 teaspoon soda
½ cup butter	1 teaspoon baking powder
2 egg yolks	2½ cups flour
½ cup cocoa in ½ cup boiling water	1 cup sour cream
	2 egg whites

Cream sugar and butter and add egg yolks and cooled cocoa mixture. Sift soda and baking powder with flour and add, alternately with sour cream, to sugar-butter mixture. Fold in egg whites beaten stiff. Bake in two greased nine-inch layer pans at moderate temperature (350°) for thirty to thirty-five minutes or until cake springs back when touched lightly with fingertip.

Benjamin Harrison's son supervises playtime at the White House, 1889, for the Presidential grandchildren. The boy in the goat cart is Baby McKee.

400

The Harrison Inaugural Ball
March 4, 1889

More than twelve thousand persons attended the ball, which was held in the Pension Office, Washington. An orchestra of one hundred musicians played. Later, a fireworks celebration was held. It included a display representing the Capitol and the White House. The menu:

Hot Foods

BOUILLON IN CUPS

STEAMED OYSTERS   OYSTERS À LA POULETTE

CHICKEN CROQUETTES   SWEETBREAD PÂTÉ À LA REINE

TERRAPIN, PHILADELPHIA STYLE

Cold Foods

BLUE POINTS IN ICE

ASSORTED ROLL SANDWICHES

MAYONNAISE OF CHICKEN   LOBSTER SALAD

COLD TONGUE EN BELLEVUE   COLD HAM À LA MONTMORENCY

BONED TURKEY À LA AMERICAINE   BREAD OF QUAIL À LA CICÉRON

PÂTÉ DE FOIE GRAS À LA HARRISON

TERRINE OF GAME À LA MORTON

Desserts

ASSORTED ICE CREAMS   ORANGE WATER ICE

ROMAN PUNCH

PYRAMID OF NOUGAT RENAISSANCE   BEEHIVE OF BON-BONS REPUBLICAN

PAVILION RUSTIC   ASSORTED FANCY CAKES

Ida Saxton McKinley

OF OHIO

First Lady 1897–1901

DELICATE, DEMANDING IDA MCKINLEY was afflicted, and she never let her husband forget it. Nor did he want to. Through thirty years she was his first and last thought. In their case it was the President rather than the First Lady who was the nation's idol. Kind, gentle, solicitous William McKinley was regarded as a kind of saint.

Ida, the daughter of a prosperous Canton banker, was graduated from a young ladies' seminary, took a trip to Europe, and after finishing a practical business course, began working as a clerk and cashier in her father's bank. It was at a picnic that she met Captain McKinley, who had been decorated for bravery in the Civil War.

Until her marriage Ida was a relatively healthy girl, but shortly after the births and early deaths of her two children, she began to suffer the attacks of epilepsy that were to continue all her life.

The McKinleys were seldom apart more than a few hours, and he spent every spare minute in her company. When he was governor of Ohio, they lived in a hotel opposite the State House. Twice each day he would leave his business or his callers and go to the window to wave to his wife. He brought her flowers. When he traveled about the country on political tours, she went with him. At each stop his first concern was to see that she was comfortably settled. Often he slipped away from meetings to make sure she was all right.

403

When the McKinleys moved into the White House, precedents were broken as every arrangement was made with her comfort in mind. Now it was the First Lady, rather than the ranking lady guest, who was seated at the President's right, so that he might help her if she had a seizure at the table. This often happened, and he would place a napkin over her face until she recovered. The excitement of the Inaugural Ball brought on an attack, and she had to be taken home.

Mrs. McKinley could not be an active First Lady—all details of White House management were in the hands of the staff, and hostess duties were carried out by relatives—but she enjoyed entertaining, always remaining seated as if she were one of the guests. In a crowded room it was easy to locate the President. He would be standing close beside her, resting a hand on her shoulder. More relaxing for both of them were the private suppers they shared, after which he read while she worked on one of the thirty-five hundred pairs of crocheted or knitted slippers that she gave to church bazaars during her husband's tenure. It was a quiet, orderly life, custom-made for Ida. The President planned it that way.

Strangely, in the end it was she who took care of him. In September, 1901, in the sixth month of her husband's second term and when she was fifty-four, Ida McKinley joined Mary Lincoln and Lucretia Garfield in the tragic role of the widow of a martyred President. The McKinleys were together on a business-pleasure trip to the Pan-American Exposition in Buffalo, New York. While she rested, he held public receptions for his many admirers. As the President was extending his hand to one man in a long line of visitors, the man—an anarchist—fired two shots from a pistol hidden in a handkerchief.

"My wife—be careful how you tell her—" were among the President's last words.

During the last eight days of his life, the First Lady amazed the nation by bearing up bravely. The frail, incompetent little woman who had been coddled, sheltered, waited on, and spared every inconvenience for thirty years now became comforter and nurse.

The American people mourned their leader. Everyone knew that his wife had ruled him sweetly, firmly, without raising her voice or a finger. He had ridden in closed carriages and lived in stuffy rooms for fear she would catch cold. He had foregone exercise and recreation to devote all his leisure time to her. Was this the reason he hadn't the vitality to recover from his wounds? Washington gossip said so; some physicians concurred. The public was not sure. It was sure of only one thing: "Mr. McKinley was a good soul."

The McKinleys Celebrate Their Silver Wedding Anniversary

[*An excerpt from the Canton, Ohio,* EVENING REPOSITORY, *February 5, 1896*]

MANY GUESTS RESPOND TO THE INVITATIONS OF MAJOR AND MRS. MCKINLEY

They are Cordially Greeted at the Pleasant Home.

Mother McKinley's Illness Prevents Her From Being Present.

THE HOUSE BEAUTIFULLY DECORATED.

Some of the Guests From Abroad.

The reception tendered by Governor and Mrs. William McKinley at their pleasant home in North Market St. Wednesday afternoon was the most brilliant affair ever given in Canton and one of the most thoroughly enjoyable and social happenings it has been the good fortune of those present to participate in. . . . The scene was a most brilliant one. Flowers elegantly arranged adorned the parlors and halls, and potted plants in abundance transformed the apartments into bowers of beauty and bright colors.

Governor and Mrs. McKinley unassisted received their guests in the bow window of the south parlor after the arrivals were ushered in by Welcome Blue. Mrs. McKinley was attired in her wedding dress of ivory satin and brocade, en traine, and trimmed in point lace and white pearl passementerie with elaborately trimmed bodice. She carried a handsome bouquet of white bridal roses. . . .

Guests from a distance arrived on the early morning trains and were conveyed in elegant equipages. The late trains are expected to bring many others from out of the city to attend the evening reception. . . .

Several hundred people walked, and carriage after carriage arrived and deposited at the McKinley home their loads, which disappeared into the brilliantly lighted and happy home of their hospitable host and hostess. The scene on the lawn and avenues leading to the Governor's residence was almost as animated as that within the house. The air was delightful, and no discomfort was experienced by those who, drawn by a kindly curiosity, gathered to watch the visitors as they alighted from carriage and car and made their way through the admiring spectators.

405

The lawn was brilliantly illuminated by two mammoth locomotive headlights, making the grounds almost as bright as day. The stone walk from the front gate to the stoop led to the front door, which was swung open, and within stood an usher, who directed the arrivals to apartments on the second floor, where wraps and outer coats were discarded. The guests then descended to the spacious hall and entered the south parlor. Each guest was warmly received with a kindly pressure of the hand of both Maj. McKinley and the lovable wife, who showed plainly the spirit of welcome and happiness that beamed from their handsome faces. The callers then dispersed to the other parlors, passing the time delightfully in social conversation and renewal of acquaintances.

Refreshments were served in the west dining room, which was prettily decorated with flowers, an elaborate piece occupying the center of the table, the whole looking brilliant in the light of a large candelabrum. Charters Bros., with a corps of assistants, served the following:

CHICKEN AND LOBSTER SALADS

MAYONNAISE DRESSING

HAM FILLING   OLIVES   PICKLES

SALTED ALMONDS

CUCUMBERS   LETTUCE

SHERBET   FANCY CAKES

FRENCH MACAROONS

ROMAN PUNCH   COFFEE

LEMONADE   CLARET

LOBSTER SALAD

Prepare a sauce with the coral of a fine, new lobster boiled fresh for about half an hour. Pound and rub it smooth, and mix very gradually with a dressing made from the yolks of two hard-boiled eggs, a table-spoonful of English mustard, three of salad oil, two of vinegar, one of white powdered sugar, a small teaspoonful of salt, as much black pepper, a pinch of cayenne, and two fresh yolks of eggs. Next fill your salad bowl with some shred lettuce—the better part of two heads—leaving the small curled centers to garnish your dish with. Mingle with this the flesh of your lobster, torn, broken, or cut into bits. Pour your sauce over the whole, put your lettuce hearts down the center, and arrange upon the sides slices of hard-boiled eggs.

ROMAN PUNCH (WITH CHAMPAGNE)

Grate the yellow rind of four lemons and two oranges upon two pounds of loaf sugar. Squeeze the juice of the lemons and oranges, cover the juice and let it stand until the next day. Strain it through a sieve, mix with the sugar, add a bottle of champagne and the whites of eight eggs beaten to a stiff froth. It may be frozen or not as desired.

Edith Kermit Carow Roosevelt

OF CONNECTICUT

First Lady 1901–1909

SOME CALLED IT "the wildest scramble in White House history"; some, "a perpetual circus." Whatever it was, it began noisily and joyously when the Theodore Roosevelts ("that gang") contentedly took over the nation's Executive Mansion.

407

"I don't think any family has enjoyed the White House more than we have," said the President.

Mrs. Roosevelt enjoyed it, too, although she must have been the busiest wife and mother who ever lived there.

Theodore Roosevelt had been married first to lovely, young Alice Lee, who died in childbirth at the age of twenty-two, leaving him with a baby daughter, Alice. After two years he married again. The bride was his childhood friend, Edith Carow. It was a perfect match; they had everything in common—background, breeding, intelligence, and vitality. Five children—four rambunctious boys and a girl—were born. This made six children at the White House, not counting the baby squirrels, guinea pigs, rabbits, snakes, field mice, birds, dogs, cats, parrots, black bears, badgers, and ponies that roamed the place for eight lively years.

The wife of the youngest man ever to serve as President (forty-two), Edith Roosevelt was forty when she became First Lady. She was a poised, self-assured, eminently sensible person who could join the vigorous fun of the Rough Rider and their children, yet pull the reins on all of them when things got out of hand. She had a fine talent for letting each member develop his own individuality.

It was a close-knit, carefree, outdoorsy family of "doers"—hikers, picnickers, horseback-riders, sailers, swimmers. The old White House stairs and corridors creaked and groaned under the punishment of stilts, roller skates, water fights, and mock Indian raids. President Teddy played tennis and medicine ball, wrestled, fenced, and practiced jiujitsu, and had scant patience with those who did not live "the strenuous life." When it all became too strenuous, the First Lady would retire to her room with a book and, at bedtime, rap briskly on the floor with her slipper to remind him.

Serene and broadminded as Edith seemed, she was high-principled and strong in her convictions. Teddy respected her judgment. Once each week she called Cabinet wives to the White House, ostensibly to sew but actually to keep abreast of Washington gossip and to instruct the ladies in the fine points of official behavior. It was said that many a career and reputation was knitted up—and some unraveled—by Mrs. Roosevelt's "Sewing Cabinet."

Theodore Roosevelt and his family, with the future Alice Roosevelt Longworth standing in the rear

Teen-ager Alice Roosevelt, the first White House deb since Nellie Grant and a strong-minded young lady who demanded champagne for her debut but did not get it, became the nation's darling. Songs were written about Princess Alice; a shade of blue was named for her; yachts were christened by her. The public eagerly followed her trips abroad, her coming-out party, and her spectacular wedding, in 1906, to Nicholas Longworth of Ohio. Today, at eighty, Mrs. Longworth is one of Washington's most distinguished residents.

The First Family, though independently rich, prided themselves on sensible management. They could entertain lavishly when the occasion demanded, but for the most part, they lived simply. They were great favorites of the White House staff because they knew what they wanted and expected to receive it but were not overly critical and were quick to praise. Moreover, they were interesting people. "TR" was one of the best-liked Presidents ever; he received the greatest majority vote of any candidate up to his time.

During this period the long-awaited, half-million-dollar renovation of the Presidential mansion took place. Executive offices were erected in the west wing and offices moved outside the main house. Buffalo heads and elk antlers—souvenirs of the President's hunting trips—were used freely as decorations. State dinners were moved from the inadequate Dining Room to the East Room, which proved a beautiful setting but so far from the kitchens that soup and fish were cold and ice cream melted before they reached the tables. The Dining Room was then enlarged, and dinners were once again served there. Years later, it was discovered that too much had been done too hastily. Poor supports and fire hazards had not been replaced and corrected, only covered by paint and plaster in the one-hundred-year-old house.

In 1905 President Teddy gave his niece, Eleanor, in marriage to Franklin Delano Roosevelt, a distant cousin who, in twenty-eight years, was to bring the famous family name back to the White House.

Edith Roosevelt's Favorite Recipes

MY GRANDMOTHER'S INDIAN PUDDING

3 pints scalded milk   7 tablespoonfuls Indian meal

Stir milk and meal together while hot. Cool. When mixture is cold, add five eggs, a half pound of raisins, four ounces of butter. Spice and sugar to your taste. [*Note:* Mrs. TR forgot to add that this pudding should be baked in a slow oven, 275°, for a couple of hours.]

SPICE CAKE

1 cup butter	4 cups flour
2 cups sugar	2 teaspoons baking powder
1 cup milk	1 teaspoon ground cinnamon
4 eggs	½ teaspoon nutmeg

Suggestion: Use half of recipe with two teaspoons of baking powder to two cups of flour. Bake in two layers at 375° or in a nine-by-thirteen pan at 350° till cake springs back when touched lightly in the middle, about thirty-five minutes.

[*Note:* Mrs. Roosevelt contributed the Indian Pudding recipe to *The Congressional Club Cookbook* of 1927 and the Spice Cake recipe to a cookbook compiled by the ladies of Waupun, Wisconsin, in 1905.]

PHILADELPHIA SAND TARTS

1 pound sugar	3 eggs (leaving out white
1 pound flour	of one)
½ pound butter	Vanilla flavoring

Roll thin, cut into small cakes, brush surface with white of egg, sprinkle with sugar and cinnamon and bake.

[*Note:* For best results, bake in a moderate oven, 350–375°, ten to fifteen minutes.]

CHEESE ON TOAST ☆

Soak one cup of bread crumbs in one cup of milk for fifteen minutes. Melt one tablespoon of butter and add one cup of grated cheese, the bread crumbs, a half teaspoon of salt, a good pinch of paprika, and a pinch of mustard. Stir constantly till cheese is melted, then blend in lightly one beaten egg and cook only for a moment or two longer. Serve on hot, crisp toast immediately.

[*Note:* The Sand Tart and Cheese Toast recipes are in Mrs. Roosevelt's own handwriting at the Roosevelt home, Sagamore Hill, Oyster Bay, New York.]

ALICE ROOSEVELT LONGWORTH ON HER WEDDING DAY, WITH HER
HUSBAND AND FATHER

412

Favorite Recipes of Alice Roosevelt Longworth

[Daughter of President Theodore Roosevelt]

EGGPLANT WITH SPAGHETTI OR RICE ☆

Peel the eggplant and cut in thin slices. Add a little salt to each slice and press under a heavy weight for one-half hour. Fry in butter until tender. Cook the spaghetti or rice. Make tomato sauce. When ready to serve, put first in the center of the dish a layer of spaghetti or rice, then a slice of eggplant, then another layer of spaghetti or rice, another slice of eggplant, and so on. Pour the tomato sauce around the layers and serve.

SAVORY RICE ☆

Chop onions very fine and fry in butter in saucepan until well cooked. Mix pepper and salt with well-cooked rice and add to onions. Add good chicken stock, place in casserole and cook in oven until tender. Do not stir after it is put into the oven. Chicken livers or small pieces of any kind of meat greatly improve the flavor of this dish, but if these are added it should not be more than fifteen minutes before serving.

[*Note:* This recipe and the one above are from *The Congressional Club Cookbook.*]

MARKETING LIST
1902

1 pound oatmeal	$ .06	1 pound cheese	$ .20
Coffee	.35	1 pint vinegar	.05
¼ barrel flour (enough		2 heads celery	.08
for 1 month)	1.50	1½ pounds rump steak	.24
2 pounds sugar	.10	Oysters	.25
2 lemons	.03	2 pounds beef	.24
1 pound dates	.10	3 pounds butter	.75
1 quart peanuts	.05	½ peck potatoes	.10
1 pint molasses	.10	2 heads cabbage	.10
1 package baking soda	.03	1 dozen eggs	.20
2 pounds rice	.12	1 quart onions	.10
5 pounds cornmeal	.18		

413

Helen Herron Taft

OF OHIO

First Lady 1909–1913

" *. . . the President of the United States. . . . Now that meant my husband!* "

WILLIAM HOWARD TAFT wanted to be a Supreme Court justice. His wife wanted him to be President. In the end both got their wishes.

"My wife is the politician," Taft often said.

Helen's father was a Cincinnati judge and a former law partner of Rutherford Hayes. As a girl she had visited at the White House. Probably these early experiences accounted for her interest in politics and the active role she always took in her husband's affairs. She was the first First Lady to walk in, unannounced, on the President's official meetings. Interested, informed, and discerning, she saw no reason why she should not. She attended almost every important conference until a slight stroke curtailed her activities. Many people thought that "pushing too hard" had brought it on. Her keen mind was not affected, however, and she made a remarkable recovery.

The Tafts had met at a bobsled party when she was eighteen. They discovered a mutual interest in dramatics, dancing, literature, and politics. Their three-month wedding trip through Europe was the first of many journeys they were to make together.

414

When Taft was appointed governor-general of the Philippines, she and their three small children joined him enthusiastically. She loved Manila and the social life that his position imposed. With wisdom and diplomacy she and her husband established deep friendships with the people of the Islands. When he was recalled to the States to serve as Secretary of War, the Filipinos staged a mass protest.

In Washington she became a member of Mrs. Roosevelt's "Parlor Cabinet." With this background she had a clear picture of the role of First Lady when she stepped into it at forty-eight. Always a determined person, she did not hesitate to make her wishes known and to put her ideas into effect even if it meant breaking long-established traditions:

On Inauguration Day she rode beside President Taft on the return trip to the White House. (Always before, the outgoing President had accompanied his successor.)

Believing that only a woman could competently manage the executive mansion, she replaced the long-time steward with a housekeeper.

Six Negro footmen in blue livery and with silver trays now received cards at the front door instead of the century-old police guard. Furthermore, she insisted that all employees be clean-shaven, an order that caused many a handlebar mustache to quiver indignantly before it came off.

Shocked by the careless usage of White House silver and linens, she added to the supply, then saw to it that the staff handled it with almost-reverent care.

President Taft, a genial, outgoing man, had a problem—food—too much, too rich. By far our largest President (six-foot-two, over three hundred pounds), he was a confirmed steak-for-breakfast fan who constantly snitched on his diets. Eventually, he developed gout. He was somewhat embarrassed when it became known that a new bathtub, which could accommodate four average-size men, had been ordered for him. (He had got stuck in the old tub and had had to be helped out.) The President was light on his feet, however, and he and Mrs. Taft joined a class that danced in the Blue Room to the music of a Victor Talking Machine.

The First Lady received three days a week in the candle-lit Red Room, and the President, proud of her flair for entertaining, liked to receive with her. The staff was annoyed by his habit of inviting last-minute guests to dinner, but Mrs. Taft was a flexible hostess.

Nostalgia for their Island days led her to plan summer parties on the terrace till bugs and dampness drove guests inside. Undaunted, she arranged for Potomac Park to have a "luneta" such as she had enjoyed in Manila. It was an oval drive with a bandstand at each end

415

where concerts were given two evenings a week for the pleasure of Washington residents.

Taft was the first President to receive an annual salary of seventy-five thousand dollars, the first whose servants were paid by the government, the first to have an automobile, the last to keep a cow. Washington's Japanese cherry trees, which bloom each spring around the Tidal Basin and along Riverside Drive, are a living memorial to Mrs. Taft. She conceived the idea and arranged for the planting of three thousand trees, which were a gift from the City of Tokyo.

In 1913 the Tafts—he with relief, she with regret—turned over the White House to the Woodrow Wilsons.

Favorite Recipes of Helen Taft

CHICKEN CROQUETTES

Chop cold boiled chicken (or turkey) very fine. Season with pepper, salt, a little nutmeg and onion. Mix a large tablespoon of butter and two of flour. When well mixed and warmed, add a pint of cream seasoned with a little salt. Let it stand a minute, then stir the mixture into the meat. When cold, take a spoonful of the mixture and dip into two eggs, slightly beaten, then into bread crumbs. Roll lightly into shape. Fry in boiling lard.

[*Note:* Use heavier white sauce: six tablespoons butter, two-thirds cup of flour to one pint of liquid.]

SPICED CHERRIES OR DAWSON PLUMS

Seven pounds of fruit, four pounds of sugar, one quart of vinegar, one ounce whole cloves, one ounce whole cinnamon. Place fruit and spices in alternate layers in kettle and let stand overnight. Boil sugar and vinegar together, pour hot over fruit, and cook all together one minute.

MUFFINS

One quart of milk, a half-pound of butter, warmed together; add four eggs, well beaten, flour to make a batter, a half-pint of good yeast, salt to taste. Bake in muffin tins.

PRESIDENT TAFT AND HIS FAMILY, WITH
ROBERT A. TAFT AT RIGHT

417

The above recipes were taken from an old cookbook which was, according to Charles P. Taft, of Cincinnati, "long a favorite in the Herron family and used by my mother in the White House." Mr. Taft, younger son of the President, also remembers that his mother had a favorite recipe for Tomato Halibut which has been lost through the years. Perhaps it was similar to this halibut recipe from the early 1900's:

BAKED HALIBUT WITH TOMATO

Freshen halibut as usual. Cover bottom of baking dish with two tablespoons each of chopped onion, celery, and parsley. Moisten with melted butter and lay halibut steak on top. Dot fish with butter. Bake twenty minutes, adding more moisture if necessary. Remove fish to hot platter and make sauce as follows: Add to the vegetables in the pan two cupfuls of strained tomatoes thickened with a little flour in cold water. Strain over the fish. Garnish with mounds of boiled rice.

MRS. TAFT'S DESSERT

1 cup powdered sugar	6 egg whites, beaten very light
2 teaspoons cocoa	6 egg yolks, beaten
1 teaspoon coffee	Cream for whipping
1 teaspoon vanilla	

Mix first six ingredients. Bake in one thin pan in a moderate oven for about ten minutes. Beat cream very light and spread it over cake. Roll up cake and cream. Put chocolate icing over it, and put whipped cream in stripes at the end.— *The Congressional Club Cookbook*

Ellen Lou Axson Wilson

OF GEORGIA

First Lady 1913–1914

"Isn't it lovely, Children?"

WOODROW WILSON liked women. He enjoyed their company more than that of men, believing they had "deeper sensibilities and finer understanding." Fortunately, Ellen Wilson understood and never showed the slightest jealousy. All his adult life he was surrounded by the fair sex:

his first, then his second wife, three daughters, many women friends, and the hordes of suffragettes who continually picketed the White House for "Votes for Women."

Ellen Wilson brought the fine arts to the White House. A gentle Southern lady, she had given up a promising art career to marry her childhood friend, Woodrow Wilson. Both were the children of Presbyterian ministers. When they entered the White House their three daughters were in their twenties, and Ellen had time for her sketching and landscape design. She gave many garden parties and ordered the dining table moved to one end of the state dining room so that guests might gaze at her gardens rather than at Teddy Roosevelt's moose heads.

As she explored the backyard of Washington—the alleys, tenements, and shacks—Ellen's sensitive nature and artistic eye were shocked by the squalor. Owing largely to her efforts, Congress passed a bill to eliminate the slums.

The Wilson women pampered and petted their lord and master and were a responsive audience on the evenings when he recited, danced,

419

sang, mimicked, or performed some other little vaudevillian feat. Wilson, a great theater buff, had always thought that—had he not been president of Princeton University, governor of New Jersey and President of the United States—he could have been a success in show business. He was a Southern gentleman who refused, even as President, to precede the ladies. "No politics at the table," he ruled, so his wife, though she was familiar with his speeches and his philosophy, knew little of his practical political life. The second Mrs. Wilson was to know much more. . . .

Ellen Wilson served one year as First Lady and saw two of her daughters married in the White House before she succumbed to a kidney ailment at the age of fifty-four. Dying, she begged Dr. Cary Grayson to "take care of Woodrow." He promised.

Edith Bolling Galt Wilson

OF VIRGINIA

First Lady 1915–1921

". . . my stewardship . . ."

THERE WAS LITTLE Dr. Grayson could do for the despondent, grieving President beyond prescribing long walks in the fresh air. Then, one day, the perfect tonic presented itself—the handsome Mrs. Edith Galt, daughter of a Virginia judge and widow of a prominent Washington jeweler. Mrs. Galt was dark-eyed, dark-haired, and dimpled; her voice, soft and musical. A successful career woman who had carried on her

420

husband's business, she was forty-two (the President was fifty-seven). For the first time in months, the White House staff heard The Boss humming and whistling.

It was a whirlwind courtship, carried on under the watchful eyes of the Secret Service. Political associates who feared a second marriage might hurt Wilson's chances of re-election almost succeeded in preventing the wedding. But it took place in the bride's home, in December, 1915. In 1916 Wilson was re-elected. In 1917 the United States went to war.

From the beginning the First Lady was the President's trusted confidante. As war pressures mounted, he turned more and more to her as cheerful companion and intelligent and sympathetic listener. Night after night she sat with him coding and decoding cables to and from Europe. The day often began at six in the morning and ended at midnight. He was in a constant state of fatigue, and she, although she did not know it, was in training for heavier responsibilities to come.

On the feminine side, Mrs. Wilson was kept busy setting an example for the women of the country as Red Cross volunteer and relief worker. The White House served wheatless and meatless meals, raised a war garden, observed fuel-saving regulations. Sheep were turned loose on the lawn of the Executive Mansion to crop the grass and save manpower; their wool was sold at auction and brought thousands of dollars for the Red Cross. There was virtually no entertaining except of military groups. At lawn parties for wounded soldiers, the President helped serve cake and ice cream.

After the Armistice the Wilsons toured Europe, then returned to travel across the United States. At every stop the President made a fervent plea for the support of the League of Nations. This enormous effort took its toll; Wilson collapsed in Colorado and, back at the White House, he suffered a stroke.

Edith now began the most unusual job a First Lady has ever had: "carrying on" for the President of the United States. Nurse, companion, executive secretary, she enlisted the aid of Dr. Grayson in keeping news of the stroke from the nation. White House gates were locked; sentries were posted. It was the First Lady who met reporters and government officials, who summed up problems and carried to the President's bedside those she considered most pressing, hoping against hope that soon he would recover and resume his work. Some people criticized her tactics as underhanded or highhanded; others defended her faithfulness. To charges that she had tried to "run the government" she always answered that she had made no decision except that of when to present matters to the sick President. Wilson never fully recovered, and in 1921

Warren Harding was elected President, bringing to a close the one and a half years during which the United States had no active leader. It was the end of a period that a newsman called "Mrs. Wilson's Regency" but that she, herself, modestly referred to as "my stewardship."

The Wilson Wedding Supper
December 18, 1915

OYSTER PATTIES

VIRGINIA HAM   BONED CAPON   CHICKEN SALAD

BISCUITS WITH MINCED HAM

CHEESE STRAWS   ROLLS

PINEAPPLE ICE   CARAMEL ICE CREAM

WEDDING CAKE

FRUIT PUNCH   COFFEE

BONBONS   SALTED ALMONDS   CHOCOLATES

WAR BREAD—1918

1 cup rye meal
1 cup graham flour
½ cup flour
1 teaspoon cream of tartar
1 teaspoon soda
1 teaspoon salt

¼ cup molasses
1⅛ cup sour milk
1 egg
2 tablespoons melted
    shortening
½ cup raisins

Mix dry ingredients, add molasses, sour milk, well-beaten egg, shortening, and raisins cut in pieces. Mix thoroughly and bake in a greased bread pan.

[*Note:* This recipe was one of those approved by Herbert Hoover, food administrator during World War I, as a means of saving wheat, eggs, sugar, and dairy products.]

CHEESE STRAWS 1 ☆

1 cup sifted flour
½ teaspoon baking powder
½ cup (¼ pound) butter

1 cup shredded cheddar cheese
3 tablespoons cold water

Sift flour and baking powder. Cut in butter and cheese with pastry blender. Blend in water. Form straws with a cookie press (using star plate) on ungreased cookie sheets. Cut into desired lengths. Bake eight to ten minutes at 375°. Makes three to four dozen straws.

CHEESE STRAWS 2 ☆

½ pound butter
  Paprika or cayenne pepper

2 cups flour
½ pound grated American cheese

Cut butter into dry ingredients; add cheese, working it into stiff dough. Roll thin, cut into even strips, and bake as above.

PRESIDENT AND THE FIRST MRS. WILSON AND THEIR
DAUGHTERS

423

Florence Kling DeWolfe Harding

OF OHIO

First Lady 1921–1923

*"I have only one real hobby
—my husband."*

THE GATES OF THE White House, which had been closed by Mrs. Wilson, were thrown wide open by the Hardings. They were Just Folks from Back Home in Ohio, and they wanted to make everyone feel welcome.

"We will never be inaccessible to the public," declared sixty-year-old Florence Harding, who was only a little less bedazzled than her husband by living in the White House, though she had helped engineer the move there.

Warren Harding, a handsome, hail-fellow-well-met who liked golf, poker, chewing tobacco, and toothpicks on the dinner table, never believed himself suited to the office of President. It was one of the accurate judgments of his life. He was nominated in the first place because seasoned politicians thought he "looked like a President." A former small-town newspaper editor and a born joiner, Harding seemed to look upon his political colleagues as loyal lodge brothers, and when some of the brothers betrayed his trust, he was bewildered and hurt.

Florence Harding was as unsophisticated as her easy-going husband, but shrewder. The daughter of a banker who was the richest man in Marion, Ohio, she had been married and divorced when she met Harding, owner of the Marion *Star*. He was five years younger than she and, perhaps, attracted by her positive ways. Her father opposed their friendship and, after the marriage, it was several years before father and daughter, passing on the street, would speak.

424

Florence was a go-getter. As the bike-riding circulation manager of the *Star*, she sold advertising and subscriptions, made collections, trained carrier boys, and helped build the newspaper. Later, she just as efficiently helped push her husband to the Ohio Senate, then to the United States Senate. ("I made Warren Harding," she said.)

He might not be the *best* President, Harding once said, but he hoped he would be the *best-liked*. His wish was very nearly a prediction. He was far from the best, and he was well liked. Both Hardings were hospitable and gregarious people, kindly and gracious, who entertained practically every night and seldom dined alone. Always willing to lend her presence to public affairs and good works, Mrs. Harding received daily, made many visits to the war-wounded at Walter Reed Hospital, and gave large parties for veterans at the White House, wearing her old hat "so the boys can find me." She showed remarkable endurance for a woman with a serious, chronic ailment. The Duchess—as his poker-playing friends called her—was a congenial "mixer" at the President's famous stag parties upstairs, where the liquor was as plentiful as the pork-and-sauerkraut, though Prohibition was then the law of the land.

Her garden parties amid the roses and magnolias were unexcelled. The scarlet-clad Marine Band played on the lawn, where the President and First Lady received. Beverages and ices, sandwiches and cakes were served from long tables beneath gay, striped awnings and eaten on green settees under the trees. Inside and outside, the White House had the carefree atmosphere of an exclusive country club.

Vivacity and enthusiasm—real or feigned—were Mrs. Harding's fortes; she worked hard at being continually "thrilled." Some people found this touch of artificiality tiresome, but her friends defended her stoutly. Always well groomed, she had a cared-for pink and white skin and a precisely waved coiffure. She was a stylish dresser; her trademark, a black velvet throat-band fastened with a diamond pin.

More than just a hostess, the First Lady exercised much influence in the President's appointments and managed to prevent passage of a bill which would have provided a permanent home for the Vice-President. (She had never liked the Coolidges.) She was alert to political undercurrents and perhaps was not as surprised as the President when ominous rumblings from the Veterans' Bureau and the Department of Interior indicated that all was not well with the administration. It was at about this time that she became especially interested in fortune-tellers and other clairvoyants who might help her pierce the uncertain future.

Saddened by the suspicion that some of his buddies had betrayed him, President Harding with his wife set out on a journey to Alaska.

425

Upon their return to San Francisco, he died unexpectedly. While he lay in state in the East Room, Mrs. Harding began her one-woman campaign to collect his letters and personal papers—"for sentimental reasons," she explained. She destroyed everything she found. If it was not the work of a patriot, it was the act of a loyal partner (for the Hardings were always a team) and of a canny newspaperwoman who could envision sensational headlines.

The storm broke with revelations of scandals, conspiracies, misplaced funds, graft, and "deals," and there followed suicides, murders, and prison sentences for villains the President had thought were his friends.

A little more than a year later Mrs. Harding died. Then they were both gone—the two small-towners who had ventured over their heads in the deep waters of political intrigue.

Favorite Recipes of Florence Harding

HARDING WAFFLES ☆

2 eggs	1 pint milk
2 tablespoons sugar	1 pint flour
1 teaspoon salt	2 heaping teaspoons
2 tablespoons butter	baking powder

Beat the yolks of the eggs and sugar together. Add salt, melted butter, milk, and flour. Beat the whites of the eggs and add with baking powder the last thing before baking.

SANTA ANA BREAD

When preparing dinner, boil four or five large potatoes until well done. Measure one large cooking spoon of flour, one of sugar, one of salt, and a tablespoon of fat. Moisten with cold water. Stir smooth and scald with the boiling potato-water. Stir well and cool with cold water until lukewarm. Add to this one cake of dry yeast, previously moistened, two

President and Mrs. Harding with Marie Curie and others

cups of mashed potatoes, and let stand until morning. Sift four sifters full of flour (hard wheat preferred) and warm through. Stir into this the liquid yeast made lukewarm and mix stiff. Let rise in a warm place and make into loaves when raised double size. Bake in moderate oven until done.

MRS. WILL HAYS'S SOUTHERN CHICKEN PILAU ☆

Cut up and stew a fat hen in water enough to almost cover it. When almost tender add from two to three cups of uncooked rice and let stew slowly until the chicken is thoroughly done and the rice has absorbed the liquor. The rice must not be stirred, but care must be taken that it does not stick. All of the broth should be absorbed by the rice. Season well. Serve on platter with the chicken surrounded by the rice. In the South red pepper is used, but this is optional.

[*Note:* Will Hays was chairman of the Republican National Committee and later President Harding's postmaster-general. He resigned to become Hollywood's "movie czar," head of the Hays Office for Censorship.]

Grace Goodhue Coolidge

OF VERMONT
First Lady 1923–1929

"I love people."

LOVELY GRACE COOLIDGE, age forty-four, was the popular member of this White House team. Charming, gracious, friendly, her sparkling personality drew people to her; she "loved them all" and felt fortunate to be in a position where she could meet great numbers. Before her marriage to the man who was to be governor of Massachusetts, vice-president, and President, Grace had been a teacher of the deaf. This occupation must have helped her develop the patience she would need to cope with a picky husband who was, however, devoted to her. His famous "stinginess" ended where she was concerned.

Never had any President said so little or saved so much as "Silent

Cal." A dry, taciturn, poker-faced Vermonter who preached "moral fiber" and practiced penny-pinching thrift, Coolidge was not a man the nation could warm to. The respect that Americans felt for this rock of integrity was better than affection, however. After the scandals of

429

the previous administration, respect was long overdue in Washington. Though Coolidge had been a member of Harding's cabinet, not one breath of suspicion ever was blown his way.

As President, he pored over menus and household accounts looking for little extravagances, ordered the embarrassed staff to shop at supermarkets, taught the cook to concoct a nutritious and cheap cereal food, cut down on the amount of meat served at state dinners, had haircuts at breakfast to save time, held early-hour meetings because people could be fed more economically at breakfast than at luncheon, put off having the White House roof repaired until he was sure of being elected for a full term, and set a record for simplicity by breaking the custom of providing lunch for officials at his inauguration.

But as Grace Coolidge's husband, Complex Cal was quite different. Extravagantly fond of pretty clothes for her, he would spy a dress in a store window and order it sent home for her approval. Often she did not approve. Her taste was excellent though quiet, while his ran to vivid colors, fancy hats, and fussy gowns. He did not want her to wear a dress a second time at state functions.

"The biggest part of the Administration," Grace was often called, though she took no active part in state affairs, made no speeches, and scarcely knew many of the Cabinet members and their wives. She simply was nice to people, flashing smiles and waving at crowds and giving extra-warm handshakes and kind words to guests in reception lines who were being hustled along by the President. Once he "greeted" two thousand people in an hour, briefly and silently touching each hand, pushing it past, and reaching for the next. She was indulgent with him and often slipped away from afternoon parties early so that she could be home when he arrived. He was upset if she was not there. The White House staff learned to live with his idiosyncrasies—which included nicknames and practical jokes—and they liked him for his casual way with them.

The First Family felt a reverence for the executive mansion and its traditions. At Grace Coolidge's urging, Congress passed a resolution authorizing the acceptance of authentic furnishings as gifts from private citizens. Valuable old pieces that had been stored away were sought out and restored. As her personal gift Mrs. Coolidge crocheted a spread for the Lincoln bed, completing one square each month during her stay. Many other improvements were added: sewing, pressing, and cedar rooms, wardrobes, cupboards, storage and linen cabinets, servants' rooms and baths. The most dramatic addition was the First Lady's "Sky Parlor," a sunroom with glass on three sides, built above the

South Portico. Later Presidents and their families were to enjoy this cheerful, cozy hideaway.

The old White House that had seen so much heartache went into mourning again in 1924 when Calvin, Jr., age sixteen, died of blood poisoning, resulting from a blister on his foot.

Guests at the White House during the Coolidge terms included Marshal Foch, General Pershing, Queen Marie of Rumania, the Prince of Wales, and Charles Lindbergh, just back from his news-making flight over the Atlantic. Strangely, in view of the President's economical ways, his administration was the most expensive up to that time. More employees had been hired, and a law had been passed that said the

THE COOLIDGES POSE AT THE WHITE HOUSE

431

government would pay for all official entertaining. Guests at the Coolidge receptions benefited little from this largesse, however.

Reception Menu:

ICE WATER AND PAPER CUPS

Both items were in short supply. If you gave them all they wanted, the President confided to an aide, people would stand around all evening drinking and never go home.

Mrs. Coolidge Keeps House

[Grace Coolidge's typewritten instructions to the household staff at "The Beeches," Northampton, Mass., the Coolidge home after the President's retirement]

Breakfast...... 7:30 to 8:15, usually about quarter of eight

Lunch........12:30 promptly

Dinner....... 6:00 promptly

Sundays, about the same hour for breakfast, lunch at 1:00, and dinner at 6:00.

Care of own room, hall, and bathroom on third floor, kitchen, pantry, and cellar stairs. Also, sweep and mop floor of butler's pantry when doing the kitchen floor.

Kelvinator should be defrosted every week or ten days. Garbage pail should be washed often.

Dogs are fed about 5 o'clock P.M. Alternate Kennel Ration and Cale, adding grated raw carrot. Left-over muffins are broken up in Beauty's food. After breakfast, in the morning, she has a dish of rolls or a little bread in warm milk. Beef from soup stock and left-over vegetables may be mixed with ration. Occasionally, I get a little raw meat to mix in. Do not give any veal.

Time off every Thursday after luncheon work is done and every other Sunday after lunch, beginning with this Sunday, January 25.

Do not hesitate to try new recipes. We like surprises. Good cooking requires time, study, material, and experimentation.

For breakfast, Mr. Coolidge has melon, cereal with bacon and coffee. My breakfast consists of fruit, thin buttered toast (one slice) or dough-nut, and coffee.

For lunch, when alone, Mr. Coolidge has a soup and dessert, while

I have a salad or left-overs, done up in some interesting way, and dessert.

For dinner Mr. Coolidge has a soup, while I am served with a small portion of some green salad with French, Roquefort, or Russian dressing. This is followed by a meat course. Then Mr. Coolidge has some sauce and a hot muffin. (He also has a muffin served with his soup.) I have a piece of cake or a cooky. This may sometimes be varied with some form of pudding. When guests are present, there will necessarily be some changes.

The cereal usually served for breakfast, unless otherwise planned, is made of two parts whole wheat to one part rye. This is cooked in a double boiler for about five hours or until the wheat kernels burst open. A quantity sufficient for several mornings may be cooked, kept in the ice chest, and required amount re-heated for the morning meal. [*Note:* This is the famous "thrifty cereal" which President Coolidge taught the White House cook to make.]

Whole wheat bread is made at home. White bread will be bought. Do not pour gravies and sauces over meat, etc. Serve in separate dish.

Keep a list of commodities required on kitchen pad. Telephone orders are placed before 10 A.M, and I go to market nearly every morning for fresh meat and vegetables. The milk man comes a little before eleven. Get cream from him. Usually we require ½ pint, more if making ice cream, mousse, etc. Vermont butter store man leaves 2 dozen eggs every Wednesday morning. If we need more, I can get them at market.

MRS. COOLIDGE'S ICE BOX COOKIES ☆

1 cup butter or Crisco
   (if Crisco, use a little less
   and salt it)
2 cups brown sugar
3½ cups flour

1 teaspoon soda
½ teaspoon salt
1 cup nut meats
2 eggs, well beaten

Cream butter and sugar. Sift flour, soda, and salt three times. Add nuts, add eggs and flour. Mix all thoroughly and pack into mold (long narrow bread pan) and let stand overnight. Next day, unmold, slice very thin, and bake in moderate oven. Do not grease mold or baking pan.

[*Note:* Bake these at 375° for ten minutes, and they will be nice and moist and chewy. Bake them a little longer if you want them crispy. Housekeeping schedule and cooky recipe, courtesy of Mrs. Sidney A.

433

Bailey, personal friend of the Coolidges and present owner of "The Beeches."]

COOLIDGE PIE CRUST

2 tablespoons shortening	Cold water
1 cup flour	(about 3 tablespoons)

Cut fat into flour. Add water slowly, using only enough to hold the dough together. Roll and bake in a hot oven.

[*Note:* The Coolidge pie crust seems a little short on shortening, doesn't it?]

SALAD DRESSING ☆

2 eggs	¼ cup vinegar
1 tablespoon dry mustard	¼ cup water
Salt ·	1 tablespoon olive oil
Paprika	

Beat eggs and add dry ingredients. Stir in vinegar, water and olive oil and cook in the upper part of the double boiler until thick, stirring constantly.

NORTHAMPTON BAKED BEANS ☆

1 pint California beans	1 teaspoon dry mustard
1 teaspoon soda	¼ pound salt pork
½ cup dark-brown sugar	

Pick over and wash the beans. Soak overnight. In the morning, parboil the beans until the skin breaks very easily. Before taking from the stove, add soda. As soon as the water foams up well, remove from the stove and drain and rinse the beans in fresh water. Place them in a bean pot, add sugar and mustard. Score the pork and place it in the center of the pot, sinking it until the rind is level with the top of the beans. Cover with boiling water and place in the oven. Add more water from time to time as needed. Bake eight hours. If a gas range is used, gas may be saved by baking the beans in a top oven placed over the simmer burner.

MRS. DAWES'S CREAM CHEESE SALAD ☆

Three cakes cream cheese dissolved in ½ pint lukewarm cream. Add 1 tablespoon chopped almond and pimiento and salt to taste. Add ½ pint of whipped cream and ½ envelope of gelatin which has been dissolved in a little of the warm cream. Mold in a ring mold. Serve on lettuce with mayonnaise dressing in center of mold.

[*Note:* Mr. Dawes was vice-president under President Coolidge.]

CORNMEAL MUFFINS ☆

2 cups cornmeal	2 eggs, well beaten
1 cup flour	½ cup sugar
1 cup sweet milk	2 tablespoons baking powder

This quantity will make fourteen muffins.

[*Note:* President Coolidge was not satisfied with his White House muffins until his wife presented the cook with this recipe "from home."]

CUSTARD PIE

¾ cup sugar	2½ cups milk
1 tablespoon flour	Pinch of salt
2 eggs, beaten	

Mix sugar, flour, eggs, milk; then add salt. Dust a little nutmeg on top after pie is baked. Bake in hot oven (450°) ten minutes, then in slow oven (300°) till custard is firm when tested with silver knife.

[*Note:* We tried President Coolidge's favorite custard pie, and it was too runny for our family. However, it *is* economical—only two eggs; perhaps that is what he liked best about it. Every American to his own taste!]

BUTTERSCOTCH PIE ☆

1 cup brown sugar	2 tablespoons flour
1 cup milk	1 teaspoon cornstarch
2 tablespoons butter	½ teaspoon salt
2 eggs	1 teaspoon vanilla

Beat sugar, milk, and butter together in the upper part of the double boiler. Beat egg yolks; add flour, cornstarch, and salt. Add to the mixture in the double boiler and cook until it thickens, stirring constantly. Cool and fold in beaten egg whites and vanilla. Place in a baked pie shell and frost with whipped cream.

If I've talked you out of trying Mr. Coolidge's Thrifty Custard Pie, try Mrs. Ervin's Quick Custard Pie. You'll love it.

QUICK CUSTARD PIE ☆

4 slightly beaten eggs
½ cup sugar (or, even better,
    ¼ cup white sugar and
    ¼ cup brown sugar)
¼ teaspoon salt

1 teaspoon vanilla
2½ cups milk, scalded
9-inch unbaked pastry shell,
    not too thick
Nutmeg or cinnamon

Thoroughly mix eggs, sugar, salt, and vanilla. Slowly stir in hot milk. Pour into unbaked shell. Dash top with nutmeg or cinnamon. Bake in very hot oven (475°) five minutes, reduce heat to 425°, and bake ten minutes or longer till knife inserted comes out clean. Cool or serve chilled.

Lou Henry Hoover

OF IOWA
First Lady 1929–1933

A MATURE FIGURE with placid features and white hair arranged in classic style, Mrs. Herbert Hoover appears, in portraits, a woman who never did anything more exciting than preside at teas. In reality, her whole life was an adventure story.

The daughter of a banker who had hoped for a son, Lou Henry was as much her father's pal as a boy could have been. Sharing his love of the outdoors, she was at home in field and forest. She learned to ride, fish, hike, pitch a tent, and build a campfire. Her ability to adapt to rugged circumstances was to prove useful to her as the wife and comrade of a world-wandering mining engineer.

Herbert Hoover met the slim, athletic blonde at Stanford University, where she was the only girl in his geology class and the first to be graduated with a geology major. Later, from the gold fields of Australia, where he was working, Hoover cabled his proposal of marriage. She cabled back one word: "Yes." Within a few hours after the wedding the young couple set sail for the Orient, where he had accepted a job.

The following years found them visiting almost every country together. Threats of disease, war, and bandits did not deter the young bride from following her husband into the interior of China. The Boxer Rebellion broke out, and the Hoovers helped defend the besieged city of Tientsin, she braving bombs and bullets to nurse the wounded and distribute scarce rations. While he served as chairman of the American Relief Committee during World War I, she helped organize the American Woman's Hospital. Both their sons were born in London. Wherever they lived, Lou established a home "with good taste and economy," he said.

At age forty the Quaker orphan boy from Iowa was a millionaire. He became United States Food Administrator in World War I and served without salary. He went to Washington as Secretary of Commerce, choosing this demanding position instead of a lucrative partnership in a mining firm.

Lou Hoover was fifty-three when her husband was elected President. Though wealthy, she remained a direct, natural person who drove her own car and dressed simply in clothes suited to the active life she preferred. As National President of the Girl Scouts, she participated in the girls' classes, hikes, and camping trips and gave them a house in Washington for their national headquarters.

Mrs. Hoover's combination bedroom-office at the White House was filled with books, newspapers, and notebooks that testified to her scholarly interests. She spoke five languages and, for recreation, read sociology and economics. Together, she and the President translated rare scientific works. They filled the White House with books, art objects from their travels, and Chinese porcelains, which they collected. The second-floor sitting room was turned into a miniature conservatory

437

with vines, ferns, and plants, lending an outdoor look. Talking movies were installed. Interested in the history of the mansion, Mrs. Hoover succeeded in finding a few authentic pieces to furnish it. She kept three personal secretaries busy. In spite of her activities, not many people felt that they really knew the serious, austere First Lady.

Entertaining was almost continuous during the Hoover tenure, and

PRESIDENT AND MRS. HOOVER WITH HERBERT HOOVER, JR. (LEFT), HIS WIFE, AND ALLEN HOOVER

438

the staff learned to expect last-minute extra guests. The Hoovers are remembered as setting the best table in First Family history. Nothing but the best was ever served, and cost was no object. When expenses exceeded the official allowance, the President paid.

The Great Depression overtook the administration and, upon defeat for re-election, the Hoovers retired to the home she had designed years before—a white stucco hilltop house in Palo Alto, California. She died in 1944 at the age of sixty-eight.

President Hoover never really retired but was often called upon by future administrations for aid and counsel. Ninety years old in 1964, this great humanitarian and sage elder statesman lives in New York. With each passing year he is held in greater affection, admiration, and respect by the people of the United States and the world whom he has served so faithfully for more than a half-century.

Favorite Recipes of Lou Hoover

Many of Mrs. Hoover's favorites originated with Mary E. Rattley, who was the Hoover cook during the years when Mr. Hoover was Secretary of Commerce.

MARY RATTLEY'S SPOON BREAD ☆

One pint of milk, a half cup of Indian meal. Cook this into a porridge and when cold add two eggs, well beaten, a piece of butter the size of a small egg, scant tablespoonful of sugar, teaspoonful of salt. Add a little milk if needed to make it rather thin. Beat this all very well and bake in a slow oven from thirty to thirty-five minutes in a well-greased tin.

MARY'S MUSHROOM SOUP ☆

One pound of mushrooms, chopped fine; paprika; one pint of chicken stock; one pint of water, cold; one pint of cream, thin; one tablespoon of flour; whipped cream. Let mushrooms stand in cold water two hours; simmer on slow fire about thirty minutes, strain juice, add chicken stock, well-seasoned. Add cream and flour mixed in cold milk until smooth. When perfectly smooth, run through a fine strainer. Just before serving add two tablespoons of whipped cream.

439

MARSHMALLOW SWEET POTATOES ☆

Boil six sweet potatoes. Mash through a potato masher to remove all strings. Add butter, grated nutmeg, salt to taste, cream enough to make a soft consistency, and a half pint of ground walnuts. Put into a baking dish, bake for ten minutes, cover the top with marshmallows, brown as a meringue. Serve at once. Serves six to eight persons.

VENISON

Fashion into small cutlets. Dip in olive oil, fry in deep fat exactly like doughnuts until done as one likes, perhaps five minutes, but one should experiment with a small bit first. Sprinkle with salt and pepper, serve immediately. The cutlet may first be rolled in bread crumbs, corn meal, or batter, but this makes them much greasier.

[*Note:* This recipe applies also to moose, elk, reindeer, bear meat, or any tough or dry meat, as frequently cooked by mountain people. The recipe probably was used by the Hoovers on their camping trips. They were veteran campers and maintained a retreat in the Blue Ridge Mountains while he was President. "It is too bad we do not have other recipes they used while camping and fishing," says Philippi Butler, Mrs. Hoover's former secretary. "They would make quite a superlative campers' cookbook!"]

MARY RATTLEY'S ASPICS ☆

One quart of juice strained from ripe tomatoes; one tablespoon of sugar; salt to taste; dash of ginger; one tablespoon of vinegar; one package of gelatin, well dissolved. Fill the aspic molds half full. These should first stand in ice-cold water for some time. Mix cream and Roquefort cheese together. Season to taste and place in the half-full mold. Add the remainder of the juice but not until the first half is almost firmly set. Aspic to serve with cold or any wild meat may be made in the same way from the juice of pickled peaches: one pint juice, one package gelatin.

ROLLED TOAST ☆

Cut very thin bread that will roll without crumbling; spread with soft butter; roll, starting at one corner, into as tight a roll as possible without breaking the bread. Fasten by piercing with a toothpick. Toast slowly. Remove toothpick and serve. Bread may first be dipped in conserve or spread with cheese or cinnamon and sugar.

[*Note:* Mrs. Hoover contributed the above recipes to *The Congressional Club Cookbook* in 1927.]

THE COOLIDGES DINE WITH THE HOOVERS

Here is the dinner served when President and Mrs. Hoover entertained former President and Mrs. Coolidge at dinner, 1929:

CONSOMMÉ

CURLED CELERY

ROLLED TOAST AND SALTED ALMONDS

BROOK TROUT WITH TARTARE SAUCE

WHITE POTATO CURLS

CUCUMBER ASPIC

CHICKEN SUPREME WITH SPANISH RICE

SWEET POTATO CROQUETTES

GRASSED BEANS   CLARIFIED APPLES

HEARTS OF LETTUCE AND ASSORTED CHEESES

TOASTED CRACKERS

VANILLA ICE CREAM IN MOLDS

PINK CRYSTAL PEARS

HOMEMADE POUND CAKE

CANDIES   FRUITS

COFFEE

RECIPES FROM

"Mr. Hoover Asked for Some More"

by Mary E. Rattley

HIS FAVORITE BREAKFAST OMELET ☆

Heat slowly in buttered pan two teacups minced ham. Beat six eggs, put into a second hot buttered pan and set in hot oven about three minutes. Fold one-half ham into center of omelet, and roll omelet over carefully. Pour remainder of ham and melted butter over top. Serve hot at once.

MARYLAND BROILED SHAD ☆

Take one Potomac shad, boned, and put into hot buttered pan with salt and pepper to taste. Place roe with shad. Spot with bits of butter, and baste with chicken stock which has been boiled down till good and strong. Broil slowly till very brown. Leave in oven ten minutes. Baste with remaining stock in pan. Garnish with parsley and lemon.

CUCUMBER AND WHIPPED CREAM SAUCE ☆
[*delicious with shad or any other fish*]

Chop, don't grate, one large fresh cucumber. Drain in wire sieve till pretty dry. Have ready one and one-half cups whipped cream to which you have added one-half teaspoon salt, one tablespoon vinegar, and two tablespoons sugar. Before serving, fold in cucumber carefully.

VIRGINIA HAM

Soak a not-too-old Virginia ham a night and a day. Scrub and scour thoroughly. Place in ham boiler, skin side down. Cover with cold water, add two cups brown sugar, two whole carrots, and two cups vinegar. Bring to a boil and simmer slowly. Cook till skin puffs on the back a little. Remove from fire, let stand in water till nearly cold. Remove skin, trim off fat, rub with homemade currant jelly. Sprinkle with cloves and fine bread crumbs. Brown in oven ten minutes and serve hot or cold.

PERFECT CAKE ☆

⅓ cup butter
1 cup sugar
2 eggs
2 small cups flour

2 teaspoons baking powder
½ cup milk
1 teaspoon vanilla

Cream butter, sugar, and egg yolks together; sift flour with baking powder; add flour and milk alternately to egg mixture, beating after each addition. Fold in stiffly beaten egg whites and add vanilla. Turn into well-buttered round mold and bake thirty-five minutes in a slow oven. Fill center with whipped cream and pour hot chocolate sauce over all, or fill center with fruits.

[*Note:* A simple cake but perfect, Mrs. Rattley says, if made right.]

Anna Eleanor Roosevelt

OF NEW YORK

First Lady 1933–1945

"Some people probably won't like some of the things I am going to do. . . . I hate the idea that I might ever lose touch with people."

ELEANOR ROOSEVELT, who served longer than any other First Lady and who was called by many, "First Lady of the World," was known and loved and disliked by more people than any other President's wife in history. Whether one saw her as a great humanitarian and devoted public servant or as a publicity-seeker overly fond of the limelight depended largely on one's political leanings. Through the years an ever increasing number of Americans crossed party lines to offer her their

443

esteem and admiration. So did the high and mighty and the poor and lowly of other countries.

Eleanor was a Roosevelt before she married a Roosevelt—her handsome distant cousin, Franklin. Painful awareness that she was the ugly duckling in a family of swans clouded her early years. Her mother was a society beauty who was disappointed by her daughter's plain looks and often said so; her father was a charming world-traveler with a "drinking problem." Both died before Eleanor was ten, and she was sent to live with her grandmother, who brought her up on a diet of Duty and Self-Discipline.

At home and abroad Eleanor was an outstanding student, popular with other girls and with her teachers, but she was not a belle. Her good mind and sweet manner attracted the "best catch" in New York, however. Though Franklin's domineering mother had opposed the youthful marriage, it took place in 1905 with the bride's uncle, President Theodore Roosevelt, giving her away. Mother-in-law Roosevelt immediately built a home for the newlyweds next door to her own, chose their furniture, and hired their servants. Years later Eleanor was to remark wistfully that she never had had a house or furnishings of her own choosing. Instead of becoming embittered, however, she proceeded to outgrow this natural desire, trading it for larger interests so that, by the time she reached the White House at age forty-nine, she was little concerned by the interior decorating problems that had preoccupied so many First Ladies. People became the hobby, interest, and ruling passion of her life. It was in warm personal relationships with all kinds of human beings —not in refurbishing an old mansion—that Eleanor found her creative satisfaction.

For the first fifteen years of her marriage, she lived the quiet, predictable life of a young society matron overshadowed by a dynamic husband, six children (one of whom died in infancy), and a possessive, dictatorial mother-in-law. From her father she had learned compassion for the poor and afflicted, and she spent much of her spare time in charitable work. A new dimension—politics—was added to her experience when her lawyer-husband became state senator, then Assistant Secretary of the Navy, but she remained largely in his shadow until the

The Roosevelts pose at Hyde Park on Christmas Day, 1932

fateful day when he was stricken, at age thirty-nine, with polio. On that day one kind of life ended for Eleanor, and another began.

Convinced that he should be as active as possible rather than retire as an invalid to Hyde Park (which his mother begged him to do), Eleanor assumed the heavy duties. She became his "legs," traveling where he could not travel, investigating, observing. From the information she provided, he made the decisions. Though terrified of public speaking, she forced herself to make speeches, helping in his campaigns for the New York governorship and the Presidency. With her sharp mind and her keen social conscience, it was inevitable that she could draw conclusions of her own which did not always jibe with his. She made no attempt to be uncritical when she disagreed.

"I shall be myself," she often said.

The traditional picture of the First Lady had been that of a gracious hostess who presided, received, christened, shook hands, thought much perhaps but said little, particularly of a controversial nature. Mrs. Roosevelt could not fit into this mold. She spoke her mind in editorials and columns, broadcasts and lectures, and press conferences (for women reporters only). She continued to observe living and working conditions for the "ill-clothed, ill-housed, ill-fed one-third of a nation." She visited farm migrants, sharecroppers, slum-dwellers, and prisoners. She founded a furniture factory for unemployed young farmers. She served in soup kitchens. She taught English. She championed social justice and better opportunities for underprivileged children, youths, women, minority groups. Not content merely to observe human suffering, she had to try to do something about it and often kept after Congress until it appropriated money for a housing project or some other relief measure.

"Here comes Mrs. Roosevelt!" became a rally cry, a battle cry—and, to some, a joke.

During World War II, under the army code name of "Rover," she toured Europe, England, the Caribbean, the Pacific, Guadalcanal, outposts and islands, talking to enlisted men in camps and hospitals. (She traveled thirty-eight thousand miles one year; after that, they lost count.) Newsmen and Secret Service men panting after her called her "indefatigable." Throughout the war she was a prime target for political snipers and a ready subject for caricatures, kindly and otherwise. They did not seem to bother her.

Back at the White House, life moved fast. Meetings, mail sessions, dictation, phone calls, press conferences, luncheons, tours, teas, dinners, receptions. The staff was shocked by the way she waited on herself. It was twelve years of congenial chaos, continual entertaining of all kinds of people, and an open-house atmosphere. With five children and thirteen grandchildren coming and going, it was no place for antiques, and valuable pieces were moved to storage. Mrs. Roosevelt had no time for furnishings, fashions, or food as "status symbols." What she did have time for, acquaintances remember, was the small, kindly gesture, for sympathetic listening. Rarely did one of her critics or political enemies meet her and talk with her and come away still disliking her.

She loved her family but was often absent from them. Years before, she had decided that she did not want to live only through her children, as her grandmother had done. The Roosevelt children worked out their own destinies, made their own mistakes, married, divorced, remarried. When they needed her, she came quickly, but she did not interfere.

In the midst of all the busy-ness the President, whom she had begged not to seek a third or fourth term, died suddenly. Mrs. Roosevelt's life was not over. Still ahead of her were her jobs as United States representative to the United Nations and chairman of its Human Rights Commission, a task she considered her most important. A great-grandmother past seventy, she continued her work, still catching midnight trains and planes here and abroad. Foreign dignitaries visiting here sought her out as the American second in importance only to the President. She died at age seventy-eight, in 1962. The shy, homely child who had wanted to feel close to somebody left behind countless friends—known and unknown—who felt very close to her.

History will judge Eleanor Roosevelt as it judges all First Ladies. It may praise or criticize her but one thing is certain—it will not overlook or soon forget her. She will not join the ranks of shadowy wives of whom historians say: "What kind of woman was she? What did she try to do? We don't know very much about her. . . ."

Favorite Foods of the Roosevelts at the White House

The family of President Franklin Roosevelt was much too busy coming and going to give a great deal of thought to food, though they could entertain elegantly if the occasion demanded. Their social lists were the longest in history; reception guests often numbered fifteen hundred. A staff of forty was maintained, with extra emergency help on call. Mrs. Roosevelt gave parties "in series," sometimes as many as three teas for different groups in one afternoon. Food was ordered in almost wholesale quantities, with daily deliveries at the White House service door. The huge electric ranges in the kitchen could cook more than two hundred dinners at one time. Light refreshments were served at state receptions: grape juice, mixed fruit punch, cake, salted nuts, and candies.

When dining *en famille* the Roosevelts preferred simple menus. Their all-time favorite was scrambled eggs, served every Sunday night no matter how important the guests and prepared in a chafing dish by Mrs. Roosevelt. Sweet breads and rolls were always on the table.

Other favorites of the President were fruit cake, pumpkin pie, oranges, Strawberry Romanoff, fish chowder (made from a recipe of his Delano ancestors of Fairhaven, Massachusetts), and *kedgeree*, a concoction of flaked white fish, rice, and hard-boiled eggs. The family also liked Italian Rice, simmered in chicken broth with onions, and pecan or walnut pie. President Roosevelt usually had breakfast in bed and was served lunch in his office from an electrically heated lunch wagon.

Mother-in-law Roosevelt was somewhat distressed when the First Lady decided to serve "good, plain American food"—including picnic hot-dogs—to the King and Queen of England on their visit here in June, 1939.

During the royal visit an overloaded table tipped, spilling food and dishes, and a waiter tripped and fell with a tray of glasses and beverages. It could happen to any hostess, said Mrs. Roosevelt with a smile, her poise unshaken.

The Roosevelts' Private Luncheon for King George VI and Queen Elizabeth

MINTED MELON BALLS

JELLIED BOUILLON

BROILED SWEETBREADS WITH MUSHROOMS

ASPARAGUS WITH SARATOGA CHIPS

HEARTS OF LETTUCE WITH ROQUEFORT DRESSING

STRAWBERRY SHORTCAKE

COFFEE

Famous visitors at Hyde Park, 1939, with the President's mother in the center

State Dinner for the King and Queen

[*Note:* This was one of the grandest occasions in White House history. The gold service was used, and covers were laid for 82 guests.]

CLAM COCKTAIL

CALF'S HEAD SOUP

BROILED FILET OF FLOUNDER

MUSHROOM AND WINE SAUCE

SLICED TOMATOES

BONED CAPON   CRANBERRY SAUCE

PEAS   BUTTERED BEETS

SWEET POTATO PUFFS

FROZEN CHEESE AND CRESS SALAD

MAPLE AND ALMOND ICE CREAM

COFFEE

WINE WITH DINNER

Sunday Family Dinner

JELLIED BOUILLON

FRIED CHICKEN

CORN ON THE COB

POTATOES

STILTON CHEESE SALAD

CARAMEL ICE CREAM

COFFEE

Formal Luncheon, 1937

CREAMED PEA SOUP

CELERY AND OLIVES

CAPON

CUBED SWEET POTATOES TOPPED WITH TOASTED MARSHMALLOW

STRING BEANS

AVOCADO SALAD

RUM PARFAIT

LITTLE CAKES WITH CANDIES AND NUTS

COFFEE

FISH CHOWDER [*Down East Recipe—1891*] ☆

Fry five or six slices of fat pork crisp in the bottom of the pot; take them out and chop them into small pieces; put them back into the pot with their own gravy.

Cut four pounds of fresh cod or sea bass into pieces two inches square and lay enough of these on the pork to cover it. Follow with a layer of chopped onions, a little parsley, summer savory, and pepper, either black or cayenne. Then a layer of split Boston or butter or whole-cream crackers that have been soaked in warm water until moistened through but not ready to break.

Above this put a layer of pork and repeat the order given above: fish, onions, seasoning [not too much], crackers, and pork until your materials are exhausted. Let the topmost layer be buttered crackers, well soaked. Pour in enough cold water to barely cover all. Cover the pot, stew gently for an hour, watching that the water does not sink too low. Should it leave the upper layer exposed, replenish cautiously from a boiling tea kettle. When the chowder is thoroughly done, take out with a perforated skimmer and put into a tureen. Thicken the gravy with a tablespoonful of flour and about the same quantity of butter. Boil up and pour over the chowder. Serve sliced lemons, pickles, and stewed tomatoes with it, that the guests may add them if they like.

451

KEDGEREE ☆
[an old-time favorite from the East Coast]

2 cups cooked rice   ½ cup cream
4 hard-cooked eggs, chopped   4 tablespoons butter
3 tablespoons parsley, chopped   Salt and pepper
2 cups cooked flaked fish

Combine and heat.

Sometimes sautéed onion and curry powder are added along with flour for thickening. Chicken broth may be substituted for cream. In the past this dish was often served warm with fried tomatoes for breakfast.

Favorite Foods of the Roosevelts at Hyde Park*

President Roosevelt liked sea food—lobster when it was available, salmon, flounder, cod, halibut, or dried codfish. He also had a weakness for griddle cakes—sweet-milk pancakes rather than those made with sour milk.

FISH ASPIC ☆

2 tablespoons gelatin   2 cups clear soup stock or
¼ cup cold water   2 bouillon cubes in 1 pint
½ teaspoon salt   water
⅛ teaspoon black pepper   Juice of ½ lemon
     2 cups flaked fish

Dissolve the gelatin in a quarter-cup of cold water, add salt, pepper, soup stock or bouillon, lemon. Strain into molds to one-half inch deep. When aspic has hardened, fill molds with flaked salmon or other cold fish, add the rest of aspic jelly and allow all to harden. To serve, unmold on a slice of tomato or on lettuce and garnish with sliced tomatoes, cucumbers, or hard-cooked eggs, and you will have almost a meal.

*From "Our Hospitable and Home-Loving First Family," by Mary H. Culbertson, Better Homes and Gardens Magazine, 1934.

FISH AND VEGETABLE SALAD ☆

2 cups cold boiled fish
   (canned salmon or tuna
   may be used)
1 cup mayonnaise
1 cup coarsely chopped celery

1 tablespoon capers or
   chopped pickles
1 cup cooked peas
2 medium-sized cooked beets
2 hard-cooked eggs

Mix the fish and mayonnaise, celery, capers or pickles, and peas, taking care not to break the fish into too small pieces. Pile lightly on crisped lettuce leaves and garnish with alternate slices of cold boiled beets and hard-cooked eggs.

RHUBARB AND ONION PICKLE ☆

[*Note:* This condiment has delighted palates in Old England for 100 years or more. Subtle, delicious and easy to make.]

1 quart cubed rhubarb
1 quart chopped onions
1 pint vinegar
2 pounds brown sugar
1 tablespoonful salt
1 tablespoonful ginger

⅛ teaspoonful cayenne
½ teaspoonful paprika
1 teaspoonful each black pepper,
   cloves, mace, allspice,
   nutmeg, cinnamon

Boil all together over moderate heat, stirring occasionally to prevent sticking until it has reached the consistency of chili sauce. Seal in bottles or jars. Good served with codfish.

POTATO DRESSING FOR DUCK ☆

[enough for 2 ducklings or 1 large duck]

½ cup butter
1 finely chopped onion
2 cups mashed white potatoes
1½ cups stale bread crumbs

2 teaspoonfuls salt
½ teaspoonful pepper
2 eggs

Melt the butter and fry the onion until soft but not brown. Add mashed potatoes, bread crumbs, seasonings, and well-beaten eggs. Mix together thoroughly and proceed to fill duck. With a teaspoonful of marjoram added, this dressing is good for geese.

PORK AND SAUERKRAUT ☆

Lard your pork with small slivers of garlic before roasting and while your kraut is heating add caraway seeds to your taste. Two teaspoonfuls of seed to a quart of kraut is not too much.

CORNED BEEF ☆

3-pound piece of beef	3 tablespoonfuls salt
(brisket or rump)	½ tablespoonful saltpeter
3 tablespoonfuls brown sugar	

Put beef in a bowl and cover with water, adding sugar, salt, and saltpeter. Put bowl in a cool place for three days, turning the meat every day. Cook meat slowly in this same liquid until tender, adding six whole cloves and a small stick of cinnamon if the meat is to be served cold, omitting spices if it is served hot.

Mrs. Henrietta Nesbitt was the chief housekeeper and meal-planner at the White House during the Roosevelt terms. She had been a neighbor of the family at Hyde Park, New York, and was, according to Mrs. Roosevelt, "the best housekeeper I know." At the First Lady's request, she went along to Washington to keep the executive mansion running smoothly. Mrs. Nesbitt always insisted that the favorite dishes of the First Family were no more elaborate than those the average home-maker put on her table. Simplicity was the keynote and good, plain American food was the preference of the Roosevelts.

Red Stamps, Blue Stamps, and Ration Points

When war came to American kitchens in December, 1941, housewives faced new problems. With only sixteen points to be divided among meats, canned fish, butter or margarine, cooking fats and oils, and cheeses, these saving measures were suggested:

1. Serve fresh fish once or twice each week.
2. Serve meatless main dish, rich in protein, once each week.
3. Eat out once each week.

Meat substitutes: poultry, fish, game, cheese, eggs, milk, soya beans, peanuts, and peanut butter.

454

Shortening substitutes: bacon, sausage, and pork fat; chicken, goose, and duck fat; drippings from roasts; fat skimmed from soups and stews; beef suet.

Sugar substitutes: honey, molasses, corn syrup, maple syrup, sweet syrup from canned fruits.

To save coffee and sugar when entertaining: remind guests to bring their own!

SUGAR-SAVING ICING

1 teaspoon gelatin
¼ cup cold water
2 egg whites

⅓ cup sugar
½ teaspoon vanilla

Add gelatin to cold water, then dissolve over hot water. Beat egg whites stiff and gradually add sugar, beating well. Add vanilla and dissolved gelatin, beating constantly.

Elizabeth Virginia (Bess) Wallace Truman

OF MISSOURI
First Lady 1945–1953

"The White House walls should be kept intact."

BESS TRUMAN, a solid, sensible "woman of Independence," had no desire to be a celebrity. As successor to Eleanor Roosevelt, she was somewhat in the position of Eliza Monroe, who had followed busy Dolley Madison. Like Mrs. Monroe, she insisted on being herself. She made no attempt to escape her responsibilities, as had some re-

455

luctant First Ladies, but handled the job conscientiously while still insisting on her right to be as anonymous as possible.

One of her earliest decisions was to hold no press conferences and grant no interviews. Her rare public statements were made through her secretary, and reporters' questions had to be submitted to her the same way.

Mrs. Truman seemed especially modest and retiring in contrast to the peppery, plain-speaking President. The Trumans were a close threesome. Bess succeeded admirably in her intents to help her husband as much as possible without becoming involved in controversy and to keep twenty-one-year-old Margaret from developing "princess fever" while she was the belle of the White House. If Mrs. Truman was not a public idol as more colorful First Ladies had been, she was respected as a mature, down-to-earth "real person."

Bess and Harry Truman were schoolmates from the fifth grade through high school. After a long friendship and romance, they were married at ages thirty-four and thirty-five. Five years later their only child, Margaret, was born. When Truman went to Washington as United States senator, Mrs. Truman served as his secretary. After being vice-president only three months, he succeeded to the Presidency upon the death of Roosevelt, in one of the most critical periods in history—the fourth year of World War II.

Sixty-year-old Bess Truman was not a politician. She was interested in household affairs, which she managed efficiently, in the White House gardens, and in her family, which included her elderly mother. Always busy with official entertaining, she had little time for personal interests, but she did organize a Spanish class for cabinet wives at the mansion. She liked baseball and bridge and, homesick for friendly, unofficial conversation, once invited "the girls" of her Independence bridge club to the White House for a few days of homespun fun.

The Presidency was now bigger business than ever, socially as well as politically. Almost ten thousand guests were entertained at the inaugural reception following Truman's re-election, and the Presidential salary was raised to one hundred thousand dollars a year.

Upon entering the White House, Mrs. Truman and Margaret had ordered the family quarters of the "big, bare barn" decorated in cozy, feminine style. Soon, the work was all to be done over. Swaying chandeliers and sagging floors, detected by the President's keen eye, led to a thorough inspection, which revealed that the elegant house, underneath its paint, was in hazardous condition. The walls were standing, said one horrified inspector, "purely from habit."

For the next three and a half years the First Family lived and entertained at Blair House, while the White House was completely rebuilt at a cost of more than five and a half million dollars. When authorities debated whether to tear down the decrepit mansion completely or to leave the outer walls standing for sentimental reasons, Bess Truman's opinion that the walls should be kept intact was observed. The original shell was left as the whole inside was scooped out, marked, and stored, to be reassembled later, piece by piece, much as a giant jigsaw puzzle. The day that Mrs. Truman moved to Blair House, she made another of her rare pronouncements: "This is a mess!" said the nation's Number One Housewife.

In 1952, shortly after returning to the most attractive, convenient White House in history, President Truman announced that he would not run for another term. The First Lady happily looked forward to going home to Independence.

Margaret Truman, the apple of Daddy's eye, had enjoyed a normally gay young womanhood in spite of having to date under chaperonage of the Secret Service. Birthday parties on the Presidential yacht, slumber parties in the Lincoln bed, travels abroad, and a debut as a concert singer filled in her years as a White House belle, and a few years later she married Clifton Daniel, a New York newspaperman. She is now the mother of three sons.

EZIO PINZA AND MARGARET TRUMAN ON TELEVISION, SPRING, 1952

Favorite Recipes of Bess Truman

OZARK PUDDING ☆

1 egg
¾ cup sugar
2 tablespoons flour
1¼ teaspoons baking powder
⅛ teaspoon salt

½ cup chopped nuts
½ cup raw apples,
   finely chopped
1 teaspoon vanilla

Beat egg and sugar a long time until very smooth. Mix flour, baking powder, salt, and stir into sugar-egg mixture. Add nuts, apples, and vanilla. Bake in a buttered pie tin in a 325° oven thirty-five minutes. Serve with whipped cream or ice cream.

SMALL MEAT LOAF ☆

2 eggs
¾ cup bread crumbs or oatmeal
¾ cup milk
2 tablespoons chili sauce
1 teaspoon Kitchen Bouquet
1 tablespoon Worcestershire
   sauce

1½ teaspoon salt
1 tablespoon bacon grease
2 pounds ground beef
   (or 2 pounds ground veal)
1 pound ground veal
   (or 1 pound ground pork)

Beat eggs in bowl, add other ingredients, then meat. Bake forty-five minutes in well-buttered pan. [Put in hot oven for a few minutes, then reduce heat to 350°.] Serves eight.

TUNA AND NOODLE CASSEROLE ☆

⅓ package noodles
1 pint milk
  Flour
¼ pound sharp cheese

⅛ pound butter
1 can tuna
  Salt and pepper
2 hard-boiled eggs

Boil noodles in salt water, remove, and drain. Make white sauce, add cheese and butter. Drain tuna, add all ingredients, pour into buttered casserole. Bake in moderate oven thirty minutes. Serves four.

Persimmon Pudding was a special request of President Truman when he stayed at the French Lick–Sheraton Hotel, French Lick, Indiana. Here are several versions of that midwestern and southern favorite, beginning with the one served to Mr. Truman:

FRENCH LICK PERSIMMON PUDDING ☆

1 quart persimmon pulp
1 cup sweet milk
2 cups sugar
4 eggs
1 teaspoon cloves
4 cups flour

1 cup butter
1 tablespoon nutmeg
1 tablespoon cinnamon
1 teaspoon allspice
2 teaspoons baking powder

Mix ingredients thoroughly and bake in moderate oven (350°) about forty to fifty minutes.

HOOSIER PERSIMMON PUDDING ☆

Take one and a half quarts of persimmons, mash and rub them through a coarse sieve or fine colander, add two eggs well beaten, three-fourths cup of sugar, one pint sweet milk, a half-cup of butter cut in small bits, a little ground cinnamon and nutmeg. Then add flour enough to make a stiff batter. Bake in moderately hot oven.

SOUTHERN PERSIMMON PUDDING ☆

2 cups persimmon pulp
3 eggs, separated
1 tablespoon melted butter
1 cup sugar
1½ cups flour

¼ teaspoon salt
1 teaspoon soda
1 teaspoon baking powder
1 teaspoon cinnamon
2 cups buttermilk

Sieve persimmons and add egg yolks and melted butter. Beat well. Add sugar, beat again. Sift flour with salt, soda, baking powder, and cinnamon. Add to persimmon mixture alternately with buttermilk. Fold in stiffly beaten egg whites. Pour into greased two-quart casserole. Bake forty to fifty minutes at 350°. Serve with cream or whipped cream.

459

Mary Geneva (Mamie) Doud Eisenhower

OF IOWA

First Lady 1953–1961

"My hobby—fixing up homes for other people to live in; my principal job—looking after Ike."

MRS. DWIGHT ("Call me Mamie") EISENHOWER was an attractive addition to the White House. Thirty-seven years as an army wife, from lieutenant's bride to five-star general's lady, had taught her the mechanics of getting along with people. At official affairs, stiff with protocol, she knew how to turn a bright face to her public, give warm handclasps, say the right things. Friendly, informal, and uncontroversial, she won friends easily and quickly made herself at home in the Executive Mansion.

As the perkiest grandmother ever to occupy the White House, she was an inspiration to other mature women. In her sunny smile and youthful fashions it was easy to glimpse the popular, piano-playing teen-ager of 1916 who had won the heart of Second Lieutenant Eisenhower, of West Point. It was easy to forget that through the years she had had more than her share of worry as the wife of a soldier who became Supreme Allied Commander in World War II. Their son, John, served overseas at the same time. (The Eisenhowers' first child, David Dwight, had died in 1921 at the age of three.)

In thirty-seven years they moved about thirty times. "Start packing" became a familiar phrase. She once said that she had "kept house in everything except an igloo." Texas, Maryland, Kansas, Colorado,

460

Georgia, Washington, the Canal Zone, the Philippines, Paris, New York
. . . The White House was another new post, and fifty-seven-year-old
Mamie found no difficulty in continuing the role of Ike's hostess, which
she had filled so ably during all his previous assignments.

Mamie was born in Iowa, one of four daughters of a prosperous
cattleman and meat-packer who retired at thirty-six and moved his
family to Colorado for his wife's health. Their winters were spent in
Texas, where Mamie met Lieutenant Ike. After their marriage on July
1, 1916, their first post was Fort Houston, where they lived in two rooms
and ate their meals at the officers' club while the lieutenant gave his
bride cooking lessons. It is rumored that Mamie's mother advised her,
"If you never learn to cook, you'll never have to!" Whether or not
there is a grain of truth in the story, it is a fact that Mrs. Eisenhower
never has been a culinary enthusiast, though cooking is one of the
General's hobbies—an ideal arrangement, many a kitchen-bound housewife might agree!

A slight heart-murmur and inner-ear imbalance kept the First Lady
from enjoying robust health. Always charming in public, she insisted
on maintaining a private life as well. When demands of her position
became excessive, she simply retreated, calling upon Mrs. Richard
Nixon, wife of the Vice-President, or a Cabinet wife to pinch-hit for
her. Visiting clubwomen, who expected to see the First Lady in person,
sometimes grumbled. The President, ever concerned about his wife's
health and happiness, heartily approved.

Neither a housewife, politician, nor crusading intellectual, Mrs. Ike
enjoyed, outside "working hours," the companionship of her family—
husband, mother, sister, son, daughter-in-law, and four grandchildren.
She liked to shop for feminine fashions—pretty clothes, costume jewelry,
and perky, youthful hats—and her extensive wardrobe was one of her
chief hobbies. Seemingly pliable, she knew her own mind. From time
to time the ever critical public would suggest that she adopt a new
hair style to replace the famous "Mamie Bangs," but the bangs remained, and since the ladies could not banish them, many simply
copied them.

In the newly rebuilt White House there was little decorating to be
done except in the family quarters, where Mamie's feminine taste was
reflected in shades of pink and roses. Seventy servants kept the household
running smoothly; still, the First Lady was busy meeting with staff
heads, answering mail, and entertaining. She was finicky about the
appearance of the mansion and liked everything "just so." One of her
most important personal projects was the completion of the all-Presidents

461

china collection that Mrs. Benjamin Harrison had begun. Mamie saved time and energy and, of course, invited criticism by cutting down on receptions and handshaking, substituting smiles and waves.

For relaxation the President painted in oils and putted on the green he had installed on the White House lawn. Together he and the First Lady enjoyed bridge, canasta, movie-watching in the White House theater and television-viewing while eating their dinners from trays in front of the set. Such simple pleasures, sometimes shared with close friends, occupied more of their leisure time after the President suffered a heart attack and stroke and underwent an abdominal operation.

THE EISENHOWERS ON THE FORMER PRESIDENT'S
SEVENTY-FIRST BIRTHDAY

He recovered from all three. Meanwhile, formal entertaining had been greatly curtailed.

Popular President Ike and his Lady celebrated their fortieth wedding anniversary in the White House and, at the close of his second term, moved on to their next "post"—a red-brick farmhouse in Gettysburg, Pennsylvania. It was to be, they hoped, a permanent assignment.

Favorite Recipes of the Eisenhowers

PRESIDENT EISENHOWER'S RECIPE
FOR VEGETABLE SOUP ☆

[*Note:* Ask any housewife how to make Vegetable Soup, and she will answer briskly: "Boil soup meat and add cut-up vegetables." For a male cook it isn't so simple, especially when he is Chief Executive of the United States. No one could ask for more explicit instructions than President Eisenhower's.]

The best time to make vegetable soup is a day or so after you have had fried chicken and out of which you have saved the necks, ribs, backs, etc., uncooked. [The chicken is not essential but does add something.]

Procure from the meat market a good beef soup bone—the bigger, the better. It is a rather good idea to have it split down the middle so that all the marrow is exposed. In addition, buy a couple pounds of ordinary soup meat, either beef or mutton or both.

Put all this meat, early in the morning, in a big kettle. The best kind is heavy aluminum, but a good iron pot will do almost as well. Put in also the bony parts of the chicken you have saved. Cover with water, something on the order of five quarts. Add a teaspoon of salt, a bit of black pepper, and if you like, a touch of garlic (one small piece). If you don't like garlic, put in an onion. Boil all this slowly all day long. Keep on boiling till the meat has literally dropped off the bone. If your stock boils down during the day, add enough water from time to time to keep the meat covered. When the whole thing has practically disintegrated pour out into another large kettle through a colander. Make sure that the marrow is out of the bones. Let this drain through the colander for quite a while, as much juice will drain out of the meat. [Shake the colander well to help get out all the juice.]

Save a few of the better pieces of meat just to cut up a little bit in small pieces to put into your soup after it is done. Put the kettle containing the stock you now have in a very cool place, outdoors in the winter time or in the icebox. Let it stand all night and the next day until you are ready to make your soup.

You will find that a hard layer of fat has formed on top of the stock which can usually be lifted off since the whole kettle full of stock has jelled. Some people like a little bit of the fat left on and some like their soup very rich and do not remove more than about half of the fat.

Put the stock back into your kettle, and you are now ready to make your soup.

In a separate pan boil slowly about a third of a teacupful of barley. This should be cooked separately since it has a habit, in a soup kettle, of settling to the bottom, and if your fire should happen to get too hot it is likely to burn. If you cannot get barley use rice, but it is a poor substitute.

One of the secrets of making good vegetable soup is not to cook any of the vegetables too long. However, it is impossible to give you an exact measure of the vegetables you should put in because some people like their vegetable soup almost as thick as stew; others like it much thinner. Moreover, sometimes you can get exactly the vegetables you want; other times you have to substitute. Where you use canned vegetables, put them in only a few minutes before taking the soup off the fire. If you use fresh ones, naturally they must be fully cooked in the soup.

The things put into the soup are about as follows:

1 quart can of tomatoes
½ teacupful of fresh peas. (If you can't get peas, a handful of good green beans, cut up very small, can substitute.)
2 normal-sized potatoes, diced into cubes of about ½-inch size
2 or 3 branches of good celery
1 good-sized onion, sliced
3 nice-sized carrots diced about the same size as the potatoes
1 turnip diced like the potatoes
½ cup of canned corn
A handful of raw cabbage cut up in small pieces

Your vegetables should not all be dumped in at once. The potatoes, for example, will cook more quickly than the carrots. Your effort must be to have them all nicely cooked but not mushy at about the same time. The fire must not be too hot, but the soup should keep bubbling.

464

When you figure the soup is about done, put in your barley, which should now be fully cooked. Add a tablespoonful of prepared gravy seasoning and taste for flavoring, particularly salt and pepper and, if you have it, use some onion salt, garlic salt, and celery salt. [If you cannot get the gravy seasoning, use one teaspoonful of Worcestershire sauce.]

Cut up the few bits of the meat you have saved and put about a small handful into the soup.

While you are cooking the soup do not allow the liquid to boil down too much. Add a bit of water from time to time. If your stock was good and thick when you started, you can add more water than if it was thin when you started.

As a final touch, in the springtime when nasturtiums are green and tender you can take a few nasturtium stems, cut them up in small pieces, boil them separately as you did the barley and add them to your soup (about one tablespoonful after cooking).

GREEN TURTLE SOUP ☆

[*Note:* This recipe of President Eisenhower was included on the menu for the dinner he gave in honor of the president of Mexico and the prime minister of Canada, April, 1956, at The Greenbrier, White Sulphur Springs, West Virginia.]

Cut off the head from a live green turtle and drain the blood. Remove the four flappers from the turtle with a sharp knife; divide the back and belly into four parts and put the whole (without the intestines) in boiling water for about three minutes.

Now lift the pieces from the boiling water. While they are still warm, remove the skin with a coarse cloth, then wash the pieces well and lay them in clean water with a sufficient amount of mixed vegetables, bay leaves, thyme, a little garlic, lemon skin, parsley, and season with salt and pepper.

Let the whole cook from two and a half to three hours. Strain and cut the turtle meat into small cube-size pieces and place in a pot, covering with sherry. Put the strained turtle broth into a clean pot; add chopped beef, fresh mixed vegetables, whites of eggs, bay leaves, garlic, cloves, parsley; season with salt and pepper and cook this again for three hours.

Strain the turtle broth with a cheesecloth; wash the pot in which you have just finished cooking and put into it again the strained broth. Keep the whole hot.

465

To obtain a more delicate and more spicy flavor prepare the following: add to sherry wine, thyme, rosemary, bay leaves, coriander, sage, basil, black and white pepper. Heat and strain and according to your taste add this to the turtle soup before serving.

PRESIDENT EISENHOWER'S
OLD-FASHIONED BEEF STEW ☆

[*Note:* Mr. Eisenhower often prepares this marvelous beef stew for fellow campers at his hunting and fishing lodge.]

20 pounds stewing meat (prime round)	1 bunch bouquet garniture (thyme, bay leaves, garlic, etc., in cloth bag)
8 pounds small Irish potatoes	
6 bunches small carrots	3 gallons beef stock
5 pounds small onions	Salt, pepper, and Accent
15 fresh tomatoes	

Stew the meat until tender. Add the vegetables and bouquet garniture. When vegetables are done, strain off two gallons of stock from the stew and thicken slightly with beef roux. Pour back into stew and let simmer for one-half hour. This will make sixty portions.

To adapt the above recipe to average family use (six portions) it is suggested that you use about one-tenth of the ingredients, as follows:

2 pounds stewing meat (prime round)	2 fresh tomatoes
	Assorted spices
1 pound small Irish potatoes	2½ pints beef stock
1 bunch small carrots	Salt, pepper, and Accent
¾ pound small onions	

Cook as in above recipe, straining off one cup of stock from stew instead of the two gallons.

MAMIE EISENHOWER'S BAKED CARAMEL CUSTARD ☆

6 tablespoons sugar	⅛ teaspoon salt
2 cups scalded milk	½ teaspoon vanilla
3 eggs	

Caramelize four tablespoons sugar [heat sugar until light brown and of caramel flavor, stirring constantly]. Add to the scalded milk. Add slightly beaten eggs, remainder of sugar, salt, and vanilla. Strain. Pour into baking cups or dish. Bake in slow oven (300°) about three-quarters of an hour or until custard is set.

MAMIE EISENHOWER'S FUDGE ☆

4½ cups sugar
  Pinch of salt
  2 tablespoons butter

1 tall can evaporated milk
  (1⅔ cups)

Boil sugar, salt, butter, and milk six minutes, stirring constantly. Pour this boiling syrup over:

12 ounces German sweet
  chocolate
12 ounces semi-sweet
  chocolate bits

1 pint marshmallow cream
2 cups nut meats

Beat until chocolate is all melted. Pour into pan. Let stand a few hours and store in tin box.

Jacqueline Bouvier Kennedy

OF NEW YORK

First Lady 1961–1963

"I am, first, a wife and mother; second, the First Lady . . . ."

JACQUELINE KENNEDY, First Lady of the New Frontier, brought to the White House a combination of youthful glamor, talent, and taste never before seen in the old mansion. The youngest First Lady of this century (thirty-one) and the third youngest in history, she had—as had her husband, the youngest elected President—a style all her own.

467

The handsome, vigorous, intellectual Kennedys, with their boundless enthusiasm and energy and their keen interest in literature, music, art, history, and sports, as well as politics, waked up staid Washington and quickened the pace of life throughout America. From the day of the inauguration the world was aware that a new generation had taken command.

To a quickly captivated public, Jacqueline Kennedy seemed a blend of the best in many Presidents' wives:

THE KENNEDYS LEAVING CHURCH ON EASTER SUNDAY

468

Her gentle Virginia connections and her love of riding to hounds recalled Martha Washington;

Her fondness for sunny yellow in decorating and her flair as a hostess suggested Dolley Madison;

Her classic taste in decor and her preference for French furnishings revived the Monroe era;

Her youth, beauty, and chic reminded historians of Julia Tyler;

In her role of devoted mother, eager to protect her children from excessive publicity, she was as appealing as Frances Cleveland;

Her plans for "restoring" the White House were successful beyond the dreams of First Ladies Garfield, Harrison, Coolidge, and Hoover;

In her personal problems—the President's serious illnesses, her own difficulties in bearing children, the death of her newborn son—she had to summon the fortitude displayed by Abigail Adams and other pioneer First Ladies.

It was clear from the beginning, however, that she was a copy of none of her predecessors but a sturdy individualist with a mind of her own. More than willing to contribute her special talents, which were artistic and scholarly, to the position, she soon learned, as had the many other wives or hostesses of Presidents, that nothing a First Lady does is ever quite "right" nor quite "enough." There are always criticisms and demands for more. The restrictions of the job, which had been the bane of every First Lady from Mrs. Washington to Mrs. Eisenhower, must have seemed especially irksome to a privileged and high-spirited girl who had always been free to pursue her own interests. She had the flexibility of youth on her side, however, plus a deep desire to do nothing that would hinder her husband's career. She worked hard to fulfill her historic role without sacrificing her convictions. These convictions included her right to enjoy a private life with her family.

"I will be, first, a wife and mother; second, the First Lady," she said with determination.

The wife of our thirty-fifth President, Jacqueline was born in fashionable Southampton, New York, in 1929, the first child of a socially prominent couple. Her father was a handsome, dashing society figure, descended from an old French family. Her mother was a belle, an expert horsewoman, and a "Lee of Virginia."

A pretty, intelligent, temperamental little girl—sometimes described as stubborn—Jacqueline early showed marked talents for writing and sketching. Educated at private schools and colleges here and abroad, she majored in the history of art and American history. At eighteen she was named Debutante of the Year and later won *Vogue's* Prix de Paris competition for college women with a flair for fashion, art, and creative writing. After graduation she became a career girl—reporter-photographer for a Washington newspaper, for which she covered Queen Elizabeth's coronation. She also interviewed for the paper a handsome bachelor-senator twelve years her senior. Senator John Fitzgerald Kennedy was a World War II hero; later he would become the Pulitzer Prize-winning author of *Profiles in Courage*, a book about brave Americans in government.

The Bouvier-Kennedy wedding, a highly publicized event, took place in 1953 in Newport, Rhode Island, in the presence of six hundred guests. Three years later the Kennedys' first baby was stillborn. In the next four years they became the parents of two children, Caroline and John, Jr. As she awaited the birth of the latter, born shortly after his father's election to the Presidency, Mrs. Kennedy forced herself to overcome a lifelong aversion to crowds and took an active part in her husband's campaign.

Early in his administration Jacqueline was heard to protest that she had been "turned into a piece of public property"—a complaint that all First Ladies have expressed in one way or another. (Thomas Jefferson had said: "When a man assumes a public trust, he should consider himself as public property.") Soon she learned to conform where she must, to refuse when she could, to contribute her best talents to the job, ignore criticism, and accept, with resignation, the public's insatiable curiosity about her private life and its mass copying of "The Jackie Look"—bouffant coiffure, pillbox hats, and A-line dresses.

Lucy Hayes was the first First Lady to accompany her husband on political trips. Eleanor Roosevelt was the first to travel thousands of miles on semi-official business. Jacqueline Kennedy was the first to travel the world, alone or with relatives, in pursuit of rest, recreation, and pure pleasure. There was some public grumbling about her jaunts, of course; it is interesting that there was not more. Perhaps the people realized that this First Lady—wealthy in her own right and with a multi-millionaire husband—was merely "living in the style to which she was accustomed." More likely, they recognized her as a prime political asset and a credit to her country. Wherever she went she charmed heads of state and crowds of citizens. An accomplished linguist, she spoke to people in their own language—French, Spanish, or Italian. As French crowds cheered "la belle Jaquie," the President good-naturedly introduced himself as "the man who came to Paris with Jacqueline Kennedy."

"It seemed such a shame, when we came here, to find hardly anything of the past," she said shortly after moving into the White House. Furnishings of the one hundred-thirty-room mansion were a hodge-

MRS. KENNEDY ON ONE OF HER MANY TRAVELS

podge of antiques, reproductions, and modern. The one-hundred-fifty-year-old house at 1600 Pennsylvania Avenue had been waiting, it seemed, for a mistress with the scholarly awareness and artistic taste necessary to restore it to something approaching its original glory. Jacqueline appointed a Fine Arts Committee of museum experts, curators, historians, and knowledgeable private citizens. The committee, which sought out authentic pieces and private donors and approved each change or purchase, used no public funds; thus the First Lady avoided charges of high-living, free-spending extravagance that had tagged other administrations.

In the past, First Families could dispose as they pleased of furnishings in their temporary home. Now a new law made the White House a national museum and everything in it part of a permanent collection. If a First Family does not want to live with a piece, it goes to the Smithsonian Institution for safekeeping. Never again can there be a President Arthur Auction.

A fascinating event took place in February, 1962, when Mrs. Kennedy led forty-six million Americans on a television tour through the mansion, showing them the results of her committee's research and hard work.

Official Washington had no cause to complain, as it did in Van Buren's day, about the "sameness" of parties at the White House. The Kennedys scored with their original entertaining. French cuisine appeared on the menu probably more frequently than at any time since Thomas Jefferson's day. (It was the First Lady who leaned to the French; the President's tastes were as American as New England fish chowder. He was especially fond of soups.)

Dinners were shortened to four courses to allow more time for such after-dinner entertainment as dancing in the East Room, a concert by renowned Spanish cellist Pablo Casals, and a performance of Shakespearean plays—the first time The Bard had played the White House.

The Kennedys' interests were egg-head, arty, and diversified; their style was dramatic. Nobel Prize winners were feted at a White House dinner for the first time in history in April of 1962. The first fireworks to be rocketed from the White House lawn lighted up the Washington sky after a state dinner in 1963. George Washington's white, pillared home in Mount Vernon, Virginia, was the setting for a gala affair in July of 1961. Guests came down the Potomac by boat, strolled the

THE STATE DINING ROOM, 1962, READY FOR
AN OFFICIAL DINNER

candlelit rooms, and viewed, from the wide veranda, the Salute to the President by a color guard and fife and drum corps dressed in colonial uniform.

In August, 1963, Mrs. Kennedy gave birth prematurely to a son, Patrick, who died two days later. She took a two-week recuperative vacation in Greece and the Mediterranean. Then, back home at the White House, she prepared to accompany her husband on a political trip to Texas.

"All the problems that arise for my husband I feel with him, all through their development," she had once remarked. Still she had shied away from such trips. For some reason she now changed her mind and decided to go along. She told a friend, "He needs my help."

On November 22, 1963, while seated beside his First Lady in a motorcade moving slowly through cheering crowds in Dallas, Texas, President John F. Kennedy was assassinated. He was forty-six years old, the youngest American president to die. Jacqueline Kennedy, at thirty-four, had become the widow of a martyred President. Three women before her had shared this sad distinction—Mary Lincoln, Lucretia Garfield, Ida McKinley. She knew their stories well.

Within a few hours she was back in Washington, helping to plan the rites and ceremonies that would be conducted before the eyes of the world. She made no plea for personal consideration or privacy. The only wishes she expressed were for services befitting an eminent statesman. Some of the traditions observed at her request dated back to the early days of this Republic; some derived from the funeral of Abraham Lincoln. Her small children firmly in hand, the First Lady took part in public ceremonies. With thousands of other mourners, she walked in the funeral procession.

In Britain it was said of her: "She has what the United States always has lacked—dignity." President Kennedy himself might have called the erect, black-veiled figure "a profile in courage."

She had been an aristocrat so gently reared that, until well into adulthood, she had known little of cold reality, nothing of brutality. Now, in the great trial of her life, the stubborn determination of her childhood served her well, as did her thoroughbred training, her grasp of American history, and the democratic example set by her husband. Like many Presidents' wives before her, she sometimes may have wished that he could be less the Chief Executive, more husband and father. But in those closing, critical days she rose above personal wishes and private grief to give the President to his country, and she herself became "first of all, the First Lady."

473

Favorite Recipes of Jacqueline Kennedy

CONSOMMÉ JULIENNE ☆

2 small carrots, scraped
1 leek
1 stalk celery
2 slices turnip
1 tablespoon butter or
    margarine
3 cabbage leaves, shredded
½ medium-sized onion,
    sliced thinly

⅛ teaspoon salt
    Dash of pepper
⅛ teaspoon sugar
4 chicken bouillon cubes
    dissolved in 4 cups boiling
    water
    Chopped parsley

Cut carrots, leek, celery, and turnip into very thin strips about two inches long. Melt butter in a small saucepan over low heat. Add carrots, leek, celery, turnip, cabbage, onion, salt, pepper, and sugar. Cover and cook about five minutes, until vegetables are tender. Combine with chicken bouillon. Simmer five minutes. Serve with garnish of chopped parsley. Serves six.

PRESIDENT KENNEDY'S FISH CHOWDER ☆

2 pounds haddock
2 ounces salt pork, diced
2 onions, sliced
4 large potatoes, diced
1 cup chopped celery

1 bay leaf, crumbled
1 teaspoon salt
    Freshly ground black pepper
1 quart milk
2 tablespoons butter

Simmer haddock in two cups water for fifteen minutes. Drain. Reserve broth. Remove bones from fish. Sauté diced pork until crisp, remove and set aside. Sauté onions in pork fat until golden brown. Add fish, potatoes, celery, bay leaf, salt and pepper. Pour in fish broth plus enough boiling water to make three cups of liquid. Simmer for thirty minutes. Add milk and butter and simmer for five minutes. Serve chowder sprinkled with diced pork. Serves six.

474

BOULA-BOULA [*American Soup*] ☆

2 cups freshly shelled
   green peas
1 tablespoon sweet butter
  Salt and white pepper

2 cups canned green
   turtle soup
1 cup sherry
½ cup whipping cream

Cook the green peas in boiling salted water. Strain through a fine sieve or an electric blender to get a puree; reheat it. Add one tablespoon sweet butter, salt, and white pepper to taste. Blend with the green turtle soup and one cup of sherry. Heat to just under the boiling point. Put the soup into serving cups. Cover each cup with a spoonful of unsweetened whipped cream. Brown topping under the broiler.

ICED TOMATO SOUP ☆

6 large ripe tomatoes,
   coarsely chopped
1 onion, chopped
¼ cup water
½ teaspoon salt
  Dash of pepper

2 tablespoons tomato paste
2 tablespoons flour
2 chicken bouillon cubes,
   dissolved in 2 cups
   boiling water
1 cup heavy cream

Combine tomatoes, onion, water, salt and pepper in a saucepan. Cook over moderate heat five minutes. Combine tomato paste with flour and add to tomatoes with chicken bouillon. Simmer gently three minutes. Rub mixture through a fine sieve. Chill several hours. Before serving, add cream. Season to taste with more salt if necessary. Garnish each serving with a thin tomato slice if desired. Serves six.

SALAD MIMOSA ☆

¼ cup olive oil
1 tablespoon wine vinegar
½ teaspoon salt
  Dash of pepper

⅓ clove garlic, finely minced
2 quarts crisp salad greens
2 hard-cooked eggs,
   finely chopped

Combine oil, vinegar, salt, pepper, and garlic in a jar with a tight lid. Shake vigorously. Arrange greens in salad bowl, add dressing, and toss thoroughly. Sprinkle with chopped egg. Serves six.

475

BELGIAN ENDIVE ☆

8 stalks endive	1 teaspoon salt
4 tablespoons melted butter	½ teaspoon sugar
Juice of one lemon	½ teaspoon white pepper
¾ cup chicken stock	1 teaspoon paprika

Wash and drain endive. Place in ovenproof baking dish. Pour over endive, butter, lemon juice, stock, salt, sugar, and pepper. Cover dish and bake in moderate oven (325°–350°) for forty to forty-five minutes. Remove cover and place under broiler until golden. Sprinkle with paprika and serve.

POLENTA ☆

[Italian version of cornmeal mush]

1 pint of water	2 eggs
1 teaspoon salt	Breadcrumbs
1 tablespoon olive oil	4 tablespoons butter
6 ounces cornmeal	

Bring water to rolling boil. Add teaspoon of salt and olive oil. Gradually pour in cornmeal, stirring constantly. Cook for twenty minutes, stirring occasionally. Remove from stove and pour into greased baking dish. Cool and cut into squares. Dip in egg, roll in breadcrumbs, and fry in butter until golden brown.

POLENTA ED UCCELLETTI ☆

2 ounces each, diced Swiss cheese and diced prosciutto ham	1½ pounds lean veal, prepared as for scaloppine
3 ounces chopped lean pork	3 tablespoons butter
½ teaspoon each salt and pepper	Flour
¼ teaspoon each thyme and sage	¾ cup white wine
1 whole egg	½ cup chicken broth

Mix cheese, ham, pork, salt, pepper, sage, thyme, and whole egg in bowl. Divide veal into individual servings. Place two tablespoons cheese and ham mixture in center of each piece. Roll the scallopine and secure with toothpicks. In an ovenproof casserole, melt the butter. When it begins to turn light brown, sprinkle a little flour over the veal

476

rolls and place in casserole. Turn veal rolls until they are golden brown, add white wine, and cook for two minutes, then add chicken broth, cover and bake in 375° oven for ten minutes. Serves six to eight.

POTATOES SUZETTE ☆

3 large baking potatoes
2 tablespoons butter
   or margarine
3 tablespoons heavy cream
1 egg yolk, well beaten
   Salt and pepper
1 tablespoon grated
   Parmesan cheese

Heat oven to 400°. Bake potatoes until fork-tender, about one hour. Cut in halves lengthwise, scoop out pulp without breaking shells. Mash pulp thoroughly. Add butter, cream, and egg yolk. Beat vigorously until light and fluffy. Season with salt and pepper. Spoon mixture into shells, sprinkle tops with cheese. Bake fifteen minutes until tops are golden-brown. Serves six.

POULET À L'ESTRAGON ☆

3 whole chicken breasts
1 onion, thinly sliced
1 carrot, thinly sliced
¼ teaspoon dried tarragon
½ cup white wine
3 tablespoons butter
   or margarine
3 tablespoons flour
½ teaspoon salt
   Dash of pepper
2 tablespoons butter
   or margarine
1 egg yolk, slightly beaten
3 tablespoons heavy cream

With poultry shears cut breasts in halves along the backbone. Pull off the skin. Place chicken, onion, carrot, tarragon, and wine in a large saucepan. Add just enough water to cover chicken, about four cups. Cover and bring to a boil over moderate heat. Lower heat and simmer gently about twenty-five minutes until fork-tender. Remove chicken and keep warm. Strain liquid, then cook over high heat until it is reduced to two cups. In a heavy saucepan melt the three tablespoons butter; stir in flour, salt and pepper. Gradually add the two cups of chicken broth, cook and stir over moderate heat until thickened and smooth. Add the two tablespoons butter, simmer gently five minutes, stirring occasionally. Combine egg yolk and cream. Stir into hot sauce. Arrange chicken breasts on a warm serving platter and pour the hot sauce over them. Serves six.

CASSEROLE MARIE-BLANCHE ☆

1½ pounds cooked,
    drained noodles
1 cup cream-style
    cottage cheese
1 cup commercial sour cream

½ teaspoon salt
⅛ teaspoon pepper
⅓ cup chopped chives
1 tablespoon butter
    or margarine

Heat oven to 350°. Combine noodles, cheese, sour cream, salt, pepper, and chives. Pour into a buttered two-quart casserole and dot top with one tablespoon butter. Bake about thirty minutes until noodles begin to brown. Serve immediately. Serves six.

BAKED SEAFOOD CASSEROLE ☆

1 pound canned or
    frozen crabmeat
1 pound shrimp, cooked,
    shelled, and deveined
1 cup mayonnaise
½ cup chopped green pepper
¼ cup finely chopped onion

1½ cups finely chopped celery
½ teaspoon salt
1 tablespoon Worcestershire
    sauce
2 cups coarsely chopped
    potato chips
Paprika

Heat oven to 400°. Combine crabmeat, shrimp, mayonnaise, green pepper, onion, celery, salt, and Worcestershire. Pour into a buttered two-and-a-half-quart casserole. Top with crushed potato chips. Sprinkle with paprika. Bake twenty to twenty-five minutes until mixture is thoroughly heated. Makes about eight servings.

LOBSTER CARDINALE ☆

6 1½-pound lobsters
8 cups boiling water
¾ cup butter or margarine
4 tablespoons flour
1½ teaspoons salt

2 tablespoons dry white wine
4 tablespoons chopped
    canned mushrooms
1 tablespoon grated
    Parmesan cheese

Drop lobsters into rapidly boiling water. When water returns to a boil, cook lobsters fifteen minutes; remove and cool. Boil the water rapidly until it is reduced to two cups. Place each lobster on its back and with a sharp knife cut membrane the entire length of the body. Remove and discard the stomach portion, which is under the head. Remove meat from claws and body and cut into one-inch pieces. Place

478

body shells in a shallow baking pan. Melt four tablespoonfuls of butter in a saucepan, add flour and salt. Gradually add the two cups reduced liquid, stirring constantly until smooth and thickened. Cook fifteen minutes, stirring frequently. Add wine, mushrooms, and the remaining butter. Spread a little sauce in the bottom of each shell. Add lobster meat. Top with rest of sauce and sprinkle with cheese. Place three to four inches from heat in a preheated broiler and broil about five minutes until mixture is hot and lightly browned. Serves six.

DINNER IN HONOR OF ANDRÉ MALRAUX, 1962

The Menu for the Malraux Dinner

CONSOMMÉ MADRILENE IRANIEN

LOBSTER EN BELLEVUE

STUFFED BAR POLIGNAC

POTATOES PARISIENNE   FLORIDA ASPARAGUS

PHEASANT ASPIC

CREAM PUFFS WITH NUTS

479

LEMON ICE ☆

4 cups water

3½ cups sugar

1 cup fresh or frozen lemon juice

1 tablespoon grated lemon rind

Combine water and sugar in a saucepan, bring to a boil, and boil five minutes. Cool. Add lemon juice and rind. Pour into two refrigerator trays. Place trays in freezer. When mixture is frozen to a mush, remove to a cold bowl and quickly beat with a rotary beater until smooth. Return to trays and freeze again; remove mixture to cold bowl and quickly beat until smooth. Return to trays and freeze until firm, about two hours. Serves six.

CRÈME BRÛLÉE ☆

3 cups heavy cream

1-inch piece vanilla bean

6 tablespoons sugar

6 egg yolks

½ cup brown sugar

In upper part of double boiler heat three cups of heavy cream with vanilla bean. In a bowl beat sugar with egg yolks until light and creamy. Take out vanilla bean and stir warm cream into yolks very carefully and slowly.

Return mixture to double boiler, over boiling water. Stir constantly until custard coats a spoon. Then put into a glass serving dish and place it in the refrigerator to set. When ready to serve, cover top of custard completely with brown sugar, using a half-cup or more. Place the dish on a bowl of crushed ice and place custard under broiler flame until brown sugar melts and caramelizes. Keep watching it, for sugar will burn. Serve immediately.

SOUFFLÉ FROID AU CHOCOLAT ☆

2 squares unsweetened chocolate

½ cup confectioner's sugar

1 envelope gelatin (unflavored)
   softened in 3 tablespoons
   cold water

1 cup milk

¾ cup granulated sugar

1 teaspoon vanilla extract

¼ teaspoon salt

2 cups heavy cream

Melt chocolate squares over hot (not boiling) water. When entirely melted, stir in the confectioner's sugar, mix well. Heat milk just enough so that a film shows on the surface, then stir it into the melted chocolate slowly and thoroughly. Cook, stirring constantly, until the mixture reaches the boiling point. Do not boil, however. Remove from the heat and mix into it the softened gelatin, the granulated sugar, vanilla extract, and salt. Put in the refrigerator and chill until slightly thick. Then beat mixture until it is light and airy-looking. In a separate bowl beat heavy cream until it holds a shape, then combine the two mixtures, pouring into a two-quart soufflé dish or serving bowl. Chill two or three hours in refrigerator or until ready to serve. Serves six to eight.

HOT FRUIT DESSERT ☆

1 orange
1 lemon
½ cup light brown sugar, packed
¼ teaspoon ground nutmeg
1 8¾-ounce can
    pineapple tidbits

1 8-ounce can apricots
1 8¾-ounce can
    sliced peaches
1 17-ounce can pitted
    Bing cherries
Commercial sour cream

Grate the rind from the orange and lemon; add to brown sugar with nutmeg. Cut orange and lemon into very thin slices. Drain and combine fruits. Butter a one-quart casserole and arrange fruits in layers, sprinkling each layer with some of the brown-sugar mixture. Bake thirty minutes. Serve warm with a spoonful of sour cream on top. Serves six to eight.

Dinner for the President of Pakistan
MOUNT VERNON, VIRGINIA
July 11, 1961

AVOCADO AND CRABMEAT MIMOSA   HAUT-BRION BLANC 1958

POULET CHASSEUR

COURONNE DE RIZ CLAMART   MOET ET CHANDON IMPERIAL
BRUT 1955

FRAMBOISES À LA CRÈME CHANTILLY

PETITS-FOURS SECS

DEMITASSE AND LIQUEURS

481

Luncheon in Honor of Amintore Fanfani,
Prime Minister of the Italian Republic
THE WHITE HOUSE
January 16, 1963

BRAISED ROCKFISH DAUMONT

ROAST LAMB DAUPHINE

STRING BEANS

SALADE MIMOSA

SAVARIN ALMINA

DEMITASSE

Claudia Alta (Lady Bird) Taylor Johnson

OF TEXAS

First Lady 1963–

"I am on stage for a part
I never rehearsed . . . ."

THE FINE FRENCH HAND of elegant, formal Jacqueline Kennedy had brought great distinction to the White House. Now the mansion was to have a folksy, western brand impressed upon it by a friendly, outspoken First Lady from Texas with the whimsical name of Lady Bird. The nickname was bestowed upon her at a tender age by a doting nurse

482

who said she was "as pretty as a lady bird." Her husband and close friends call her "Bird." "I learned long ago to make peace with that name," she says.

The First Lady Bird of the United States is the second Mrs. Johnson in history to be "called to the White House by a national calamity." The first, Eliza Johnson, was Mary Lincoln's successor. Eliza, one of our most retiring White House wives, left both politics and social life to the rest of her family. The resemblance between the two Mrs. Johnsons ends with the name.

So petite and warmly feminine is Mrs. Lyndon B. Johnson that magazine writers, at first, portrayed her as a typical housewife whose main interests were "home decorating and home movies." It was a far-from-accurate picture of the most politically experienced woman who ever moved into the President's House—a woman who, for thirty years, had been a politician's wife and whose specialty was "going along and saying howdy to the voters." She has been the personal and political helpmate of a man who served twelve years in the House, twelve years in the Senate (where for six years he was majority leader and called "the most influential man in Washington"), and three years in the vice-presidency. So often was Lady Bird called upon to stand in for President or Mrs. Kennedy that she became known as Washington's No. 1 Pinch-Hitter.

Lady Bird Johnson's first contribution to her husband's career, thirty years ago, was her inheritance from her mother. This provided the financial cushion that permitted her bridegroom to pursue his primary interest—politics. In addition, the bride quickly proved herself a vote-getter for him on the campaign trail. Childless for the first ten years of her marriage, she traveled with him, made political speeches, once enrolled in a public-speaking course that she might plead his cause more effectively. While Congressman Johnson was on active duty with the Navy in World War II, she worked, without salary, in his Washington office "to keep the lines of contact open with the people of the tenth district of Texas."

Social demands made of the First Lady are not likely to overwhelm her. As a senator's wife, she entertained Washington bigwigs at barbecues and buffets in her basement recreation room. As the wife of the vice-president, in a larger home, she gave bigger and more formal parties for important international figures. Always the charming hostess, her winning, womanly ways do not conceal from astute acquaintances her observant eye and keen ear and facility for mental note-taking. (She likes to think of herself as an extra pair of eyes and ears for her husband.) Underneath the soft exterior is a firm businesswoman who

483

knows how to drive a shrewd bargain. She handles all family money and household details.

"Lyndon is always prodding us to look better, learn more, work harder," says the First Lady, who admits that her dynamic husband is "an exciting man to live with, an exhausting man to keep up with, a good man in a crisis." Hard-working himself, impulsive and impatient, sometimes short-tempered, the President tends to be perfectionistic and to demand top performance from family and staff alike.

Mrs. Johnson's keen business sense may be attributed in large part to her close association with her father, a prosperous land-owner and general-store proprietor in Northeast Texas. Her mother was a gentle Alabaman who was interested in culture and justice for Negroes (unusual for a small-town southern woman of her time). When her mother died, Lady Bird was only five. From then on, her life was spent mainly with men—her father ("Mr. Boss") and her two older brothers. From them she gained an understanding of business transactions and an

LYNDON B. JOHNSON CUTS HIS BIRTHDAY CAKE, A FEW
MONTHS BEFORE HE BECAME PRESIDENT

insight into the workings of the masculine mind. It was good training for her role as wife of a Chief Executive who expects her to show independence and resourcefulness in handling business matters for which he has no time. Fortunately, she has the kind of well-organized mind that moves efficiently and alertly from one project to the next.

"Elasticity" is the most important trait a First Lady can possess, she has said. Indeed, it requires great patience and flexibility to cope with an outgoing husband who, on Christmas Day, 1963, kept twenty-three hungry relatives waiting while he conducted a horde of reporters on a spur-of-the-moment tour of the LBJ ranch house. Turkey and trimmings were well-cooled and the First Lady a bit flushed when the tour ended one hour later.

As a "political wife," Mrs. Johnson has been compared to Mrs. Franklin D. Roosevelt. There is this difference: Mrs. Roosevelt carried on a semi-official, political life of her own, while the present First Lady has no aspirations except for her husband. For thirty years her life has belonged to him and, through him, to his political associates and the voting public. Apparently, she would not have it any other way. From the beginning, she has shown a willingness—almost an eagerness—to make herself and her family available to the public. She gives no impression of trying to save a private life for herself and her husband and children, as so many First Ladies, from Martha Washington to Jacqueline Kennedy, have tried desperately to do. She is an old enough hand at politics to know that this is virtually impossible. Congressional wives and others who, for years, have hungered in vain for a glimpse of the White House "upstairs" are now being treated to frequent tours of the second-floor family quarters.

Such a glamorous and demanding life could not have been foreseen by the shy Lady Bird who was born December 22, 1912, in Karnack, Texas, and who grew up "rather alone" in that small town. After being graduated from high school in Marshall, Texas, at fifteen (third academically in her class), she attended St. Mary's Episcopal School for Girls in Dallas, where classmates remember her as "sweet but retiring." She was graduated in 1934 from the University of Texas in Austin with degrees in liberal arts and journalism. Shortly after, she met a self-made, politically ambitious young high school speech teacher named Lyndon Baines Johnson. It was a whirlwind courtship. He proposed almost immediately; she, a more prudent type, thought it over for two months. They were married in a simple ceremony at St. Mark's Episcopal Church in San Antonio, November 17, 1934— only a few hours after she had said "Yes." Just before the wedding, a friend was quickly dispatched to the nearest jewelry store to bring back

485

a selection of rings. Lady Bird still wears the modest diamond she chose that day.

The new Mrs. Johnson invested her inheritance from her mother in a run-down, debt-ridden radio station in Austin (little knowing that she was making a down-payment on a future Summer White House!). Through long hours of work and close attention to both programming and financial reports, she built the station into a paying business. Today it is the only commercial television station in Austin, and the family owns interests in several other Texas stations. Until recently, when the holdings were turned over to trustees, she served as chairman of the board. Over a period of twenty years, profits from the stations have made possible the purchase of four cattle ranches complete with well-furnished and decorated ranch houses.

On the banks of the Pedernales River, in Johnson City, Texas, sixty-five miles from Austin, stands the Summer White House—a rambling, thirteen-room stone and frame ranch house. A sign at the entrance reads "LBJ ranch," and from the flagpole fly the American flag, the Presidential flag, and the Texas flag. Concrete stepping stones around the pool bear signatures of famous figures who have visited there. Thirty telephone lines to the house and numerous outlets around the pool take care of official calls, and golf carts scurry about the 300 acres carrying messengers. Near the back door of the house are an airplane hangar and landing strip. The eighteen-hundred acre ranch is twelve miles away.

LBJ is the "trademark" of the family. There are Lyndon Baines, Lady Bird, Lynda Bird, Lucy Baines; there was even the late Little Beagle Johnson. Some Washingtonians find all this LBJ-ing as appealing as the "you-alls"; others, on the far side of the political fence, call it "corny." None, however, has been known to turn down a recent LBJ invitation to the White House or the ranch.

After ten years of marriage Mrs. Johnson gave birth to Lynda Bird on March 19, 1944. On July 2, 1947, Lucy Baines was born. Both girls have been brought up to appreciate the importance of their father's position and the obligations that go with it and seem as agreeable as their mother about sharing the public spotlight. Lynda, a tall, brown-eyed brunette, is of marriageable age. She would be the seventh daughter of a President to be married in the White House. Maria Monroe was the first; she was wed there in 1820. Others were Elizabeth Tyler, Nellie Grant, Alice Roosevelt, and President Wilson's two daughters, Jessie and Eleanor.

Now that the click of teen-age high heels has replaced the patter of little feet in the mansion, the Secret Service once more is busy chaperoning dates and dances—its first such assignment since Margaret Truman was the daughter of the White House.

Fashionwise but conservative Lady Bird Johnson is sure to make America's "best-dressed" list, though she hopes women will not concentrate on her wardrobe. Not label-conscious, she buys what she likes, favors yellow and red because they complement her fair skin, blue eyes, and black hair, which are more striking in person than in photographs. The President is particular about the clothes his "three girls" wear, and purchases are subject to his approval. In feminine fashion, as in everything else, he knows what he likes—bright colors, slim skirts, high heels. He keeps an eye on their weight, too, and periodically puts them all on his own low-calorie diet. (The First Lady is five-foot-four inches tall and works at keeping her weight at a hundred and ten pounds.) All three try hard to please the head of the household. He could please them by not working as long and hard as he does. Since a severe heart attack eight years ago, they worry about him. "But there's no stopping him," his wife sighs. "Short of nagging."

Mrs. Johnson sees herself as a "balm, sustainer, and sometimes a critic" for her husband, who values her advice. In the little spare time they spend together, they enjoy walking or riding over the Texas ranch land they both love.

She does not plan to redecorate the White House, already so skillfully restored by Jacqueline Kennedy's Fine Arts Committee, but to give the Committee a free hand in continuing its research and restoration. In the family quarters upstairs, however, LBJ touches have been added —southwestern art objects and paintings of the Texas hill country by native artists.

The First Lady sums up her personal philosophy gained through sharing a long, always busy, often hectic married life with Lyndon Johnson: "From him I've learned that to put all the brains and heart and skill you have into the job of trying to make your government work a little better can be a wonderful life for a man and his wife. . . ."

Favorite Recipes of Lady Bird Johnson

NOCHE SPECIALS ☆

Cut tortillas into quarters and fry in deep hot fat until brown and crisp on both sides. Drain and put about one teaspoon of grated cheese and a slice of jalapeño pepper on each quarter. Place in hot oven until well heated and cheese begins to melt. Serve at once.

PEDERNALES RIVER CHILI ☆

4 pounds chili meat
1 large onion
2 cloves garlic
1 teaspoon ground oregano
1 teaspoon comino seed

6 teaspoons chili powder
  (more if needed)
2 cans tomatoes
Salt to taste
2 cups hot water

Put chili meat, onions, and garlic in large heavy boiler or skillet. Sear until light-colored. Add oregano, comino, chili powder, tomatoes, salt, and hot water. Bring to a boil, lower heat and simmer about one hour. As fat cooks out, skim.

PICKLED OKRA ☆

Fresh okra
1 quart white vinegar
½ cup water

For each pint jar:
1 teaspoon dill seeds
1 hot red pepper
1 hot green pepper
2 cloves garlic

Place a half-teaspoon of dill seed in bottom of each sterilized jar. Wash okra and pack as tightly as possible in jars—being careful not to bruise. Add a half-teaspoon dill seed, the red and green peppers, and garlic. Bring vinegar, water, and salt to boil and pour this hot mixture over the okra. Seal and allow to stand two weeks. Serve icy cold. Makes approximately four pints.

CHESS PIE ☆

2 cups sugar
1 heaping tablespoon flour
½ pound butter

4 eggs
½ teaspoon vanilla

Mix sugar and flour together and add to butter. Blend until light and fluffy. Add eggs one at a time, beating after each addition. Add vanilla and pour into unbaked pie shell. Bake in 300° oven until knife inserted comes out clean—about one hour.

[*Note:* Chess Pie (or Chess Cake) is a very old recipe. Compare Mrs. Johnson's recipe with the following one.]

CHESS CAKE—1879

Make shells of pie crust and bake before putting in the following cooked filling: one cup of butter, two cups of sugar, yolks of six eggs, a very small teaspoonful vanilla. Beat well together and fill the shells, placing some pretty jelly in the center of each. Place in the oven to brown slightly. Eat entirely fresh.

SPINACH PARMESAN ☆

3 pounds spinach
6 tablespoons Parmesan cheese
6 tablespoons minced onion

6 tablespoons heavy cream
5 tablespoons melted butter
½ cup cracker crumbs

Cook the cleaned spinach until tender. Drain thoroughly. Chop coarsely and add the cheese, onion, cream, and four tablespoons of butter. Arrange in a shallow baking dish and sprinkle with the crumbs mixed with the remaining butter. Bake for ten to fifteen minutes.

LADY BIRD'S STRAWBERRY ICE BOX PIE ☆

1 17-ounce package
    marshmallows
1 box frozen strawberries or
    2 cups fresh strawberries,
    sweetened to taste

1 cup whipping cream
1 cool pastry shell

Put marshmallows in double boiler. Add two tablespoons of strawberry juice. Cook until marshmallows are dissolved. Mix strawberries and marshmallows thoroughly. Chill about two hours. Fold in whipped cream to marshmallow mixture and pour into pastry shell. Chill until firm.

PASTRY SHELL ☆

1 cup flour
2 tablespoons shortening
1 teaspoon salt

3 tablespoons cold water
1 tablespoon sugar

"BACK TO THE CHUCK WAGON, BOYS!"

West German Chancellor Ludwig Erhard got a taste of American hospitality, Texas-style, in January, 1964, when President and Mrs. Johnson entertained with a barbecue in his honor at the LBJ ranch. Four hundred guests were served from western chuck wagons. They ate at long tables covered with red checkered cloths and lighted with lanterns. The menu:

BARBECUED BEEF RIBS

HICKORY GRAVY

RANCH BEANS

SOURDOUGH BISCUITS

GERMAN POTATO SALAD

TEXAS COLE SLAW

HOT FRIED PIES

TEXAS-GERMAN CHOCOLATE CAKE

COFFEE

THE BARBECUE FOR WEST GERMAN CHANCELLOR ERHARD

It was a fine blend of German *Gemuetlichkeit* and Texas git-up-n-go. The Lone Star attraction was the chocolate cake which was baked from a recipe brought to Texas by German pioneers in the early 1800s. Here is the recipe:

TEXAS-GERMAN CHOCOLATE CAKE ☆

5 ounces butter	8 egg whites
3 ounces sugar	2½ ounces granulated sugar
8 egg yolks	5 ounces cake flour
6 ounces sweet chocolate, melted	8 ounces clear apricot jam

Work butter and three ounces sugar until fluffy. Add yolks of eggs, two at a time, beating well after each addition. Stir in the melted chocolate. Beat egg whites stiff but not dry; add two and a half ounces sugar gradually. Fold into egg-yolk mixture alternately with sifted flour. Pour into a round ten-inch buttered mold. Bake at 300° fifty to sixty minutes or till done. Cool and brush whole layer with apricot jam and ice completely with chocolate fondant icing.

LBJ CRAB CASSEROLE ☆

1 cup grated cheese	2 tablespoons melted butter
2 egg yolks	¼ cup cracker crumbs
2 cups white sauce	(Ritz type)
2 cups crabmeat	

Add cheese to hot white sauce, stir until melted, and remove from heat. Add beaten egg yolks gradually, then crab meat. Turn into casserole. Mix butter and cracker crumbs together and sprinkle on top. Bake in moderate oven for thirty minutes.

FRIED PIES ☆

2 pounds fresh dried apples	3 slices lemon (⅛-inch thick) chopped fine
3 slices orange (¼-inch thick) chopped fine	

Cover fruits with cold water and let come to a boil. Simmer a few minutes until almost done. Add two pounds granulated sugar and a quarter-pound real butter. Remove from fire and let sit overnight in refrigerator.

OLD WORLD GREETING FOR THE NEW FIRST LADY AS
CHANCELLOR ERHARD PREPARES TO KISS MRS. JOHNSON'S
HAND ON ARRIVAL AT WHITE HOUSE FOR AL FRESCO
FORMAL DINNER

Next day make pastry with very little shortening; whip to make it tough. Roll out as any pie dough; cut circles with No. 10 can. Put approximately one and a half ounces of fruit on one side of pastry; fold pastry over and crimp edges with wet fork. Fry in shallow pot of deep fat till lightly browned.

492

Since President Johnson's heart attack nine years ago, he has followed a sensible, low-calorie diet. Following are two calorie-saving desserts that appear frequently on his menu—old favorites with modern twists, excellent for dieters:

PRESIDENT JOHNSON'S SPANISH CREAM ☆

1 tablespoon gelatin	3 eggs, separated
¼ cup cold water	1 teaspoon Sucaryl
1 cup scalded milk	1 teaspoon vanilla

Soften gelatin in cold water for five minutes; add milk. Combine egg yolks and Sucaryl, add gelatin mixture and cook over hot water five minutes, stirring constantly until sugar is dissolved. Cool and chill until slightly thickened. Add vanilla and fold in stiffly beaten egg whites. Turn into mold and chill until firm. Serves six.

And *The White House Cookbook* ends almost as it began—with Floating Island, the glamorous and delicious custard that Mrs. John Adams (see her favorite recipes) served at her White House reception in 1801. Probably it has been served, at some time, by every First Family. This is the way it is prepared at the White House today:

PRESIDENT JOHNSON'S FLOATING ISLAND ☆

2 eggs, separated	1 tablespoon Sucaryl
2 cups scalded milk	1 teaspoon vanilla
A pinch of salt	4 tablespoons powdered sugar

Beat egg yolks well. Add a little hot milk to them and stir, then pour yolks into two cups of hot milk and mix well. Pour into top part of double boiler and cook only until liquid coats spoon, no longer. Cool quickly and add salt, Sucaryl, and vanilla. Beat egg whites until stiff. Add four tablespoons powdered sugar to egg whites, one tablespoon at a time, beating after each addition. Pour custard into dessert dishes and put egg whites on top of each. Garnish as you wish with your favorite jam, jelly, or fruit.

493

Every Four to Eight Years . . .

Into the White House, "America's Living Room," moves a new First Family, ambitious, idealistic, hopeful of giving their best—and human. A new First Lady becomes the mistress of one of the most important mansions, historically and politically, in the world. Here America's great have lived and died. At night, many occupants have said, their ghosts rustle and whisper through the halls.

Each new First Lady brings with her a unique background and personality, along with fresh ideas that will inspire and influence millions of women. At the end of her stay, she may say, with Abigail Adams, "I can return to my own home and be happier," or, with Julia Grant, "These were the happiest years of my life." Not once in her White House years will she know the sometimes-blessed anonymity of the average woman whose triumphs and failures do not make the front pages. Everything the First Lady does or says during this period will be reported in tomorrow's newspaper and will stand for all coming generations to review and condemn or defend. "It is a terrible responsibility," said Lucretia Garfield.

The benign old White House is quite used to new beginnings and to new decision-makers in its family apartment as well as its executive offices. Only "little" decisions are made by Presidents' wives, of course, but time and again these have influenced the course of American history. State dinners, receptions, teas, press conferences, tours, visitors, personal appearances, speeches, autographs, portraits, letters, requests, a graduation, a wedding . . . and always the old question, pondered by hostesses everywhere: "What shall I serve?"

Working days are long in the White House for First Ladies as for Presidents.

494

Acknowledgments
and
Index

ACKNOWLEDGMENTS

The author wishes to thank the following individuals and organizations for their help in the preparation of this book:

Former President Herbert Hoover; Mrs. Lyndon B. Johnson; Mrs. John F. Kennedy; Mrs. Dwight D. Eisenhower; Bess Abell, secretary to Mrs. Johnson; Marta M. Miller, assistant to Mrs. Johnson; Pamela Turnure, secretary to Mrs. Kennedy; Charles P. Taft; Martha L. Willingham; Mrs. Sidney A. Bailey; Mrs. Frederic B. Butler, former secretary to Mrs. Hoover; The Harry S. Truman Library, Philip C. Brooks, director; The Franklin D. Roosevelt Library, Elizabeth Drewry, director; The Congressional Club of Washington, Mrs. Clifford Davis, president; The Ladies' Hermitage Association, Steve S. Lawrence, custodian; James Buchanan Foundation for the Preservation of Wheatland, Mrs. Gordon Parker, curator; Hugh A. Lawing, park historian, Andrew Johnson National Monument; Grant House, Sadie Allen, custodian; Polk Memorial Auxiliary, Mrs. T. P. Yeatman; Rutherford B. Hayes Library, Watt P. Marchman, director; Stark County (Ohio) Historical Society, E. T. Heald, director; The Canton (Ohio) *Repository;* The Muncie (Ind.) *Evening Press;* The Library of Congress, Reference Division; Theodore Roosevelt Home, Mrs. Harold Kraft, curator; Tea Council of the United States, Beryl Walter; French-Lick Sheraton Hotel, Jeane Woolsey; The Greenbrier, Margot Coley; Victor O. B. Slater, chairman, Fairhaven (Mass.) Chamber of Commerce; Mrs. Charles Leonard; Miss Edith Carrell; Mrs. L. K. Halliday; Mrs. Omer H. Foust; Mrs. Will Hays, Jr.; Mrs. Bernard Perry; Mrs. Gerald Buckley; Cecil Beeson, president, Blackford County (Ind.) Historical Society; The Milwaukee *Journal*, Clarice Rowlands; The Milwaukee Public Library; The Wauwatosa (Wis.) Public Library; Jeanne Clark; Mrs. John Stedje; Mrs. Claude Weber.

The main source for the old recipes in this book was:

The White House Cook Book, by Mrs. Fanny Lemira (Camp) Gillette and Hugo Ziemann, editions of 1887, 1889, 1891, 1894, 1899, and 1901.

Other sources were:

Mrs. Winslow's Domestic Recipe Book for 1865, Boston, Mass.

Center Church Cook Book, compiled by the women of the Crawfordsville (Ind.) Presbyterian Church, Christmas, 1879, rev. 1894.

The Capitol Cookbook, by Mrs. Fanny Gillette, 1896.

The New World's Fair Cookbook and Housekeeper's Companion, by Mrs. M. E. Porter, Prince George Court House, Va., 1891.

The Presidential Cook Book, by Mrs. Fanny Gillette, 1901.

Social New York Under the Georges, 1714–1776, by Esther Singleton, D. Appleton & Co., New York, 1902.

The Waupun, Wisconsin, Cook Book, 1905.

20th Century Cook Book, A Feast of Good Things, by Lillian V. Wyrick, Angola, Ind., 1905.

Old advertisements appeared in *Ladies' Home Journal*, issues of 1891, 1893 and 1900, *Harper's Bazaar*, issues of 1891 and 1893, *The Cosmopolitan*, issues of 1890, *The Elite News*, issues of 1887, and in some of the cookbooks mentioned above.

497

ACKNOWLEDGMENTS

Permission was granted to quote from the following published works:

The *Congressional Club Cookbook* of 1927, copyright The Congressional Club of Washington (Thomas Jefferson's Cookbook and other selected recipes)

"Mr. Hoover Asked for Some More," *Collier's*, Copyright 1929

42 Years in the White House, by Irwin Hoover, copyright 1934, Houghton Mifflin Co., Boston

Gone With the Wind, by Margaret Mitchell, copyright 1936, The MacMillan Co., New York; permission granted by Stephens Mitchell

Abraham Lincoln's favorite recipes, The Milwaukee *Journal*

Favorite foods of the Roosevelts, recipes reprinted from *Better Homes and Gardens*, copyright 1934, Meredith Publishing Co., Des Moines

"My Window," by Myrtie Barker, The Indianapolis *News*, for Funeral Pie

Favorite recipes of their mothers, mothers-in-law and grandmothers were contributed by the following good cooks:

Mrs. Edward Aldinger, Cincinnati Sauerbraten and Kartoffel Klosse; Mrs. Earl Anderson, Chinese Pork Chops; Mrs. William E. Ervin, Galettes; Mrs. John Fulton, Turban of Salmon, Caper Salad, and Butterscotch Cookies; Mrs. Wirth Gadbury, Finger Pie; Mrs. Thomas G. Gordon, Pompey's Head, Spoon Bread, and Beaten Biscuits; Mrs. Byron T. Hawkins, Gram's Coffee Cake and Date-Nut Bread; Mrs. W. J. Lemasters, Skillet Meal, Meat Loaf, Great-Aunt Gertrude's Biscuits, Mexican Wedding Cakes, Oatmeal-Apple Cake and Pecan Pie; Mrs. Kenneth S. Mann, Homemade Noodles, Caramel Tarts and Corn Pudding; Mrs. Walter E. Maile, Jr., Rhubarb Pie; Mrs. George K. Meyer, Coffee Cake and Press Cookies; Mrs. Kenneth P. Milbradt, Sauce for White Cake; Mrs. Frederic Mohr, Fastnachts; Mrs. O. H. Ratcliff, Sherry-Ambrosia Salad and Ginger Cookies; Mrs. John E. Smith, Grandma's Pancakes and Holiday Snow Pudding; Mrs. Otto Wernicke, Kalv Dans, Krum Kake, Fattigman, Banana Bread, Biscuits and Mincemeat Crescents; Edith Carrell, Layover for Meddlers.

Thanks, too, to my agent, Scott Meredith, for his helpful advice. Special thanks to Mrs. Howard G. Ervin. And thank you, Boze ("the first shall be last").

INDEX

HOUSEHOLD HINTS AND RECIPES

501